NOUS·SOMMES·PRETS
SIMON FRASER UNIVERSITY
W.A.C. BENNETT LIBRARY

GUNBOATS, CORRUPTION, AND CLAIMS

Recent Titles in
Contributions in Latin American Studies

Brutality and Benevolence: Human Ethnology, Culture, and the Birth of Mexico
Abel A. Alves

Ideologues and Ideologies in Latin America
Will Fowler, editor

Family and Favela: The Reproduction of Poverty in Rio de Janeiro
Julio César Pino

Mexico in the Age of Proposals, 1821–1853
Will Fowler

Reinventing Legitimacy: Democracy and Political Change in Venezuela
Damarys Canache and Michael R. Kulisheck, editors

Sugar and Power in the Dominican Republic: Eisenhower, Kennedy, and the Trujillos
Michael R. Hall

Tornel and Santa Anna: The Writer and the Caudillo, Mexico 1795–1853
Will Fowler

Exiles, Allies, Rebels: Brazil's Indianist Movement, Indigenist Politics, and the Imperial Nation-State
David Treece

One of the Forgotten Things: Getulio Vargas and Brazilian Social Control, 1930–1954
R. S. Rose

The Abolition of Slavery in Brazil: The "Liberation" of Africans Through the Emancipation of Capital
David Baronov

Beyond the Ideal: Pan Americanism in Inter-American Affairs
David Sheinin, editor

Oil, War, and Anglo-American Relations: American and British Reactions to Mexico's Expropriation of Foreign Oil Properties, 1937–1941
Catherine E. Jayne

GUNBOATS, CORRUPTION, AND CLAIMS

Foreign Intervention in Venezuela, 1899–1908

Brian S. McBeth

Contributions in Latin American Studies, Number 20

GREENWOOD PRESS
Westport, Connecticut • London

Library of Congress Cataloging-in-Publication Data

McBeth, B. S. (Brian Stuart), 1951–
Gunboats, corruption, and claims : foreign intervention in Venezuela, 1899–1908 / by Brian S. McBeth.
p. cm.—(Contributions in Latin American studies, ISSN 1054–6790 ; no. 20)
Includes bibliographical references (p. –) and index.
ISBN 0–313–31356–3 (alk. paper)
1. Venezuela—Foreign relations—1830–1935. 2. Political corruption—Venezuela. 3. Castro, Cipriano, 1856?–1924. I. Title. II. Series.
F2325.M39 2001
987.06'312'092—dc21 00–035357

British Library Cataloguing in Publication Data is available.

Library of Congress Catalog Card Number: 00–035357
ISBN: 0–313–31356–3
ISSN: 1054–6790

First published in 2001

Greenwood Press, 88 Post Road West, Westport, CT 06881
An imprint of Greenwood Publishing Group, Inc.
www.greenwood.com

Printed in the United States of America

The paper used in this book complies with the Permanent Paper Standard issued by the National Information Standards Organization (Z39.48–1984).

10 9 8 7 6 5 4 3 2 1

To John Alfred, an indomitable spirit.

Contents

Acknowledgments

I am most grateful for the assistance rendered by the Public Record Office, the Archivo Histórico de Miraflores, and the following British and Venezuelan libraries: The Bodleian Library, The British Library, the Biblioteca Nacional, and the Library at the Latin American Centre, University of Oxford. I owe much to Senator Dr. Ramón J. Velásquez for his patience and countless hours of discussion. I owe a big thanks to both Malcolm Deas and Dr. George Philip for their comments on the manuscript and for their general encouragement. For any errors of omission or commission I alone am accountable.

Abbreviations

AHM	Archivo Histórico de Miraflores
AHMSGPRCP	Archivo Histórico de Miraflores, Secretaría General de la Presidencia, Correspondencia Presidencial
AMLR	Archivo de Manuel Landaeta Rosales
Asphalt Trust	The Asphalt Company of America, which subsequently became The General Asphalt Company
Asphalt Company	The General Asphalt Company
BAHM	Boletín del Archivo Histórico de Miraflores
BATT	Biblioteca de Autores y Temas Tachirenses
Bs.	bolivars
CAB	Cabinet Office
CO	Colonial Office
DDCS	Diario de Debate de la Cámara de Senado
DS	Department of State
FO	Foreign Office
FCC	French Cable Company
HAHR	Hispanic American Historical Review
HMSO	His Majesty's Stationery Office
MinRelExt	Ministerio de Relaciones Exteriores
MinRelInt	Ministerio de Relaciones Interiores
NY&B	New York & Bermudez Company

PP	Parliamentary Papers
SAJ	The South American Journal
UCV	Universidad Central deVenezuela
Warner-Quinlan	Warner-Quinlan Asphalt Company

Introduction

Four different Tachirense dictators ruled Venezuela from 1899 to 1945. These dictators traced their political birth to the invasion of the country by a small band of rebel exiles led by Cipriano Castro on May 23, 1899. Táchira at the time was a political and cultural backwater that appeared to have more in common with neighboring Colombia than with the rest of the country. Nevertheless, through a combination of luck and the exceptional political ability of one dictator in particular, Venezuela was ruled by these men from the mountains for almost half a century.

A series of internal and external political crises characterized Castro's government from 1899 to 1908. Any of these crises seemed capable of toppling him. The first major external crisis was with Colombia in 1901. Castro had a vision, inspired no doubt by Simón Bolívar, to work with other countries to form a grand Liberal alliance against the Conservatives. As part of this strategy, Castro backed General Rafael Uribe Uribe's bid to secure the Colombian presidency in 1901, supplying him with arms and forcing the sister republic to break off diplomatic relations with Venezuela. In December 1901, after confronting a number of minor internal political crises, Castro then faced the biggest threat to his regime. Castro's erstwhile friends, most of them Liberal *caudillos* who had been instrumental in getting him to the presidency in 1899, combined under the leadership of Manuel Antonio Matos to start the Revolución Libertadora. At one stage Matos controlled most of the country with the exception of Caracas, the capital city, and the Andean states. To compound the government's troubles in the middle of this revolution, Great Britain, Germany, and later Italy instituted a "peaceful blockade" of Venezuela in December 1902 to get the government to honor the claims that various foreign nationals had pursued over a number of years. At the outset of the Libertadora revolution, Juan Vicente Gómez, the vice president and Castro's closest supporter and *compadre*, was named head of the expeditionary force that was assembled to crush the rebels. It was during this rebellion that Gómez showed his true military capacity, which saved the regime from the rebel forces. After several skirmishes and combats he was seriously wounded in the thigh during a battle in Carúpano on May 6, 1902, against Nicolás Rolando. After his recovery Gómez was appointed acting president; from July 5, 1902 to March 20, 1903 he dealt with the "peaceful blockade" and was instrumental in bringing much needed reinforcements of arms and ammunition to the besieged government troops of Castro at La Victoria, who eventually defeated the Matos army in central Venezuela. Gómez finally pacified the country on July 21, 1903, when he defeated the last bastion of rebels in Ciudad Bolívar under Nicolás Rolando. Gómez returned in triumph as a national hero to La Guaira on August 3 of that same year. From then on Gómez's military skill would go unquestioned, acknowledged by friend and foe alike, as the regime's ablest military man after Castro. Gómez's popularity soared for the first time since his arrival in Caracas and would stand him in good stead in the coming years. Although Gómez had dealt with the foreign trading houses in his native Táchira, it was in Caracas that he came into greater contact with foreigners and the representatives of foreign powers, especially during the "peaceful blockade." This was important because the Castro regime steadily alienated a number of foreign powers, leaving Gómez to pick up the pieces after he came to power in December 1908.

Castro's regime also had an immensely stifling effect on the economy of the country as Castro and his cronies awarded themselves all sorts of monopolies to line their pockets. This was also associated with Castro's policy of antagonizing foreign capital, which led eventually to the rupture of diplomatic relations between Venezuela and the United States, France, and the Netherlands. Many of the problems with the foreign powers were self-inflicted, brought on by Castro's greed and the government's need for funds. A number of foreign powers, especially the United States, France, and the Netherlands, placed a great deal of pressure on Castro to get him to be more conciliatory toward their nationals and their assets. Once this failed, the foreign powers were left with the choice of either taking the issue into their own hands or abandoning the fate of their nationals to Castro.

A great deal has been written about the Castro government and, in particular, the "peaceful blockade."[1] However, what is new in this book is our contention that the extreme behavior of certain foreign powers during the period in question was provoked by the actions and avarice of Castro, whose posturing has been wrongly interpreted as a sign of fervent nationalism. During this period the United States seriously considered intervening in the country, while the Netherlands' seizure of Venezuelan gunboats precipitated the political crisis that ultimately brought Gómez to power. The behavior of Castro is a painful but salutary reminder that it is often extremely difficult to bring to justice a ruler who does not play by recognized rules or who chooses to change the rules, especially if that country is large and difficult to subdue militarily.

This book looks at how Castro, an obscure politician from the backwater state of Táchira, reached power in 1899. It then examines the nature of the foreign claims on the country and the intervention that took place because of the ill-treatment of foreign capital and nationals. It looks in detail at the foreign companies that got into trouble with Castro because their contracts were subject to contradictory interpretation, while backing a revolutionary uprising that failed to achieve power. The reaction of the Venezuelan government, which at times was driven by corruption on the part of Castro, is detailed with special reference to the "peaceful blockade" and a number of other claims. Finally, the consequences for both parties are examined. The international repercussions of the Castro administration should not be underestimated. U.S. foreign policy, for example, was modified as a result of the "peaceful blockade" while the French and Dutch governments realized the limit of their power to influence events in far-flung places such as South America. The consequences for Castro were monumental as he lost the biggest prize of all. The political crisis that developed in Venezuela as a direct result of the foreign claims led to both the rupture of relations with the Netherlands, France, and the United States and the threat of intervention because of the appalling treatment of their nationals. The crisis culminated in the December 19, 1908, *coup d'etat* that brought Gómez to power. From then until his death in 1924, Castro remained an exile, mostly in Puerto Rico, forever dreaming of toppling his erstwhile friend. Meanwhile, Gómez ruled the country until his death on December 17, 1935.

NOTE

1. See for example: Velásquez, Ramón J., *La Caida del Liberalismo Amarillo. Tiempo y Drama de Antonio Paredes*, Caracas, Ediciones Venezuela, 1960; Sullivan, William M., "The Rise of Despotism in Venezuela: Cipriano Castro, 1899–1908," PhD. diss., The University of New Mexico, 1974; Herwig, Holger H., *Germany's Vision of Empire in Venezuela, 1871–1914*, Princeton, Princeton University Press, 1986; Hood, Miriam, *Diplomacia con Cañones, 1895–1905*, Caracas, Ediciones de la Presidencia, 1975; Picón Salas, Mariano, *Los Días de Cipriano Castro*, Caracas, Ediciones Garrido, 1953; Alarico Gómez, Carlos, *La Amarga Experiencia (El Bloqueo de 1902)*, Caracas, Ministerio de Educación, 1983; Brandt, Carlos, *Bajo la Tiranía de Cipriano Castro. Su Desgraciada Actitud durante el Bombardeo*

y el Bloqueo de 1902, Caracas, Editorial Elite, 1952; Gallegos Ortiz, Rafael, *La Historia Política de Venezuela, de Cipriano Castro a Pérez Jiménez*, Caracas, Imp. Universitaria, 1960; Gilmore, Robert, *Caudillism and Militarism in Venezuela, 1810–1910*, Athens, Ohio State University Press, 1964; Fenton, P. F., "Diplomatic Relations of the United States and Venezuela, 1880–1915," *Hispanic American Historical Review* 8:3 (August 1928) 330–57; and Platt, D. C. M., "The Allied Coercion of Venezuela 1902–03: A Reassessment," *Inter-American Economic Affairs* 15:4 (1962).

1

Táchira Comes of Age

At the end of the Wars of Independence from Spain, Táchira was administered from neighboring Mérida, only becoming a fully independent state under the 1864 constitution. A few years later this was reversed by the 1881 constitution, which grouped together the three Andean states of Táchira, Trujillo, and Mérida into one large state, the "Gran Estado de los Andes," with the old states becoming *secciones* or dependencies.

The mainstay of the Tachirense economy was coffee, which was first grown in 1798 but only assumed importance in the economic structure of the region and the country during the last quarter of the nineteenth century. The reason for its slow development was the state's chronic small labor pool. The growing of coffee is labor intensive because the beans have to be handpicked at harvest time. Other regions of the country, such as the central and eastern states, did not have a surplus population to transfer to the coffee-growing region of the Andes. However, the Wars of Independence and the Federal Wars of the 1860s had the demographic effect of shifting the population away from the *Llanos* (plains) to the mountainous regions of the Andes. At the same time many Colombians also arrived, bringing with them their commercial acumen and expertise as well as their ability for hard work, skills that would be put to good use in developing the coffee industry. The state's population between 1880 and 1890 grew by 21.8 percent from 83,521 to 101,709. The bulk of this increase occurred in the western coffee zones of San Cristóbal and Rubio. The size of the boom, however, should be kept in perspective. Táchira's coffee production between 1883 and 1898 accounted for only 18 percent of the national total, producing 33,090 tons during the period in question, while the rest of Venezuela yielded 188,719 tons.[1]

The development of coffee production in the Andes was associated with small-scale farms that were owned mainly by families. The mountainous conditions of the region were not suitable for the development of a *latifundio* type of plantation, and extensive landowning was confined to the district of Rubio in western Táchira. Toward the end of the nineteenth century, coffee became the most important commercial crop in the region, and the economic boom it fostered gave rise to the development of a nascent capitalist class that was willing to take risks and develop the region economically.

The German trading houses that had been active in the region since the 1860s also grew in commercial importance with the coffee boom. They acted as commercial banks, advancing credit to the coffee producers and using the following year's crop as collateral. At the same time they supplied the region with imported merchandise. The role that the foreign traders played at this time should not, however, be overemphasised. The local moneylenders of Táchira were far more important and competed directly with the German trading houses. The municipal records of San Cristóbal and Rubio that Muñoz examined indicate that in those cities the "majority of the moneylenders were Venezuelans and that the German firms were responsible for only a small number of the total registered loans."[2] Castro, of urban middle-class background, educated in Pamplona, Colombia, and the country's first Tachirense president, took a clerical job in the German trading firm of Van Diesel & Co. in San Cristóbal.[3] His brother, Celestino, was engaged during the same period in "small scale commercial and financial activities,"[4] lending money at a monthly interest rate of 2.5 percent. Many of the German trading houses, such as Van Diesel & Co., had their headquarters in Venezuela. They had relative autonomy from Germany, and their expanding network of rural stores served to increase demand for coffee and hence production as the Tachirense merchants often purchased coffee and stockpiled it until they could ship it to the German warehouses in the large cities. However, toward the end of the 1880s the German trading houses began to assume a more dominant position, undertaking a systematic campaign to "exploit the coffee boom and expand operations throughout the Andes."[5]

A NASCENT MIDDLE CLASS

As a consequence of the coffee boom in the 1880s and 1890s, rural wages in Táchira were the highest in the country. The economic prosperity that the coffee boom brought to the region contributed toward the formation of a nascent middle class among a "sizeable segment of the urban residents of the coffee zone."[6] Táchira's coffee income allowed it to import many goods from abroad, mainly from Colombia. A U.S. diplomat described the trade in manufactured articles from Santander, Colombia, as intense. At the same time the region's prosperity also attracted many Colombian teachers, who generally settled in the western coffee zone and began to raise the educational standards of the state, producing a generation of well-educated youths at the end of the nineteenth century. These youths experienced keen dissatisfaction at job prospects and believed that they were the vanguard of a better future, not only for the region but for the country as a whole.

Táchira's geographical isolation made it extremely difficult for the central government in Caracas to destroy the autonomy of the state's dispersed communities. A direct result of this regional isolation was an inefficient local government and an inadequate infrastructure, both of which constrained the state's economic development. There was no direct link with Caracas, so the quickest journey to the capital entailed first going to Colombia, then travelling to Maracaibo, taking a boat to Curacao, and then going to Puerto Cabello or La Guaira. The Young Turks of the state wanted to foster a better transportation system to facilitate and expand trading and commercial ties with the rest of the country.

Despite the regional isolation of Táchira and the close links it had with Colombia, the commercial and political interests of its citizens were firmly rooted in Maracaibo and Caracas. The Tachirense nationalists wanted greater participation in the central government. Such a wish was achieved with Castro in 1899, ending forty-five years later with the October 18, 1945, coup that toppled the government of Medina Angarita. Of the Andean rulers, Gómez, who toppled his *compadre* Castro in 1908, ruled the country the longest, remaining in power for twenty-seven years.

CASTRO AND GÓMEZ: THE EARLY YEARS

Juan Vicente Gómez was born on July 24, 1857, in the hacienda El Recreo in La Mulera, near Rubio in Táchira. Cipriano Castro was born fifteen months later on October 12, 1858, in La Ovejera de las Lomas Altas, near Capacho. Gómez came from a relatively well-off rural family that owned a coffee farm; he went to a primary school run by Ramón Navarro while his sisters were taught at home by Braulia Santander. Pedro Cornelio,[7] Gómez's father, proposed that Gómez study medicine at Bogotá or Caracas. In contrast, Castro did not have a rounded education, with a contemporary observer suggesting that to speak to him about art was like "casting pearls before swine."[8]

Gómez grew up during Táchira's coffee boom of the 1880s, which together with the relative geographical isolation produced a nascent middle class that was willing to take risks and develop the region economically. This appalled the neighboring *merideños*, who could not fathom "the pragmatic and unabashed capitalistic spirit of San Cristóbal."[9] Gómez's intelligence and capacity for hard work made him stand out "above the general level of the small landowners of the region,"[10] while "there were no other families with greater power than the Gomezes, the Castros and the Bellos"[11] in Cúcuta, San Antonio, or Lobatera.

With Gómez's business activities and farm prospering he began to assume regional importance. This led him to join Colonel Evaristo Jaimes in 1886 to protest against the excessive abuse of power that local *jefes civiles* had perpetrated with the connivance of General Espíritu Santo Morales, president of the Andes. Castro received his first political lesson in June 1886 when he joined Pepe Rojas Fernández's local rebellion against Espíritu Santo Morales. The rebel forces of Evaristo Jaimes gathered at Los Capachos, where they were met by General Morales, who on June 23, 1886, ordered an attack against the city. Although Jaimes was killed during the fight, the government army was forced to retreat, with Castro giving chase. Later Castro was ambushed but escaped, managing to attend the funeral of Jaimes the following day, where he met Gómez for the first time, striking a lasting friendship and introducing to him Pepe Rojas Fernández and Camilo Merchán.

Morales led two thousand men on a renewed attack on Capacho, but Castro defeated him again. On June 29 at Boquerón the government troops were completely routed. The rebel movement triumphed in Táchira, with Castro entering San Cristóbal in a victorious procession on July 5, the country's independence day. The two most distinguished military commanders in the rebel campaign were Castro and Pepe Rojas Fernández. The government feared that the rebellion would get out of hand, so they appointed the latter as governor of the Federal Territory of Amazonas. However, he was murdered before he could take his appointment.[12]

In the ensuing years a series of reforms were instituted in Táchira, bringing the region more closely into the national political arena. In 1888, Castro joined Carlos Rangel Garbiras, the newly appointed president of Los Andes, as leader of the Sección Táchira, but differences between them soon developed because they represented antagonistic forces in the region. Rangel Garbiras was perceived as a defender of the interests of the rich and powerful groups of Táchira, whereas Castro's power base lay in the rural areas among the small farmers of the state.[13] These differences would eventually drive them apart. In 1890 Castro, who was now a regional power in his own right, was appointed commander of the government's army in Táchira. A year later he became a deputy at the National Congress, representing Táchira and supporting President Andueza Palacio.

CASTRO WIDENS HIS HORIZONS

The political problems that bedevilled Venezuela during the last twenty years of the nineteenth century were due, to a large extent, to the power struggle between Antonio Guzmán Blanco and Joaquín Crespo. The former assumed power after a bloody battle in 1870 when the conservatives, who had ruled since the end of the Federal Wars in 1863, were defeated. The method of government of the Liberal party, which ruled until 1888, was for each president to be surrounded by "his personal group exploiting, according to circumstances, local political reactions and conceding to a greater or lesser extent power to local people."[14] Guzmán Blanco wanted above all to mould his "backward and savage country in the image of prosperous societies he had come to know across the seas. He admired both Yankee industriousness and the culture of the Second Empire in France."[15] In 1873 Venezuela's first Military Code was enacted. The code replaced Spanish titles, commands, and formations with American and Prussian models. Another code issued in 1881 modernized the army even further. This code set the army at 3,000 soldiers, 253 generals, and 97 colonels. It also sharply increased salaries. A year later a navy academy was created, and in 1890 the first army academy was established.

In 1884 Guzmán Blanco, known as *El Ilustre Americano*, appointed Joaquín Crespo as his successor. During Crespo's presidency the economy declined, and because of his incompetence Guzmán Blanco rapidly returned from Europe. Crespo handed over power to Guzmán Blanco in 1886. However, Crespo kept a "ring of iron"[16] because he was able to appoint the judiciary, the state presidents, and the legislators of the different states for the next four years, whereas the presidential period would last only two years. In addition, Crespo had selected and appointed the congressmen for the next two periods, naming his friends who would secure his reelection. This caused a major rupture in Guzmán Blanco-Crespo relations, with the former departing for Europe and leaving Hermógenes López in charge. At the same time Crespo also retired to Europe.

Guzmán Blanco's intention was to appoint biennial presidents from Europe. In 1888 various candidates came forward, although the idea was for the Liberal Party convention to elect the president. Crespo was one of the candidates, but Guzmán Blanco was determined to continue his domination of the political life of the country and proposed that Juan Pablo Rojas Paúl be designated president. Rojas Paúl turned out to be a popular choice and a good administrator, and he was followed by Andueza Palacio, who tried to extend his period to four years "judging that this would be sufficient time to raise the federalist flag from the autonomy of the state departments."[17] The strongman of the regime was Sebastián Casañas, "the Iron Chancellor" as he was known, who got the municipalities and state congresses to approve the increase in tenure from two years to four. The National Congress, in turn, needed to sanction such a move to reelect Andueza Palacio. From his Guárico *hato*, Crespo declared such a move illegal, stating that any reforms would take effect in 1894. However, Andueza Palacio remained in power and suspended Congress. Crespo was then left with no choice but to launch his Revolución Legalista in 1892. Sebastián Casañas, at the head of an army of four thousand men, was sent to subdue the wayward rebel. Meanwhile, in Táchira, the Baptistas, Araujos, José Manuel Gabaldón, and Victoriano Márquez Bustillos, the latter state president, took up Crespo's banner against Andueza Palacio. Castro, however, defended the government's position. On his suggestion, General José María González, head of the Táchira frontier army, appointed Gómez to the rank of colonel.

On March 20, 1892, Castro left for Colón with a small army that included Emilio Fernández, Francisco Croce, Francisco Antonio Colmenares Pacheco, Pedro María Cárdenas, Pedro Murillo, and Modesto Castro. This army sought to relieve González's reduced army, which was being attacked by his old enemy Espíritu Santo Morales. After twenty hours of hard battle, Castro defeated Morales whose army scattered in disarray. In El Topón, General Eliseo Araujo, who had arrived in San Cristóbal to reestablish order as president of the Andes after Márquez Bustillos joined the rebels, was decidedly beaten on March 22, 1892 by General José María González, commander of the border troops, and Colonel Juan Vicente Gómez, commander of the sectional troops, and later joined by Castro,[18] forcing Araujo to flee the state. Later at Táriba and Caneyes, Castro and Gómez defeated the government troops and then followed the rebels to Palmira and San Juan de Lagunillas, entering triumphantly in Mérida at the head of three thousand men.

Castro's plan to carry the fighting to Caracas was debated, with some arguing that his duty was to protect the Andes. However, Castro's reasoning won the day, and preparations were made to march toward the capital. This plan was halted when General José María García Gómez delivered a message from Andueza Palacio, which brought the sad news that the government had capitulated. Castro remained adamant about proceeding to Caracas, but the pessimism of García Gómez persuaded him to desist in his quest. As a result Crespo, after seven months of hard fighting, was able to consolidate his power with his government. More authoritarian than Andueza Palacio, Crespo appointed General Espíritu Santo Morales, Castro's old enemy, to take over in Táchira. A conspiracy against Castro had already taken place, with General Croce Moreno maneuvering to take over power from him by joining up with the Rangelistas, the followers of Rangel Garbiras. However, as soon as General Morales arrived in San Cristóbal and assumed power, he threw out Croce Moreno. Castro was left with no alternative but to resign his army commission and seek refuge in Colombia, with Gómez following closely after him.

Castro's campaign to defend the Palacio government meant that his *hacienda* in Táchira had been destroyed, with his personal loss estimated at Bs 10,000.[19] In the neighboring republic, Castro acquired the small estate of Bella Vista in a region near the frontier town of Cúcuta, with the financial assistance of Gómez.[20] Gómez acquired the Buenos Aires estate, close to his *compadre*. Most of Gómez's children with Dionisia Bello were born here, including José Vicente Gómez and Ali Gómez, his favorite, who would die in the 1918 influenza epidemic.[21] Over the next seven years Gómez built up a successful business of cattle ranching and coffee production, amassing a small fortune that was estimated at Bs 30,000.[22] This enabled Gómez to finance both Castro's trips to Caracas and the 1899 invasion. During this period Castro spent his time planning his political return, and meeting many of the leaders of Colombian Liberalism such as Carlos Díaz Irwin and Benjamín Ruiz.

Castro was a frequent visitor to Gómez's *hacienda*, with the conversation always focusing on how to depose Crespo. The Venezuelan President wanted to get the fiery Táchira rebel on his side by persuading him to join the government in exchange for Castro handing over the arms that he had hidden in Colombia for the country's Liberals. Alirio Diaz, Crespo's Colombian private secretary, invited Castro to Caracas. However, the president's overtures went unheeded, and Castro instead put forward his own ideas about reorganizing the country. The result was a stalemate, with Castro returning to his exile in his *hacienda* in Colombia. In the second of his two trips to Caracas, which were financed by Gómez, Castro returned to the capital in 1893 to speak to Crespo about the deteriorating political situation in the Andes. However, this time he was ignored and dismissed with the scathing remark that "he is an indian who is too big for his boots."[23]

MOCHO HERNÁNDEZ

Crespo's victory, however, had managed to unify the old *liberalismo amarillo* of Guzmán Blanco against the rising tide of conservatism that José Manuel (Mocho) Hernández propounded. Crespo allowed his former enemies, who were not revolutionaries, to form a Representative Cabinet of Opposition that was led by Manuel Antonio Matos. This neutralized part of the opposition but entailed giving Matos the treasury portfolio, which backfired as the enemies of the new finance minister also wanted to be part of the government. At the same time Crespo also initiated a period of open elections, an action that was vigorously taken up by the conservative Mocho Hernández, who earned his nickname at the age of seventeen when his right arm and neck were wounded in the battle of Los Lirios at the beginning of the Septenio.[24] Mocho Hernández, who had led a colorful career, cofounded with Alejandro Urbaneja the Partido Democrático during Rojas Paúl's time. In 1897 Urbaneja proposed the formation of the Partido Liberal Nacionalista with Mocho Hernández at its head. The party's goals included adopting traditional liberal principles and "promising to establish the democratic practices which had not been fulfilled and to suppress corruption and those lucrative business ventures which for too long had been considered as part of the government's largesse."[25] A committee composed of Alejandro Urbaneja, Jorge Nevett, David Lobo, Miguel Páez Pumar, Cristóbal Soublette, and Pedro Manuel Ruiz launched the presidential candidacy of Mocho Hernández in May 1897.

The official government candidate was Ignacio Andrade. After the Revolución Legalista, Andrade had been minister of Public Works and Education and became the second most powerful man in the country when he was elected president of Miranda, which up to 1898 comprised the states of Miranda, Aragua, and Guárico.[26] From his exile in Curacao, Rojas Paúl also launched his candidacy. Other contenders with no hope of winning, such as Pedro Arismendi Brito, Francisco Tosta García, and Juan Francisco Castillo, also entered the race.

Mocho Hernández used the latest electioneering techniques, which he had seen in action in the United States during the presidential campaigns of William Jennings Bryan and William McKinley. During his campaign Mocho Hernández "organised an intensive program of tours, speeches, mass meetings, explaining his program, which consisted of a restatement of all the liberties that had been consistently trampled in Venezuela for over half a century."[27] Mocho Hernández was an incessant campaigner, who, at the start of the campaign, had only Bs 2,000, but who never lacked money because of the enthusiasm that he was able to convey to the public. He canvassed for support across the country, visiting the Aragua valleys, La Guaira, Maiquetía, and Macuto. This was the first time that an election campaign using modern electoral techniques had been conducted in the country.

Jacinta Parejo de Crespo, wife of Crespo, was opposed to Andrade's candidacy and gave her support first to Claudio Bruzual Sera and then to Custodio Milano. In official circles as well, Andrade was not given much support. Many wanted Crespo to launch his candidacy, but he stood resolute in not seeking reelection.

When the polls opened on September 1, the government flooded the cities with peasants armed with *machetes*, who took over the electoral tables and prevented people from depositing their ballots. The result was that Andrade won with 406,610 votes to 2,203 votes for Mocho Hernández, 203 votes for Rojas Paúl, 152 votes for Guzmán Blanco and 31 for Nicolás Rolando. Congress duly confirmed the result, electing Andrade who, according to Lecuna, was "a stooge."[28] Crespo, who had divided the country into five military areas, with himself commanding the most important central zone, ensured that the country accepted the result.

Mocho Hernández, who felt that he had been robbed of the election, wanted to rebel immediately against the fraud. However, he was unable to leave his house in Caracas because he was under virtual house arrest, as his home was being watched constantly. An escape plan was devised in which Mocho Hernández feigned sickness with only David Lobo, his doctor, seeing him. Later, Eloy Escobar, secretary to Urbaneja, arrived dressed in dark glasses and a thick beard accompanied by two ladies. After a suitable time Mocho Hernández left the house disguised as Eloy Escobar, heading first for the home of his friend Felipe Llamozas and then hurrying to Escobar's own house. During the short time at his disposal before his departure from Caracas, Mocho Hernández issued many orders and despatched numerous letters to his supporters around the country. At 1:00 A.M., Mocho Hernández, accompanied by Eloy Escobar and his adviser Juan José Michelena, left for the house of Rafael Ramos, a train conductor in Palos Grandes who lived near the train station. Ramos hid him in the luggage compartment where repair equipment was usually kept in case of emergencies. Ironically, Crespo lived opposite the station.

At dawn the following day, José María Escobar and Vicente Lecuna, Mocho Hernández's agents, arrived at the station to accompany the important "parcel" for part of its journey. Escobar's final destination was Guárico and Apure, while Lecuna headed for Falcón and Lara to finalize arrangements for the forthcoming uprising. At 3:00 P.M., after what must have been an extremely uncomfortable journey, Mocho Hernández arrived in Valencia. However, he was only released from what had become almost a torture chamber at 8:00 P.M. Mocho Hernández immediately left for La Loma, from where he rode on horseback to General Evaristo Lima's *hacienda* of La Queipa. After lengthy discussions it was decided that March 2 would be the most suitable date on which to launch the rebellion. However, the uprising started on March 1, when Mocho Hernández and three hundred peasants took up arms with his Grito de Queipa.

Crespo took control of the government forces and immediately pursued Mocho Hernández. However, Crespo was killed by a stray bullet at Mata Carmelera on April 16, 1898, precipitating a national crisis that shook the foundations of the *liberales amarillos*. The new government of Andrade was placed on the defensive as it was now a foregone conclusion that the popular Mocho Hernández would enter Caracas unopposed and form the next government. However, at the insistence of Matos, Ramón Guerra was named head of the government's armed forces. Ramón Guerra managed to capture Mocho Hernández at Churuguara in Cojedes state in June and he was taken to Caracas and imprisoned.

By the beginning of 1899 the *liberales amarillos* were divided into the Crespistas, who were "resentful and conspirators" as Velásquez has called them, and the Andradistas who were formed by the brothers of Ignacio Andrade and by Febres Cordero, Troconis, Arvelo, Carrillo Guerra and Leopoldo Baptista. The Crespistas would later surround and support Ramón Guerra because he had saved the country from the rule of Mocho Hernández, thereby preventing the dreaded Conservatives from gaining enough power to replace the deceased Crespo as president of the Miranda state. Andrade, fearful of the real intentions of Guerra, did not want to give him so much power, preferring to split the state into its three constituent parts: Miranda, Aragua, and Guárico with Pepe Rojas Fernández; Morales and Guerra their respective presidents, and the Crespistas, after realizing that their influence was waning, supporting Guerra. Andrade would further erode Guerra's power base by making him replace some of his officers, thereby pushing him into rebellion on February 19, 1899, at Calabozo. Guerra proclaimed Guárico an autonomous state and accused Andrade of violating the constitution. Andrade ordered General Augusto Lutowsky to take three thousand men to Calabozo. Generals Manuel Guzmán Alvárez and Lorenzo Guerra also converged with battalions from Guárico, forcing Ramón Guerra to seek refuge in Colombia.

TACHIRA'S INVOLVEMENT IN NATIONAL POLITICS

Táchira at the close of the nineteenth century had the highest per capita income of Venezuela. However, during this time there was a drastic decline in coffee prices that produced a great deal of discontent among the urban middle-class population of the state, who perceived that the policies that the Federal Government pursued, such as an increase in taxation and higher import duties to pay off the country's foreign debt, diminished their economic opportunities, especially those of the educated middle class and the small farmers. Many frowned on civil disorders because it was only with peace and order that business could prosper. However, many of the *bachilleres* suffered from the economic depression, and there were no "industries with gratifying perspectives to employ those people."[29] It must have occurred to many of them to incorporate themselves more fully into national politics in what Rangel calls "participating in the adventure of the Venezuelan civil wars."[30] The nascent middle class of Táchira, however, was dissatisfied with the general state of affairs of the country. It was predominantly from this group and the young, urban sector of Táchira that Castro drew his strength in 1899, forming a movement of "high school students transformed into warriors,"[31] as Rangel so eloquently described the rebels that invaded Venezuela that year.

ANDRADE IS NAMED PRESIDENT

Upon his appointment as president on February 28, 1898, Ignacio Andrade sought to release the hold that the deceased Crespo still had on the country and to consolidate his own power by splitting the country back into its twenty states and granting them full autonomy. The *secciones* of the Andes state, for example, would have their status upgraded to that of a full state. By doing this Andrade had to appoint new legislative and judicial bodies, both at the national and state level. He would then get rid of the Crespistas by appointing his own men while at the same time further consolidating his power. Such a move was a solid legal blow against the Crespo political machinery because it attracted to the Andrade camp those people who wanted to recover their old political power. It also lessened the influence of the state presidents. Anyone who opposed Andrade's move, such as the members of the Supreme Court, would be jailed under the pretext that they were conspiring against the government. The measure had the added attraction that it could be applied immediately, as there was no need to change the constitution because according to Bello Rodríguez, the interior minister, all that was necessary under the 1864 constitution was for Congress to approve the change.

Nevertheless, Andrade's action caused violent opposition within the Liberal Party. The Crespistas and Anduecistas united with Francisco Tosta García, while José Landislao Andara and Ramón Ayala joined the old *guzmancista*, Francisco González Guinán. They all argued that the country's political division would not be immediate and could only be applicable during the presidential period following its approval, which would start on January 1, 1902. In Táchira the vexed question of representation of the state at the national level increased political unrest. In January the Asambleas Legislativas met to proclaim the independent wishes of the Trujillo, Mérida, and Táchira *secciones*, which formed the Andes state. The Trujillanos decided to breakaway, forming their own independent state, while Mérida and Táchira chose to form a smaller state whose president would be Espíritu Santo Morales. They chose La Grita as the new capital, an idea well received in Táchira but causing consternation in Mérida. The Merideños appealed to Andrade, but he gave Morales all the support he needed. It was time for Castro to place his political marker.[32]

CASTRO PREPARES TO INVADE VENEZUELA

During his period of exile Castro was constantly visited by people who kept him in touch with events in Caracas. In early 1898 he held talks with Carlos Rangel Garbiras, his old adversary and head of the Nacionalismo in the Andes, at La Donjuana in Colombia. However, an agreement could not be reached because his old foe wanted a dual leadership structure with him as civil chief and Castro as military chief. This was unacceptable to Castro because he reasoned that two leaders would weaken their position. In reality both men felt that they should be the sole leader of the revolution. The *liberales continuistas* of Andueza Palacio and José Ignacio Pulido had gone into exile after their defeat in 1892 by the *liberales legalistas*. However, they had returned to the country with the death of Crespo and were not willing to give up without a fight. They viewed Andrade as a conservative because of his social background and considered themselves to be the "real trustees of the purity of the yellow liberal cause."[33] The result was that the Anduecistas began to conspire to end Andrade's rule. Cipriano

Castro was one such Anduecista who had been in exile since 1892. Pulido, Ayala, and Andueza Palacio invited him to participate in the rebellion, designating him chief of the Andes state.

On February 28, 1899, Castro sold a life policy to Gómez for $1,298 with a surrender value of $5,000 so that he could travel to Caracas to confer with Andrade about what political role he could play in the future. In exchange for supporting Andrade, Castro demanded the presidency of the Andes, but he was unable to put his views to the president because Mendoza Solar, secretary to Andrade, prevented a meeting from taking place between the two men. At this snub Castro immediately put into effect his plan to topple Andrade and seize power, which he had spent so much time mulling over at his *hacienda* in Colombia.

On his return journey back to his status of political exile in Colombia he stopped at Curacao, where he was able to enlist the support of an important group of Venezuelan Anduecistas exiles on the island, including José Ignacio Pulido, Juan Pietri, and Ramón Ayala.[34] In Maracaibo, at the home of Don Felipe Arocha, who was the foster uncle of Castro's wife and ran a large trading house, a number of important business leaders promised to support Castro in his revolutionary quest. During the rest of the year Castro kept busy seeking support for his plans by forming a Centro Directivo del Partido Ciprianista. Lucio Baldó was president of the committee, and other members included Santiago Briceño Ayesterán, Rafael María Velasco Bustamante, Román Moreno, Pedro Pablo Rodríguez, Trino Niño, and Ramón Buenahora. The committee later expanded with the incorporation of other Liberals such as Colonel Régulo Olivares, General Froilán Prato, and General Obdulio Cacique. Although Castro funded the initial expenses, most of the financial backing came from Gómez, the successful entrepreneur.

The objective of the rebels was to acquire power in the Andes and then take over the country. Castro also informed his small band of supporters in the center and western areas of the country of the purpose of his actions so that he could count on their backing. He declared that the first man to enter "the capital triumphantly would be accepted as the chief of state, with everybody having to acknowledge and support him."[35] Many took up his offer, but the government squashed all their attempts. In Caracas, General Esteban Chalbaud Cardona, Castro's second in command who had travelled to Caracas to communicate the news to the rebels, was imprisoned.

A CONSTITUTIONAL CRISIS

The new national administrative structure posed a tricky constitutional question because the seven states mentioned in the first article of the 1881 constitution no longer existed, implying that the constitution needed to be reformed completely. Consequently, Congress met on February 20, 1899, to discuss these matters. It essentially became a constitutional assembly, with all legislative and governmental powers from the president downward becoming provisional until the constitutional matters had been resolved. To compound the government's difficulties, the year would be an economic disaster, with coffee prices plummeting and revenues shrinking as imports fell. The country also suffered from a smallpox epidemic, a locust plague that destroyed many of the crops, and a long draught that decimated cattle stocks.

The idea of returning the country to twenty states was not in dispute. However, the way to obtain this result divided Congress into two distinct camps: the *Inmediatistas* who were supported by Andrade and who wanted to immediately create the twenty states, and the *Constitucionalistas*, who preferred to amend the constitution first to create the twenty new states. The *Inmediatistas* proposed returning to the political division of the 1864 constitution by changing the second clause of the constitution, which allowed the creation of provisional states and the appointment of interim officials within the new states. When it came to a congressional vote on this proposal, Andrade's supporters won by sixty-six votes to twenty-five. On April 22, Congress enacted the formation of twenty states in Venezuela, with the large states of Bermúdez, Miranda, and Andes splitting into smaller entities. Such an outcome amounted, according to Velásquez, to a *coup d'etat* "in which the soldiers were replaced by deputies and senators and the rifles for ballot papers."[36] At the beginning of May, Andrade and Bello felt sufficiently strong to release Mocho Hernández from prison, reasoning that all Liberals would unite with them against the Conservatives.

Castro did not agree with the result, arguing that the changes that Congress had approved were unconstitutional. However, the constitution allowed the creation of such entities on a provisional basis while it was debated in Congress, and the appropriate amendments to the constitution had been enacted. Castro had nevertheless found the pretext he needed to launch his revolution, and so he began to rally his supporters by setting up local committees in Táchira for the restoration of the constitution. In Capacho the committee was composed of Pedro María Cárdenas, Rafael María Velasco, Evaristo Prieto, Jorge Bello, and José María García Gómez. In San Cristóbal, Ovidio Salas, José Antonio Dávila, Joaquín Garrido, Gumersindo Méndez, César Ibarra were ready to spring into action, while in Táriba, Santiago Briceño Ayesterán, and Clodomiro Sánchez were ready. Other Castro supporters were dotted about the state, with Juan Alberto Rámirez in Rubio, Luis Varela in Santa Ana, Régulo Olivares and Florentino Vargas in Lobatera, Maximiano Casanova in Palmira, Régulo Olivares' brothers in Colón, and Roberto Pulido in San Antonio. In Tovar, Mérida state, Eulogio Moros was in charge of Castro's supporters. Many of Castro's strongest allies, such as Régulo Olivares, Santiago Briceño Ayesterán, and Pedro María Cárdenas, travelled to Colombia to cross the border with him. However, there was one last attempt to get Andrade to change his mind in the form of a memorandum proposing that Castro be appointed president of Táchira. Andrade rejected the suggestion, something that he would live to regret. By October he would be in exile in Curacao, and Castro would start his nine-year rule of the country.

NOTES

1. Arturo Guillermo Muñoz, "The Táchira Frontier, 1881–1899: Regional Isolation and National Integration in the Venezuelan Andes," PhD. diss., Stanford University, 1977, p. 126.
2. Ibid., p. 138.
3. William M. Sullivan, "The Rise of Despotism in Venezuela: Cipriano Castro 1899–1908," PhD. diss., The University of New Mexico, 1974, p. 73.
4. Muñoz, p. 138.
5. Ibid., p. 132.
6. Ibid., p. 143.
7. Gómez's ancestors came from Colombia and were involved in the independence movement. Gómez's grandfather was José del Rosario García Bustamante, who was the son of Eleuterio García Rovira, a neogranadine hero and brother of Custodio García Rovira, a martyr of Colombia. José del Rosario García Bustamante, Gómez's grandfather, was born in Cúcuta. He owned La Mulera in Táchira. He had three sons with Ana Dolores Gómez Nieto, his common-law wife: Pedro Cornelio, Fernando, and Silverio. Pedro Cornelio, Gómez's father, inherited La Mulera. José del Rosario García Bustamante married María Concepción Bustamante, who was related to him. They had two sons, Eleuterio and José Rosario García. Through the Bustamante surname came the family relation among Gómez, José María García, José Rosario García and Rafael Velasco Bustamante.
8. Pedro José Domínici, *Un Sátrapa. Notas sobre una Tiranía*, Paris, n.p. 1901, p. 21.
9. Muñoz, p. 40.
10. Pablo Emilio Fernández, *Gómez el Rehabilitador*, Caracas, Jaime Villegas Editor, 1956, p. 63.
11. Ibid., p. 65.
12. The crime was never solved.
13. Ramon J. Velásquez, *La Caida del Liberalismo Amarillo*. Tiempo y Drama de Antonio Paredes (Caracas: Ediciones centauro, 1991) p. 207.
14. Vicente Lecuna, *La Revolución de Queipa*, Caracas, Ed. Garrido, 1954, p. 17.
15. Julian Nava, "The Illustrious American: The Development of Nationalism in Venezuela under Antonio Guzmán Blanco," *Hispanic American Historical Review* 45:4, November 1965, pp. 428, 527–43.
16. Lecuna, p. 18.
17. Ibid., p. 39.
18. Santiago Briceño Ayesterán, *Memorias de Su Vida Militar y Política*, Caracas, Tip. América, 1948, p. 26.

19. Equivalent to $49,000 in 1999. This is a rough estimate and is used for illustrative purposes.

20. Enrique Bernardo Núñez, *El Hombre de la Levita Gris (Los Años de la Restauración Liberal)*, Caracas, Ediciones Elite, 1953, p. 17.

21. Others include Josefa, who married Carlos Delfino; Flor, who married José María Cárdenas; Graciela, who married Julio Méndez; Servilia, who married Ignacio Andrade Sosa; Gonzalo, who married Josefina Leyva; and José Vicente, who married Josefina Revenga.

22. Equivalent to $145,000 in 1999.

23. Carlos Siso, *Castro y Gómez. Importancia de la Hegemonía Andina*, Caracas, Editorial Arte, 1985, p. 145.

24. Lecuna, p. 42.

25. Ibid., p. 46.

26. Ignacio Andrade's father was General Escolástico Andrade, a hero of the Wars of Independence. Andrade finished his schooling in the United States and was a man "of ample knowledge and with an excellent background in business administration." (Zoilo Bello Rodríguez, *Archivo Político*, Caracas, Ediciones de la Secretaría de la Presidencia y del Ministerio de la Defensa, 1979, Prologue by R. J. Velásquez, p. vii).

27. Nikita Laureano Harwich, "Cipriano Castro and the 'Libertadora' Revolution. A Hypothesis in Historical Development," Senior Honors History Seminar Paper, Duke University, 1971–72, p. 48.

28. Lecuna, p. 60.

29. Domingo Alberto Rangel, *Los Andinos en el Poder*, Caracas, n.p., 1964.

30. Ibid., p. 67.

31. Ibid., p. 67.

32. A. Arellano Moreno, *Mirador de Historia Política de Venezuela*, Caracas, Imp. Nacional, 1967, p. 191.

33. Zoilo Bello Rodríguez, *Archivo Político*, Caracas, Ediciones de la Secretaría de la Presidencia y del Ministerio de la Defensa, 1979, Prologue by R. J. Velásquez, p. viii.

34. See Domínici.

35. Briceño Ayesterán, p. 37.

36. Velásquez, p. 204–5.

2

Castro Invades

In the small hours of the night of May 23, 1899, Castro, a small man with a thick beard, big eyes, and not forty-two years old, slipped across the border into Táchira with fifty-seven[1] followers, launching his Revolución Restauradora. His objective was to restore the old constitution, which he argued would give the country a strong central government that would stimulate and ensure the general progress of Venezuela. These sentiments were reiterated by General Juan Vicente Gómez, his right-hand man and the main financier of the venture. At the same time that Castro invaded the country, the various Castristas revolutionary committees also took up arms. In Palmira, 180 men "armed normally"[2] and led by Santiago Briceño Ayesterán marched toward Capacho, where all the other revolutionaries were to meet.

The following day Castro reached Independencia, where he issued a proclamation stating that Congress and Andrade had "trampled on the Constitution when the April 22 agreement on the political organization of the republic was sanctioned and approved."[3] Castro wanted the establishment of the state's autonomy, but this had to be done "in a legal way without anger or intransigence, and, above all, without trampling on the Constitution or the current laws."[4] Castro was not against the state's autonomy *per se*, but he objected to the current use of such a concept because it could lead to a dictatorship. Castro's appeal was initially embraced by a small group of people, mainly Tachirenses, while in Mérida only José María Méndez joined him. In Trujillo, where the Araujos and Baptistas had been Castro's supporters, the state remained at the sidelines of the rebellion. In

Barquisimeto only five hundred Larenses joined his rebellion. Castro's revolt was then composed almost entirely of Tachirenses. It would be a mistake, however, to view Castro's revolution as a regional one. It was, as Muñoz observes,[5] a nationalistic one that had a strong desire to strengthen the federal government rather than repudiate it.

When Castro arrived in Capacho he organized his army, which would soon swell to one thousand five hundred men. Their immediate problem at this stage was not manpower but insufficient arms and ammunition. The forces of the government stationed in the Andean states were also minute, almost nonexistent. They were armed with small quantities of poorly maintained mauser carbines. Juan Pablo Peñaloza in San Cristóbal had fifty soldiers at his disposal, while Espíritu Santo Morales in Mérida and Rafael González Pacheco in Trujillo had under their command one hundred soldiers and fifty soldiers respectively. Therefore, Castro was not unduly worried about the local ill-equipped soldiers, but he needed to strengthen his forces to face the expeditionary force that the central government would send once it became clear that his rebellion had not petered out after a week.

GOVERNMENT REACTS

Antonio Fernández, a former commander of the army, former Defense Minister, and a regional *caudillo* in Barlovento, was dispatched by Andrade with an army of six hundred men to deal with Castro. This suited Andrade, who wanted to get rid of Fernández for his own political reasons as he was an important member of the Liberal Party of the Barlovento region of the Miranda state. Castro spent two months campaigning in Táchira against Fernández, whose tactics were "attacking the enemy at the crack of dawn and avoiding concentrating all his forces in one place."[6] Fernández did not see the point of defeating an obscure regional nuisance such as Castro, preferring to conserve his army for later events where he could achieve greater glory. This allowed Castro to lift the siege of San Cristóbal and head toward Mérida, where further differences between the Liberals and Conservatives would allow him to reach Barquisimeto with ease. Castro was not only an undoubtedly good fighter, but he was also lucky in that his opponents were distrustful of each other "with a host of intrigues and mysterious errors that signalled the breakdown and contradiction under which *andradismo* was debated in the Cordillera."[7] In addition, much of the ammunition supplied to government forces was useless, as it was the wrong caliber for their muskets.

In Trujillo the central Conservative figure was Juan Bautista Carrillo Guerra, who was an intimate friend of Andrade and had been the state president since April 1899. The Liberals, such as the Baptistas and Araujos, were more interested in local political fights against Conservatives such as

Carrillo Guerra and González Pacheco than in pursuing the small Castrista army. Nevertheless, Castro faced Rafael González Pacheco, the Agente del Ejecutivo Nacional. He was a courageous and astute Trujillano politician who left Trujillo city with three-hundred men to cut off the rebel leader and prevent him from reaching Mérida. But Juan Bautista Carrillo Guerra gave González Pacheco the wrong ammunition and rifles, and so he had to abandon the fight against Castro in Tovar.

The rebel forces were better organized due in large measure to the efforts of Gómez, who occupied the key post of quartermaster general, ensuring that vital supplies and ammunition reached the fighting men. Gómez's efforts meant that the insurrectionists during the campaign would not lack anything because "there was Gómez ever vigilant, watching everything."[8] Gómez also took part in three battles, one siege, and five skirmishes. The most important of these were at Tononó on May 24, at Las Pilas on May 27, at San Cristóbal on May 28, and at Páramo Zumbador on June 27. Gómez was also at the siege of San Cristóbal and was involved in the battle of Cordero against the troops of Fernández. On August 6, Gómez defeated general Rafael González Pacheco at Tovar, and on August 26 he was involved in the Parapara combat in Yaracuy. He reached Carababo in September, where he participated in the combat of Nirgua on September 8 and in the large battle of Tocuyito on September 14.

Castro's progress to Caracas was swift after he broke out of Táchira in early August. His advancement went almost unimpeded because the government decided to do battle closer to Caracas. Over forty-two days Castro's army covered 540 kilometers to reach Tocuyito, in Carabobo state, on September 12. The same morning that Castro arrived at Tocuyito, Diego Bautista Ferrer, the war minister, and Antonio Fernández, the president of Aragua, led an army of four thousand six hundred men out of Valencia to do battle against Castro. However, the rebel leader from Táchira was able to rout them because Andrade had given equal command to both Ferrer and Fernández, old enemies who did not consult each other. The government troops dispersed in a disorderly, panic-stricken manner, even managing at one stage to attack each other. Ferrer returned to Valencia and the city was evacuated. The population, in near panic, wanted to escape the wrath of Castro, thus allowing the almost deserted city to be taken unopposed by the rebels.

Although the government had received a set-back at this stage, it still controlled most of the country. The rebels held only Motatán in Trujillo and now Valencia, where Castro was surrounded by new influential friends such as Ramón Tello Mendoza, Manuel Corao, Julio Torres Cárdenas, Eduardo Celis, and José Rafael Revenga. It was at this point that Andrade decided to take command of the government troops himself, leaving Caracas on September 14 and meeting with the routed troops in La Victoria, where they had retreated. In Caracas, Bello Rodríguez was appointed secretary general with Fernando Arvelo replacing him at the interior ministry. There were now two factions within the government. The *liberal amarillos* were headed by Bello Rodríguez. The Nacionalistas were headed by Arvelo, who took a secret plan to Mocho Hernández, who was in jail, to form a new government that would be composed mostly of Nacionalistas.

SUPPORT FOR CASTRO IN THE COUNTRY

The intermittent civil wars that affected the country also brought unrest among the commercial elite of the country because it was bad for business. In addition, the foreign debt that Guzmán Blanco and subsequent governments incurred had practically mortgaged Venezuela to foreign countries, placing an undue burden on customs taxes and making imported goods expensive while constraining economic growth. There was a general feeling that it was necessary to bring law and order to the country as this would possibly lift the country out of its economic nightmare. Simón González Chacón, for example, wrote at the time that because the country was in total disorder, it needed a strong hand to put it back on an even keel. The Liberals, who under Andrade's government had suffered politically, saw the increasingly successful Castro as the savior of their own causes.[9] If Castro was able to bring both the Conservatives and the Liberals together and to use some of the younger generation who were not tainted by corruption, then "only this way will he manage to keep the country from falling over the threatening edge of the steep slope and thus manage to remould the country under the Restoration banner, opening new horizons and bright perspectives for the future of the people."[10]

In Caracas the political situation deteriorated for Andrade when he heard that General Víctor Rodríguez, the vice president, was organizing a coup against him, forcing the president to return to Caracas. In La Victoria, Luciano Mendoza refused to command the government troops unless Fernández was sacked as president of Aragua state and Ferrer was removed from his post of war minister. Andrade was reluctantly forced to accept this, appointing Agustín Carullo, the governor of Caracas, as head of Aragua state and Isidoro Widerman, the former military chief of Caracas, as war minister. The majority of the country's military leaders, however, remained loyal to Andrade. Nicolás Rolando in eastern Venezuela and Gregorio Segundo Riera in Coro offered to concentrate their troops near Caracas to fight Castro. Luciano Mendoza would now command an army of four-thousand men to fight the upstart from Táchira.

In spite of Andrade's military support his political power was inexorably waning. On September 16, a few days after the decisive battle of El Tocuyito, the Liberals of Caracas, headed by Matos, met outside Valencia and declared their support and adherence to Castro's Revolucíon Restauradora.[11] Andrade's position was becoming more untenable as the crisis deepened and the country's economic situation deteriorated further, with the government facing bankruptcy because the national coffers were empty. Although the rebels only controlled a small part of the country, Andrade felt that he had no support and knew he was beaten. Andrade's own political decline owed much to corruption among his supporters. This stemmed from his method for unifying the Liberal party by giving most of them "preference in the best state offices"[12] and from the government's bad administration of the public works program.

THE VALENCIA PROCLAMATION

On September 25, Castro issued his Valencia Proclamation in which he once again accused Andrade of becoming a dictator, stating that

> The country was eager for legal practices and in need of a normal, honest and pure administration, but general Andrade far from paying attention to such an urgent need, chose instead to concentrate on personal politics, taking away from some States their Constitutional Magistrates, and imposing his capricious authoritarian regime above the law, and ending by degrading the foundations on which our system rests, breaching the Constitution to reach the monstrous agreement of April 22 which violently created twenty autonomous states and in turn made the President of the Republic into a Dictator.[13]

A delegation headed by José Manuel Revenga was dispatched to see whether Andrade would accept a negotiated peace settlement with Castro. However the president would only contemplate such a move if the Partido Liberal was recognized as the dominant force in national politics, reasoning that if Castro accepted such a situation the war could come to an end and a new political organization for the country could be achieved. On September 28, General Bello Rodríguez, Andrade's secretary general, left Caracas for La Victoria to establish contact with Castro. Together with Celestino Peraza, who represented the military, Rodríguez entered into talks with the rebel leader in the president's name, although Andrade remained ignorant of the basis on which negotiations would take place.

Castro's terms were well defined and remained essentially the same as those contained in his Independencia Proclamation. In addition, he wanted an eight-day truce and promised that there would be no victors nor vanquished, that there would be no special favors for any regional groups, and that all personal and property rights would be respected. In return, he wanted to share power equally with Andrade's supporters, but the president would have to resign until constitutional elections had been held. After a number of false starts a workable peace agreement was tacitly arranged on October 1 at the small Carabobo town of San Mateo. This was stillborn, however, as Andrade rejected the negotiations because he considered General Celestino Peraza a traitor and had sent specific instructions on September 23 to Luciano Mendoza not to appoint him to the talks with Castro. Although Andrade wanted to preserve Venezuela's peace and institutions, he was not going to surrender to the man from the mountains, a view endorsed by the cabinet on October 2 when it denounced the San Mateo accord as unacceptable. On their return to La Victoria, Bello Rodríguez and Peraza were intercepted by Fernando Arvelo, the interior minister, who revoked their commission for assuming greater powers than had been initially assigned to them.

Castro was no longer a regional problem that could simply be ignored. He was now firmly on the national political map after his victory at Tocuyito. It became increasingly clear to Andrade that his own political situation would deteriorate further if he did not extend an olive branch to Castro. Andrade sought the counsel of Manuel Antonio Matos, the most important Liberal in the country,[14] who in turn feared that the president, who was no longer sure of the political support he commanded from the Liberals, would free Mocho Hernández to obtain the backing of the Nacionalistas. Such a move could conceivably hand the presidency to the Mochistas because of the split within the Liberal Party. It was thus clear that to prevent the Mochistas from assuming power, a deal would have to be worked out with the *cabito*, as Castro was to be called later.

Matos therefore accepted his appointment as *Delegado de la Paz*, leaving Caracas with José Manuel Revenga on October 3 to negotiate a new settlement with Castro. They were unavoidably delayed at La Guaira because the Spanish stokers refused to work on the Venezuelan gunboat *Miranda* until their wages had been paid in full. Once the dispute was settled, the Peace Delegation finally departed on October 4, followed closely by Francis Loomis, the American Minister, on the USS *Detroit*. Matos was convinced that Andrade was about to release Mocho Hernández to the consternation of all Liberals. He informed Castro at their first meeting that if this occurred, Vice President Rodríguez, former Defense Minister Ferrer, Caracas Commander in Chief Francisco González Espinosa, Army Inspector Domingo Monagas, General Francisco Batalla, and he would intervene to prevent it from happening. It was clear to Castro after this meeting that Andrade's days were numbered and that the presidency was his for the taking before Mocho Hernández was released from jail. Castro needed to act quickly to secure the presidency for himself, as the move to release Mocho Hernández in Caracas might be imminent.

THE NATIONALISTS

The directors of the Partido Liberal Nacionalista, Alejandro Urbaneja, David Lobo, Ricardo Castillo Chapellín, Régulo Franquiz, Pedro Tomás Vegas, and Eloy Escobar, worked with the interior minister, Fernando Arvelo, to reach a secret agreement in which Mocho Hernández would be immediately released from prison. Andrade, in turn, would reciprocate and hand over the presidency of the country to him to destroy the "military and political alliances which the Liberals in the government headed by Vice-President Rodríguez were forging to favour general Castro."[15] Moreover, Andrade would then name him *Jefe del Ejército Nacional* and appoint a new cabinet in which the former president would be able to name five of the ministers "with the rest designated by Hernández under the clear understanding that the War and Navy Ministry would be included in the latter group."[16]

The position of the rebels had its weaknesses as their army had not grown significantly since it had taken up positions in Valencia. Only Martín Marcano in Barcelona and Diego Colina in Coro had pledged their support to Castro. The government, on the other hand, had four thousand well-armed, provisioned men in La Victoria, with a further one thousand five-hundred in Caracas. Practically the whole country was in government hands, so it is difficult to understand the fear that the government had of a Castro victory. Andrade attempted a further peace settlement through Mendoza on October 9, when he requested that the U.S. State Department arrange a private meeting with him and Castro on the USS *Detroit*. Castro travelled to Maracay to wait for the arrival of Andrade, who did not show up. Castro was furious at this snub and negotiations ended. Castro, however, still honored the truce set for October 14.

The role played by Matos further distanced Andrade from his commander in chief, with both men no longer trusting each other. After further protracted debate with Andrade, Matos reached Valencia to negotiate a meeting with Castro to create a national accord. On October 14, Matos saw Castro once again in his camp and proposed a peace agreement and the establishment of the Congreso de Plenipotenciarios from the twenty states, of which half would be appointed by the president and the other half by Castro, that would meet in Caracas on October 28 to oversee the resignation of Andrade. President Andrade would place at Castro's disposal the National Armoury until October 28, and half the government's revenue would accrue to the rebel leader. Castro also wanted to include a clause that reappointed the twenty-five congressmen who had voted against the government in April. It is difficult to understand why the government was willing to hand over power, as the rebels were in a much weaker position.

The following day, October 15, a meeting that would decide the destiny of the country took place between Luciano Mendoza and Castro in San Mateo, in a car of the Ferrocarril de Venezuela. Because no agreement was reached the truce was extended further so that Mendoza could consult the president. However, Andrade was furious at this. He demanded an explanation from Mendoza, who argued that a further truce had not been granted but that "in recognition of the intervention by Matos and authorised by a presidential order, [he] had opted to wait rather than be the cause of a split."[17] Andrade also found unacceptable the clause in the peace treaty that "made the twenty-five parliamentarians, which during the sessions of the Chamber in April were opposed to the constitutional reform and abstained from voting, members of the Plenipotentiary Congress."[18] Castro, on the advice of Matos, Víctor Rodríguez, Andueza Palacio, and Guillermo Tell Villegas Pulido, would later agree to drop this particular clause. Andrade now threatened the Liberals and Castro with freeing Mocho Hernández from La Rotunda prison. It is from this point onward that Mendoza ceased to support the president.

Andrade, who was becoming more isolated politically, was now left to play with the Mochista option, something that the Liberals knew only too well. The Nacionalista coup was expected at any time. The Liberals, led by Ministers Diego Ferrer and Francisco González Espinoza, were also preparing to take emergency measures to check the Conservative threat, especially as Andrade seemed incapable of doing anything. During the evening of October 19, Andrade had a long conversation with Matos, who informed the president that his days were numbered. At around midnight "a mortar exploded in the hall of Matos home,"[19] and the immediate thought was that the Mochistas were responsible for the attack. By dawn, Andrade was receiving news of a possible military uprising in Caracas. When he tried to get hold of General Antonio Orihuela, the *Jefe de la Guardia Civil Montada* he received no reply. For that matter he heard nothing from Diego Ferrer, Governor Pedro Alcántara Leal, or Commander Francisco González Espinoza because, like himself, they were planning their next move.

At this stage Andrade ordered all political prisoners to be freed, planning to take Mocho Hernández with him to Macuto, a seaside resort next to La Guaira. However, nobody listened to his orders. It was at this moment that the president finally realized that all was lost. He left for La Guaira where he departed on the *Bolivar* for the British West Indies on the evening of October 20. Ironically, at the time of Andrade's departure Matos was frantically trying to get hold of him to inform him of Castro's acceptance to the changes in the peace treaty.

A NEW PRESIDENT

In Caracas there was general confusion when Vice President Rodríguez assumed the presidency on October 20, as he was unable to decide on his next move. One group of Liberals, the Continuistas, who were headed by the former presidents Andueza Palacio and Villegas Pulido, advised that Castro should be given the presidential chair. However, the writer Jacinto López, Rodríguez's new secretary general, had another idea, which was to surround the new president with capable people who could give him sound advice. As a first move López advised Rodríguez to appoint his own cabinet. However, Matos opposed this move because he wanted a president whom he felt he could control, and insisted that power should be handed over to Castro. But López maintained that Rodríguez could continue and informed him that he already had a number of people who would be willing to form part of the new government. In addition, he argued that government forces controlled most of the country, so that to relinquish power as suggested by Matos would be "total irresponsibility, an act without glory, and of collective treason."[20] A compromise proposal was to appoint a *junta* composed of José Ignacio Pulido, Cipriano Castro, and Luciano Mendoza. However, Rodríguez found López's advice to go it alone the most compelling. He appointed a new cabinet that was headed by Juan Francisco Castillo, the opposition presidential candidate whom Andrade had defeated, and was composed of Eduardo Calcaño, Manuel Clemente Urbaneja, Juan Pablo Rojas Paúl, Diego Bautista Ferrer, Heriberto Gordon, and José Rafael Ricart.

Twenty-four hours later, however, the views of Matos prevailed. On October 21 the new government declared its intention of handing over power to Castro. A commission headed by a former president, Guillermo Tell Villegas Pulido, and composed of Manuel Modesto Gallegos, Torcuato Ortega Martínez, Bernabé Planas, Carlos Urrutía, and Elias Rodríguez left Caracas for Valencia to offer the presidency to Castro and to sign a peace treaty with him. The commission planned to accompany him on his triumphant march to Caracas. Under Article 151 of the constitution the government could enter into such treaties to bring acts of civil war to an end. It was argued that the rebel forces had superior power compared to the government, which was clearly untrue. Castro accepted the presidency and the entourage left for Caracas, stopping at Maracay, where the peace treaty was signed between Castro and Rodríguez's representatives.

Castro, who had just celebrated his forty-second birthday, was accompanied by Matos and Luciano Mendoza on his train journey to Caracas. Castro arrived on October 22 to be met by a host of public officials, and "then conducted in an open carriage to the presidential palace through streets lined with government troops and curious onlookers."[21] That evening at a sumptuous banquet given by Vice President Rodríguez, most of the high government personalities came to the Casa Amarilla to congratulate Castro, who declared that his administration would bring "new men, new ideals and new procedures." The following day in the Salón Elíptico of the capitol, Rodríguez formally handed over power to Castro, whose first political act was to free all political prisoners, including Mocho Hernández.

However, Castro had arrived in Caracas a virtual prisoner of the troops of Luciano Mendoza and Loreto Lima, which were superior in numbers and in quality to Castro's own two thousand men in Valencia. Consequently, instead of appointing new faces to his administration Castro was forced, out of political expediency, to include in his new cabinet old Liberal *caudillos* such as Andueza Palacio, Guillermo Tell Villegas Pulido, Juan Pablo Rojas Paúl, Juan Francisco Castillo, Victor Rodríguez, Luciano Mendoza, Ramón Guerra, Celestino Peraza, and José Ignacio Pulido. In addition, Mocho Hernández, the lifelong enemy of the *liberales amarillos*, was appointed to Castro's new cabinet as development minister. Castro's new cabinet had the merit of uniting all Liberal factions, something that Crespo and Andrade had failed to do. Although Andrade had abandoned the country, he still had the support of Juan Pablo Peñaloza, Nicolás Rolando, Gregorio Segundo Riera, and Antonio Paredes, who could all muster sufficient support to mount an attack on Caracas. However, Andrade advised his supporters on October 26 to work with the new government. Antonio Paredes, however, refused to hand over the Puerto Cabello fort until certain promises were made. Ramón Guerra and Julio Sarría were sent to dislodge Paredes with a land and sea attack on the fort, which started on November 11. Paredes finally surrendered two days later and was sent to prison at La Rotunda in Caracas.

To the dismay of the Tachirenses, Castro's original backers, there was not one Andino in his first cabinet. They only managed to secure "secondary and tertiary positions in the bureaucracy, a monopoly of high offices in Táchira, a few important posts in the Federal District, and some staff positions in the armed forces."[22] This was not unreasonable, however, given that in the latter stage of the campaign they had played a relatively minor role in Castro's quest for power. Castro reached power by default. As Sullivan observes, as long as he "had to rely on traditionalists for military and financial support, old men, old ideas and old methods would prevail. The Caracas elite would not have accepted a superimposed hierarchy of *andinos*."[23] Castro did not want to challenge directly the Guzmán Blanco system that had ruled the country for over forty years. During his administration Castro would imprison many people who had previously defended his actions and who hoped for a permanent democratic change. However, Castro would not be anybody's puppet, as the old *caudillos* would soon realize. The appearance of the men from the Andes changed the political landscape of the country forever because they upset the political equilibrium that Guzmán Blanco and his Liberal supporters had developed between the commercial bourgeoisie and the local regional *caudillos*. The result was that the local *caudillos* would increasingly see their position in jeopardy and would later rebel against Castro, with Mocho Hernández the first to go against him.

MOCHO HERNÁNDEZ

Mocho Hernández did not accept his appointment as development minister because he wanted two other Nacionalistas to accompany him in the cabinet. During the night of October 26, Mocho Hernández, Samuel Acosta, and a few loyal supporters slipped out of Caracas toward the Tuy valley, seeking Loreto Lima, whose troops were stationed between Valencia and Tinaquillo. From his *Cuartel General de Las Tejerías* Mocho Hernández, as Jefe Supremo de la Revolución Nacional, issued a Proclamation that accused Castro of betraying his ideals by maintaining all the old *liberal amarillos* in power. After a number of battles and skirmishes that did not make any military sense, Mocho Hernández ended up in Guayana toward the end of 1899. Nicolás Rolando, as president of that state, felt increasingly isolated from Castro because he appeared to favor his regional rival, José Antonio Velutini. Rolando suggested to Mocho Hernández that the two should join forces to restore the regions' autonomy, starting with Guayana. The movement known as the *Movimiento Reintegrador* promised to install in Caracas a plural government in which the followers of Mocho Hernández would be involved. However, first Mocho Hernández needed to "retire to Trinidad while the States of the Federation accepted the *rolandista* cause."[24] The nationalist leader, as expected, did not agree with all this and was opposed to a pluralist type of government, wanting instead to see the autonomy of all twenty states recognized as the 1864 constitution stated. Unable to agree, Rolando sent General José Manuel Pañaloza to apprehend Mocho Hernández, who retired to the center of the country to start peace negotiations with Castro through General Valentín Pérez. These negotiations came to an end when Mocho Hernández found out that Castro had appointed Ramón Guerra, his old enemy during the days of the Queipa revolution, as his chief negotiator. General José Antonio Dávila, *comandante de armas of Carabobo*, was then sent against Mocho Hernández, who was in Casupo. He managed to escape with 10 men, only to be captured the following day in Tierra Negra. At the same time Nicolás Rolando fled to Trinidad, where he organized an opposition movement against Castro. In June 1900, Mocho Hernández was transferred to the San Carlos fort in Zulia state.

CASTRO IN CARACAS

When Castro travelled to Caracas, his troops were billeted in Valencia. They entered the capital on November 2 under the command of Gómez, who had been appointed commander in chief and whose appearance was described by a contemporary as that of "a good-natured hick who did not intend to hide or disguise anything."[25] Gómez was later appointed governor of the Federal District; on February 22, 1900, he was named military chief of Táchira state and given the difficult task of pacifying the state, which was still resentful from their lack of participation in government. When Gómez arrived early in March, his message was one of unity, putting aside old differences among them in order to build a new future.[26] In a few months Gómez managed to reestablish some order out of the chaos that the local administration had fallen into, creating the "union of the Tachirense family and thereby consolidating local institutions; awarding generously the services and efforts of his supporters while at the same time avoiding reprisals and thus giving absolute political guarantees who up to then had been opponents."[27] Gómez would carry this conviction with him all through his long political life.

The new regime was vulnerable to all sorts of pressure because Castro's political base was very insecure, and any support that the Andes offered was far away. To ensure that he remained in power and also to break his dependence on Matos, Castro soon built his own political base in the shape of a national army. Castro's first move was to outfit, provision, and station several thousand Andinos in Caracas. On February 28, 1900, he created the quartermaster generalcy to distribute military supplies and to collect arms following the mustering out of troops. Although Venezuela's first military code was enacted under Guzmán Blanco in 1873, it was only under Castro that the army began to be modernized. At the same time Castro announced the need to establish a proper navy to patrol the country's coastline with the purchase of "cruisers, gunboats, transport ships for the navy and a flotilla of auxiliary sailboats."[28] He also created the Arsenal de la Marina. A naval school and an admiralty was also established, featuring its own officers and a proper career structure. All these changes pointed to the army becoming more centralized and homogeneous, taking away prime political power from the regional *caudillos* and vesting it with the central government. After 1903 the government had thirty battalions of well-fed, clothed soldiers who were also copiously armed, because Castro had procured great quantities of arms for his regime.

Castro's rule would soon come into conflict with the regional *caudillos*, such as Nicolás Rolando and Luciano Mendoza, the former in Trinidad, trying to organize an opposition movement with other Andinos, such as Rangel Garbiras and Peñaloza. Rolando managed to acquire arms in Grenada and was waiting to confer with other *caudillos* when Celestino Peraza, a former presidential secretary and minister of development, launched his own rebellion on December 14, 1900, from Las Mercedes, speaking to the country in the name of a new party, the Republicano Liberal.[29] Peraza's rebellion soon petered out, but then General Pedro Julián Acosta in eastern Venezuela took up arms in the name of Nicolás Rolando, who in turn launched his own rebellion in January 1901, which he labelled as his "*cumanesa-margariteña* guerrilla." Among Rolando's supporters were the Ducharme brothers, who knew all the hiding places in the Orinoco swamp lands. Although the terrain was difficult, Gumersindo Méndez was finally able to defeat the rebels. As soon as Acosta was defeated, General Juan Pietri, who was instrumental in the 1892 Revolución Legalista, started an uprising against Castro in Carabobo state. Pietri was soon captured in

Magdaleno but Castro ordered his release, although his closest officers were imprisoned in La Rotunda. This disparate group would align themselves in 1901 with the old liberal elite, headed by Matos, to form the Revolución Libertadora and try to depose Castro.

On February 20, 1901, Castro addressed Congress for the first time when he delivered the annual presidential speech for that year. The last time Castro had been at the capitol was in 1890 as deputy for the Andes state. The Asamblea Nacional Constituyente, which had been assembled to legitimize the current political situation, elected Castro provisonal president for the period from March 29, 1901, to February 26, 1902. Gómez was named first provisional vice president and Ramón Ayala was named second vice president. After the close of the 1901 Asamblea Nacional Constituyente the old Liberal politicians tried to establish a political party to impede Castro's plans.

RELATIONS WITH COLOMBIA

The close ties of Táchira with Colombia and Castro's own affinity to the Liberals in the neighboring republic during his long sojourn there led him to dream of forming a grand alliance to get rid of the Conservatives in Colombia. When he achieved power, Castro assisted the Liberals in their quest to topple the *godos*. Castro's dream did not stop there. He wanted more than anything to recreate Gran Colombia with a Venezuelan as its president. This was something that his great friend, the Colombian Liberal Rafael Uribe Uribe, constantly fed to his imagination. The two, along with Eloy Alfaro of Ecuador, wanted to start the "empire of liberalism in America,"[30] which would also extend to other like-minded presidents in the area such as José Santos Zelaya in Nicaragua. To make the concept valid the bastion of conservatism, Colombia, had to be defeated. Consequently, on May 17, 1900, Castro invited Zelaya to join his grand-unification plan with the former countries of Gran Colombia. The plan was simple in its conception. Castro would invade Colombia from the east, while Eloy Alfaro in Ecuador invaded from the south. Zelaya in the north would overrun Panamá, and the Colombian Liberals would undermine the government of the country. After the fall of Bogotá, an expeditionary force of five thousand men would sail to Managua to assist Zelaya in conquering the rest of Central America.

The Colombian government appeared to be living in a permanent state of panic because of all the help that Castro was giving to the Liberals. Of the forty thousand rifles that the Venezuelan government acquired in Europe, it was thought that ten thousand were destined for the Colombian revolutionaries. The arms were shipped to Táchira under the pretext that they were needed to maintain law and order. The thousands of exiled Colombian Liberals and soldiers waiting to return to their country were the beneficiaries of this policy. Castro judged that this was the right moment to help his Colombian Liberal friends.

The Conservative Colombian government of José Manuel Marroquín, however, decided to preempt Castro by supporting the invasion plans of the Venezuelan revolutionaries led by Rangel Garbiras. On July 26, 1900, Rangel Garbiras led four-thousand men across the border into Táchira. The army was a motley group of people whose main aim was to pillage the surrounding countryside while shouting " 'Down Castro,' 'Long Live Mocho Hernández,' 'Down with the Reds,' 'Long Live Rangel' "[31] while they broke down doors and "destroyed shops and housing, burnt clothes and furniture, while shooting over the heads of peaceful neighbours."[32] The principal objective of the invading army, which was more akin to a pillaging horde, was San Cristóbal and its large arsenal. However, because it had wasted valuable time pillaging the border towns of Ureña, San Antonio, Capacho Viejo, Capacho Nuevo, Palmira, and Táriba, Celestino Castro was able to organize the defenses of the city,[33] with the South side of the city guarded by the Colombian general Uribe Uribe. On July 28, the battle of San Cristóbal started, ending at sunset the following day. The rebels suffered casualties of eight-hundred men dead and wounded, compared with the government losses of three-hundred men.

Marroquín's plan had failed. Instead of the rebels gaining access to the arsenal at San Cristóbal, the Castro government was able to increase its own supply of weapons by acquiring the arms and ammunition of the retreating invading army. Cipriano Castro then mobilized General Cardona, the president of Mérida, Pedro Araujo, the president of Trujillo, and Régulo Olivares, the president of Zulia, to form an army of five-thousand soldiers to march to Táchira under the command of General Uribe Uribe, who defeated the invading army of Rangel Garbiras. In August, Rangel Garbiras and the Nacionalistas tried again to invade the country by San Faustino, but they failed.

With the rout of Rangel Garbiras' army, General Uribe Uribe convinced Castro that a two-pronged attack on Colombia by way of the Guagira and the plains of Arauca would gain victory for the Liberals in Colombia. Consequently, on August 4, 1901, Castro ordered General Rufo Nieves and Marcelino Cedeño to proceed with two battalions of men to Paraguaipoa on the Guagira peninsula. A second expeditionary force was sent to Apure to enter the country via the Arauca plateau. At the same time the president of Ecuador, Leónidas Plaza Gutiérrez, was poised in the south, ready to invade Colombia. Castro's plans did not meet with universal approval, however. General Pulido, Castro's war minister, resigned because he thought the plan would fail, as the country did not have the financial resources for such an endeavor. Ramón Guerra, Andrade's old enemy, replaced Pulido as the new minister of war. He approved the plans, sending fifteen hundred men to the Guagira peninsula.

Castro should have heeded General Pulido's warnings because only a few hundred men returned from the disastrous campaign. It was a shambles because of the appallingly bad logistics, for which General José Antonio Dávila was blamed. The advancing army was met by a Colombian Liberal general, José M. Castillo, at the town of Pueblo Treinta with only one hundred men. Castillo urged the Venezuelans to turn back because the Atlantic army that he wanted to create with Uribe Uribe was not feasible. However, Carmelo Castro, the younger brother of Cipriano Castro, opted for a frontal attack on Rio Hacha. Dávila was not sure of success. Nevertheless, Generals Dávila, Castillo, and Carlos Echevarría sailed into Rio Hacha, threatening to bombard the town if it did not surrender. While the municipal council was debating the ultimatum, the French warship *Suchet* arrived, requesting that hostilities be delayed until all foreigners had been evacuated. General Dávila agreed. As negotiations proceeded, the Colombian warships *Alexandre Bixro* and *Pizón* entered the bay, landing twelve hundred troops and three hundred boxes of ammunition. This forced the Venezuelans to retreat down the coast to Punta La Vela. The Venezuelan forces were later decimated when they were ambushed at Carazua, with six hundred men killed and three hundred taken prisoner. In Caracas no news of this tragedy was given. The government instead paraded the Colombians who had been captured when Rangel Garbiras invaded Táchira. As a result of this debacle, diplomatic relations between the two countries were severed and would remain so until 1909. The United States offered to mediate the dispute between the two countries in 1901, but Colombia rejected this offer.

Castro had arrived in power by default with little political experience outside Táchira and under the auspices of Matos. Castro had to form a government after a long military campaign and start to administer a country he hardly knew. It is not surprising that there were no Andinos in Castro's first cabinet. He depended instead on old Liberal strongmen such as Andueza Palacio, Guillermo Tell Villegas, and Juan Pablo Rojas Paúl. Castro would have to learn his politics fast if he was to survive in Caracas, and he also faced the challenge of stimulating an economy that had endured two years of continuous political upheaval.

NOTES

1. With Castro were Gómez, Joaquín Garrido, Manuel Antonio Pulido, Froilán Prato, José María Méndez, Emilio Fernández, Elias Sayago, Régulo Olivares, Pedro María Cárdenas, Miguel Contreras, Guillermo Aranguren, Luis Varela, José Antonio Dávila, Jorge Bello, Maximiano Casanova, Secundino Torres, Ramón Moreno, Santiago Briceño Ayesterán, Eulogio Moros, Andrés Amaya. Also Gómez's brother Aníbal, Castro's brothers Carmelo and Trino were there. There were also youngsters such as Eliseo Sarmiento, Roberto Pulido, Graciano Castro, Clodomiro

Sánchez, Elias Sayago, Felipe Peralta, Calixto Escalante, T. Morales Rocha, Benjamín Olivieri, Ovidio Salas, Teófilo Velasco, Manuel Rugeles, José R. Dávila, Salvano Briceño, José María García, Rafael María Velasco, and Eleázar López Contreras.

2. Santiago Briceño Ayesterán, *Memorias de Su Vida Militar y Pólitica* Caracas, Tip. América, 1948.

3. Ambrosio Perera, *Historia Orgánica de Venezuela*, Caracas, Editorial Venezuela, 1943, p. 222. For a further discussion on the campaign itself see Emilio Constantino Guerrero, *Campaña Heroíca. Estudio Histórico-Militar de la Campaña Dirigida en Venezuela por el General Cipriano Castro, Como Jefe de la Revolución Liberal Restauradora en 1899*, Caracas, J. M. Herrera Irigoyén y Cia., 1903; Ignacio Andrade, *Cómo Ilego Cipriano Castro al Poder;* Ayesterán, *Memorias de Su Vida Militar;* Picón Salas, *Los dias de Cipriano Castro*, Caracas, Ediciones Garrido, 1953; and, Ramón J. Velásquez, *La Caida del Liberalismo Amarillo.* Tiempo y Drama de Antonio Paredes, Caracas, Ediciones Venezuela, 1960.

4. Perera, p. 222–23.

5. Arturo Guillermo Muñoz, "The Táchira Frontier, 1881–1899; Regional Isolation and National Integration in the Venezuelan Andes," PhD. diss., Stanford University, 1977.

6. Picón Salas, p. 45.

7. Ibid., p. 48.

8. Pablo Emilio Fernández, *Gómez el Rehabilitador*, Caracas, Jaime Villegas, Editor, 1956, p. 98.

9. Simón González Chacón, *El Imperio del Desorden. Realidad Política*, Caracas, Tip. del Comercio, 1899, p. 11.

10. Ibid., p. 16.

11. Juan Sánchez, *Narración Histórica al Partido Liberal. Aclaratoria a Mis Compatriotas*, Caracas, n. p., undated.

12. Ignacio Andrade, *¿Porqué Triunfó la Revolución Restauradora? Memorias y Exposición a los Venzolanos de los Sucesos 1898–1889*, Caracas, Ediciones Garrido, 1955, p. 27.

13. Perera, p. 223.

14. Matos was born on January 8, 1847, at his father's hacienda of Campanero, near Puerto Cabello. At the age of twelve he was sent to school in New York. At fifteen he went to Europe. In 1868, at the age of twenty-one, Matos started a small trading house in La Guaira. In 1875 he married Maria Ibarra, sister of Guzmán Blanco's wife.

15. Velásquez, p. 236.

16. Ibid., p. 237.

17. Ibid.

18. Ibid.

19. Ibid., p. 238.

20. Ibid., p. 239.

21. William M. Sullivan, "The Rise of Despotism in Venezuela, Cipriano Castro, 1899–1908," PhD. diss., The University of New Mexico, 1974, p. 132.

22. Ibid., p. 151–52.

23. Ibid., p. 151–52.

24. Velásquez, p. 252.

25. Estebán Roldán Oliarte, *El General Juan Vicente Gómez. Venezuela de Cerca*, México: Imprenta Mundial, 1933, p. 235.

26. See Jefe Civil y Militar del Estado Táchira, Juan Vicente Gómez, 'A los habitantes del estado', San Cristóbal, 2 March 1900 in Tobias Arias O., *Relieves Máximos*, Caracas, n. p., 1930, p. 16.

27. Roldán Oliarte, p. 34–35.

28. Velásquez, p. 267.

29. In 1893, Alejandro Urbaneja founded a Partido Republicano Liberal that was transformed in 1896 into the Partido Liberal Nacionalista.

30. Velásquez, p. 271.

31. Ibid., p. 275.

32. Ibid., p. 275.

33. Velásquez mentions a number of young men who fought in the battle of San Cristóbal. They subsequently became important people in the government:

Juan Alberto Ramírez

Timoleón Omaña

Pedro Murillo

Arturo Omaña

Pedro María Cárdenas

Ruben, Marcelino, and Antonio Cárdenas

Francisco Antonio Colmenares Pacheco

Aniceto Cubillán

Roman Moreno

Abigail Olivares

Rafael Rojas Fernández

Froilán Prato

Abel, Abraham, Eliseo, Manuel, Marco Antonio Parada, and

Manuel Angarita

3

Foreign Capital and Intervention

When Castro came to power in October 1899, he found the country in a dire state as a result of six years of fiscal chaos and two years of continuous civil war. This was a time of low prices for the country's main agricultural exports. Many of the coffee and sugar plantations had been abandoned. A high foreign debt also meant that no new loans could be secured overseas. The national debt, which amounted to Bs 190 million, had not been serviced since Crespo's time. The government owed the Gran Ferrocarril de Venezuela Bs 710,274, while the gunboats *Zamora* and *Crespo* had been remortgaged after they were purchased in 1896 with a loan. Finally, the Arbitration Tribunal on the Guayana-Venezuela border dispute was owed Bs 400,000.

Agriculture, especially coffee, the leading export crop, had suffered enormously during Castro's invasion, affecting the Andes and the central region of the country. Coffee was fetching low prices on the international markets, which had "the most disastrous effect upon commerce and brought great suffering to all branches of industry"[1] especially in the western part of the country. The value of coffee exports declined from Bs 19,314,600 in 1898 to Bs 13,517,675 in 1900.[2] The position worsened in 1901 when prices dropped from Bs 1.25 to Bs .52 per pound, while a severe drought that affected the whole country severely restricted output that year. The position in eastern Venezuela was better, with British Consul C. H. de Lemos reporting that the civil disturbances of 1899 had no material effect on trade in the region, but he stated that the outlook for 1900 did not "indicate any prospect of improvement."[3] The *Financial News* of London reported in July 1899 that Venezuela would attract attention during the following decade for its almost exhaustless mineral deposits that included "everything from iron in abundance to gold and diamonds."[4] This would also be the source of Castro's biggest problems.

When the new administration took over in 1899, it promised to work for economic recovery. This pleased people who were advocating greater industrial development, such as José Rafael Ricart, who in 1903 criticized the local capitalists or "men of talent" for failing to develop the country industrially because he felt that this was "a very secondary theme for them,"[5] with the result that the "usurer marcantilism" and the imports of goods took their toll on the local economy. Although Castro appeared to offer some hope for the future, the economy worsened during the next few years because of the pernicious monopolies that he awarded to himself and his cronies.

When Castro arrived at the presidential palace in October 1899, he soon found that the government was facing a severe budget deficit. There were two options to reduce the fiscal deficit: float an international loan or impose higher import tariffs. At first Castro attempted the former, sending special commissioners to Europe at the end of 1899 to negotiate a large loan in exchange for the salt monopoly and a special tax on alcohol, but the mission failed. Castro persisted, stressing to A. Pietri Daudet in Antwerp that "more important than consolidating the peace process in the country was the top priority of reestablishing, reviving and reinvigorating our foreign credit facilities."[6] Castro appointed the Belgian consul Andree Rohl, as the country's special financial agent during the early part of 1900 to secure from the American Syndicate in New York a loan for $35 million. The negotiations were proceeding well until *Seligman Brothers* demanded part of Venezuela's customs receipts as collateral. Rohl was then instructed to negotiate a loan with the Disconto Gesellschaft of Berlin, which declined because it was already owed money by Venezuela. A couple of years later the bank played an instrumental role in getting Germany to press for the "peaceful blockade" of Venezuela. Without a large foreign loan forthcoming the government was forced to alleviate the plight of the coffee and cocoa producers by increasing exports. On May 1, 1901, the export duty levied on these items was abolished. To compensate for the loss of revenue the government increased its general import levy by a further 12.5 percent, bringing it to 25 percent. On January 12, 1901, the government had previously imposed an export duty on gold of Bs 100 per kilogram.

However, the government coffers remained empty. Castro appointed General Fabricio Conde Flores[7] as a Comisionado Extraordinario del Gobierno to borrow Bs 1,000,000[8] during December 1900 from the Banco de Venezuela to meet the government's ordinary daily cash requirements. The money ran out in January 1901, so Castro asked Matos to negotiate a new loan. The banks, however, were reluctant to lend any more money as they did not feel that the regime was stable enough. Matos advised the government to raise between Bs 500,000 and 600,000 by private subscription from friends and foes alike, each contributing about Bs 5,000 each. Such a move was rejected. Matos was the country's wealthiest man, a major shareholder in both the Banco de Venezuela and Banco de Caracas, and the president of the latter. He finally persuaded the banks to lend the government the small sum of Bs 500,000, which was not enough. Matos informed Castro that more money would only be forthcoming once the government's budget plans were known, something that the president refused to disclose. The government was in a real bind. Andueza Palacio, the former president and now chancellor, proposed threatening to imprison the bankers if they did not comply and taking the money by force from the banks. The bankers, including Matos, J. B. Egaña, Carlos Echeverría, H. Valarino, and Eduardo Montauban, refused. Castro marched them down the street to the La Rotunda prison. After two days the bankers were shunted to the Caño Amarillo railway station and threatened with being locked up in the San Carlos fortress in Zulia. Such an experience was enough for them to relent and they agreed to provide the loan in exchange for their freedom. Matos was the only banker who refused. He was returned to La Rotunda, where he was detained for a few more days and then freed.

FOREIGN CAPITAL

The panacea of attracting foreign capital as a way of improving a country's economic performance and finances was as attractive then as it is now. At the beginning of Castro's regime the prospects for developing the large asphalt deposits of the country were improving. In 1900 a German company acquired the asphalt deposits near the mouth of the Pedernales tributary of the Orinoco river. In 1901, George Washington Crichfield, an American citizen, acquired from Pedro Guzmán the asphalt deposits that were situated near the Limón river. The ensuing conflict that developed between Castro and foreign enterprises started soon after he took power. On October 5, 1900, an executive decree rescinded the Orinoco Shipping and Trading Company's monopoly to navigate the Macareo and Pedernales channels of the Orinoco delta. The foreign companies defended their interests as best they could. The growing opposition to Castro's administration was mainly financed by foreign companies, especially an American asphalt company, the New York & Bermudez Company (NY&B), and the French Cable Company (FCC). The NY&B provided Matos with up to $145,000 to finance his revolution in 1902, and the FCC would be instrumental in keeping the rebel leader informed on the movement of government troops.

THE ASPHALT CONNECTION

Horatio Hamilton, a small, thin man with a large nose and a full beard, was born in Belfast in 1852. Without much of a formal education he made his way to the United States of America. Later he found himself in Venezuela, selling the biscuits that Vanderveer & Holmes of New York produced. While in Caracas, Hamilton fell in love with Mercedes Smith, the sister of Alberto Smith, and married her on October 12, 1883. The Smith family was very close to Guzmán Blanco, the president of the country, who awarded the lucky groom an asphalt concession as a wedding gift. The Hamilton concession of September 15, 1883, carried the exclusive right for the exploration and exploitation of any asphalt and other natural products of the forests found in the state of Bermúdez. The asphalt element of the document was initially secondary to the lumbering clause of the concession, which led to the processing of the precious woods found in the state. Hamilton and his partner Jorge A. Phillips had already been awarded an asphalt concession in 1883 that covered the whole country, but it was not exploited.

Hamilton left for the United States soon after his honeymoon to negotiate his concession. On October 24, 1885, Thomas H. Thomas, William H. Thomas, and Ambrose H. Carner of New York formed the NY&B to acquire Hamilton's concession with an authorized share capital of $1 million in ten thousand shares of one hundred dollars each. NY&B issued one thousand shares initially, mainly to the brothers William H. and Thomas H. Thomas. Four other shareholders, Melvin Stephens, Edward Williams, and H. B. and N. S. W. Vanderhoef, received a small equity stake of between 10 to 20 shares each. The company's capital at this stage consisted of a $10,000 loan[9] which was awarded by Moses Taylor & Company. On November 16, 1885, after the NY&B was registered, the concession was acquired by issuing Hamilton nine thousand shares, with the vast majority ending up in the hands of Guzmán Blanco.

Thomas H. Thomas became president of the company with Carner as secretary. Hamilton travelled to Venezuela in November 1885 to become the general administrator. The approval of the transfer of the title to the NY&B by the Venezuelan government took place on December 9, 1885. Carner left for Venezuela to start the lumbering and cattle operations. Carner would remain in Venezuela until 1896, when he left the country, allegedly suffering from ill health. However, the real reason for his departure was his mismanagement of the property.[10] Carner later returned to the country, becoming a pivotal character in the NY&B's dispute with the Castro administration.

The development of the wood and cattle resources of the concession did not fare well with the company. They were left with their asphalt deposit as their only exploitable commercial asset. The new company was potentially a serious competitor to the Trinidad Asphalt Company of New Jersey, which was owned by the Barber Asphalt Paving Company. Its main asset was the Trinidadian pitch lake, the largest asphalt deposit in the world. Barber concentrated production on Trinidad because it offered better communications with the United States. In addition, production could be shipped more easily from the island. Barber had guaranteed to pay the colonial authorities an annual royalty of $50,000. Venezuela's production at the time was 10 percent of the British colony's production. Barber's Trinidadian interests produced 220,000 tons between 1896 and 1897, compared with Venezuela's 18,000 tons. The Venezuelan asphalt deposit had the potential to become a large producer, which would mean that prices would fall. This would be prevented if they came under the control of Barber.

By 1893 the NY&B was running out of money. They had to turn to Barber for help, who agreed the following year to extricate the company out of its dire financial straits in return for 85 percent of the company's equity. The NY&B became a subsidiary of the Trinidad Asphalt Company. The Barber Asphalt Paving Company injected $500,000 of new capital into the company by issuing further shares to increase its paid-up capital to $12.5 million. On December 15, 1897, Barber formed the New Trinidad Lake Asphalt Company in London to replace the Trinidad Asphalt Company of New Jersey and to tap the British capital markets. The British company owned all the bond issue and 99.8% of the common stock of NY&B. Although the company erected a $100,000 processing plant in Venezuela in 1900, the government up to then had only received $28,904 in royalties, less than $2,000 per year since the time of the original grant and just over half the sum guaranteed by the company to the government of Trinidad in one year.

DOWNTURN IN ASPHALT

In 1898 the asphalt business went into a recession because of the Spanish American War and a duty of three dollars per ton that was imposed on all asphalt imported into the United States. It was around this time that the Barber Company and General Francis V. Greene[11] started their quest to monopolize the world asphalt business. On June 28, 1899, they formed the Asphalt Company of America. The Company had an authorized capital of $30 million in six-hundred thousand shares with a par value of fifty dollars, of which only 10 percent was paid up. Its other source of capital was a bond issue to the value of $30 million with a 5 percent coupon. The purpose of the new company was to consolidate all the asphalt trusts in the United States, including the NY&B, into one corporate structure. John M. Mack, a Philadelphia politician and paving contractor, wanted to join Barber's party. However, the price of his company, $4 million, was too high and the offer was rejected. Not to be outdone, Mack founded the National

Asphalt Company in New Jersey on May 3, 1900, with a market capitalization of $35 million. Mack gathered all the small paving contractors to compete against the Barber trust. Mack's fellow directors included Arthur Wollanston Sewall and Brigadier General Avery Delano Andrews.

Mack's company began to have an impact on the profitability of the Asphalt Company of America, which had also overextended itself financially with an annual interest charge of $1.5 million.[12] It was in serious financial trouble and had to approach Mack with a merger plan. The plan was accepted, provided that the Barber trust raised $6 million with a further bond issue. In effect, Mack turned his company into the Asphalt Company of America, with the Philadelphia politician becoming the chief operating officer on January 3, 1901. He pushed Amizi Lorenzo Barber, the previous owner, out of the company.

The interest on the company's bonds, which was due on January 4, 1901, was covered from its sinking fund. However, the company collapsed in October 1901 because it could not service the interest on the debentures issued to its shareholders. The National Asphalt Company and the Asphalt Company of America passed into the hands of the liquidators in December 1901. After protracted negotiations the assets of both companies were reorganized, and the shareholders were offered equity in the General Asphalt Company, a new venture incorporated in New Jersey on May 19, 1903. The company received an injection of $6 million of new capital from Henry C. Everdell. General Francis V. Greene assumed the presidency, with Mack as first vice president, General Avery Delano Andrews as second vice president, and Arthur Wollanston Sewall as treasurer. Once the dust settled with the reorganization in May 1903, fifty-four out of the sixty-nine world corporations dealing with asphalt were incorporated into the General Asphalt Company. The company was distributed into four divisions: the NY&B, the New Trinidad Lake Asphalt Company, the South American Asphalt Paving Company, and the Barber Asphalt Paving Company.

DEVELOPMENTS IN VENEZUELA

Soon after Barber left the Asphalt Company of America in 1901, Carner resigned and the two joined with Count Henri Courcier de Julvecourt to form the Pan American Asphalt Company on October 20, 1902. Orray E. Thurber, who had been the Treasurer at the National Asphalt Company, also joined Barber in his new venture. At the same time Barber formed the A.L. Barber Asphalt Company, which despatched Carner to Caracas to obtain the annulment of the Hamilton concession. Carner from now on would be an open enemy of the Asphalt Trust.

Prior to Carner's arrival in Caracas the validity of the Hamilton concession had already come under attack. Antonio Cervoni, a former NY&B manager in Guariquén, joined Mateo Guerra Marcano, Antonio Branchi, and José Francisco Micheli (hereinafter referred to as Cervoni and associates) to file a claim on January 28, 1897, with Luis Esteban Bianchi, a local magistrate at the parish of Unión in the district of Guariquén. The claim was for a tract of about three hundred hectares of land where an asphalt mine called La Felicidad was located. This was situated on the eastern side of the valley of Usirina, adjacent to one of the channels formed by the Orinoco drainage system in the Gulf of Paria. The area was known as Majajul, and it was where the Bermúdez asphalt lake was also situated. Guerra Marcano, a lawyer and politician of some prominence who had been a deputy for the province of Cumaná, a deputy at the National Congress, and a former interior and justice minister, was the driving force in securing the title to La Felicidad. A close inspection of NY&B's mining deeds had revealed to him that an error in the original survey placed the property twenty kilometers from Guariquén and 180 meters above sea level. The location of La Felicidad was only ten kilometers from Guariquén, and therefore it was clearly on a different part of the pitch lake hence it was a separate claim.[13]

On June 22, 1897, Nicolás Rolando, the president of the state of Bermúdez, granted Cervoni and associates a provisional title for two years. President Crespo granted the definitive title for La Felicidad to Cervoni and associates on November 30, 1898. However, the NY&B title was a thorn in their plans, so they sought to have it cancelled. On January 3, 1898, they filed a petition with Carlos León, the development minister, to annul Hamilton's concession, something that President Crespo approved the following day. The government's reasoning was that it had not received any revenues from the exports of the area's natural resources as stated in the concession because the company had only concentrated its efforts on the exploitation of the asphalt deposits.

Carlos León, who was now the NY&B's attorney, allowed for a suitable delay for the new administration of Ignacio Andrade to settle in, then filed a petition on April 11, 1898, with the new minister for Agriculture, Commerce and Industry[14] for the revocation of the decree. The petition was referred to P. Febres Cordero, the attorney general. On May 28, 1898, he held that the executive decree of January 4, 1898, was null and void because the government could not rescind a contract that had been approved by the president of the state and that Congress had subsequently confirmed. The Federal Court confirmed this view on August 23, 1898.

In a separate development on February 18, 1898, Eduardo Capecchi, Julio Figuera, and Antonio Vicentelli Santelli filed a claim for the Venezuela asphalt mine, which was located in the same area. They received provisional title on June 13, 1898. The claim, however, had to be abandoned because of an error discovered in preliminary proceedings. As a result the same people joined with General Fabricio Conde Flores,[15] a new partner and a front for Castro and his cronies (as the NY&B would discover later),[16] and filed a claim in February 1900 to an asphalt mine that they discovered and named Venezuela. The mine was situated on a different part of the Guanoco pitch lake. The development minister approved this claim on October 24, 1900.

WARNER AND QUINLAN

The merger of the Asphalt Company of America and the National Asphalt Company in 1901 brought a new dimension to the industry by their desire to control "all the principal sources of asphalt production."[17] In Syracuse, New York, Warner-Quinlan Asphalt Co., owned by Charles M. Warner and Patrick Quinlan, was a prominent paving contractor. As large purchasers of asphalt they did not want to be at the mercy of one company. So they looked for an alternate supplier, sending Patrick Sullivan to Venezuela in 1899. Sullivan soon came into contact with the owners and promoters of La Felicidad traveling with a surveyor to Guanoco. After taking legal advice both in the United States and Venezuela, Sullivan felt that the NY&B could not maintain a claim to the part of the pitch lake called La Felicidad. Quinlan and Henry Willard Bean travelled to Caracas in March 1900. They visited La Felicidad, which Sullivan then acquired on their behalf by paying $40,000 in cash on May 25, 1900.[18]

The NY&B immediately brought a case against Warner and Quinlan in the United States, claiming that the deed given to them was in "effect only a quit claim."[19] This view was not upheld as the title deed to La Felicidad was perfectly legal and "acquired in conformity to law, and that it was the only legal title ever granted by the Government for the mine in question."[20] The NY&B had some powerful allies in the United States. Senator Boies Penrose of Pennsylvania argued the company's case very clearly and forcefully on Capitol Hill. The result was that the State Department informed William Russell, the U.S. charge d'affaires in Caracas, that he should protect the interests of NY&B. Three weeks later on October 13, 1900, Russell was further instructed to see Castro and to inform him that any unjust assault on the NY&B's property would not be tolerated. General Greene and Avery D. Andrews, president and vice president of the NY&B respectively, visited Washington to put more pressure on the State Department to act in their favor. Greene was in a particularly advantageous position to present his company's case because he was a special consultant to President McKinley and a colleague of Theodore Roosevelt, the newly elected vice president, on the New York City Board of Police Commissioners during Mayor Strong's period in office. The Asphalt Trust's principal chemist was also a family friend of Roosevelt's.[21] The Trust also had a strong ally in Francis Loomis, as the State Department gave distorted stories to the newspapers so that "the least significant incident which occurred in Venezuela was twisted and exaggerated out of proportion and always used against Castro, with many old anecdotes brought to light again in order to benefit from them."[22] The NY&B had not been idle in Venezuela either. On March 31, 1900, Carner informed Ramón Ayala, the development minister, that Patrick Sullivan and a surveyor had made explorations on the property of NY&B with the evident purpose of making a claim. The company made five protests to the development minister. By October it was clear that Warner and Quinlan would have to do some lobbying themselves. Warner contacted Congressman Driscoll and Senator Frank Hiscock, who visited Secretary of State John Hay to argue their case. The outcome was that the secretary of state informed Russell to remain neutral in the affair.

THE LEGAL DISPUTE

The legal dispute with the NY&B was whether the La Felicidad and Venezuela mines intruded upon the property of the Asphalt Company and whether the land was included in Hamilton's original concession. To look into the matter and ascertain the veracity of the claims by all parties involved, Castro ordered Tomás C. Llamoza on July 23, 1900, to produce a report and map of the area, which he did on August 22. However, Sullivan was not happy with the outcome because the map had been drawn under the direct supervision of the NY&B. Sullivan lodged a strong protest with general Ramón Ayala.

As a way out of the impasse Ayala set up a committee on September 6 to make a report on the property. The committee consisted of one engineer from the government and two engineers from each of the parties involved. The outcome of this was that on December 10 an executive decree confirmed the title to the La Felicidad and Venezuela mines because the Hamilton concession was not a monopoly. In addition, the decree stated that the boundaries of the concession were wrong because none had been assigned. On December 14, Carner filed a protest against the decree, but the government granted Warner and Quinlan a concession on December 15 to build a railroad from La Felicidad to a nearby river. Two days later a similar contract was granted to the owners of the Venezuela mine. According to Thurber, both parties in the court case that ensued from the La Felicidad mine used illegal methods to obtain a favorable result. The case was held in Cumaná. When Warner and Quinlan, the owners of La Felicidad, were about to get a favorable sentence, the manager of NY&B bribed two judges with $10,000 in gold. The third judge heard of the procedure and immediately telegraphed Castro, who dissolved the court.

GOVERNMENT BLACKMAIL

The award in favor of the La Felicidad and Venezuela mines was the government's way of blackmailing the NY&B. In late December 1900 the Venezuelan attorney general offered to settle all the problems with the company's title in their favor in return for Castro becoming the owner of a third of the mine[23] and the payment of $400,000.[24] This was clearly unacceptable to the NY&B, so the government used a new approach. Fabricio Conde approached Carner and said that Castro had no ill feelings toward the NY&B. Castro would help the company reacquire its titles by the simple expedient of paying $400,000 and a $50,000 commission to Conde. Carner negotiated the offer down to $250,000, but he needed to get approval from New York before he proceeded with the deal.

Castro's action was such a blatant show of force against the company that Loomis, the American minister, recommended that a gunboat be sent to Venezuela to bring the government to its senses.[25] Loomis, who was getting very anxious, cabled Secretary of State Hay on December 29, 1900, that the United States should demand that the company's assets be restored. Loomis later reported that the property was about to be attacked. In defending the interests of the NY&B, Loomis was also ingratiating himself with the Republican Party, as many of the main shareholders in the Asphalt Company were part of the inner circle of the party. Loomis had headed the Republican Party's National Press Bureau during the presidential campaigns of 1884 and 1886. He also had edited the Cincinnati *Daily Tribune*, a paper founded to promote William McKinley, the then Governor of Ohio, to the presidency. When McKinley was nominated in 1896, Loomis became a campaign manager, a role he repeated in McKinley's presidential campaign of 1900.

It was clear that a settlement could be reached with Castro, but the price was far too high for the Asphalt Company. The NY&B wanted proof of the corrupt nature of the Castro government. The company wanted to strengthen its argument with the State Department so that the department could intervene on its behalf and secure the title to its property. Colonel Victor M. Backus was dispatched to Caracas in January 1901, allegedly to negotiate an amicable settlement but in reality to gather evidence of the Castro administration's corruption. Soon after his arrival Backus met with Julio Figuera, owner of the Venezuela mine, to try to reach a settlement. They finally concluded an agreement to acquire the mine for $420,000. Backus later discovered, however, that Figuera was merely acting as a front for a consortium that included Felipe Arocha Gallegos, who was the foster brother of Doña Zoila, Castro's wife. Arocha Gallegos was to receive $120,000 in commission for his services. Backus also met with General Victor Barret de Nazaris, Doña Zolia's secretary, while Castro was in an adjoining room listening to the negotiations. At the end of his trip Backus had gathered enough evidence to show that the Venezuelan government at the highest level was behind the scam. The company therefore refused to be blackmailed, deciding not to pay any money to retain its concession but instead to bring a court action against Warner and Quinlan, who would be defended by Nicómedes Zuloaga and José de Jesús Paúl.[26]

In January, Warner and Quinlan took up their case with the State Department through their lobbyist Frank Hiscock, a former Senator. The NY&B wanted to take the case to international arbitration, complaining that it had been a victim of a conspiracy that sought to despoil its property. The government countered that the decision of the development minister to grant deeds to the La Felicidad and Venezuela mines was a way of forcing the NY&B to increase its production. Although it had the largest asphalt lake in the country that produced high-quality pitch, its production record was dismal. Its production increased from 1,130 tons in 1891 to 17,981 tons in 1900. This meant that with taxes at forty cents per ton, total government revenue for the period in question was $28,904, or less than $2,000 per year. The State Department could not force the case into international arbitration until there had been a miscarriage of justice and all legal proceedings in the country had been explored. The Venezuelan judiciary, however, left much to be desired. Three of the high-court judges in the 1901 appeal did not have any legal training, as they had been appointed for political reasons.[27] The U.S. government dispatched the battleships *Hartford, Scorpion*, and *Buffalo* to Venezuela in the mistaken belief that the war vessels "would force the Venezuelan dictator to concede to American demands."[28] Castro, oblivious to the presence of the American flotilla, conducted such a vigorous press campaign that it ultimately forced Loomis to be recalled in April.

The affair dragged on through the first half of 1901, when Carlos León, the former development minister who had signed the decree with José Loreto Arismendi declaring that the company had not fulfilled its obligations, withdrew from the case because the NY&B had not paid his fees of $25,000 for services during the case on top of his usual retainer of $500. León instigated a court action against the company, which decided that his retainer covered the defense of the company's rights. At this stage Carner also retired from the company.

The NY&B's new lawyers, Claudio Bruzual Serra and Manuel Clemente Urbaneja, accused the court of "illegal favouritism"[29] with the "most flagrant deprivation of justice."[30] On August 7, 1901, Bruzual Serra made an unwarranted attack on the court for the purpose of provoking an international incident. The government so resented his action that he was arrested and imprisoned. The court also suspended the lawyers for contempt, something that the NY&B said proved the conspiracy against the company. The evidence for this was the imprisonment of both Claudio Bruzual Serra, the company's senior counsel, and Manuel Clemente Urbaneja. But as William Calhoun would later argue "if any lawyer had so conducted himself, with no greater provocation, before any of the courts of our own country he would have received prompt and severe punishment."[31]

The Asphalt Company clearly did not want to be blackmailed. As it did not have a sufficiently strong case to argue in court, it decided that the best way to retain its concession and keep its production potential dormant was to work toward the demise of the Castro administration. Consequently, when the opportunity to topple Castro became a reality, the company did not hesitate to give its wholehearted support to the venture, especially as the State Department refused to intervene in the La Felicidad court case.[32] Other foreign enterprises that were thoroughly disgusted at Castro's treatment of them joined the NY&B in supporting a certain faction of the Venezuelan opposition to the government.

NOTES

1. Vice-Consul Bodecker, "Maracaibo Report" in Acting Consul Andral, "Diplomatic and Consular Reports: Venezuela—Report for the Year 1899 on the Trade of the Consular District of Caracas" (HMSO 1900), *PP* vol. xcvii, 1900, pp. 535–57.
2. Acting Consul Andral, "Diplomatic and Consular Reports: Venezuela—Report for the Year 1900 on the Trade of the Consular District of Caracas," (HMSO 1901), *PP* vol. lxxxv, 1901, pp. 771–89. The original sterling amounts have been converted to bolivares using the exchange rate of Bs 25 = £1.
3. Consul de Lemos, "Diplomatic and Consular Reports: Venezuela—Report for the Year 1899 on the Trade and Commerce of the Consular District of Ciudad Bolívar," (HMSO 1900), *PP* vol. xcvii, 1900, pp. 529–35.
4. *Financial News*, 26 July 1899.
5. José Rafael Ricart, *El Trabajo. Consideraciones sobre las Causas de Fuerza Mayor que han Impedido el Desarrollo de Nuestras Industrias y Demostración Suscinta de la Necesidad de Abrir un Paréntesis de Paz, de Garantías y de Protección a la Propiedad y al Trabajo, sin lo Cual el Progreso Patrio Será Imposible*, Caracas, Tip. Americana, 1903.
6. C. Castro to A. Pietri Daudet, 27 September 1900 in Elías Pino Iturrieta, *Castro, Epistolario Presidencial* (Caracas, Universidad Central de Venezuela, 1974), p. 295.
7. He was finance minister in 1893 during Joaquín Crespo's second presidency.
8. Equivalent of $4,000,000 in 1999.
9. Equivalent to $200,000 in 1999.
10. The most comprehensive and lucid study on the NY&B is by Nikita Harwich V., *Asfalto y Revolución: La New York and Bermúdez Company*, Caracas, Monte Avila Editores, 1992.
11. General Francis V. Greene was a well-respected army general who had published a seminal work on army campaigns entitled *The Russian Army and its Campaigns in Turkey in 1877–78*. He met Barber while he was public works supervisor for Washington D.C. between 1880 and 1886.
12. Equivalent to $22.7 million in 1999.
13. William J. Calhoun, "Wrongs to American Citizens in Venezuela," *Senate Document No. 413*, 60 Cong. 1 sess., September 1907–1908, pp. 161–563.
14. The government of Ignacio Andrade had divided the Development Ministry into the Agriculture, Commerce, and Industry Ministry and into the Post Office and Telegraph Ministry.

15. He was Castro's *Comisionado Extraordinario del Gobierno* when he had needed money in December 1899.

16. William M. Sullivan, "The Rise of Despotism in Venezuela: Cipriano Castro, 1899–1908." PhD. diss., The University of New Mexico, 1974, p. 487.

17. Calhoun, p. 176.

18. Ibid. p. 177. The amount paid would be equivalent to $610,000 in 1999.

19. Ibid.

20. Ibid.

21. Orray E. Thurber, *Origen del Capital Norteamericano en Venezuela. La Epoca del Asfalto (1884–1907)*, trans. Angel Villasana, Barquisimeto, Editorial Nueva Segovia, 1955, p. 71.

22. Ibid., p. 72.

23. George Washington Crichfield, another aggrieved foreign investor in Venezuela, states in his book that Castro was to be paid by the NY&B $50,000 and two hundred and fifty thousand shares in the company for rendering a decision in favor of the NY&B in the Warner and Quinlan La Felicidad suit. Crichfield, G. W., *American Supremacy. The Rise and Progress of the South American Republics and Their Relations to the United States under the Monroe Doctrine*, 2 vols., New York, Brentano's, 1908.

24. Equivalent to just over $59 million in 1999.

25. Calhoun, p. 310.

26. He later became foreign affairs minister.

27. Two of the judges were not lawyers, and the third had not finished high school.

28. Sullivan, p. 319.

29. Calhoun, p. 227.

30. Ibid.

31. Ibid.

32. John Hay to Nicoll, Anable & Lindsay, 28 February 1901 in Thurber, p. 31.

4

Matos and Foreign Companies

The NY&B was the most visible foreign company in dispute with the Castro government. However, there were others, such as the Orinoco Company and the Manoa Company, that would also take part in the American claims against the Venezuelan government in the years to come. However, Castro did not single out American companies for this treatment. The French Cable Company, with French government equity participation, also came under scrutiny, as did Dutch interests. The British also had grievances, but these were small and did not warrant even the consideration of any active coercive action after the "peaceful blockade" of 1902–3.

THE ORINOCO COMPANY

Cyrenius Charles Fitzgerald first arrived in Venezuela in April 1878 as an employee of the El Callao Goldmine Company. On September 22, 1883, he was granted a ninety-nine-year concession covering twenty-two-thousand square miles of the Orinoco delta valley and the island of Pedernales. Fitzgerald raised capital through the issue of shares on the New York stock exchange. On June 10, 1884, he formed the Manoa Company with a registered capital of $5 million. The Board of Directors consisted of John A. Bowman as president, Fitzgerald as vice president, Julius Schutt, George H. Atkinson, and Judge James Troy. On June 14, 1884, the Fitzgerald concession, as it became known, was transferred to the company. Fitzgerald received $250,000 and 40 percent of the new corporation's stock, which was valued at $2 million. At the same time the company issued

12,500 shares to Guzmán Blanco and distributed a further 2,000 shares among influential Venezuelans. The company was undercapitalized as it only managed to raise $45,000 in working capital on the stock market.

At first the company tried producing sugarcane. Then they attempted goat rearing, but both enterprises failed. Cattle ranching was a mild success. The company purchased 1.5 million head of cattle with the intention of supplying the Caribbean meat market, but the competition was intense. There were eight million head of cattle in the Orinoco basin alone. The company's most successful activity became its lumbering business. The company's asphalt mine on Pedernales island was sold to the Asphalt Company of Pedernales, which was run by George Turnbull and Henry F. Stone.

Like the NY&B, the Manoa Company was unable to fulfill its obligations. On February 12, 1886, the government compelled the company to suspend its operations. The government annulled the concession on September 9. A similar concession was immediately awarded to George Turnbull, who had negotiated it with Guzmán Blanco, ostensibly because he bore a letter from President Cleveland stating that the United States would take Venezuela's side in any Guyana-Venezuela dispute. The Venezuelan government also approved a contract with Herbert Gordon, a U.S. citizen, to settle, colonize, and organize the vast territory that extended from the Imataca mountain range to the Paracaima mountains, which comprised the whole Cuyumu River. Part of the concession extended into the disputed frontier area with Guyana. Both Fitzgerald and Gordon were warned that their property would be lost if the disputed land was found to be in British hands. Gordon joined forces with Fitzgerald to exploit the iron-ore deposits at Imataca. In the meantime, Turnbull constructed a six-mile railway to the iron-ore mine at a cost of $160,000. Between 1888 and 1890 approximately three thousand tons of iron ore were produced from Imataca. However, by 1893 rebel armies had confiscated his tools and machinery. He had trouble raising additional capital so he was forced to close the mine. On March 30, 1895, Turnbull signed an optional lease with Joseph Robertson to form the Orinoco Iron Syndicate of London, which was organized to exploit the Imataca mines. On September 18, 1895, the Orinoco Iron Syndicate of London purchased the lease that the Venezuelan government had declared void and appointed Turnbull its operating manager.

In October 1894 the Manoa Company sold its potential iron-ore rights under the old Fitzgerald concession to a Minnesota group, which formed the Orinoco Company. In spring of 1895 Donald Grant of Farribault, Minnesota, travelled to Caracas with his son Samuel, John Bowman, and James Radcliffe to get the Fitzgerald concession transferred to them. However, on June 18, 1895, the development minister issued a decree that annulled Turnbull's contract because of a lack of mining activity. The minister revived the Fitzgerald concession with the exclusion of the asphalt mines of

Pedernales and the iron-ore mines of Imataca. The Americans retaliated by sending a long memorandum to the State Department, but the department felt that the matter should be decided in the local courts. To make matters worse, Turnbull's supply boat, the *New Deal*, arrived unannounced in Ciudad Bolívar. Its failure to land at a proper port of entry resulted in the company being fined Bs 248,985.17.

While this was happening in the United States, the Orinoco Company was trying to acquire the Manoa Company, Turnbull's rival. Their plans were initially thwarted when a creditor instituted proceedings against the Manoa Company in February 1896 for $15,000 owed. On November 11 of that year the Manoa Company declared bankruptcy, and its property was sold at public auction. A single bid of $500 on November 26 from George N. Baxter, who was acting for the Orinoco Company, secured the remaining assets that had not been transferred to the Minnesota company in 1894. The company envisaged the production of rubber, gold, and iron ore. On October 17 the Manoa Company ceded its concession to the Orinoco Company, which the government approved on November 20, 1895. The concession ran until 1899, the original expiration date under the 1886 Turnbull contract.

On July 10, 1895, the exclusive right to exploit the asphalt mines on Pedernales was awarded to the Minas de Pedernales Compañía, a Venezuelan company. Meanwhile, Turnbull sought to reacquire his iron-ore concession. On November 20, 1896, after the insistence of the U.S. minister, the Venezuelan government issued a decree stating that the order of the previous year did not affect the Imataca iron mines. This returned Fitzgerald's concession to the Manoa Company. A similar executive resolution of November 20, 1896, also deprived the Orinoco Company of the exploitation of its iron-ore discovery at Imataca which had been awarded to Turnbull. As a result Turnbull reacquired the iron-ore mine while the Orinoco Company acquired the remainder of the Fitzgerald concession. The Orinoco Company continued its colonization plans. In February 1897, twenty-two colonists left New York for Venezuela, with each man getting forty acres. The colonists encountered a host of severe problems, of which tropical diseases were the worst. By the middle of 1888 the company claimed that there were three-hundred colonists in the Santa Catalina area, but this was a gross exaggeration. Loomis, the American minister, visited the colony in March 1899. He was unable to find a single colonist.

On July 22, 1897, the Orinoco Company leased its rights to the iron-ore mines at Imataca, which it had lost to Turnbull's Orinoco Iron Syndicate. At the same time the local court in Ciudad Bolívar ordered the sale of Turnbull's assets to pay for the previously imposed fine. The disposal of the boat and equipment that belonged to the company only raised Bs 120,000. This was insufficient to cover the fine. As a result Benoni Lockwood, the secretary for the Orinoco Iron Syndicate, agreed to pay $23,026 for the Orinoco Company to reacquire its iron-ore lease by paying the fine in 1899.

Turnbull then filed suit against the Orinoco Iron Syndicate. The court ruled on February 21, 1899, that he was the legitimate holder of the concession. The government appealed the judgment and won in May 1899. In August a group headed by Frederick G. Corning bought the Orinoco Company and changed its name to the Orinoco Corporation. The group invested in the lessee company, the Orinoco Iron Syndicate. On October 10, 1899, the Andrade government declared that the concession held by the Orinoco Company was null and void. The new Castro government confirmed this on October 19, 1900, when it "said Fitzgerald contract and the Turnbull contract to exploit its concession was declared null and void once again."[1] In the autumn of 1900, Turnbull appealed the May 1899 decision with the support of the State Department. Turnbull's plea was that the Orinoco Company had no claim to the Imataca mines or that the rights could be sold by the Orinoco Iron Syndicate. On June 7, 1900, the court recognized Turnbull as the legitimate owner. The company lost its concession when it was forcibly evicted from the iron-ore deposits after shipping its first nine hundred tons of ore that year. On May 15, 1901, the Venezuelan government issued a certificate stating that Turnbull was the sole possessor of the title between March 13, 1888, and May 14, 1901. The authorities seized the company's steamer, *La Perla*, without compensation and awarded a separate iron-ore concession and other concessions near Manoa to Ustáriz and others.

In December 1900 the Orinoco Company declared bankruptcy. It had liabilities of $345,255 and no assets. The Minnesota group was forced to sell its company, the Orinoco Company, to the Orinoco Corporation of West Virginia, which would support the Matos rebellion in order to reacquire its valuable concession.[2] According to Carreras the biggest problem that these companies encountered was their undercapitalization. They were never "able to raise the necessary funds to carry out the programs which they planned and which the Venezuelan Government expected them to implement."[3]

THE ORINOCO STEAM SHIP COMPANY

On May 14, 1847, the Venezuelan Congress granted Vespasin Ellis, a former U.S. charge d'affaires at Caracas, a monopoly contract for the navigation of the Orinoco and Apure rivers. The Orinoco Steamship Company was formed to work the contract. However, on May 2, 1849, the concession was revoked and granted to E. A. Turpin and Fred A. Beelen, who founded the Orinoco Steam Navigation Company and placed four steamers into service. On May 14, 1869, the Orinoco River was opened to ships of all nations. In anticipation of this event the Venezuelan Steam Transport Company was formed in New York with J. W. Hancox as president. However, in October 1871 Guzmán Blanco closed the Orinoco to all the ships. General Juan F. Pérez was later awarded a seven-year contract. Pérez joined with Scandello and Treveranus to form the Orinoco Navigation Company. They managed to stay in business until 1893.

In 1886 Guzmán Blanco had opened two northernmost channels, the Macareo and Pedernales channels to trade. These were at the mouth of the Orinoco delta. President Joaquín Crespo reversed the decision on July 1, 1893, making these channels exclusive to coastal shipping. The result was that international shipping had to use Boca Grande for trade with Trinidad and other southern countries. The exclusive use of the Macareo and Pedernales channels for shipping between Ciudad Bolívar and Maracaibo over a period of fifteen years was acquired by the Englishman Ellis Grell on January 17, 1894. The concession also included the privilege of linking the islands of Curacao and Trinidad to the domestic coastal routes. Although the concession had not appeared in the Official Gazette, Grell was able to transfer his concession in June 1894 to the Compañía General Venezolana de Navegación, a local company. Four years later this company sold its rights to The Orinoco Steam Ship Company, a newly created company incorporated in London on July 14, 1898, with a capital of twenty-thousand £1 shares and a debenture of $100,000. However, U.S. stockholders controlled 99 percent of its stock. On December 12, 1898, the company purchased both the Red Star Steamship Line and the General Navigation Company of Venezuela. These companies merged to form the Orinoco Shipping & Trading Company. The driving force behind the acquisition was R. Morgan Olcott, who was a director of the Red Star Line that, along with the Compañía General Venezolana de Navegación, controlled the majority of the coastal trade of Venezuela. The major trading houses of the country did not view the merger with favor. They were worried that such a monopoly would restrict their trading activities. H. L. Boulton and Blohm & Co., which both had extensive interests in eastern Venezuela, tried without success to persuade the government to rescind the contract. President Ignacio Andrade granted the shipping company the exclusive right to establish steamship communication with West Indian trading centers, mainland ports, the river towns above Ciudad Bolívar and between La Guaira and Trinidad, and the ports in between.

The Orinoco Steam Ship Company suffered during the 1899 revolution. The company was eventually driven out of business during the Castro administration. Ramón B. Luigi, Castro's agent in Trinidad, attempted to prevent the company's steamers from sailing to Ciudad Bolívar during the *Revolución Libertadora* because it was felt that the company was assisting the rebels. When the company purchased two local shipping firms, it acquired a substantial debt that the government owed. A solution was reached whereby the company's contract would be extended from 1909 to 1915, with the government paying a small cash settlement. Despite these promises the government cancelled the company's concession on October 5, 1900. After this the government frequently commandeered the company's ships so that it was unable to trade. Olcott, the manager, complained to the interior minister in December 1901 that the company had been left with only one ship sailing between La Guaira and Trinidad. Olcott also requested protection from revolutionary activity. However, on December 14, 1901, Castro annulled the company's concession beyond 1909. The company lost all confidence of "preserving their investment."[4] They cancelled "all steam communication with La Guaira and provided General Matos with money and armaments."[5]

In January 1902 the Orinoco Steamship Company was organized in New York to take over the Orinoco Shipping and Trading Company. On April 1, 1902, Olcott transferred the assets of the old company to the new one at the request of American stockholders, who believed that Washington would be more vigorous in defending their claims. On May 31, 1902, Castro ordered the company to cease its operations because of revolutionary disturbances in the east. In 1903 the company sold its vessels to Dalton & Co. of Ciudad Bolívar, which founded the Línea de Vapores del Orinoco.[6]

GEORGE WASHINGTON CRICHFIELD

On April 20, 1901, George Washington Crichfield acquired Pedro A. Guzmán's asphalt concession in Zulia for $25,000. As soon as the Venezuelan government approved the transfer of the title, the company issued $1 million in stock and $500,000 of mortgage loans to form the United States-Venezuela Company. The terms of the concession involved the development of the asphalt deposits at Inciarte in Zulia, the construction of a railway, and the monopoly to navigate the rivers leading to Lake Maracaibo. It also obtained the privilege of importing duty-free machinery and received a special clause that exempted Crichfield from further taxes being levied on his activities. Although the company faced many problems, it eventually invested $600,000 in building the railroad. More than one thousand people were employed at the mine. In its first full year of operations, which started in July 1902, the company shipped fifteen thousand tons of asphalt and earned net profits of $100,000.[7] Castro soon turned his attention to this company, threatening to cancel its concession if it did not pay higher taxes. With such cavalier treatment by the Castro government, Crichfield felt obliged to join the Matos revolution. The company was fined Bs 24,178,336.47 on September 22, 1904, for damages caused during the Revolución Libertadora. The court arrived at this figure by taking into account the commercial discredit caused to Venezuela by the rebellion, the losses incurred by the Venezuelan economy due to the rebellion, the need to create a war tax (which generated Bs 16.8 million between February 1903 and June 1904), and the decline in custom's receipts from Bs 29.94 million in 1900 to Bs 4.08 million in 1903.

The company's contract was violated when its tax situation changed after the 1904 mining code was enacted. Its taxes increased from ten cents to forty cents per ton of asphalt, and a 3 percent levy on the gross value of tonnage exported was added. Another executive decree in June 1904 levied a further tax of eighty cents per ton on all asphalt exported. In addition, the land tax increased from $30 to $120 per hectare a year, and the code fixed the value of a ton of asphalt at $20 per ton, so that the gross levy was $1.40. A further violation of its contract was that the company also had to pay duty on any machinery imported. The United States-Venezuela-Company refused to accept the increase in export taxes that the new mining code imposed, arguing that Crichfield's concession was still valid. The government countered that as Congress had never ratified the contract, it was therefore not operative. On February 4, 1907, R. Floyd Clarke, the corporation's lawyer, informed Castro that as of April 1, 1907, the company would not be responsible for the deterioration that the lack of repair of the equipment caused. The result was that Castro granted the concession to a Venezuelan company.

THE FRENCH CABLE COMPANY

The Societe Francaise des Telegraphs Sous-Mairns, which later changed its name to the Compagnie Francaise des Cable Telegraphique (French Cable Company), received its original concession on July 25, 1887, when V. Cuenca Creus signed a contract with Venezuela to connect the country telegraphically with the outside world. A year later the first link was established between Willemstad in Curacao and La Guaira. In 1895 the company was awarded a further fifty-year monopoly to connect Caracas and the coastal towns of the country with New York. The company had a capital base of Bs 24,000,000 and received an annual subsidy of Bs 800,000 from the French government.

Prior to this on March 19, 1890, the company had established itself in Martinique, receiving an annual subsidy of fifty thousand francs from the French government. The French colony had previously awarded its subsidy to The West India and Panama Telegraph Company, but the company had a poor service record, needing in the end to be bailed out. The new company was not any better. As early as 1894 the Conseil General of Martinique complained of defective service by the new company.[8]

In 1897 the conflict became more acute when the company refused to accept the paper money of the Bank of Martinique at the ordinary colonial rate and insisted on payment for telegrams in gold or Banque de France notes. The company charged a premium of 8 or 10 percent if payment was made in paper money. On December 17 the Conseil General refused to pay the subsidy to the company unless it accepted colonial money, but "thanks to its contacts in France the Company obtained through its headquarters in Paris the payment of the FFr 50,000 in question."[9] In 1898 the Conseil General passed the same resolution with exactly the same result: the company got its money in Paris. That same year legislative elections took place, and the company sided against the political majority that had granted the subsidy in 1890. Their candidate was allowed the free use of the cable. The candidate "did not move from Paris but thanks to his *ad honoren* services to the French Cable Company was in daily and hourly contact with his friends in Martinique, receiving and forwarding up to a thousand words per day."[10] However, the service did not improve, and the conflict escalated.

The company also had problems in Guadeloupe when it had publicly complained about its lack of confidence in the paper money that the official bank of the colony issued. The company also openly flouted the commercial interests of the island. The colony began proceedings against the company in the courts in 1899. Although it had been beaten at every stage, the company raised the cry that justice had been denied to it, and it overwhelmed the Ministere de Colonies with its protests. Here again the company openly sided with political candidates. In the 1901 elections its offices were placed at the disposal of their candidate. In December 1902 the Ministere des Colonies, moved by the reiterated complaints of its service—the island had been without a cable link with Paris for six months—and the tenacity of the Conseil General, decided to take measures against the company, withholding the second half of the annual subsidy payment. The Conseil General withheld payment of the subsidy again in 1903. The following year it further reduced its subsidy to twenty-five thousand francs.

The service from Venezuela was also very poor. The international line ran from La Guaira to Curacao to Santo Domingo, then it crossed by land to Puerto Plata and Cape Haiti and New York. The inclusion of the Santo Domingo land line, which ran through the rough ground of swamps and forests, contravened the original contract. It was also very difficult to maintain. A direct link with New York was only possible, on average, between ten to twelve days a month. The rest of the time messages were conveyed by mule from one end of the island to another, which frequently meant a delay of forty-eight hours in transmitting telegrams. At the beginning of 1901 the merchants of the main cities of Venezuela complained to the company about the appalling service but to no avail. The government, as one of the parties to the contract, also tried to get the company to improve its service, complaining that several clauses of the 1895 contract had not been carried out and that an international cable had been laid between Coro and Curacao instead of a coastal cable between Coro and Puerto

Cabello. The feeling among the directors of the company was that it was living on borrowed time. They believed that sooner or later they would be obliged either to improve the service at a high cost or lose its contract. The company gradually turned to the Matos opposition in Venezuela in the belief that if they were successful, the FCC could continue to operate its shoddy monopoly. The connection with Matos started in 1895 when the French charge d'affaires, M. Quievereaux, became a close friend to many liberal *caudillos*. In 1902 Quievereaux joined the Revolución Libertadora that Matos headed with the FCC directorate and French government supporting him. In Venezuela, Quievereaux was supported by Albert Felix Jaurett, a Frenchman by birth who was a naturalized American. He had arrived in Venezuela in 1896 after a series of shady dealings in Central America. Soon after Jaurett's arrival in Caracas, he started publishing the *Venezuelan Herald*, a weekly English-language newspaper. Jaurett would play a key role in the unfolding story of corruption between Castro and the FCC during the next few years. The scenario was thus set for a number of aggrieved foreign companies to join Matos and his rebel supporters to topple the Castro regime.

NOTES

1. AHM SGPRCP Julio 1–14 1909 'Memorandum para Ministro de Fomento,' 23.6.09.

2. In the resulting U.S.–Venezuela Mixed Claims Commission of 1903 after the "peaceful blockade," Turnbull would claim Bs 6,396,000 in damages, while the Manoa Company claimed Bs 26 million. By a government resolution on October 10, 1900, Fitzgerald's concession was declared null and void, and the Turnbull concession was declared valid. The resolutions were contradictory, however, and the Mixed Commission of 1903 decided that the case should be arbitrated by Judge Harry Barge at The Hague International Tribunal. After looking at the papers, Barge declared Fitzgerald's concession to be valid, the Turnbull one invalid, and that the Venezuelan government should pay the Orinoco Company the sum of Bs 120,000, which the company had paid "the government wrongfully for the judicial auction of the Imataca mine." (AHMSGPRCP Julio 1–14 1909 'Memorandúm para el Ministro de Fomento', 23.6.09.) The reasoning behind Barge's arbitration was that Fitzgerald's concession was annulled because the Venezuelan government in 1886 could declare a contract annulled without having to give any explanations. Under the contract it only needed to give its opinion that they thought that the contract had not been fulfilled as a valid reason for annulling it. The Manoa Company's claim was dismissed because its contract specified that it had to take its case to the Venezuelan courts. The commission overruled the October 1900 decree, which in effect meant that the 1883 Fitzgerald concession was still valid. This meant that the Venezuelan government had to indemnify Bs 120,000 to the Orinoco Co because the company had been overcharged for its concession. (AHM Unclassified 'Informe al Ministro de Fomento,' Unsigned, 23.6.09.) The Venezuelan attorney

general, however, disagreed with the decision and so started a suit at the *Corte Federal y de Casación* against the Manoa Co. Limited and the Orinoco Company as holders of Fitzgerald's concession, as null and void "for nonfulfillment its obligations" (AHM Unclassified 'Informe al Ministro de Fomento', Unsigned, 23.6.09.). Turnbull transferred his title to a new company in May 1905.

3. Charles Edward Carreras, "U.S. Economic Penetration of Venezuela and Its Effects on Diplomacy: 1895–1906," PhD. diss., University of North Carolina at Chapel Hill, 1971, p. 142–43.

4. William M. Sullivan, "The Rise of Despotism in Venezuela: Cipriano Castro, 1899–1908," PhD. diss., the University of New Mexico, 1974, p. 478.

5. Ibid.

6. At the Mixed Claims of 1903 the Orinoco Company claimed $1,209,701.05, but it was awarded only $28,224.93, which Washington vigorously protested. Prior to Gómez coming to power in December 1908, the Venezuelan government owed the Red Star Line $554,550.01 for services rendered. The Orinoco Steamship Company inherited this claim, but it accepted Bs 200,000 as full payment in return for the extension of its monopoly until 1915.

7. Carreras, p. 197.

8. Throughout the West Indies there was keen competition between the French and British telegraph companies to maintain their market share. In 1888 the FCC petitioned the Spanish government for permission to carry a cable to Santiago de Cuba, but the British companies that operated there, The West India and Panama Telegraph Company, (established in 1871) and the Cuba Submarine Cable Company (established in 1875) opposed the entry of the French company because they had received certain assurances from the government that no new competition would be allowed. When the Spanish-American War erupted in 1898, the Americans wanted to cut the wires of the two British companies. As this was technically difficult to do, the American commander approached the commander of the French warship *Pouyer Quertier*, who spoke to the FCC representative. Upon hearing what he had to do, he resigned and returned to Le Havre.

9. J. E. Sauvage, "El Cable Frances," *El Constitucional, Venezuela y la Compañía Francesa de Cables Submarinos. Ruidoso Proceso. Documentos Publicados en "El Constitucional,"* Caracas, Imprenta Nacional, 1906, p. 57.

10. Ibid.

5

Matos Launches His Revolution

It had been clear for some time to Matos and others in the country that Castro's administration made no guarantees for "either domestic or foreign capital, nor any encouragement for investors."[1] Ever since his humiliation at the hands of the parvenu from Táchira whom he had helped to power, Matos had been organizing a revolution against the government. He built the most extensive, important revolutionary alliance in the country since its independence from Spain by bringing together "old and young men, Andeans and Easterners, Central people and Falconianos, Yellow Liberals and Nationalists."[2] Matos also received encouraging support from Francis Loomis, the American minister, and foreign companies such as the NY&B, the Orinoco Corporation, the Orinoco Steam Ship Company, and the FCC. It was also becoming clear to the regional *caudillos* that they would lose with Castro, who owed them very little politically as he was not linked to the "social and military oligarchies which were engendered and sustained in their prestige by the Guzmanismo regime."[3] The Matos rebellion, which at one stage would total fourteen thousand men, was a who's who of Venezuelan political life. It included most of the regional caudillos: Luciano Mendoza, Domingo Monagas, Gregorio Segundo Riera, Nicolás Rolando, Juan Pablo Peñaloza, José Manuel Peñaloza, Amabile Solagnie, Antonio Fernández, Francisco Batalla, Pedro Ducharme, Horacio Ducharme, Alejandro Ducharme, Zoilo Vidal, Pablo Guzmán, Luis Loreto Lima, R. Blanco Fombona, J. M. Ortega Martínez, and others. The following Liberal generals remained loyal to the government: José Antonio Velutini, Diego Bautista Ferrer, Rafael González Pacheco, José María García Gómez, Víctor Rodríguez, Jacinto Lara, Francisco Linares Alcántara,[4] Asunción Rodríguez, Angel Morrison, Luis Mata Illas, and Francisco Gutiérrez.

Matos was well aware of his lack of military experience and appointed two veterans to command his army. Domingo Monagas, who was in charge of eastern Venezuela, and Luciano Mendoza, who was responsible for operations in the central and western part of the country. However, the two military men were approaching eighty years of age each. They were no real match for the youthful Castro, who was almost half their age at forty-four. It was clear, as Velásquez has pointed out, that the Matos revolution had all the necessary ingredients to win except that it lacked the one great military leader who could command and mold the disparate group into one. As a result the old jealousies between the Nacionalistas and the Liberals would come into play, with each faction trying to dominate the other.

Matos headed the Revolutionary Committee, which consisted of twelve men representing the business community and the regional *caudillos*, including Luciano Mendoza, the powerful president of Aragua, and Ramón Guerra, the second vice president. Its responsibility was to plan the revolution and coordinate the activities of the regional *caudillos*. It was not long before a general consensus was reached that a steady supply of ordnance would be needed to coordinate an invasion from Colombia, Curacao, and Trinidad. In addition, internal uprisings were planned in many parts of the country. The revolution therefore faced a major disadvantage, which was the lack of adequate military supplies compared to the war machine that Castro was amassing. Arms and ammunition were in ample supplies in Europe, but the problem was to get somebody to finance such a venture. The Asphalt Company would be the ideal source to tap, as it had a strong motive for wanting Castro out of power. The marriage of convenience would be settled quickly while other foreign enterprises, such as the FCC, the Orinoco Corporation, and the Orinoco Steam Ship Company, aggrieved at their ill treatment by Castro, would also assist in the rebellion. In addition, the Colombian government, which had broken off relations with Venezuela, would help Matos in his endeavors.

MATOS AND THE NY&B REACH AGREEMENT

In the early part of 1901 Matos travelled to New York to meet Francis V. Greene, the president of the NY&B, to formalize the financial support for his revolution that had already been informally offered. The time had therefore arrived for the Asphalt Trust to reach a decision as to whether they would make a serious commitment. Greene dispatched Gilbert M. Furman on May 4 on a fact-finding mission to Venezuela to ascertain whether Matos had any chance of succeeding in his revolutionary plans.[5] Prior to Furman's trip, Henry Willard Bean, the representative of the NY&B in Caracas, had been actively engaged with the agents and associates of Matos, who were frequent visitors to his residence in the country's capital. On his arrival in Venezuela, Furman warned Bean to be more discreet in his dealings with the revolutionaries. More importantly he came to the conclusion that the Asphalt Trust should support Matos, as he was sure that the revolution would succeed. The exact amount of financial support would be negotiated in New York, depending on the estimated cost of the arms and the ship needed to take them to Venezuela.

At Bean's party to celebrate Venezuela's independence on July 5, Matos, the guest of honor, was toasted for the victory of the forthcoming revolution. Soon afterwards, on July 14, Matos and M. M. Schweizer, Bean's secretary in Caracas, travelled to New York arriving eight days later. Matos did not waste time, spending the following day, July 23, at the National Asphalt Company's offices. There he met General Andrews and the other officers of the company. The meeting started with the Venezuelan rebel stating that he had united all the regional chieftains who opposed the Castro regime. Matos stated that he had the support of many major foreign investors in the country as well as foreign government support. The Orinoco Steam Ship Company had granted Matos $25,000 to assist the revolution. In addition, they could help to transport troops and ammunition on its ships, especially between Trinidad and Venezuela. Matos could also count on the support of the FCC, which had the telegraph monopoly in the country, an invaluable source of espionage because it could report the movements of government troops to the rebels and delay government messages to its commanders. The help of the Gran Ferrocarril de Venezuela, which was German owned, was also of great assistance because it could delay the transportation of government troops by placing obstacles in the way of its locomotives, but it could also move and protect rebel troops. Matos could also count on the support of the Colombian government,[6] something that would be invaluable when it came time to acquire a ship in the United States or in Europe. Matos ended by informing Greene that he controlled a large section of eastern Venezuela where the NY&B's properties were situated, and that before long he would have total control of the area. This was not true. However, once Nicolás Rolando joined the revolution, Matos could indeed claim control over the area.

Although Matos commanded wide support, the rebels were afraid of launching a full-scale attack because Castro had substantially increased the government's arsenal. The rebels therefore needed a supply of adequate arms and ammunition. Matos proposed to the Asphalt Company that its financial assistance would be best used for purchasing arms and ammunition in Europe and a ship to transport it to Venezuela. At the end of a long meeting it seemed that the Venezuelan rebels had covered all angles and that they were assured of victory in Venezuela. The board of the company, sufficiently impressed with Matos and with their own intelligence sources that confirmed the success of the venture, decided to support Matos financially by providing sufficient funds to purchase a ship and the arms and ammunition needed for the revolution. The money would not be released, however, until the Asphalt Company was satisfied that it had been soundly invested. The company would later argue that it had no option but to fund Matos because "it was confronted by a formidable revolutionary movement which for at least some time would control its assets and would behave as friend or foe depending on what attitude it adopted towards General Matos' petition."[7]

Matos was unable to acquire a ship in the United States, possibly because he did not want to raise suspicion as the situation between the rival asphalt groups was so tense. He instead went to London to secure the ship and armaments. Greene also travelled to Europe to oversee the company's investment. In London, Matos discussed with his agent, Rodolfo de Paula,[8] the details of the ship that he wanted to purchase, leaving him with the responsibility of acquiring it when he left for Paris on August 7 to purchase arms and to discuss the remaining outstanding matters in his arrangement with the FCC. The FCC was predisposed to do a deal with him because they had nothing to lose. The coastal-cable centers would be of enormous strategic importance to the revolution. Through mutual friends Matos obtained an introduction to the company, which readily agreed to his plans.

A. Carnegie, a ship broker, was soon able to offer Matos' agent and Greene a number of possible ships for purchase.[9] Greene finally focused on the 1500 tonnes *Ban Righ*,[10] which the Aberdeen Steam Navigation Company had put up for sale. On October 26, Greene purchased the ship for the relatively large sum of $96,000, almost the entire sum promised by the Asphalt Company. To not arouse suspicion the ship was allegedly purchased by the Colombian government.

In September of that year Thurber received a phone call from Stuart G. Nelson, vice president of the Seaboard National Bank of New York, where Greene was a director. Nelson wanted to know whether he should honor the payment of a draft received from the Credit Lyonnais for the amount of US$101,336.67 drawn upon the New Trinidad Lake Asphalt Company. Although Thurber agreed that the draft should be paid without delay, the matter was eventually referred to Arthur W. Sewall, secretary and treasurer of the National Asphalt Company. In November, Sewall instructed his staff to pay the sum and to charge it to a new account opened by the NY&B called "Government Relations."[11] The sum was paid through the company's law firm, Nicoll, Anable and Lindsay, so that it would appear on the company's books and not arouse the suspicion of the employees. The money was drawn from the "legal expenses account." Matos was to communicate with the company via their lawyers. A further payment of $45,000 was made on December 28.

Meanwhile, in London the *Ban Righ* was being fitted with powerful searchlights and platforms for mounting four heavy guns. Such activity was brought to the attention of the Lord Commissioners of the Admiralty by A. T. Waters, an official of the Thames Conservancy, who rightly suspected that the ship was being fitted for war. The ship was detained on November 9 because it might breach the Foreign Enlistment Act of 1870. The Colombian government, the alleged owners, protested this treatment as they argued that the ship was their legitimate property. The Attorney General agreed to allow the vessel to sail, provided that the Colombian minister in London assured that the ship was being purchased by the Colombian government and that both Venezuela and Colombia declared that a state of war did not exist between the two countries. The *Ban Righ* was released on November 22 after receiving the assurances of G. R. Calderón, the Colombian consul general, that the ship belonged to the government of Colombia. According to De Paula the purchase of the ship was not completed until the *Ban Righ* arrived in Martinique, when the last payment was received.

Upon its release the *Ban Righ* immediately left for Antwerp, where it arrived on November 25. It berthed at the Asia dock to take delivery of a large consignment of French arms and ammunition from Paris. While at Antwerp the Colombian consul came aboard and gave Captain Willis documents that he was to deliver to Colombian government officials in Colón. A French captain of artillery, two doctors, and a friend of Matos came aboard, and De Paula received orders to transfer the ship to Matos after the last payment was made in Martinique. Further down from Antwerp the *Ban Righ* took on more arms that were labelled "hardware, musical instruments and kettledrums."[12] On November 30 the ship sailed out of the Scheldt with an all-British crew of forty-two bound for the West Indies. The crew was unaware of the type of cargo they were carrying, and it was only during the passage that Captain Willis discovered "that the holds contained 175 tons of Mausers, 180 tons of ammunition, pack-saddles, a large number of field guns and carriages, two Hotchkiss guns and the quick-firers were for the *Ban Righ's* own armament."[13] The ship carried fifteen thousand rifles and between four and six million rounds of ammunition.

When they reached Marigot on the island of St. Martin, the rebels camouflaged the *Ban Righ* and mounted the guns. The ship sailed for Fort de France, Martinique, arriving on December 21. Matos and seventy-five others, including Horacio Ducharme, Nicolás Rolando, and Domingo Monagas, then joined the ship from Trinidad. Many of the crew, who had realized that they were part of a filibustering expedition, did not want to have any part in the operation and were discharged. Of the original crew only the chief officer, second officer, two other men, and Captain Willis remained. There was some difficulty in obtaining a replacement crew, but as De Paula stated privately, the local authorities at Martinique were assisting the Venezuelan insurgents and "lent their aid in obtaining men."[14] When the ship eventually set sail, it overflowed with well-armed men. The decks were alive with "the smells of unwashed flesh, hot iron, engine oil, and black humanity, that even the continual cloud of their cigar and cigarette smoke failed to smother."[15] The ship was further strengthened with thick plates of steel that protected the more vulnerable parts. Its "armament, of modern type, consisted of several guns capable of firing 300 shots per minute, and four 10 centimetre rapid firing guns."[16] By this time a Venezuelan gunboat had arrived in Fort de France, and it shadowed the *Ban Righ*.

Matos was on the island to finalize the arrangements with the local representatives of the FCC for the use of the cable facilities and the codes to be used. The Paris office of the FCC had instructed its local office in Martinique to give Matos all the assistance he requested in his revolutionary endeavors, but to do so "in a discreet manner making sure to avoid any compromising direct connection with either you or the Company."[17] It was decided that the best way to operate without raising suspicion would be for all the managers of the Venezuelan offices to communicate the political events that occurred in their respective districts to the manager at Caracas. This would neither attract attention nor elicit comment as it was the ordinary practice in the company to communicate interesting news of all kinds to the head office. The French government was also drawn into the conflict because it was official policy for it to receive information on all French nationals from every office manager of the FCC. The managers communicated the information in a private code to the French consular agent in their district. It was not until after May 1902, however, that the FCC became fully involved. Up to then their agent in Fort de France had insisted on following strict orders. However, he perished in the Mont Pelee disaster of that year. In the confusion that ensued and with the civil war in Venezuela, the French consul, who felt that he was acting in the best interests of his country, was able to take over operations. He sent more than 200 telegrams in private code, with many more in his own handwriting. The FCC not only communicated to Matos the movements of Castro but also the condition of his forces, the strength of the garrisons faithful to him, and also manufactured bogus telegrams.

THE REVOLUCIÓN LIBERTADORA

In Venezuela, Castro received news of the Matos plot on November 21. He immediately arrested Second Provisional President Ramón Guerra and a dozen of his associates. Castro also ordered the seizure of the family assets of both Matos and Guzmán Blanco "with all interest and returns from the confiscated property to be used to finance the war effort."[18] With the arrest of Ramón Guerra and his associates, and with the *Ban Righ* nearby in the Caribbean, the revolution started when Luciano Mendoza, the Aragua provisional president, marched with a dozen followers from La Victoria to

Villa de Cura and issued a proclamation on December 19, 1901. This caught Matos unawares as he was travelling from Trinidad to Martinique to meet the *Ban Righ*. Further uprisings were scheduled for the following day in Aragua, Carabobo, Cojedes, Lara, Falcón, and Guárico. Most of the Mochistas joined the rebellion. On his return from Martinique, Matos set up his operational headquarters in Trinidad and with the help of the Orinoco Steam Ship Company and their boats *Masparro, Apure*, and *Guanare*, together with the *Ban Righ*, Matos distributed arms from Trinidad to the rebels along the Venezuelan coast.

Nobody in the government wanted to go after Luciano Mendoza, but Gómez accepted the challenge and was appointed *Jefe Expedicionario* with the central army at his command. His willingness to take on this task was explained some years later to the Mexican writer Nemesio García Naranjo in the following manner:

> That fight only offered positive results. If I was defeated, who could censor me for having suffered the same fate as general Páez? If my troops were destroyed at La Puerta, who could blame me when Bolívar's army had been defeated in the same place? So then I was covered even if defeated because it had to be acknowledged, at least, that I had refused to be intimidated by my adversary. Now, if providence helped me and I managed to defeat Mendoza and take La Puerta, then I would have carved out a future for myself and opened the way for a better destiny.[19]

It was during this civil war that Gómez showed his true military capacity by confronting and defeating most of the old *caudillos*. Gómez caught up with Mendoza at Villa de Cura[20] on December 22 and defeated him, but General Antonio Fernández came to the rescue and Mendoza got away. Two days later Gómez engaged Mendoza at Desembocadero in Guárico, defeating the rebel forces. On New Year's Eve, Gómez routed General Antonio Fernández at Las Vigas. Gómez further engaged the rebels at Los Naranjos on January 4 and at El Barrio a day later. Luciano Mendoza was defeated again on February 2 at Tinaco. Five days later Loreto Lima was routed at El Totumo, which was followed by the defeat of Guillermo Barral at Vega del Viudo and Gregorio Cedeño at Alto de Lara on February 16.

THE *BAN RIGH* DECLARED A PIRATE

Just over a week after the *Ban Righ* entered the Caribbean, the Venezuelan government declared it a pirate ship and offered a $10,000 reward for her seizure. The European powers and the United States argued against this, with the latter considering the ship to be "simply a revolutionary agent acting against Venezuela alone."[21] The United States at this stage was very anxious for Matos to succeed. It was even contemplating sending a "powerful squadron to La Guaira."[22] because it feared that the British would cut short the career of the *Ban Righ* by having one of her cruisers seize her. The British, however, had no intention of acting against the rebel ship for the same reasons as the United States. The British minister at Caracas argued that it would "probably crush the hopes of General Matos and his large party as well as of his sympathizers in the United States, whose neutrality bears, as I gather from conversation with my American colleague and others, at least a benevolent tinge towards the revolution."[23] The little enthusiasm on the part of the British to help Castro out of his predicament was due to the failure of the Venezuelan president to deal with the sticky question of the 30 percent transhipment tax on goods imported from the British and Dutch Caribbean colonies. Dr. E. Blanco, the Venezuelan foreign affairs minister, had requested earlier that exports of arms from Trinidad be curtailed. However, Haggard, the British minister in Caracas, thought that the island had to consider its own interests in light of the Venezuelan government's refusal to abolish the 30 percent surtax. Haggard replied to Blanco that the prohibition of arms was an internal matter for the colonial authorities. The Venezuelan government was also irritated that Venezuelan refugees in Trinidad could openly carry out their revolutionary plans without being sanctioned by the colonial authorities, especially as Matos had set up his headquarters on the island. However, the activities of the Venezuelan rebels in Trinidad were not carried out with the consent of the colonial government. In addition, the British government did not see why they should prohibit the entry of Venezuelan shipping to Trinidad. In the opinion of J. H. Villiers at the Foreign Office, "so long as Venezuela is not at war with another Power with whom the United Kingdom is at peace Lord Lansdowne does not think it advisable to impose any such prohibition or limitation on the entry of Venezuelan public ships into Trinidad ports."[24]

At the end of December the *Ban Righ* left Fort de France. Once the ship was in Venezuelan waters, Willis was ordered at gunpoint to capture a sloop so that fifteen hundred rifles could be distributed to rebels in Boca Uchire in Anzóategui and other parts of the coast. On January 1, 1902, the British flag was replaced with a Venezuelan one, and the ship's name was changed to *Libertador*. It dropped anchor outside the port of Willemstad on January 5 to pick up Juan Pablo Peñaloza, E. S. Morales, and Gregorio Segundo Riera. In the Gulf of Venezuela, the *Ban Righ* unloaded one thousand rifles and sixty thousand rounds of ammunition to two generals.[25] The *Ban Righ* returned to Fort de France and left on January 11 under a British flag for Colón. Captain Willis and three other British subjects remained aboard while the rest of the British crew returned to Southampton. It was at this time that Captain Willis organized a small sabotage maneuver by injecting salt water into the ship's engine, thereby rendering it useless. Willis finally decided to leave ship at Puerto Colombia, helped by an American in charge of the pier, and made his way home on the *Elbe* after disguising himself and spending two days in a bull pen on a Norwegian steamer. As a result of Willis' sabotage the ship had to put into Barranquilla for repairs. It received a military commission from Juan Tobar, general in chief of the army of the Atlantic of Colombia, on January 25, 1902.

Once temporary repairs were completed the ship sailed again. On February 7 off Cumarebo, Falcón, the *Ban Righ* fought the Venezuelan man-of-war *General Joaquín Crespo*, "reducing it to flotsam, and then bombarding the town."[26] It later sailed to Los Taques on the Paraguaná peninsula, taking aboard eighty-six men who were commanded by General Juan Sierralta Tinoco, who would form part of General Riera's two hundred-man force. This group disembarked with Peñaloza, Ortega Martínez, Calvani, and Izquierdo León at Sauca. After an initial victory, however, the superior government forces headed by Jesús Hernández forced Riera to retire.

The sinking of the *General Joaquín Crespo* provoked a strong complaint by the Venezuelan government against Colombia. But there was little sympathy for Castro because he was the chief supplier of arms to the rebels in Colombia, which prolonged an already vicious civil war in the neighboring republic.[27] On February 28, the *Ban Righ*, escorted by a Colombian man-of-war called at St. Lucia. After taking on coal it continued to Trinidad under its new name of *Bolívar*. Flying the Colombian flag, it arrived at the British colony on March 23.

Castro was furious when he heard that the *Ban Righ* had docked at Port of Spain, Trinidad. An unfavorable comparison was made between Curacao and Trinidad, when the Dutch authorities had not allowed the ship to enter the harbor and had prevented communications with the shore. Although Castro failed to understand the "bias of the English authorities,"[28] he could not believe that a "serious government such as the English one, would jeopardise nothing less than its national flag in grotesque adventures such as the Matos one."[29] The British authorities were well aware that they could not allow the colonies to be used as a base for revolutionary activity against the Venezuelan government.[30] Therefore, they did not allow the ship to take coal at the island or any other British colony in the West Indies. The *Ban Righ* was ordered to leave Trinidad immediately. The ship was unable to leave port, however, because of the Willis sabotage (which had led to the bending of the intermediate astern eccentric rod and hence disabling the ship's engines from working; there was also a defect in the condenser that prevented fresh water being used in the boilers, and all six crowns of the furnaces of the port boiler had collapsed owing to the use of salt water, necessitating that all eight furnaces be replaced). L. Backler, chief engineer of the HMS *Indefatigable*, concluded that the *Ban Righ* was not in a fit "condition to raise steam, but in my opinion one of the boilers could be temporarily patched up and made fit for use, which would give the ship a speed of about 5 knots."[31] The *Ban Righ* remained disabled in Trinidad for at least two months, but the Venezuelan government achieved its objective in that the ship would not be allowed to refit in a British port "unless and until satisfactory assurances have been received that she is a Colombian public vessel and that she will not in the future be permitted to engage in any irregular hostilities against Venezuela."[32] In spite of such friendly action the British colony had alienated the good will of the Venezuelan government regarding the imports surtax. The British minister in Caracas reported that the behavior of Trinidad "would seem likely to have finally signed the death warrant of the abolition of the 30% Surtax."[33]

GÓMEZ PURSUES THE REBELS

In Venezuela the rebellion continued unabated. On February 26, Gómez returned to Caracas. He left as *Delegado Nacional* for Western Venezuela soon afterwards on March 18 to track down the rebels who were led by Riera and Peñaloza, which Régulo Olivares, had failed to do. Gómez engaged them on April 15 at Urucure in Coro. The rebels suffered, according to Gómez, "the most disastrous defeat registered in the history of our internal struggles."[34] Gómez then pursued them for a further skirmish at Barrio Nuevo. Gómez was then sent to eastern Venezuela, where government forces headed by Vice President Ramón Ayala had not fared well. On May 4, Gómez defeated Zoilo Vidal and entered Cumaná, leaving almost immediately for Carúpano, which was defended by two thousand troops under the command of Nicolás Rolando. The attack of eight hundred government soldiers on May 6 took place by land and sea, but Rolando was able to keep them at bay. Gómez suffered a serious wound to the right thigh, and the government troops had to retreat. The government then laid seige to the city.[35] This was broken in June when the captain of the German cruiser *Gazelle* persuaded Rolando to evacuate Carúpano and then "informed the Government commanders that he would not permit the bombardment of an undefended place."[36] Despite the number of skirmishes that Gómez had won the rebels still controlled most of the country through the alliances of local *caudillos*. Meanwhile, the rebels in western Venezuela had regrouped and defeated the government troops that were headed by Arístides Tellería, the president of Falcón.

On May 15, Matos finally landed on Venezuelan soil at Guiría in eastern Venezuela. Matos was pleased with events so far. His rebel forces under Domingo Monagas controlled most of eastern Venezuela, while the armies of Peñaloza, Riera, and Solagnie "have erected an impassable barrier between the Andes and Caracas,"[37] Luciano Mendoza held control of western Venezuela from Coro to Barinas. Castro and his weakened government only held the three Andean states, Carúpano, Maracaibo, and the relatively small rectangle between Caracas, Puerto Cabello, Valencia, and Los Teques. All that remained for the rebels to do was to oust Castro and his government in Caracas. Matos ordered his forces to converge on the center of the country for the final assault on the capital city. By June the revolution was moving closer to Caracas. The rebels took Maiquetía and held up a train on the Caracas-La Guaira line. It was clear to most observers that it was only a matter of time before the Castro government fell. In La Guaira there were seven foreign men-of-war[38] at the end of June to protect American, French, German, and Dutch interests. It would not be long before British interests would also need protection as Haggard, the British minister, informed the Foreign Office. The situation for the government at this juncture seemed hopeless.

CASTRO TAKES THE INITIATIVE

While Gómez was convalescing from his thigh wound, Castro went on campaign. He left Caracas on July 5, leaving the vice president in charge of the government until March 20, 1903. With his own position acquiring more strength militarily and economically, it was during this period that Gómez began to be considered Castro's natural successor by the people he had helped in Táchira, who would eventually become his personal armed force.

Castro headed for Aragua de Barcelona, arriving on July 7 to engage the rebels. However, he did not find them because they had regrouped in the center of the country to join with the western rebel forces of Mendoza. Castro was forced to make a hasty return to Caracas because the forward ranks of the rebel eastern army reached La Pascua at the end of July. Matos was clear in his mind for the need to push toward Caracas above all other cities. However, his two chiefs of staff offered two opposing strategies, which would ultimately lead to the defeat of the revolution. The Domingo Monagas plan was to pin down government troops at La Victoria with a small army and then proceed to Caracas. Luciano Mendoza argued for a full-frontal engagement of government troops at La Victoria. The supporters of the Monagas plan received a setback when he died on September 1 of natural causes. Matos, who wanted to march to Caracas directly from Villa de Cura via Ocumare de Tuy, was opposed by Mendoza, who felt it would be bad for the army because it would mean "forcing it to make two counter-marches, one to San Sebastián and the other to El Rodeo in order to take the Tuy route."[39] Mendoza argued that Castro should be drawn to La Victoria, where he would be defeated. There is little doubt that behind this strategy was Mendoza's strong desire to avenge his 1899 defeat at the hands of Castro on the same battlefield.

The war council debated the proposals and without the presence of Monagas opted for Mendoza's plan. Matos accepted this with equanimity, but warned that the attack on La Victoria would be difficult. He stated that success was not guaranteed because they were entering the conflict with insufficient ammunition for a prolonged, hard battle, owing to the detention of the *Ban Righ* in Trinidad. Moreover, as Giacopini Zárraga has argued, "the revolutionary chiefs underestimated the intuitive military capacity of General Castro and his combative valour."[40] The rebels' momentum at this stage was lost, something that many of Matos' supporters could not understand. Castro was now in the process of assembling three large armies in the Andean states. At the same time Matos travelled to Trinidad to secure the release of the *Ban Righ*, but the British colonial government would not allow the rebels to transport arms and ammunition. The pressing need, therefore, was to acquire a new cache of arms quickly. Matos tried to smuggle out as much of his arsenal as he could from the moored, guarded ship, which was a hazardous and expensive operation. In June, while the HMS *Indefatigable* was engaged in relief work at St. Vincent, a number of Trinidadian merchants reported that they "had seen boxes of ammunition being transferred at night from the *Ban Righ* to small boats and taken by them to sloops laying in the neighbourhood."[41] Part of this cache went to General Luciano Mendoza, who was preparing an attack on Valencia. The collector of customs inspected the *Ban Righ* for arms in July. Finding that the cache was smaller, the official concluded that the missing arms had been sent to Venezuela. Security was increased, putting an end to the arms being smuggled. The collector of taxes examined the ship again in August and found that there was a "large quantity of arms and ammunition."[42] The NY&B again came to Matos' rescue by providing him with five hundred thousand rounds of ammunition.[43] Some of the ammunition was sent through Caño de la Bruja while some went to Guanoco or by another route. All of it was packed in barrels of lard and supervised by an American employee of the company named Fitzgerald.[44] Major Rafferty, who was the NY&B's manager in Venezuela, ordered Ezra D. Jeffs, the company's superintendent in Guanoco to help the rebels with food, money, and transportation. He also ordered that the company's machinery be placed at their disposal so they could clean and repair their arms. L. A. Kuhn, the NY&B's mechanic, repaired over one hundred mauser carbines, rifles, revolvers and machetes that belonged to the rebels. He also supplied them with Winchester rifles and ammunition. The NY&B's ship, the *Viking*, also transported Generals Ducharme and Ambard with Colonel Hueves to Trinidad "in order to escape being captured by government troops."[45] Rafferty also wanted Kuhn to take over as chief machinist of the *Ban Righ*, but the NY&B employee refused. Carlos Domínguez Olavarría, who acted as a central link between Trinidad and Venezuela, was employed as the purser of the *Viking*. He travelled to Trinidad and Guanoco as an employee of the company, where he carried out his subversive work from the company's office. According to Kuhn:

> [H]e usually receives all those who travel the countryside from one place to another and passed by Guanoco either going or coming. They would hand over all the

correspondence that they were carrying, he would open it, read it, would re-read it and then would send the messenger and if the latter requested it he would be offered assistance to continue with his journey.[46]

Matos also tried to get the ship released in Trinidad by getting the Colombian government to assure the British government that the *Ban Righ* was owned by Colombia, and should thus be allowed to be refitted and proceed to Colombian waters. The Colombian government finally convinced the colonial authorities at the end of the year that it had acquired the *Ban Righ*. The ship and its cache of arms moved to Cartagena, where Matos was able to transport the arms to his rebel commanders in Venezuela.[47]

THE FCC HELPS MATOS

After an initial reluctance from its employees who did not want to be involved in any illegal activities, the FCC started to transmit messages to Matos on government troop movements, using the French consul as an intelligence agent. The consul felt that he was acting in the interests of his country, and he sent more than two hundred telegrams using a private code. For example, on August 9 the consul informed the rebels that Baptista had arrived in Guiría. On August 23 the consul telegraphed that General Zapata had been appointed *Jefe de Operaciones* against the rebels in Ciudad Bolívar and that the government gunboats *Bolívar* and *Restaurador* were transporting one thousand soldiers with arms and ammunition to San Félix. The FCC communicated Castro's movements, the condition of his forces, and the strength of the garrisons loyal to the government. The company also manufactured bogus telegrams, such as the one sent to General Mata Illas from General Velutini stating that the decisive battle of La Victoria, which the government won, had been undecided and that rebel forces were marching on Caracas.[48]

THE BATTLE OF LA VICTORIA

The government's situation was critical because it only controlled the Andean states, Caracas, and the cities of La Guaira, La Victoria, Puerto Cabello, Valencia, Maracaibo, and Carúpano. The rebel Western army headed by Mendoza merged with Riera, Peñaloza, and Solagnie. This force advanced to the valley of Aragua while Matos and the eastern army were in the process of marching to Villa de Cura, where the two armies were to meet. More than sixteen thousand rebel troops eventually congregated there. Matos estimated that three thousand head of cattle needed to be rounded up to feed his men on their march to the center of the country.[49]

Castro wore a yellow bandanna as he led his army of six thousand men, which was only two-fifths the size of the rebel forces. Castro reached Ocumare del Tuy in Aragua, close to Caracas, on August 28. His troops camped by the River Tuy, but the rebel forces of the eastern army, which was between five thousand to six thousand men, were at Altagracia de Orituco, some forty-five kilometers from the government's camp. Castro headed for Valencia, reaching Los Guayos, the closest railway station to the capital of the Carabobo state, on September 7. He left five hundred men stationed in Los Teques and only nine hundred men in the Caracas barracks. A further one thousand men were expected from Trujillo. On September 22, Castro sent Garrido with fifteen hundred men to Cagua.

The rebel army, numbering some sixteen hundred men, was billeted around a number of towns surrounding La Victoria, such as Villa de Cura, Cagua, Turmero, Maracay, La Cabrera, Guacara, and San Mateo. A further two thousand rebels had intercepted the road to Caracas, cutting off Castro's line of communications, as well as the telegraph, the train line, and the telephone. The situation for Castro on the eve of the battle of La Victoria, which started on October 12 (the *día de la raza*) and lasted for twenty-one days, was critical. Defeat seemed certain. Castro's troops were outnumbered more than two to one, and his lines of communications and supplies were cut. On October 7, Matos enquired about the situation in Caracas through the good offices of the FCC.[50] After hearing that the city was almost defenseless, Matos prepared his move on Caracas to form the new government. Matos' attack plan was in the shape of a horseshoe. Generals Mendoza and Solagnie with 3000 men were at one end, and Generals Riera and Peñaloza were at the other end with another four thousand men.

On October 13, Gómez left Caracas with almost one thousand men and wagons full of arms and ammunition, something Matos soon knew because of the FCC connection. The Andean battalions, commanded by Leopoldo Baptista, Pedro María Cárdenas, and Pedro Linares Alcántara, were also headed for La Victoria. The *Ban Righ* left Trinidad with arms. On October 15, Matos ordered Pedro E. Rojas to send two thousand rifles and four hundred thousand rounds of ammunition to Pedro Orderiz in Paparo. In the meantime, the rebels used up much of their ammunition in the numerous skirmishes at the beginning of the twenty-one-day battle. Just as Matos feared, they could not muster sufficient ammunition by the time they tried to mount a full-frontal attack. Matos later explained that the revolution failed because Mendoza "was not a good fighter with the unjustified flashiness of Chupulún."[51] In addition, government troops had been able to reinforce their own supplies.[52]

On November 2, Matos ordered a retreat, ending the longest and most decisive battle in Venezuelan history. According to Sullivan, a total of three thousand men were dead or wounded. As a result of the civil war the country underwent a radical change. The battle imposed the rule of central government on the regional *caudillos*, whose influence was reduced. With the decimation of the regional *caudillos*, the war-weary population gave the government its support, "preferring autocracy and arbitrary government to unending civil conflict."[53] Moreover, it would ensure that the Andinos remained in power. Ironically, from then onward Castro took a more nationalistic outlook. For Gómez, these events marked the start of his transition from a local to a national figure of importance because as "Commander of government troops, [he] travels the country and engages with varying degrees of success all the most prestigious military chieftains of Venezuela."[54]

AFTERMATH OF LA VICTORIA

The battle of La Victoria was a resounding victory for Castro, but the subsequent behavior of the rebels showed that they were convinced that it was only a matter of time before victory was theirs. The rebels continued to hold the majority of the country. Castro's victory yielded La Victoria but little else for the government. Although the rebels had been decisively beaten, Matos only made a strategic withdrawal. The uprising continued in various parts of the country, especially in the eastern region. The rebels suffered one important setback, however, which was that their arsenal was considerably depleted. Matos retreated to the safety of Curacao to mobilize the arms he had in Cartagena. He appointed Nicolás Rolando *Jefe de Estado Superior General* for the states of Guayana, Maturín, Cumaná, and Barcelona. He appointed Juan Pablo Peñaloza *Jefe de Estado Superior General* in the west and *Comisionado Especial del Director Supremo* to reorganise and mobilize the remaining rebel forces.

Matos felt that Peñaloza, at the head of a five thousand-man army, should attack Caracas. It was unprotected because Castro had sent one thousand men to Coro with Baptista, seven hundred men to Tucacas with González Pacheco, and five hundred men to Oriente with Torres. Such a move would also serve to "clear the situation for Riera, Solagnie and Rolando, allowing them to activate and mobilise their supporters."[55] Matos learned his lesson the previous month and now "based on his experience and the confidence of his own judgement inspired in these matters"[56] also warned Rolando, Zoilo Vidal, Vásquez, the Ducharme brothers, and others not to get into petty skirmishes because they did not advance their cause. Matos encouraged "the formation of the respective armed forces in order to march to Western Guárico where I have decided that the army should meet in order to march directly to Caracas."[57] Matos also entrusted Peñaloza with the task of creating a new attack plan for Caracas.

Luciano Mendoza, who had retired to Barquisimeto, was convinced that the rebels had "a respectable and sufficient base to repel and destroy any expeditionary forces which the government sends against us."[58] All the states under Revolución Libertadora forces were loyal. All that was needed was a new supply of arms to "open immediately military operations in the centre of the republic."[59] Mendoza wanted Roberto Vargas and the other leaders of that part of the country to "move with the utmost rapidity to organise supporters, collecting arms and, if it was possible, to increase support, harassing the government, taking advantage of all circumstances to achieve victory over it."[60] Mendoza was convinced that they would soon be taking the offensive and marching on Caracas to "deliver the final blow to the tyranny."[61] It was clear that toward the end of November the rebels were once again regrouping to launch a new offensive against the beleaguered government of Castro, but their plans were thwarted when, in the middle of one of the country's worst civil wars, a group of European powers decided to call in their loans to the country.

NOTES

1. Mariano Picón Salas, *Los Días de Cipriano Castro*, Caracas, Ediciones Garrido, 1953, p. 93.
2. Ramón J. Velásquez, *La Caida del Liberalismo Amarillo. Tiempo y Drama de Antonio Paredes*, Caracas, Ediciones Centauro, 1991, p. 278.
3. Picón Salas, p. 115.
4. The first Venezuelan graduate of West Point.
5. CO 295/430 Orray E. Thurber, Sworn Statement, 17 June 04 in enclosure, Bax Ironside to Foreign Office, 10.22.04.
6. CO 295/414 Edward F. Hudson to Lord Lansdowne, 10 February 02.
7. Orray E. Thurber, *Origen del Capital Norteamericano en Venezuela. La Epoca del Asfalto (1884–1907)*, trans. Angel Villasana, Barquisimeto, Editorial Nueva Segovia, 1955, p. 32.
8. A Colombian who became a naturalized British citizen in 1876.
9. C. H. of *El Monitor* mentions that Greene inspected the *Ban Righ* in Glasgow. (*El Monitor*, 26 March, 04 in Nikita Harwich Vallenilla, *Asfalto y Revolución: La New York and Bermúdez Company*, Caracas, Monte Avila Editores, 1992, p. 321.)
10. It is a gaelic name that means female king.
11. CO 295/430 Thurber, Sworn Statement, 10.22.04.
12. Captain Willis, *The Cruise of the "Ban Righ" or How I Became a Pirate*, London, Brooks Bros. Co., 1902.
13. Willis, p. 19.
14. CO 295/414 Hudson to Lansdowne, 2.10.02.
15. Willis, p. 31.
16. Willis, p. 28–29.
17. Letter, Head Office FCC to Forte de France, Confidential, Paris, 14 December 01, J. E. Sauvage, "La Companñía Francesa de Cables Telegráficos y la Revolución Venezolana de 1902–03" in Venezuela, *Venezuela y la Compañía Francesa de Cables Submarinos. Ruidoso Proceso. Documentos Publicados en "El Constitucional"* Caracas, Imprenta Nacional, 1906. (p. 77.)

18. William M. Sullivan, "The Rise of Despotism in Venezuela: Cipriano Castro, 1899–1908." PhD. diss., The University of New Mexico, 1974, p. 257.

19. Esteban Roldán Oliarte, *El General Juan Vicente Gómez. Venezuela de Cerca*, p. 38.

20. Also known as La Puerta.

21. FO 199/162 H. W. Bowen to J. R. Pachano, 4 January 02.

22. FO 199/154 A. C. Grant Duff to Lansdowne, 24 February 01.

23. FO 420/206 Haggard to Lansdowne, 11 January 02.

24. CO 295/407 J. H. Villiers to undersecretary of State, 28 December 01.

25. FO 420/206 Sir A. Moloney to Chamberlain, 14 January 02.

26. Sullivan, p. 257.

27. CO 295/414 Haggard to Lansdowne, 18 February 02.

28. C. Castro to C. Zumeta, 8 April 02 in Pino Iturrieta, *Epistolario*, p. 307.

29. Ibid.

30. CO 295/414 R. B. Finlay and Edward Carson, Royal Courts of Justice, *Report*, 10 March 02.

31. FO 420/206 L. Backler to E. L. Campbell, 29 March 02.

32. CO 295/414 F. H. Villiers to CO, 2 April 02.

33. CO 295/414 Haggard to Lansdowne, 26 March 02. The 30 percent surtax, which would remain a source of friction between Trinidad and Venezuela for many years, was initially set up by Guzmán Blanco at the instigation of the Boulton trading house. Since then nobody wanted to offend the three main commercial houses of the country, Boulton, Blohm, and Lesend, by repealing the surtax. The trading houses felt that once the surtax was abolished both Trinidad and Curacao would become entrepots for European products, thus reducing the price of imports with the consequent impact on their revenues and

> as the smaller houses are more or less dependent on them, they form together a formidable body with which the Venezuelan Government has, or pretends to have to reckon in this matter, specially when, as is usually the case, the Government has its hands full in the Provinces and is therefore anxious to conciliate the commercial classes in the Capital, so as to have at least one "point d'appui." (CO 295/407 Haggard to Lansdowne, 5 November 01)

34. Gómez (Delegado Nacional en los estados Falcón, Lara, Yaracuy, Zulia, Trujillo, Mérida y Táchira) to Habitantes del Estado Falcón, 26 April 02 in Tobias Arias, *Relieves Máximos*, Caracas 1930, p. 20.

35. CO 295/414 Haggard to Lansdowne, 18 May 02. According to Haggard, the British minister, Gómez was transferred to Trinidad for medical treatment. If this is correct, this would only be the second time that Gómez left Venezuela during his long life.

36. FO 80/439 Haggard to Lansdowne, 5 June 02.

37. Velásquez, p. 280.

38. Two American, two German, and one each from Italy, The Netherlands, and France.

39. M. A. Matos, *Apuntes sobre la Revolución Libertadora*, Curacao, n.p., 1903, p. 5.

40. J. A. Giacopini Zárraga, "Revive con Su Ameno Verbo la Batalla de La Victoria," *Resumén* 7:81, May 25, 1975, pp. 56–62.

41. CO 295/414 Haggard to Lansdowne, 5 June 02.

42. CO 295/414 Haggard to Rafael López Baralt, 21 August 02.

43. Thurber, p. 58. Emphasis added.

44. Lindon Bates, *The Path of the Conquistadores. Trinidad and Venezuelan Guiana*, London, Methuen & Co. Ltd., 1912, p. 104.

45. Thurber, p. 51.

46. Ibid., p. 53.

47. The Colombian war minister, who paid for the acquisition from his budget, informed Carlos Rico, the Colombian foreign minister, that it would be impossible for him to make payments on the dates stipulated (February 1, a second payment two months later in April, and the third on June 1) because of the separatist rebellion in Panama and the expenses incurred by the government. The Colombian government finally paid Matos £15,000 in monthly instalments of £3,000. The defeated Venezuelan general arrived in Bogotá in August 1904 for the final payment. The purchase was equivalent to $72,000, almost $29,000 less than Matos paid in 1901, but he presumably pocketed the amount because there is no suggestion that he returned the money to the Asphalt Trust. The *Ban Righ*, which was then in Cartagena harbor, was renamed *Crucero Marroquín*. The ship at last became a bona fide Colombian naval vessel.

48. J. E. Sauvage, *La Compañía Francesa de Cables Telegráficos y la Revolución Venezolana de 1902–03* in *Ruidoso Proceso*, p. 84–86.

49. AHM Unclassified M. A. Matos to Roberto Vargas, 5 September 02.

50. Sauvage, p. 91.

51. Velásquez, p. 285.

52. For a fuller account of the battle of La Victoria see M. Sullivan, 1974; Ramón J. Velasquez; and Giacopini Zárraga, pp. 56–62.

53. Sullivan, p. 292.

54. Velásquez, p. 280.

55. AHM Unclassified M A Matos to P E Rojas, 17 November 02.

56. Ibid.

57. Ibid.

58. AHM Unclassified Luciano Mendoza to Roberto Vargas and Juan Pablo Peñaloza, 16 November 02.

59. Ibid.

60. Ibid.

61. Ibid.

6

The "Peaceful Blockade"

The dispute between various foreign powers and Venezuela had been simmering for some time. It would lead to a major confrontation between a number of European powers and the Venezuelan government. The Germans were the most aggrieved party, and it was they who initiated the action to recover their loans. This action ultimately led to the "peaceful blockade" of Venezuela. In the latter half of the nineteenth century a German consortium had financed the building of the Gran Ferrocarril de Venezuela. However, when the Venezuelan government failed to meet its payments, the German company pressed its own government to assist it in the recovery of its capital. In pursuing the claim the Germans were at one point willing to send gunboats to settle the dispute. However, the crisis was averted when President Joaquín Crespo secured a Bs 33 million loan with a 5 percent coupon from the Disconto Gessellschaft of Berlin in 1896, managing to repay part of the debt. By 1901, however, the country was Bs 6 million behind in interest arrears alone because neither the principal nor the interest on the loan had been paid since 1897. The German government demanded that Venezuela repay the interest on the outstanding loans. There were also additional claims for war damage against German property during the 1898–1900 period. The new government of Castro did not recognize these claims and it proposed instead that a Venezuelan Commission be set up to decide on the claims. Castro argued that foreigners should not be treated differently than locals were and that the problem in question was a domestic one that did not call for foreign involvement because Article 149 of the Venezuelan constitution stated that any dispute arising from a stated contract between Venezuela and a foreign entity had to be settled in Venezuelan courts. Such a clause, however, had been omitted from the Disconto Gessellschaft loan agreement.

The Germans rejected the Venezuelan solution because they had little faith in Venezuelan justice. In addition, they did not accept the principle that the claims could not be made into a diplomatic matter. The Venezuelan government would only admit that any appeal against the commission would be heard by the Supreme Court, but the Germans had little faith in the incorruptibility of the courts. They argued that the courts depended ultimately on the president's decision. The Venezuelan promises of honoring any new instruments of debt fell on deaf ears because the experience of the Disconto was sufficient proof that the Venezuelan government was incapable of honoring its debts.

It was not only the Germans who were owed money. The Venezuelan government was also in arrears on interest payments on British debts, such as the Bs 5 million loan on the Puerto Cabello & Valencia Railway, the loans on the Bolívar, Central, and Barquisimeto railways, and the debt on the Caracas & La Guaira Railway company. There was also a British request to abolish the 30 percent surtax on goods imported from Trinidad. The island was willing to ban completely the imports of arms, "which has proved so fruitful a source of complaint on the part of the Venezuelan Government,"[1] as long as the illegal tax was abolished. The British also had some minor but extremely irritating small claims stemming from the trading activity between Trinidad and Venezuela. In 1902 there were eight thousand foreigners living in Ciudad Bolívar, of which five thousand were British citizens. The total turnover of the port was about Bs 16,250,000, of which 60 percent was with Britain or with the British colonies.[2] A large number of small traders moved between the West Indies and the mainland, and the Venezuelan Navy harassed some of these people.

During 1901 the Venezuelan government treated a number of British subjects and their property poorly. On January 22 the Venezuelan gunboat *Augusto* seized half the passengers of four cargo boats, who were on their way from the island of Patos, a disputed British possession in the Gulf of Paria, to Trinidad. The following month John Craig, a fisherman from Trinidad, was heading to Patos on the *Sea Horse* when it was beached by a Venezuelan ship. The Venezuelans were "armed with cutlasses and rifles"[3] and assaulted the crew. On March 10 the *Maria Theresa* sloop, owned by a British subject but flying the Venezuelan flag, was hijacked by rebel troops at Yrapa. It was ordered to proceed to Yaguarapara, where a number of soldiers landed and then sailed for Guiría. Upon its arrival the sloop remained under the control of the rebel officer. The owner was ordered to return to Yaguarapara, receiving no compensation. While the boat was in Guiría the Venezuelan gunboat *Miranda* entered the port, "and after compelling the *Maria Theresa* to leave by firing two shots over her, immediately dispatched a boat to the vessel to enquire the destination of the latter."[4] The boat was heading for Yrapa, but when it tried to leave Guiría, the *Miranda* took the crew prisoner and then set the boat on fire, completely destroying it.[5] The prisoners were cast adrift off Point Pima.

Whatever may have been the circumstances that justified the commander of the *Miranda* in detaining the *Maria Theresa*, (and there was some evidence that "the vessel had been in communication with, if not in the employ of, the revolutionary party"),[6] British Charge d'Affaires Grant-Duff, complained that excessive and unnecessary violence had been used and that "no arguments can possibly be put forward in support of the treatment to which the sailors of the *Maria Teresa* [*sic*] were subjected when they were set adrift in an open boat."[7] Blanco, the Venezuelan foreign minister, assured Grant-Duff that the ministries of Interior, War, and Finance would investigate the circumstances under which the sloop had been destroyed. Their investigations revealed that the *Maria Theresa* was carrying arms and ammunition for the rebels, so the Venezuelan government felt that their action was justified.

In March, Venezuelan troops entered the house of James Natham Keely, a native of Trinidad and a British subject who had a coffee and cacao plantation at Rio Grande near Guiría. They arrested him and occupied his house, which was then pillaged with a considerable amount of property stolen.[8] On August 30, 1901, a Venezuelan ship detained the Venezuelan-owned sloop *Pastor*, which had set sail from Trinidad for Venezuela. After examining the ship's papers, the Venezuelans landed some of its crew on Patos island and seized some of the goods that the *Pastor* was carrying. In January 1902 the *Indiana* was seized on the River Barina. It was confiscated and carried away to the Venezuelan port of Amacurú. On May 1, 1901, the Venezuelan gunboat *Presidente Joaquín Crespo* destroyed the *In Time* in the port of Pedernales. In June the *Queen*, travelling from Grenada to Trinidad, was seized twenty miles from Carúpano. It was towed to Porlamar, where it was confiscated on suspicion of being a smuggling boat. This last incident convinced the British government to take action against Venezuela. Another factor was that the German trading houses in Venezuela had lost money since July 29, 1901, when the Catatumbo River had been closed to commercial traffic with Colombia. The German charge d'affaires argued that the "German government reserved to themselves the right to hold Venezuela responsible for their damages."[9]

THE GERMANS ACT

By 1901 the Germans felt justified in taking coercive action against Venezuela. However, they did not want to do this until they received the tacit approval of the United States, which it received on July 12 when Vice President Theodore Roosevelt informed von Steinberg, the German ambassador, that "if any South American country misbehaves toward any European country, let the European country spank it."[10] Blockading the country's ports and seizing its customs receipts were options. The only limitation was that no territory could be occupied. Although Roosevelt was determined to uphold the principles of the Monroe Doctrine, he did not "intend to stand in the way of the Powers enforcing their lawful claims nor did he intend to screen any South American Republic who had to give lawful satisfaction for these."[11] Roosevelt described his attitude in the Venezuelan affair as one of "watchful vigilance."[12] In April 1901 the German man-of-war *Vineta* arrived in La Guaira. It later left for Trinidad. There had been rumors, however, that the Germans were looking for a base in Venezuela, with a well-informed gentleman reporting to Grant-Duff that "a serviceable harbour has been discovered in Margarita which the German Government will lease for forty years as a coaling station and that it is proposed to exploit the coal mines at Guramichate—a place some distance from the coast opposite Margarita—for the use of the German navy in these waters."[13]

By the end of the year the Germans were ready to seek redress from Venezuela for the country's lack of payment. In an extensive memorandum sent on December 11, the German government informed Secretary of State Hay that if they could not obtain settlement of their claims, they would blockade the main Venezuelan ports. They added that "if this were not sufficient 'the temporary occupation' of different harbours, and the 'levying of duties in those places' "[14] would occur. Under no circumstances did they threaten "the acquisition or the permanent occupation of Venezuelan territory."[15] The Germans confined their dispute to their own claims, and no "ulterior motive of territorial aggrandizement"[16] was envisaged. The American government did not object to such a move because they were certain that "no measures will be taken in this matter by the Agents of the German Government"[17] that went beyond those stated in the memorandum. The American minister in Caracas, Herbert Bowen, was informed that there now existed a general agreement between the German and U.S. governments that on the "condition of not taking possession of any territory, Germany or any other Power may enforce the payment of its claims in Venezuela and may even send a fleet for that purpose."[18] It was at this stage that Haggard, the British Minister, proposed joining the Germans in their endeavors to force the Venezuelans to pay up. He believed that the German memorandum to the State Department showed that they were serious about enforcing their claims, and that this was an opportunity to reach an arrangement "by which our very large interests here might benefit."[19]

By early December 1901, Germany had assembled a small flotilla of four warships off La Guaira. The general feeling in the country was that the Germans meant business. Haggard hoped that the Germans were serious because it would benefit all foreign interests, arguing that another fiasco, such as the U.S. naval demonstration at the beginning of the year, would be "disastrous to the interests of foreign Powers."[20] The Venezuelan government stated that if the Germans occupied La Guaira, they would declare "it and any other place which they may occupy, free ports, and if they levy Customs, he will establish another Customs House in Caracas and levy them over again."[21] However, the collection of revenue from custom houses would be a very long, tedious affair that would occupy Germany's navy for a prolonged period. So the German government was hesitant to divert "part of their small fleet for a prolonged period for a purpose which they may not consider of quite sufficient importance to justify the sacrifice."[22] Moreover, such action by the Germans would be "tantamount to a blockade."[23] The current duties were as high as the market could bear, and government revenues were dependent on foreign imports.

Castro remained defiant even with the threat of a blockade, declaring that if the Germans advanced to Caracas, he would "destroy them as the Boers destroyed the English."[24] However, he did not believe that this would happen because "the exaggerated German matter has never constituted a danger to our relations with that Empire."[25] The foreign diplomats in Caracas felt that if the Germans did not act soon, then Castro would believe that they had backed down because of his threats. Castro had called their bluff, but the Germans had neither the resources nor the desire to force Venezuela to act on its claims. Germany made a tactical retreat, resorting to diplomacy to get its claims paid.

THE MERITS OF A "PEACEFUL BLOCKADE"

In early 1902 Germans first considered the merits of a "peaceful blockade" of Venezuela. Count von Bulow, the German chancellor, informed Kaiser Wilhelm that although such a measure would cripple the South American country financially, it had the endearing feature of making "a declaration of war against Venezuela unnecessary."[26] The Germans, however, were unwilling to act on their own. So in July 1902, Count Metternich, the German Ambassador in Britain, informed Lord Lansdowne that his government thought that "the time was approaching when it would be necessary for the Powers interested in Venezuela to put pressure on the Venezuelan Government."[27] This suggestion received a warm reception in London, as the British were now ready to confer with the Germans over their problems with the South American nation. The British were now bent on having their own claims fully satisfied after the *Queen* incident of June 1902. They were "quite ready to confer with the German Government with a view to joint action."[28] The British took the initiative away from Germany and prepared for a blockade.

The German claims against Venezuela amounted to Bs 1.7 million for damages suffered under the 1898–1900 civil war, Bs 3 million lost during the current Matos civil war, and the guarantee of interest on the capital of Bs 41 million held by German creditors in Venezuela. The British grievances against Venezuela were less severe and stemmed mainly from the unjustified attacks against British property. However, they also included claims by two British railway companies for damage by government troops during the Matos revolution and a minor complaint by the British government against the Venezuelan consul at Trinidad for irregularity in the discharge of his duties. Although the German government "recognised that there was a sharp distinction between the character of the British and German 'first line' claims,"[29] Britain and Germany decided to act together. The British coordinated the joint task force of the two countries. Vice Admiral Douglas, commander in chief of the North America and West Indies station, would be in overall command. Commodore Montgomerie was in charge of the actual blockade on board the *Charybdis*, with the vessels *Columbine, Tribune, Retribution,* and *Indefatigable* at his disposal as well as the torpedo boat destroyers *Quail* and *Rocket*. In addition, the *Alert* and the *Fantome* would also be available if needed. The Venezuelan government ignored the British complaints, refusing to countenance any claims so long as the *Ban Righ* remained in Trinidad.[30]

In their December 1901 *pro-memoria* sent to the U.S. government, the Germans had considered the imposition of a "peaceful blockade" of the country that would also involve the ships of neutral Powers "inasmuch as such ships, although a confiscation of them would not have to be considered would have to be turned away and prohibited until the blockade should be raised."[31] The British now had reservations about the effectiveness of such a move. Lansdowne felt that the blockade that the Germans suggested initially would "scarcely be sufficient for our purpose"[32] because the blockading force did not have the right to prevent neutral ships from using the ports. So any interference with the ships of a third nation would "be properly regarded by that nation as an act of belligerency implying, and only to be justified, by the existence of a state of war."[33] The only solution therefore would be for a belligerent blockade that would put "an end to all intercourse with the port, the merchant ships of third Powers being prevented from entering it by the blockading squadron."[34] Such a blockade would be considered an act of war, but Venezuela would be given a last warning before the blockade started. In addition, Britain would declare their intention "to the other Powers, including the United States."[35] An alternative view to the blockade was that of Vice Admiral Douglas, who favored seizing all Venezuelan naval vessels "until our demands are complied with."[36] This strategy was soon adopted. As a first measure of coercion the blockading powers would seize the Venezuelan gunboats. Then further action would be taken, "the exact nature of which is still under consideration."[37] The most favorable time for starting such an action was

November because it was the month with the most inclement weather. At this stage the Germans enquired whether the British "thought it desirable to invite the cooperation of the United States"[38] as they had "already ascertained that the United States' government saw no objection to the proposed naval demonstration."[39] However, Lord Lansdowne felt that it would be sufficient to give the U.S. government notice of the blockade's intentions without asking them to join. In October 1902, Lansdowne in an extensive minute set out his thoughts of the impending blockade of Venezuela and the attitude of the United States toward it, concluding that "we may assume the acquiescence of the United States, and I do not think we need do more than inform them when the time comes of our intention to act with Germany."[40] On November 1, Sir Michael Herbert, British ambassador to the United States, told Secretary of State Hay that the British government had "within the last two years had grave cause to complain of unjustifiable interference on the part of the Venezuelan Government with the liberty and property of British subjects."[41] Sir Michael elaborated by stating that every effort had been made to come to an agreement, but none had been successful. The British government was now pursuing further methods to bring pressure upon Venezuela, especially after a formal protest was lodged and the answer was wholly unsatisfactory. Hay replied by giving his tacit approval when he stated that although the U.S. government regretted the use of force against other republics on the American continent by European powers, it "would not object to their taking steps to obtain redress for injuries suffered by their subjects, provided that no acquisition of territory was contemplated."[42] The organization for the blockade continued. Lansdowne informed the British legation in Caracas about the possible German assistance in the event of a blockade, while Bowen sent William Russell, the American legation's secretary,[43] on the *USS Marietta* to the eastern coast of the country "to ascertain on the spot the true facts of the case about the efficiency of the blockade."[44]

THE POLITICAL SITUATION IN THE COUNTRY

Despite Matos' massive defeat in October, the civil war still continued. Ciudad Bolívar, which was in rebel hands at the end of November 1902, was bracing itself for another bombardment and possible sacking. Provisions were still getting through to the town because the commanders of the Venezuelan gunboats blockading the river port had been bribed, and traders sent vessels loaded with provisions without being stopped. At times they were even escorted by a government gunboat.[45] The rebels had three hundred thousand mauser cartridges in a bonded warehouse in Trinidad. The British colonial authorities now changed their tune and did not object to their export as they fell "within the range of legitimate commerce."[46] The failure of the colonial government to recognize Castro's proclamation the day after Matos left the country and sought asylum in Trinidad was considered by the Venezuelan president to be evidence of British encouragement of the revolutionaries.[47] However, the government's attention now shifted away from the civil war with Matos to the growing international crisis, which was about to erupt in Castro's face.

Castro was first informed of the intentions of Germany and Britain in early November. The Venezuelan president tried unsuccessfully to win over Germany by offering to settle its claims if it desisted in supporting Britain's action.[48] To gain time and initiative Castro requested that Victor Barret de Nazaris, the Venezuelan minister in Washington, arrange a loan with the Seligman Financial House of New York. He also asked the United States to guarantee to protect Venezuela from European powers. The United States refused to become a guarantor. As time started to run out in early December, H. G. & L. F. Blohm, the largest trading house in Venezuela, offered Castro "a private loan of 2 million Bolivars in case he opted to pay off the most pressing German claims."[49] Castro, however, was convinced that the "peaceful blockade" would not take place. He stated to the *Agencia Pumar* on December 6, the day before the British and German ministers delivered their ultimatum, that it was inconceivable that civilized nations with friendly relations with Venezuela should try to force their claims on the country when "the alleged difference is comfortably covered within the jurisdiction of our laws which are guaranteed by our justice principles."[50] A foreign blockade by the European Powers, though clearly undesirable, would have a positive political impact on Castro. It could swing the civil war in his favor because it was likely that his enemies would reluctantly have to rally around the government at the threat of hostile action. So all was not completely lost.

THE IMPOSITION OF THE "PEACEFUL BLOCKADE"

On December 7, 1902, the "peaceful blockade" was declared when "by order of our Sovereigns, we the Commanding Officers of the German and British naval forces, co-operating in West Indian waters hereby declare a blockade of the Venezuelan ports of Maracaybo [*sic*] (including San Carlos), Puerto Cabello, La Guayra, [*sic*] and . . . any other harbours on the east coast of Venezuela."[51] The HMS *Retribution* entered La Guaira to collect the British minister and consul. Castro ordered all German and British citizens imprisoned. He instructed his commanders at the country's ports that if any German or British naval forces disembarked and "were not in a hostile mood, nothing should be done against them, but if their landing was an armed one and in a hostile mood, then you will carry out your patriotic duties."[52] Gómez, as acting president during the conflict, would be the official representative of Venezuela and deal directly with the foreign powers. However, Castro as military governor would remain in effective control of the government; he would not assume the reigns of power officially until March 20 of the following year.[53]

Two days after the ultimatum was delivered the "peaceful blockade" started to be enforced. On December 9 the British and German naval vessels escorted the Venezuelan ships *23 de Mayo, Zamora, Zumbador, Ossum, Totumo*, and *General Joaquín Crespo* to Curacao while the *Margarita* was dismantled at its dry-dock in Puerto Cabello. The *Restaurador* was captured in Guanta and the *Bolívar* was held in Trinidad. Only the *Miranda* escaped. At this point Castro rallied the country, issuing a defiant speech in which he repudiated "the insolent foreign foot" and called for everyone to unite against the foreign aggressors.[54] Castro's first act was to free all political prisoners. Mocho Hernández was one of the first to gain his liberty. This delighted his supporters, particularly Alejandro Urbaneja. Liberal political prisoners such as Nicolás Rolando, Gregorio Segundo Riera, and Antonio Paredes, who were imprisoned at the San Carlos fort in Zulia with Mocho Hernández, were freed along with the Vallenilla Lanz brothers.

The Nacionalistas were opposed to the Castro government and to the Revolución Libertadora because, as Alejandro Urbaneja argued, once the Liberals gained power they would repress the Conservative opposition. It was also felt that because Castro was politically isolated the Nacionalistas would be able to gain valuable time by siding with the president at his time of greatest need, planning to depose him at a later date. It was imperative, however, to convince Mocho Hernández of this strategy. Urbaneja and Eduardo Celis travelled on December 12 to Zulia, where Mocho Hernández was detained, to confer with him. Mocho Hernández was convinced, but his price for joining the Revolución Restauradora was for Castro to institute a series of reforms and to appoint a number of Nacionalistas to his cabinet. On December 16, Mocho Hernández arrived in Caracas a free man. He conferred with Castro at Miraflores, where it was agreed that at the end of the foreign crisis Alejandro Urbaneja would be appointed foreign minister in a new cabinet that would also include Mocho Hernández. At a formal reception later that evening to celebrate the reconciliation between the two factions, Mocho Hernández placed himself publicly at "the service of the fatherland,"[55] adding that "my memories as a prisoner are buried in the furtherest corner of my dungeon."[56] Castro replied in a similar vein, referring to the two of them almost as Olympian gods when he stated that "superior men like ourselves only remember the good things; evil deeds leave no memory except in small-minded people. Let us sweep away the past and let us gallicise the law and the justice system of the fatherland on the basis of national brotherhood."[57] The following day Mocho Hernández publicly called for an end to the civil war because the foreign threat was far greater to the nation than the strife between the various factions in the country. He stated that it was time to put an end to "the devastation and slaughter"[58] in Venezuela. Guzmán Blanco, Matos' father-in-law and the former president of the country, was also willing to forget his problems with Castro in the time of Venezuela's need. He stated from his Paris home on December 13 that "I am a long way from being one of President Castro's supporters, nevertheless at a time when he is facing the foreigner, a feeling of dignity prevents me from passing judgement on his politics."[59] Matos wanted to seize the opportunity to depose Castro, arguing at the end of December that the attack on Venezuelan ports by the European Powers was against Castro and not Venezuela. He stated that it was the duty of the rebels, as they still controlled most of the country, to "continue the fight against the man who has corrupted and poisoned everything."[60]

The central-western states of Lara, Portuguesa, and Trujillo were controlled by Juan Pablo Peñaloza, Jacinto Lara, Gregorio Segundo Riera, Amabile Solagnie, and Luciano Mendoza, who boasted that "I am in a position to prevent the government from occupying even a hand-palm of any land of the States under our power."[61] The central-eastern states of Aragua, Miranda, Anzoátegui, Bolívar, and Guárico were controlled by M. Hernández Ron, J. M. Ortega Martínez, and Nicolás Rolando. Castro's position seemed hopeless now that he did not command a navy to transport his troops quickly. Matos argued that the time was ripe to attack him because the nation's sovereignty was not at stake, and therefore "there is no reason for our patriotism to be alarmed other than to deplore the conflict and its immediate effects."[62] He stated that matters would change considerably if the foreign powers did invade, as then the revolutionaries would be the first to defend the country. Matos felt that there was only one rallying call for the rebels, and that was "forward to finish with Castro, the only author of so many disgraceful acts."[63] Their main objective was the occupation of Caracas.[64] However, Matos was fighting a losing cause. The threat of foreign intervention was too great to ignore, and many people rallied around the government, lending it money for the forthcoming conflict. Even Matos lent the government Bs 200,000, the same as the Sucesión Guzmán Blanco and considerably more than the trading houses of Boulton & Co., which gave Bs 40,000, and Blohm & Co., which gave Bs 50,000.[65]

THE "PEACEFUL BLOCKADE" IS IMPOSED

The naval demonstration, which had started peacefully, turned nasty within a few hours. The German gunboat *Panther*, which was escorting the *General Joaquín Crespo* and *Totumo* gunboats to Curacao, received the order from Commander Scheder on the *Vineta* to sink the two ships and proceed to La Guaira to rescue the German consul, who was surrounded by an angry mob. The following day, December 10, Castro suggested that Venezuela could settle her differences with the United Kingdom and Germany by arbitration with Herbert Wilcox Bowen, the American minister, representing the South American country. Secretary of State Hay formally proposed this to both the British and German governments on December 13.

In the meantime the dispute escalated further. On December 12 the English merchant ship *Topaze* arrived at Puerto Cabello, causing a demonstration by the population. This forced the HMS *Charibdys* and the *Vineta* to bomb the San Felipe and Solano forts that defended the city. Further up the coast, the *Panther* sought shelter from a storm by attempting to enter Lake Maracaibo. General Jorge Antonio Bello, commander of the San Carlos fort at the entrance to the lake, fired upon the ship before the German captain could make his intentions clear. The German gunboat returned fire and bombarded the fort, which set the town on fire. The decision to bomb the fort was taken by the German commodore independently and without consulting the British.

The sinking of the Venezuelan ships and the bombardment of Puerto Cabello created a feeling of "irritation against action of His Majesty's Government and Germany"[66] in the U.S. House of Representatives. Moreover, there was apprehension at seeing the two European powers working together, with special regret that Britain was cooperating with Germany. This led to the view "in Washington that we are being made use by her."[67] In the United Kingdom too, British foreign policy was seen as following in the footsteps of Germany. There were public protests in Britain against the treatment of such a small, defenseless country. The Manchester chapters of the Peace Society and the Inter-Arbitration Association passed a resolution on December 23 that expressed its "deep regret that acts of War have been committed by the order of the Government against the Republic of Venezuela, and emphatically protests as citizens against such proceedings being commenced without any previous explanation to the representatives of the people."[68] The following day, the London branches of the Inter-Arbitration Association and the Peace Society passed a resolution on the Venezuelan war, renewing "its protests against the action of the government of Great Britain and Germany towards Venezuela."[69]

Under pressure from the Matos revolution, on December 16 Castro appointed Bowen to arbitrate in the conflict, which Germany and Britain accepted under certain conditions. Castro felt that Venezuela had won a moral victory now that the European powers had accepted arbitration. As part of the warming of relations, a couple of days later Captain Molke of the German navy gave a lavish banquet for Castro and his entourage. On the same day Secretary Hay assured Count Von Quadt, the German charge d'affaires, that he was confident of getting the Venezuelan affair settled quickly because he "considered it highly desirable to reach a settlement soon for both public and Congress were nervous and excited."[70] The U.S. government was under certain pressure because the Venezuelan imbroglio could blow up into a regional crisis. Congress easily approved a resolution demanding that Roosevelt ensure that the Monroe Doctrine had not been violated.

Italy, which had now joined the other two European countries, and the United Kingdom agreed to arbitration. However, the Germans, who had most at stake, were delaying matters. President Roosevelt, under certain domestic pressure, brought the Germans to the arbitration table by delivering an ultimatum: Admiral Dewey and his squadron would set sail to prevent any Germans from landing on Venezuelan soil. The German Kaiser suggested that Roosevelt act as arbiter, something that the president was willing to do. Hay persuaded him against it because the United States also had outstanding claims against Venezuela, and he felt that it was inappropriate for them to judge the case. Hay managed to get Roosevelt's approval to have the matter settled at the Permanent Court of International Arbitration at the Hague. On December 25 the Germans agreed to arbitration and all foreign claims against Venezuela were sent to The Hague for judgment.[71] Hay's "strong recommendation" produced the desired result, and all the Powers agreed to arbitration on December 27.

On December 19 the Venezuelan government appointed Bowen as their representative at The Hague, conferring full powers on him to act as arbitrator. Bowen was a "genuine and haughty New England aristocrat, whose ancestry could be traced back to the early seventeenth century."[72] He had graduated from Yale in 1876, where he had been William Howard Taft's classmate, and from Columbia Law School in 1881, with special training in diplomatic and international law. Bowen was also an accomplished musician, a poet and an art connoisseur and scholar of wide achievement who spoke French, German, Italian, Spanish and Persian fluently. In Venezuela, Bowen would not associate with many American businessmen because they were beneath his own social standing. During the negotiations at The Hague, Bowen proved to be a considerable hindrance to the European Powers. Lansdowne observed that he was not willing "to facilitate an equitable settlement but to create dissensions between the powers. We should therefore not be sorry to break off negotiations with him."[73] At the beginning of February both Germany and Italy were still not happy with the protocols, but finally an agreement was reached on February 13, 1903. Bowen signed the protocols with the blockading powers and, a few days later, with the United States and several other creditor nations. The result was that the blockade was lifted.[74]

The protocols provided that Venezuela would set aside 30 percent of its customs receipts at its two main ports of Puerto Cabello and La Guaira for the payment of the awards of the Mixed Commission (set up to adjudicate the laws and settle claims). Belgian officials would take charge of the customs houses if Venezuela did not comply with the arrangement. Venezuela also promised to make arrangements that would assure the regular service of the bonded debt. It is interesting to note that Roosevelt did

Table 6.1
Outcome of the Mixed Commission

	Claim (Bs)	Granted (Bs)	Success rate (%)
UK	14,743,523	9,401,268	63.8
Italy	39,844,259	2,975,906	7.5
Germany	7,376,685	2,091,909	28.4
France	17,891,613	2,667,079	14.9
USA	89,410,952	2,269,543	2.5

Source: Arellano Moreno, *Mirador de la Historia*, p. 202.

not object to the provision that might have given a European government control of the customs houses. The Permanent Court of International Arbitration at The Hague decided that the blockading powers should receive preferential treatment. This was a dangerous precedent because it meant that the court had decided in favor of a power that used force, placing countries that resorted to violence at the forefront of any settlement.

The protocols settled some of the outstanding claims against Venezuela (see Table 6.1). The United Kingdom was the most successful country, getting almost 64 percent of its outstanding claims, while the United States only achieved a meager 2.5 percent. With the money set aside from the customs receipts, the blockading powers' settled claims were paid off in full by 1907. Those of the other claimant countries were paid off by 1912.

MATOS DREAMS OF ENTERING CARACAS

Throughout the period of the blockade Matos continued to urge his supporters to march against Caracas. He outlined his initial plan of attack on the city on January 23, 1903. The rebel troops would support General Riera to take Coro and "make the coast ours"[75] to recover Tucacas "for the free movement of resources for the army through that port"[76] and to recover Barquisimeto, which was now once again in government hands, for the defense of San Felipe.[77] Toward the end of January 1903, Matos sent a memorandum to Ortega Martínez, the *Delegado Especial de la Jefatura Suprema*, stressing that the principal objective of the rebel cause was to occupy Caracas "for which you will determine the manner and way of achieving it with the swiftness and accuracy of movement so that the plan will not fail."[78] The plan was for the *Ejército de Oriente* to march through the Tuy valley with two thousand men to "break through at Boquerón"[79] and then occupy Los Teques. A further two hundred men would then take Lagunetas or Lajas, cutting all telegraph and railway lines. The rest of the army would march to Petare, to the east of Caracas, and to Baruta in the south, to mount an attack against the capital. At the same time some two thousand men would take La Guaira.[80]

Matos felt that General Antonio Fernández had enough men in Guárico, Aragua, and Carabobo to attack Caracas. Matos advised them that if the attack was unwise, then they should provoke further uprisings in Carabobo, and join the rebel army in Barquisimeto to take Puerto Cabello, "a military base and source of resources which will give us an immense advantage."[81] Matos also stressed that "the fatherland is at stake, therefore we have to take advantage of Castro's inactivity owing to his errors and arbitrariness in order to save Venezuela of its ruin, disrepute and shame abroad."[82] The western army, however, was in a shambles with little fighting spirit left.

The biggest threat to Castro's "Chief-Army Administration," as Velásquez labelled the government, was Rolando and his Barlovento army. Rolando had inherited the political mantle of Domingo Monagas in eastern Venezuela, and he had the potential to emerge as the new leader of the Liberals. Moreover, he was planning to attack Caracas now that the western army was in a shambles; its three main leaders, Peñaloza, Riera, and the old fighter Luciano Mendoza, were fighting for its overall leadership. During Easter week a section of Rolando's army arrived in Petare and Guatire, almost the outskirts of Caracas. Many parishioners stayed away from the religious services because of the intense fighting at the outskirts of Caracas. It was even rumoured that Rolando was about to enter the capital city because he had secured a large cache of arms. Under such intense pressure it was natural for the government to deal with Rolando first, then go after the relatively easy target of the western army later. Once the "peaceful blockade" was lifted Castro went on the offensive. Gómez was appointed to mop up the rebels in the Barlovento region and eastern Venezuela, where Rolando's army was stationed. Gómez was accompanied by Diego Bautista Ferrer, who had completed a military course in France, and Francisco Linares Alcántara, who was the first Venezuelan to graduate from West Point. They left La Guaira on April 2, 1903, with one thousand five hundred men. They disembarked in Higuerote in pursuit of Rolando in the Tuy valley. The large cache of arms that Rolando was expecting had landed in the country, but he would only get a small amount because other leaders, such as Ortega Martínez and Doroteo Flores, also needed arms. The Nacionalista generals José Rafael Luque and Juan Quintana, who were now collaborating with the government, surprised Ortega Martínez at Paparo on April 4, preventing him from reaching Rolando with reinforcements at El Guapo, where he was stationed and which Gómez was about to attack. The rebel leader had three thousand men. He waited in vain for ammunition, which was secretly hidden on the road to Batatal, and for reinforcements and food supplies. Gómez stationed his own troops on the north flank while Linares Alcántara led the western-flank attack against

Rolando. The battle lasted from April 11 to 14. It ended when Generals Hernández Ron and Fernández defected to the government with the second *cuerpo del ejército*, and the rebels ran out of arms and ammunition. Rolando was forced to retreat back to eastern Venezuela, relieving Caracas of his threat. The government paid a heavy price for this victory, suffering one thousand two hundred casualties. On May 14, Rolando and twenty of his defeated officers, including José Manuel Pañaloza, Zoilo Vidal, and Cruz Monagas, headed on board the *Apure* and *Guanare* for their last stronghold, Ciudad Bolívar. While Rolando remained in the city preparing for a possible defense against an attack from the government, a number of other officers left for Trinidad to secure further ordnance.

After Rolando's defeat at El Guapo, Gómez returned to Caracas to reorganize the troops who would accompany him in his next campaign, which was to dislodge the rebels from their strongholds in western Venezuela. On April 23, Gómez disembarked at Coro. However, after finding that Matos was in Tucacas, Gómez left immediately in pursuit of the rebel leader. Matos, upon hearing that Gómez was about to reach Tucacas, ordered Colonel Bruno López to delay his disembarkation while he headed for Coro, the state capital. However, Gómez defeated Generals González and Mogollón and took Tucacas on May 2. He then left for Santa Rosa, where he was joined by Rafael González Pacheco, a regional Trujillano *caudillo* and Castro's chief strategist against Matos. At Yumare, Gómez defeated Peñaloza, who was forced to retreat to Barquisimeto. Government troops continued the pursuit of the remaining rebels and engaged them at Palma Sola on May 20. Gómez's main military objective was to take Barquisimeto, which was defended by Peñaloza, Amabile Solagnie, and José Rafael Montilla. Gómez began his two-pronged offensive on the city on May 21. González Pacheco attacked the city from the side, where the cemetery and the railway station was situated, while Gómez concentrated on the Santa Rosa side. Meanwhile, General José Antonio Dávila struck from the Cerro Manzano. It did not take long to secure the city. Gómez entered Barquisimeto a day later, and the defending generals fled. The remaining rebel troops fell back to Coro, where it was rumoured that Matos, Riera, and Lara had gone to meet with Peñaloza. Gómez caught up with the rebels on June 2 at Matapalo. The fighting continued until June 5, when the combined forces of Matos, Riera, and Lara were defeated, leading to the reestablishment of government control over the states of Lara and Falcón. It was during these campaigns that Gómez became acquainted with some of the young officers, who would later form part of his own government after 1908, such as Félix Galavis, León Jurado, Moros, Vivas, Cárdenas, and López Contreras.

A despondent Matos joined Armando Rolando, Santos Domínici, Riera, Solagnie, Peñaloza, and Lino Duarte to return to Curacao on June 10. The following day an extremely tense meeting took place among all the rebels on the island during which Matos explained that the civil war was over for him because he could not continue the struggle. Matos' position was made perfectly clear in a fly-sheet memorandum that he issued the following day in which he urged all rebels to lay down their arms and return to civilian life. Nicolás Rolando in Ciudad Bolívar, with an army of three thousand men, and a few pockets of resistance outside Cumaná were the only territories left under the control of the rebels.

GÓMEZ PURSUES ROLANDO

After his victory at Matapalo, Gómez returned to Caracas to regroup his men and plan his eastern Venezuelan campaign. On June 27, Gómez, as *Delegado Nacional* and *Jefe del Ejército de Oriente*, with José Rosario Garcia, his secretary general, left La Guaira on board the *Restaurador* with Román Delgado Chalbaud at the helm, accompanied by the naval vessels *Bolívar* and *Zamora*, which transported his two thousand-man expeditionary army. The army disembarked at Cumaná. On July 2, led by Antonio Paredes and Manuel Morales, the army defeated the rebels at Soro and Campo Claro outside Irapa, near Cumaná. Gómez then turned his attention to Ciudad Bolívar, which was under the command of Nicolás Rolando and remained the only rebel stronghold in the country. Gómez embarked his troops in four ships and headed for the old city on the Orinoco River, reaching Santa Ana on July 10. After a long march of eighteen hours the expeditionary army arrived just outside Ciudad Bolívar, setting up camp at Cañafístola.

Gómez tried to get Rolando to agree to a peaceful surrender, but the man who a year earlier had repelled Gómez's attack on Cumaná refused. On July 12, Monseigneur Antonio María Durán, the bishop of Guayana, Luis Brokman, the German consul, and Jess Henderson, the American consul, joined a large representation of the commercial and social elite of Ciudad Bolívar to meet with Rolando. They tried to get him to surrender, pointing out that the rebels had capitulated in the rest of the country as Matos' Curacao manifesto had made perfectly clear. Rolando wanted to negotiate with Gómez directly, setting out a number of proposals for his consideration. Gómez consulted Castro over this, who agreed to grant the rebels the safe conduct outside the country in exchange for the enemy handing over all their arms and ammunition. The exception was General Ramón Farreras, who would be tried for treason because he had initially handed over the city to Rolando. The rebel leader agreed to negotiate. On July 13, Monseigneur Antonio María Durán, the German, French, and American consuls, and General Peñaloza met with José Rosario García, Gómez's secretary, to work out the details of the surrender. On July 14, Peñaloza, Rolando's chief negotiator, arrived to settle the surrender, but he delayed setting a final date.[83] Negotiations for a peaceful surrender broke down on July 18. Gómez and General Araujo surrounded the city and started their attack at 3:00 A.M. on July 19. Emilio Rivas, who was in Soledad, joined Gómez's forces and "positioned himself dominating the Orinoco shore and part of the south of the city until he was very close to enemy lines."[84] Eustoquio Gómez commanded the rear. Government ships bombarded Ciudad Bolívar while the USS *Vancroft* and French gunboats acted as observers and cared for some of the wounded. The offensive ended when the rebels surrendered on July 21. More than one thousand four hundred men were either wounded or dead.[85] Nicolás Rolando and his remaining army surrendered to Gómez. The government captured a large cache of arms, which included 3,275 rifles, 4 canons, one machine gun, one box of dynamite, 264 grenades, 450 explosive pots, 528,000 rounds of ammunition, and 6,020,000 percussion caps.[86]

When Castro heard the news of Gómez's resounding victory in Ciudad Bolívar, he declared July 21 to be the *Día de la Paz*. He called Gómez the *Salvador del Salvador*, while Congress bestowed on him the title of *El Pacificador de Venezuela*. On August 3, Gómez returned to Caracas on board the *Restaurador*, reaching the capital a national hero. Castro and his ministers travelled to La Guaira to welcome the "only victor in all places."[87] On August 5, Gómez entered Caracas "to the noisiest ovation registered by the annals of time, passing through very expensive triumphal arches which for the first time had been made in Venezuela (illuminated at night by precious electric light) and accompanied by the citizens of Caracas which received him as Venezuela's Peacemaker."[88]

During the Revolución Libertadora, Gómez could have easily crossed over to the rebel side at any time, but he chose to remain loyal to Castro because "his formal obligation was above any personal ambition."[89] Gómez had been in four battles, three sieges, and eleven skirmishes, adding to his military experience in 1899 when he had been in four battles, four sieges, and six skirmishes.[90] From now on Gómez's military skill would go unquestioned, acknowledged by friend and foe alike as the regime's ablest military man after Castro. Gómez, as some contemporary writers of the time acknowledged, "invokes valour, loyalty and honour at its highest level."[91] He increased his popularity while building up his own power base of Andino soldiers, discreetly kept at his brother's Juancho's farm in Aragua, close to Caracas.[92] Although Castro, as Arellano Moreno points out, initiated the political integration of the country and the demise of the regional *caudillos*, stating in his 1903 message to Congress that he was proud to have defeated the "famous historical rule of petty chieftains, killed by my own hand, at the same battlefield,"[93] it was Gómez who completed the project some years later.

THE AFTERMATH OF THE REVOLUCIÓN LIBERTADORA

The Revolucíon Libertadora showed the government how vulnerable it was to a large rebellion and how poorly prepared it was to tackle it without a well-equipped professional army. Consequently, the government set about the immediate task of reorganizing the army. Francisco Linares Alcántara, Diego Bautista Ferrer, and the Chilean Samuel McGill took on this task. Castro wanted his army to be prepared for small-scale internal revolts, similar to those encountered during the *Libertadora* revolution. At the same time the Military Code of the country was reformed. At the suggestion of Francisco Linares Alcántara the construction of the Military Academy was sanctioned on July 4, 1903, with funds of Bs 1.3 million. It was completed, appropriately enough, on the seventh anniversary of the Revolución Restauradora, May 23, 1906. The vast majority of the cadets at the school were from Táchira, with a sprinkling of Trujillanos and Merideños. Castro also created the Estado Mayor General, which would control all praetorian activities, meaning that the promotion of officers in the future would be based on merit. The Plano Militar de Venezuela was also commissioned, and Castro also sent his brother Carmelo to receive military training at the Manlius Military School near Syracuse, New York. However, it was Gómez, with his vast experience gained during the Revolución Libertadora, who would become the most instrumental person in consolidating the military. After 1903 he "served as special adviser to the army and saw to it that defense expenditures went toward meeting the needs of the cadres."[94]

The impact of the changes were soon felt. In December 1903 the government imported fifteen thousand mauser carbines and seven million cartridges, bringing its total reserves to forty thousand mausers with fifteen million rounds. The government also had a number of Hotchkiss field and mountain cannons and a Canet siege gun of the Creuzot works. The following year, Bs 300,000 was spent at La Victoria on the construction of new barracks, and a further Bs 41,554 went toward refurbishing Puerto Cabello's destroyed forts. On December 5, 1904, the Junta Superior de Instrucción Militar within the War Ministry was created, with General José María García Gómez, Gómez's cousin, its first director. The living conditions of the soldiers also improved. In November 1903 the value of rations trebled from Bs 0.50 to Bs 1.50, while measures were introduced to stamp out speculative abuse of the men's remuneration by paying in cash rather than in kind. Finally, the commanders were instructed to give proper shelter and clothing to the rank and file. The navy was also modernized. August 28, 1905, Castro ordered a floating dock to be built at Puerto Cabello to reduce the country's dependence on American and British ship-repair facilities. It was expected that the lower maintenance costs of the ships and the new dockyard would act as a base for the establishment of a modern fleet with Castro setting aside Bs 500,000 for its completion. It was felt that the role of the dockyard would be similar to that played by the Military Academy in the formation of the new army. On March 28, 1906, all marine operations were transferred from La Guaira to Puerto Cabello. The forts of Vigia, Libertador, and San Carlos in Maracaibo were also strengthened. The army's food and accommodation had improved significantly by 1905, with the feeling in certain sectors that "the miserable conditions had disappeared from our barracks."[95]

THE POLITICAL DIMENSION

With the demise of the regional *caudillos*, Castro and his motley crew of what remained of the Liberal party in the country were now more in control of the country's destiny. Many Nacionalistas followed the advice of Urbaneja and incorporated themselves into the government, from where they felt they could manipulate Castro. Their influence waned as soon as Mocho Hernández left for Washington on July 9, 1903, as the country's new *Enviado Extraordinario y Ministro Plenipotenciario*. Mocho Hernández prior to his departure, had extolled his followers to support the government in its efforts to bring peace to the country by placing it on a sound democratic base. Urbaneja, who was the Foreign Affairs Minister, remained as the Nacionalistas' political leader in Mocho Hernández's absence. Soon differences between the Nacionalistas and the government erupted, especially at the local level, notably in Yuruary where Governor Anselmo Zapata ruthlessly pursued the Conservatives. In spite of these local problems the Nacionalistas continued to support the government. Régulo Olivares advised the Conservatives of Maracaibo that the Castristas were assimilating their ideals. Soon their dreams were shattered, starting with Urbaneja's replacement as Foreign Affairs Minister by the Liberal Gustavo Sanabria in November 1903. It was clear that the Nacionalistas had three options, as Velásquez writes, which were "to join the Castrismo and to form part of the top administrative echelons, sharing with the Liberal Restoration its historical responsibilities, such as doctor Alejandro Urbaneja had done, go into exile or abandon politics and concentrate on private activities."[96]

With the defeat of Rolando and with the issue of foreign claims reviewed in The Hague, Castro felt that his luck had returned to him. He felt politically strong again and free to follow his own instincts without having to refer to any of the established political forces. In addition, the old scourge of the Liberals was now in Washington. However, Mocho Hernández did not take long to remind Castro that the series of reforms that they had agreed to a year earlier, when he had given his support to the government, had not been enacted. However, Castro had no intention of honoring the pact, despite the fact that Mocho Hernández had insisted on them to improve state institutions, because the current system was "introduced by the men from the 'Historical Petty Chieftains', who have led us up a disastrous path, until arriving at the blockade of our ports by the foreigner."[97] The country was still officially in a state of war. There were many political prisoners, among them many Nacionalistas, and numerous press attacks against the Mochismo.

At the same time Castro wanted to be reelected and sought the support of Mocho Hernández to join him or at least accept his new proposals. However, Mocho Hernández refused, bluntly stating that this was a travesty of the agreement that he had reached with the *cabito* the previous year. He refused to return to Caracas in February 1904 to confer with the president. Castro remarked scathingly that Mocho Hernández was "intellectually incapable of adapting to the changes that the events of the period had imposed on the people and society."[98] Castro accused Mocho Hernández of acting immorally by representing the country in Washington while at the same time attacking it. Castro reasoned that if Mocho Hernández did not like the government then he should not have accepted the position. He stated that many of the political prisoners whom Mocho Hernández claimed to be Nacionalistas were only petty convicted criminals and that generals such as Hernández Ron and Gimón Pérez "continued detained because they refused to hand over their hidden cache of arms."[99] In spite of this drawback, Congress in 1904 appointed Castro provisional president with Gómez as first vice president and José Antonio Velutini as second vice president.

Although Venezuela had been humiliated at the hands of the European powers, it served indirectly to maintain Castro in power. The defeat of Matos and his supporters was a turning point in Venezuelan history because it started the slow process of molding the country into a cohesive modern state. This would continue for another four decades. However, with the end of the Revolución Libertadora, Castro took the first tentative steps toward the creation of a modern state. Castro also turned his attention toward strengthening the armed forces to secure his own power base. The decimation of most of the traditional *caudillos* at the time had two immediate effects. First, it allowed Castro greater scope to pursue his own pecuniary interest, unhindered by opposition. Secondly, it brought Gómez into the forefront of politics as a political figure in his own right.

NOTES

1. CO 295/407 W. H. D. Haggard to Lord Lansdowne, 24 April 01.
2. FO 80/444 C. H. de Lemos to Haggard, 27 August 02.
3. "Correspondence respecting the Affairs of Venezuela, 1902," *PP*, Cd 1372 CXXX, pp. 681.
4. CO 295/407 A. C. Grant-Duff to Eduardo Blanco, 9 April 01.
5. Ibid.
6. "Correspondence respecting the Affairs of Venezuela, 1902," pp. 681.
7. CO 295/407 Grant-Duff to Blanco, 9 April 01.
8. The total damage was $300 for broken furniture; $300 for broken goods; $1,000 for loss of cacao crop; $1,500 lost in cash; $500 for a cutter (CO 295/407 F. A. Maingot to A. C. Grant-Duff, 1 March 01.)
9. FO 80/439 Haggard to Foreign Office, 25 September 02.

10. Henry F. Pringle, *Theodore Roosevelt: A Biography*, London, Jonathan Cape Ltd., 1931, p. 283.
11. CO 295/414 Haggard to Lansdowne, 13 December 01.
12. Howard C. Hill, *Roosevelt and the Caribbean*, Chicago, The University of Chicago Press, 1927, p. 200.
13. CO 295/407 Grant-Duff to Lansdowne, 7 April 01.
14. CAB 37/63 File 144, FO Minute Initialled L. (presumably Lansdowne) 17 October 02.
15. Ibid.
16. CO 295/414 Haggard to Lansdowne, 13 December 01.
17. CAB 37/63 File 144, FO Minute Initialled L., 17 October 02.
18. CO 295/414 Haggard to Lansdowne, 13 December 01.
19. Ibid.
20. Ibid.
21. Ibid.
22. Ibid.
23. Ibid.
24. Ibid.
25. Castro to J. E. González Esteves, 8 January 02 in Pino Iturrieta, *Epistolario*, p. 301.
26. Count Von Bulow to Emperor William, 20 January 02, in E. T. S. Dugdale, *German Diplomatic Documents, 1871–1914*, New York, Barnes & Noble Inc., 1930, vol. 3, p. 161.
27. Lansdowne to Buchanan, 23 July 02, in G. P. Gooch and H. Temperley, *British Documents on the Origins of the War*, London, HMSO, 1928, vol. 1, p. 153.
28. "Correspondence respecting the affairs of Venezuela, 1902," p. 681.
29. FO 420/206 Lansdowne to Buchanan, 11 November 02.
30. Memorandum for communication to the German ambassador, 22 October 02 in G. P. Gooch and H. Temperley, vol. 1, p. 155.
31. CAB 37/63 File 144, FO Minute Initialled L., 17 October 02.
32. Ibid.
33. Ibid.
34. Ibid.
35. Ibid.
36. "Correspondence respecting the affairs of Venezuela, 1902," p. 681.
37. CAB 37/63 File 161, FO Minute Initialled L., 24 November 02.
38. FO 420/206 Lansdowne to Sir F. Lascelles, 19 August 02.
39. Ibid.
40. CAB 37/63 File 144, FO Minute Initialled L., 17 October 02.
41. FO 420/206 Lansdowne to Sir Michael Herbert, 1 November 02.
42. FO 420/206 Herbert to Lansdowne, 13 November 02.
43. Russell had been the Legation's Secretary since 1895, and he would remain in the position until 1904, leaving to become the Charge D'affaires in Panama and minister in Bogotá for a short while before returning to Venezuela as Minister in 1905.
44. FO 80/439 Haggard to FO, 25 July 02.
45. CO 295/415 C. H. de Lemos to Haggard, 20 November 02.

46. FO 420/206 Lansdowne to Haggard, 21 November 02.

47. *The Times*, 22 November 02.

48. Count Von Metternich to German Chancery, 26 November 02, in Dugdale, p. 195.

49. Holger H. Herwig, *Germany's Vision of Empire in Venezuela 1871–1914*, Princeton, Princeton University Press, 1986, p. 102. In addition, Blohm financed Bowen's mediation efforts in 1903.

50. Castro to Agencia Pumar, 6 December 02 in Pino Iturrieta, p. 312.

51. CAB 37/63 File 144, Foreign Office Minute Initialled L., 17 October 02.

52. Castro to Grals, J. T. Arria, Torres, Bello, Mora, and Silverio, 12 December 02 in Pino Iturrieta, p. 315.

53. Manuel Landaeta Rosales, "Rasgos Biográficos del General J. V. Gómez" in Venezuela *Conjuración*, p. 399.

54. Part of Castro's Alocución was the following:

> The insolent foreign foot has profaned the sacred soil of the fatherland. An unusual deed in the history of civilization without precedent, without possible justification, a barbarous act, because it infringes the most rudimentary rights of men." Castro added that: "I am willing to sacrifice everything at the august altar of the fatherland; everything including what could be called my resentments owing to our domestic differences. I no longer remember the unpleasant events of the past. I have erased from my thoughts as a politician and warrior all that was hostile towards achieving my goals, all that could have left a painful wound in my heart. All that is left ahead is Bolívar's luminous vision of the fatherland, which is the same as mine. (Francisco Salazar Martínez, *Tiempo de Compadres. De Cipriano Castro a Juan Vicente Gómez*, Caracas, Librería Piñango, 1972, p. 29)

Castro's speech was written by Eloy González at the presidential office in Miraflores. (Enrique Bernardo Núñez, *El Hombre de la Levita Gris (Los Años de la Restauración Liberal*), Caracas, Ediciones Elite, 1953).

55. *El Constitucional*, 17 December 02 in Venezuela, *Venezuela ante el conflicto con las Potencias Aliadas-Alemania, Inglaterra e Italia en 1902 y 1903*, Caracas, Tip. Universal, 1905, vol. 2, p. 313.

56. Ibid., p. 314.

57. Ibid.

58. Ibid., p. 138.

59. Ibid., p. 143.

60. Velásquez, *La Caída del Liberalismo*, p. 318.

61. AHM Unclassified L. Mendoza to R. Vargas, Barquisimeto, 19 December 02.

62. AHM Unclassified M. A. Matos to Pedro Ducharme, 'Circular', 23 December 02.

63. AHM Unclassified Matos to Ducharme, 25 December 02.

64. AHM Unclassified Matos to Vargas, 20 December 02, and Matos to Eleázar Urdaneta, 27 January 03.

65. Venezuela ante el Conflicto vol. 1, p. 143. Castro himself contributed Bs 40,000.

66. FO 420/206 Herbert to Lansdowne, 16 December 02.

67. Ibid.

68. FO 80/440 The Inter-Arbitration Association and The Peace Society, Manchester, 23 December 02.

69. FO 80/440 The Inter-Arbitration Association and The Peace Society, London, 24 December 02.

70. Count Von Quadt to German Chancery, 18 December 92, in Dugdale, p. 175.

71. William Roscoe Thayer, *The Life and Letters of John Hay*, London, Constable & Co. Ltd., 1915, vol. 2, p. 288–89.

72. Harwich op. cit., "Cipriano Castro," p. 177.

73. Lansdowne to Herbert, 7 February 03, in G. P. Gooch and H. Temperley, vol. 1, p. 171.

74. On April 11, 1903, Bowen received the medal of Legión de la Defensa Nacional—Second Order. General Jorge Antonio Bello, commander of the fortaleza de San Carlos, received the Legion de la Defensa Nacional—third Order. (*Recopilación de Leyes y Decretos de Venezuela*, Doc. 8898, Vol. 26, p. 62)

75. AHM Unclassified Matos "Memorandum," 23 January 03.

76. Ibid.

77. Ibid.

78. Matos "Memorandum—Toma de Caracas," 27 January 03, printed in *El Constitucional*, taken from J. M. Oliveros.

79. Ibid.

80. Ibid.

81. Ibid.

82. Ibid.

83. Gómez to Nicolás Rolando, 14 July 03, in Tobias Arias, *Relieves Máximos*, Caracas, n.p., 1930, p. 21–22.

84. Pedro Luis Blanco Peñalver, ed., *El Libro de la Paz*, Caracas, Lit. y Tip. del Comercio, 1929, p. 14.

85. Gómez suffered 239 men dead and 405 wounded, while Rolando had 800 men dead or wounded.

86. Arias, p. 25–26.

87. Estebán Roldán Oliarte, *El General Juan Vicente Gómez. Venezuela de Cerca*, Mexico, Imprenta Mundial, 1933.

88. Landaeta Rosales, pp. 397–403.

89. Roldán Oliarte, p. 51.

90. Landaeta Rosales, p. 400.

91. Esteban D. González, *La Obra de Castro y los Hombres de Castro*, La Guaira, Tip. La Equitativa, 1904, p. 13.

92. R. Tello Mendoza, *Ligeros Rasgos Biográficos del General Juan Vicente Gómez*, Caracas, Tip. Universal, 1904.

93. Velásquez, p. 285.

94. William M. Sullivan, "The Rise of Despotism in Venezuela: Cipriano Castro, 1899–1908." PhD. diss., The University of New Mexico, 1974, p. 396.

95. C. Castro, *Comentarios a los Mensajes del General Cipriano Castro. Homenaje de Justicia al Restaurador de Venezuela. Editoriales de "Patria y Castro" de Calabozo*, Caracas, Imprenta Nacional, 1905, p. 19.

96. Velásquez, p. 336–37.

97. José Manuel Hernández to Castro, 15 February 04, in José Manuel Hernández, *Ante la Historia. El General José Manuel Hernández, Jefe del Partido Lib-*

eral Nacionalista al General Cipriano Castro, Presidente de los Estados Unidos de Venezuela, Philadelphia, 1904, pp. 10–11.

98. José Manuel Hernández to Castro, 19 March 04 in Hernández, *Ante la Historia*, p. 16.

99. Ibid.

7

Castro: Xenophobe or Blackmailer?

Although the Revolución Libertadora was Venezuela's worst civil war since the Federal Wars in the nineteenth century, the country now appeared to be heading for a period of economic prosperity. Coffee prices increased 50 percent in 1904. This was clearly a substantial boost to the country's revenues because coffee exports accounted for 45 percent of the country's total exports by value. Asphalt production was also showing promising signs, with production increasing by 427 percent, from 3,355 tons in 1902 to 14,338 tons in 1903. This improvement was soon halted by the new mining code of 1904, which increased surface and export taxes on asphalt. This brought production by the US-Venezuela Company to an almost complete standstill in Zulia. In the east the NY&B ceased operations because its property was expropriated for failing to comply with its contract. The new mining code clearly disturbed the country's mining industry, with all "European interests suffering considerably from the retrograde and narrow-minded policy of the President and his entourage."[1] American influence on the country was increasing despite the pessimistic report that W. Handley, the U.S. Vice Consul in Trinidad, wrote on April 14, 1904. Handley's report on trade with South America complained that U.S. trade in the region had only increased 5 percent during the last thirty years whereas trade with the rest of the world had more than doubled.[2] In spite of this the United States was Venezuela's main trading partner, closely followed by the United Kingdom and Germany (Table 7.1). In the United Kingdom there were fears that U.S. trade would soon overshadow British goods in the region.[3]

Table 7.1
Venezuela's Foreign Trade Held by Various Countries During 1904–1906 (percent)

	Imports		Exports	
	1904–1905	*1905–1906*	*1904–1905*	*1905–1906*
US	29.5	30.2	34.4	31.1
UK	24.3	29.8	11.2	8.0
Germany	24.4	19.7	4.9	5.3
Holland	4.8	6.9	15.0	14.6
France	8.9	6.1	19.3	25.4
Spain	4.6	4.8	3.8	3.6
Italy	3.1	2.1	6.6	0.4
Cuba	—	—	10.3	11.1
Others	0.4	0.4	0.5	0.5

Source: Vice Consul E.F. Gray, *Diplomatic and Consular Reports: Venezuela. Report for the Year 1906 on the trade of the Consular District of Caracas* (HMSO 1907), vol. xciii, 1907, pp. 825–35.

MONOPOLY POWER

Castro, with some justification, did not look favorably on foreign enterprise, although he was willing to curry their support when he needed money. According to Sir Vincent Corbett, a British minister in Caracas, Castro from the very beginning of his rule exhibited a "marked anti-foreign bias and a complete disregard of the rights of foreign subjects"[4] and an ill-conceived economic policy that was supposed to free Venezuela from foreign companies and foreigners so that the country's resources would be developed by his countrymen. However, rather than spearheading the establishment of a strong native capitalist class, Castro appeared to award monopoly concessionary rights as if they were spoils of war. Cattle, alcoholic beverages, tobacco, matches, coastal and river trade, salt production, and other industries were all under the exclusive domain of monopolies that the government granted. Starting in 1899, Castro, Gómez, and other government officials acquired large cattle ranches in Guayana, Apure, and the central states. Gómez had the exclusive right to supply meat to the cities of Caracas, Puerto Cabello, and a few others. Moreover, the flourishing cattle trade with the West Indies, mainly to Cuba, Trinidad, and Curacao, represented Bs 18 million or 10 percent of the country's export trade from 1903 to 1904. Castro and Gómez controlled this business, while Antonio F. Feo had the exclusive contract to transport beef from Guanta in Anzoátegui state to Puerto Cabello and then to Havana, Cuba.[5]

With the defeat of the Liberal elite and the regional *caudillos* in 1903, Castro now felt free to grant more monopolies "in exchange for stock in the new companies."[6] Over the next few years he placed an even stronger stranglehold on the economy by creating other monopolies. Such action had two advantages for Castro: it generated an immediate source of revenue for him, his cronies, and the government, and it paid back any political favors to his associates. According to an opposition paper in Paris, Castro had a stake in the following monopolies: flour, salt, pasta, cigarettes, matches, lottery, mail, gas, and electricity. Castro was also paid 20 percent of the value of the official paper used for drawing up contracts, generating Bs 24 million per year in revenue. Castro also had a stake in the steamers that crossed Lake Maracaibo and a half share in the Gran Ferrocarril del Táchira that had been taken away from the Roncajolo family. Both the Compañía Vapores del Orinoco and the Dalton Trading House[7] also belonged to Castro, Gómez, and Corao. According to the same opposition newspaper, Gómez had the milk monopoly in Caracas and Maracay, the exclusive contracts to supply coal to Caracas, alcohol to Carabobo, and the abattoir and cattle transport monopoly in Caracas. In July 1904 the Castro government established the liquor monopoly and proposed the establishment of a tobacco monopoly, which together with the existing cattle monopoly would "place the remaining trade of the country in the hands of officials of the Venezuelan government."[8]

On January 18, 1905, Castro created a special tax on cigarette paper of Bs 0.25, which only a few select manufacturers could purchase. On June 23 of the same year Castro decreed that all salt sites would be closed with the exception of Araya and Coche in Nueva Esparta, placing three thousand salt miners out of work in Zulia alone. This was to prepare the award of a new salt monopoly, which was acquired by Albert Pam, a British subject, on October 25, 1905. In addition to getting the exclusive right to work the salt mines and salt deposits at Araya and Coche, Pam also acquired the monopoly to distribute and sell salt throughout the country. With the consent of the Venezuelan government, Pam transferred his concession to the Venezuelan Salt Monopoly Company on November 8, 1905.

In July 1905 further monopoly concessions were awarded to Jaime F. Carrillo for the exclusive right to exploit sugarcane and to establish textile plants in Carabobo state. Francisco Terán gained the exclusive right to exploit all the natural resources of Venezuela's coastal region, with the exception of fish stocks, which was controlled by somebody else. Carlos Zuloaga gained an exclusive fifteen-year contract to manufacture glass and crystal in the country. José Hilario Mora gained an exclusive twenty-five-year contract to produce flour. Simón Bello gained a fifteen-year monopoly to develop the phosphates and guano deposit on Orchila island.[9] On December 31 of the same year, General Miguel Carabaño obtained the exclusive right to sell tobacco and manufacture liquor in return for an annual payment of Bs 480,000. On February 5, 1906, Castro awarded a ten-year monopoly on cigarette and cigar manufacturing in return for Bs 800,000 in tax payments during the first year and thereafter Bs 1 million annually. In the same year, Manuel Tejera was granted the monopoly on match production, with the government levying a tax of Bs. 0.02 per box sold. Tejera established a British-registered limited company, The National Match Factory of Venezuela, with a capital of Bs 5 million, of which he received Bs 2.8 million in shares or 40 percent of the company's equity.

CASTRO'S BROKEN PROMISES

The economic stranglehold that the country experienced was far removed from the promises that Castro made in 1899, when the population expected a strong government to unite the nation and bring an end to the ceaseless wars that had taken place, and to provide political stability that would allow the country to recuperate from the high import tariffs levied to pay off Venezuela's foreign debts.[10] The result, however, was different. The various monopolies had a stifling effect on the country's economy. They destroyed, for instance, the small artisan industry in tobacco manufacture. Part of the government's lame justification for the award of so many monopolies was that labor was difficult and costly to obtain because of the country's small population. The government stated that "the capacity of production by cultivation or manufacture is consequently very limited, and it is found easier and more lucrative to collect natural produce than to employ labour in the agricultural pursuits."[11] While the government was assured that some revenue would be generated from these sources, it also made Castro and his cronies very wealthy. The *El Universal* in 1909 estimated that between 1906 and June 1908, Castro repatriated Bs 6,476,177[12] to his German bank account. In his native Táchira, Gómez had dealt with the German trading houses, but it would be in Caracas that greater contact with foreigners and the representatives of foreign powers would be established.[13]

CORPORATE BLACKMAIL

With the Matos revolution over and the foreign claims that had led to the "peaceful blockade" being decided by either the Mixed Commission or the International Court of Arbitration, Castro needed to raise revenues. He did this by blackmailing the large foreign companies that were operating in the country for not honoring their contracts. Such a move was seen as part of a conscious effort to drive away foreign capital. In cases such as the NY&B and FCC, Castro sought, with justification, compensation for their involvement with Matos and his revolution. It would later emerge that other companies had actively assisted the Matos revolution, adding more grist to the mill.

The Warner and Quinlan case against the NY&B had been in the courts for a number of years. The legal advice given to Castro was that Warner and Quinlan would win their case, meaning that there would be two foreign companies operating the area, with neither benefiting Castro directly. Toward the end of 1903 rumors began to circulate in Caracas that the NY&B had been involved in financing and assisting Matos' revolution. Carner was instrumental in spreading these rumors. He had conclusive evidence of the NY&B's involvement with Matos, which Barber in the United States had forwarded to him in Venezuela.

Carner, Barber, and Castro each wanted the Guanoco deposits for themselves. If Warner and Quinlan were allowed to win their case, Castro would be faced with having to get rid of two American asphalt companies to get any direct benefit from the asphalt deposits himself. Castro felt that he had a watertight argument against the NY&B on two counts: first, that it had not worked its concession adequately and, secondly, the *coup de grace*, that it had assisted the Matos rebellion. It therefore made sense, Castro reasoned, to allow the NY&B to win the case against Warner and Quinlan. Then he could focus on the NY&B, where the Venezuelan government had a much stronger argument to strip it of its concession. Once this was achieved he could blackmail the company for it to retain its concession, knowing full well that the company had no real defense. If this strategy failed, the asphalt lake could be worked by a third party to the benefit of all, including the Venezuelan government, which would increase its revenues from this source compared to its hitherto meager takings.

Warner and Quinlan's case against the NY&B, which had dragged on for a number of years and would eventually cost the American asphalt company $417,897.18,[14] came to a head on January 28, 1904, when the Federal Court of Cassation rendered its final decision on the case. It handed down a very lengthy opinion. It stated that the plaintiffs had based their action on their proposal to work the mine, but that the NY&B had argued that this title was not valid because it was situated within the concession granted to it in 1885. The NY&B also argued that by virtue of Hamilton's concession, the government could not grant title to La Felicidad. The title to La Felicidad, the NY&B alleged, was null and void because the so-called mine was part of the asphalt lake that the company had possessed and exploited during the previous fourteen years. It was also argued that there was no other known asphalt lake in the district except the one that the company was exploiting. The company therefore pleaded limitation in support of its title and denied that Warner and Quinlan were the proper plaintiffs. The court therefore decided that the NY&B had the exclusive right for asphalt mining and that no other mining concession could be allowed, concluding that "whatever might be the situation of the properties the fact remained that in that territory no mining concessions for asphalt could be awarded while the exclusive right of the company, under contract, remained in force."[15] The NY&B thus won its case against Warner and Quinlan even though its Hamilton concession from a constitutional viewpoint was objectionable. It was at this time that the rumor about the Matos complicity with the NY&B started, with Nicómedes Zuloaga and José de Jesus Paúl, who would later become Foreign Minister, engaged as lawyers for Warner and Quinlan.

The decision against Warner and Quinlan was based entirely on Hamilton's contract, which was judged to be still in existence and that vested in the company the exclusive and paramount right to exploit the mines within the territory named during the time of its concession. However, William Calhoun, the American judge who was sent by President Roosevelt to look into these matters later argued, "the soundness of this decision on principle may well be questioned, because it is a very serious question whether or not the Hamilton contract was constitutionally or in any sense a legal and binding obligation asserted as a legal bar to the preemption of mining claims by other parties."[16] The argument against the constitutionality of Hamilton's contract was conclusive because under the 1874 constitution the mines located in each state belonged to the state government. The national government only took over the administration of the mines on March 13, 1883, when President Guzmán Blanco issued a decree so that the mines could be administered under a uniform system. Although this decree was in force when Hamilton acquired his concession on September 15, 1883, the first article of the decree declared that all mines were the property of the state in which they were situated, but that they should be governed by a uniform system of exploitation. The fourth article of the decree provided that no mine could be exploited unless the federal executive had previously granted a concession. A close examination of Hamilton's contract revealed that the extent of its application, the variety of the subjects it embraced, and the manner of is execution "did not conform to the mining law then in force, and was not part of a 'uniform system of exploitation' as authorised by the Constitution and as prescribed by the decree of 1883."[17] The decision of the Federal Court in Warner and Quinlan's case expressly declared that Hamilton's contract created for twenty-five years a "special situation" for the exploitation of asphalt and other natural products in the state of Bermúdez. The legal argument then was that such a "special situation" excluded the contract from the uniform system of the 1883 decree, thus making it "objectionable from a constitutional point of view."[18]

EVIDENCE ON THE NY&B AND MATOS SURFACES

There is little doubt that the Venezuelan government was well aware of the legal arguments in favor of Warner and Quinlan. The question then was why did Castro allow the NY&B to win its case when Warner and Quinlan had a clear legal right to its asphalt title? The answer was that

Castro now wanted to exclude both companies from exploiting the Guanoco asphalt lake, as new evidence came to light on the NY&B's involvement with the Matos revolution. In addition, the government had a strong case to strip the NY&B of its title because of a lack of proper work on the concession. Castro could sue for damages from the Matos revolution and reap the political benefits of being the victim of an attack by a foreign company. Once both foreign companies ceased to have legal title, the asphalt concession could then go to a third party, and Castro could share in the profits and possibly exert greater control in the matter.

As soon as the decision was given in favor of the NY&B, a rumor started to circulate in Caracas that the Venezuelan government believed that the company's officials had aided the Matos revolution by supplying money for the purchase of the *Ban Righ*. It was at this stage that Amzi Lorenzo Barber put into place his plan to get the NY&B's concession rescinded and break the General Asphalt Company's monopoly in the supply of asphalt in the United States. Carner, who had been the NY&B's manager in Caracas up to 1896, left New York for Venezuela with information on the Asphalt Company's involvement in the Matos revolution. Upon his arrival in Caracas he started feeding the relevant details of the case to his old friend Andrés José Vigas, who was the director of *El Monitor*. Carner also endeavored "with the assistance of certain New York capitalists to obtain the annulment of the Hamilton concession."[19] After a number of meetings with Castro, Carner returned to New York in April 1904, informing Barber that Venezuela's president was willing to do a deal as long as the Barber interests marketed the asphalt, something that they were happy to do. In early June, Carner was back in Caracas. He handed over to Castro the documents that proved the complicity of the NY&B in financing the acquisition and the refitting of the *Ban Righ*, which the Venezuelan government would now use to bring a lawsuit against the company.

At this stage the NY&B concession only had four more years to run. Robert Wright, the manager of the company in Caracas, felt that these rumors were unfounded and that if any officials were implicated, they no longer worked for the company. The company knew that it was in trouble, but it felt that "it would be impossible to rely on Mr. Bowen's help and assistance in view of his strained relations with the Venezuelan Govt. [*sic*] and of his alleged friendship with Mr. Carner."[20] To seek the help of the British government the assets of the NY&B were transferred to the New Trinidad Asphalt Company which had strong U.K. investment backing. The company had debentures of $1.71 million still outstanding, which were held almost exclusively by British residents of the United Kingdom. Sir Robert Herbert and Sir Charles Rivers Wilson were the trustees for the debenture holders. The Asphalt Trust, however, remained the beneficial owner of the equity issued. Only three hundred shares out of the total fifty thousand issued were in British hands. Thus the United States would be ultimately responsible for securing any payment for damages incurred at the hands of the Venezuelan government.

The confiscation of the NY&B's property and the award of the assets to another company would have a prejudicial impact on both asphalt companies because the price of pitch would fall and revenues to Trinidad "would be materially affected if the company lost the control over the Venezuelan Pitch Lake which they now exercise through their interests in the New York and Bermudez Company."[21] Hugh Clifford, the acting governor of Trinidad, was blunt in his assessment that the colony would suffer if "the control of the Venezuelan 'pitch lake' were to pass into the hands of an independent Company which would be a formidable rival to the New Trinidad Lake Asphalt Company."[22]

Armed with Carner's damaging information, Lució Baldó, the interior minister, and M. F. Arroyo Parejo, the attorney general of Venezuela, summoned Robert Wright, the managing director of the NY&B, to a meeting in early June. The government demanded as "compensation for not bringing the two proposed suits"[23] for complicity with Matos either a lump sum of Bs 50 million or Bs 10 million and the cancellation of the Hamilton concession. If the company did not pay this sum to Castro, then the government would be forced to sequestrate its property. Wright rejected the proposals outright. A second meeting took place where all the above were joined by J. B. Bance. The identical proposition was repeated with the same result. Wright argued that the company had complied with all of the contract's terms and had never aided any revolutionaries. The government requested as security from the company a deposit of Bs 20 million before sending in the Receiver.

MATOS GETS THE SAME TREATMENT

As negotiations with the NY&B continued Castro turned his attention to get Matos to pay for damages that his revolution caused. At a cabinet meeting in early July most ministers agreed that Rafael López Baralt, the Interior Minister, should issue a resolution bringing Matos to trial. López Baralt, however, argued that it was the collective responsibility of the executive branch to bring the rebel to trial. General Ferrer, the Defense Minister, disagreed with López Baralt's thesis because it would place the executive in an absurd position, as Matos would never return to stand trial from Bogotá, where he was currently living.[24] The impasse was resolved after a change of cabinet. On July 12, Pedro Vicente Mijares went to court to sue Matos for Bs 24,178,038.40, the estimate made by Lució Baldó, the new interior minister, for damages that the country suffered because of the insurrection. The court decided that there was a case to answer, and Matos' property was expropriated. Matos would eventually reach an out-of-court

Table 7.2
Asphalt Production from Guanoco, 1891–1900 (tons)

Year	Production
1891	250
1892	1,130
1893	1,743
1894	7,038
1895	3,025
1896	5,654
1897	11,990
1898	11,825
1900	17,981

Source: William J. Calhoun (Special Commissioner), *Wrongs to American Citizens in Venezuela, Senate Document* No. 413, Vol. 24 60 Cong. 1 Sess., September 1907–08, pp. 161–563, p. 229.

settlement by paying Bs 60,000, which was distributed by Doña Zoila among the Caracas poor.

THE NY&B'S CASE NOT SO EASY TO RESOLVE

Wright appears not to have consulted the New York office before he rejected the government's proposal. He felt that the claim was so preposterous that there was no need to inform his superiors. The negative response of Wright left the Venezuelan government with no other option but to instruct Arroyo Parejo, the Attorney General of Venezuela, to file a suit in the Federal Court and Cassation of Venezuela on July 20. The suit asked for the cancellation of the concession, the sequestration of the company's property, and damages for the noncompliance of its contract because the company had concentrated its efforts entirely on the production of asphalt and had not fulfilled its other obligations during the twenty-one years that it had held its concession. The government argued that the contract had been granted to the company for the purpose of developing the state's natural resources by all means possible. Furthermore, the suit declared that production of asphalt had been on a small scale (see Table 7.2), hence revenues to the government had been negligible, and that the company had not canalized any of the rivers, an obligation in its contract. Thus the government's suit was for the dissolution of the NY&B's contract and for the recovery of damages incurred by reason of its failure to execute the contract.

In its defense the company claimed that it had performed all its obligations, presenting several affidavits (by R. Velásquez, T. C. Llamozas, Germán Jiménez, and M. A. Ponce) that attested to the fact that the rivers had been canalized. However, the company's defense was not convincing. It bordered on being evasive and discursive by insisting that its only obligation was toward the exploitation of asphalt and that any other tasks were "optional privileges, the exercise of which, or any of them, was entirely discretionary with the company."[25]

According to Judge William J. Calhoun it was recognized that the government was entitled to a judgment of "forfeiture or cancellation" of the Hamilton contract because the NY&B "had not performed the obligation by it assumed, to explore and exploit the natural products of the forests and uncultivated lands in the State of Bermúdez,"[26] and because the company did not plead or prove any release from such obligation or any excuse, or any justification for such nonperformance. However, the judge added that the sequestration of the company's property as a way of bringing about its cancellation was not justified because the contract was not a lease, and the government had not claimed, nor did the evidence show, that the canalization of the Guarapiche river or any other river had any connection with Hamilton contract beyond the fact that such requests were provided for by the "second additional articles."[27] This was a separate agreement from the original concession, creating its own obligations and providing its own compensation so that a breach of the covenants in the later, more independent contract could not be considered a "breach of the original contract or made the basis for a sequestration of the company's property in a suit to cancel the original contract."[28] The failure to canalize rivers was the only evidence offered in support of the government's sequestration right, although it was very slight "and the granting of the right without notice to the company and its execution by a civil officer supported by the army and navy has, at least, the appearance of oppression and a perversion of justice."[29] Moreover, as early as June 14, 1887, the government had notified Hamilton, who was then the manager, that it would not allow the company the exclusive navigation rights if it canalized the Guarapiche river. The company argued that this amounted to a repudiation of the second additional article and relieved the company from any further obligation. In addition, the property of the company did not come under the contract and should not have been sequestrated, while the assessment of the damages against the NY&B for breach of the Hamilton contract had been made without the company's participation and with insufficient facts supporting the assessment. Finally, the land and mining title of the NY&B were ignored in the sequestration proceedings, so the possession of the property by the government was in contravention of the company's titles and rights. The day after the complaint was filed the judge ordered a summons to be served on the company, and the Hamilton concession was declared to be a lease. At the same time an order of sequestration was issued. Carner was appointed Receiver, appearing before the judge on July 22 to accept the appointment and be sworn in to take charge of his duties.

When the news reached Bowen, he telegraphed the State Department, advising that the U.S. government should take immediate action in "defence of the interests of the company"[30] unless the Receiver was removed and the NY&B reacquired its property. Bowen also proposed that "an American fleet should be sent to La Guaira at once."[31] He added that if the assets of the NY&B had not been returned within twenty-four hours of the gunboats appearing off Venezuela's coast, then the "Custom House be seized there and that also the one at Puerto Cabello, and that both of them be held until full satisfaction shall have obtained by us."[32]

On August 8, 1904, the British Government was asked to support the NY&B because it was a subsidiary of The New Trinidad Lake Asphalt Company, a British-registered company that was in turn owned by the General Asphalt Company.[33] The issue for the British government was whether the contract was a lease, and therefore whether the Venezuelan government was justified in sequestrating it. However, the British decided not to enter the dispute because although "the New Trinidad Lake Asphalt Company own the Common stock and Debenture issue of the New York and Bermudez Company, a large portion of the shares of the British Company are held in America and that the policy of the latter is controlled by an American Trust Company."[34] Although Lord Lansdowne considered the claim to be an American one, the British were to give limited support because it had to consider the personal well-being of the one hundred British subjects working at Guanoco in 1904, most of whom were "ill-treated in order to make them work on the Pitch Lake."[35] The British government reacted by informing the Venezuelan government that British subjects were being compelled to work at Guanoco by Carner, and that he should abstain from any improper treatment of British workmen. The British placed the HMS *Tribune* on alert at Trinidad to be available if required to protect British citizens.

On July 22 the summons issued for the NY&B was returned as served on Robert Wright, manager of the NY&B. That same day Wright filed a petition with the judge that agreed that to call the company's contract a lease was a perversion of its terms. Wright asked for the order to be revoked, but this was denied on July 25. On July 28, Carner arrived at Guanoco on the Venezuelan gunboat *Bolívar* with an armed military escort to ensure that there would be no breach of the peace. To avoid any complications with the British government, Carner sent back a large number of British workmen in August. On August 21 the Venezuelan government informed O. Bax-Ironside, the British minister, that no cruelty had taken place against British workmen during the recent Guanoco handover but that there were still a few British citizens in the area.

In August, Carner chartered the ship *Kennett* to load the first asphalt from Guanoco to North America. This was to the detriment of the New Trinidad Lake Asphalt Company, and a large share of the profits found its way into Castro's pocket.[36] The Venezuelan government at this stage felt that an armed U.S. intervention was imminent, and Castro ordered "the new guns at Puerto Cabello and La Guayra to be at once placed in position."[37] It seemed, especially to Bax-Ironside, that the "only logical conclusion to the present situation appears to be the adoption of coercive measures by the United States' Government against the Venezuelan Government: should such measures be undertaken it is to be hoped that they will prove of a more effective nature than the late blockade."[38] Moreover, Bax-Ironside thought that the intervention should be aimed at directly deposing Castro because if the American action was only "confined merely to bringing pressure on the Government to turn out the Receiver from the asphalt property, the President will, at a later date interfere with the British Company, and British interests . . . predominate here."[39] The United States, in spite of the advice received from its diplomatic representative in Caracas, was not contemplating any forcible action at the time. It did, however, enter a formal written protest on August 8 against the Venezuelan government. It received a reply that, according to Bax-Ironside, bordered on the insolent. Bowen sent a further protest note on August 16, requesting that the company be fully repossessed of its property.

REVOLUTIONARY SUIT

The NY&B was proving to be a more difficult problem than Castro had imagined, as it was now threatening to escalate into an international dispute with the United States. On a more positive note, the asphalt production at Guanoco was increasing which benefited Castro's bank balance and the country's revenues. It was time to play Castro's trump card, which was the involvement of NY&B with the Matos revolution. On September 22, 1904, the Attorney General began a civil suit against the company to recover damages for its alleged involvement with the Matos rebellion, estimated at Bs 24,178,336.47. The sum included the following: the need to create a war tax (which generated Bs. 3,867,530.74 between February and June 1903 and Bs. 12,928,870.34 between July 1903 and June 1904); the decrease in customs receipts (from Bs. 29,940,888.96 in 1900–01 to Bs. 6,081,429.42 in 1902 to Bs. 4,079,185.45 in 1903); the losses incurred by the Venezuelan economy as a result of the war; and the commercial discredit that the war caused to Venezuela. It should be noted that the NY&B was not the only foreign company singled out for this type of treatment, as Castro also claimed a similar amount from both the FCC and Matos. In addition, the Venezuelan government was also claiming Bs 12 million from the Puerto Cabello-Valencia Railway for damages caused during the Revolución Libertadora.

General Andrews had agreed to finance Matos' revolution to the tune of $145,000. He later argued that they were forced into doing this to protect the company's property while the revolution was under way, "but without reaching any understanding or obligation for the use of said sum. The money was provided by the Asphalt Company of America, following orders received from the National Asphalt Company."[40] General Andrews also declared that the company had spent $400,000 on legal fees to defend its property, of which $145,000 went to Matos and the other $255,000 was used "in all sorts of other expenses, fees for other lawyers, the cost of maintaining an organisation in Caracas, legal consultants, commissioners, and all the personnel that is needed there; travelling expenses, telegrams, lawyers in New York; there was a great deal of diverse expenses related to the work of that year."[41] According to Norman Hutchinson, the U.S. consul, the affidavits presented in the case against the NY&B regarding the Matos rebellion and the testimony given by O. E. Thurber were "considered of an exceedingly hearsay character by Captain Wright and other parties here and certainly, without further evidence, the Venezuelan Government's new charge against the company would be lacking the legal conception of good evidence."[42]

To place more pressure on the NY&B and to ameliorate American intervention plans by currying public opinion in the United States, José de Jesús Paúl travelled to Washington in September as the new Venezuelan minister. He started legal action against the Asphalt Company for nonfulfilment of its contract.

THE SEQUESTRATION ORDER IS CONFIRMED

On October 4, 1904, the judge presiding over the NY&B's appeal against the sequestration of its property rendered his decision in favor of the government. Therefore, the reasons for the confiscation remained in force and the former decree was confirmed. The commission that the court appointed to determine how much the NY&B should pay for its breach of contract decided "in Bs 1,500,000 or some $300,000."[43] The company immediately appealed the decision on October 5, 1904. According to its lawyers, the NY&B faced three alternatives, which were to ask for its properties back, to request the Venezuelan government for a prompt and impartial hearing, or to seek help from the United States, asking them to seize the customs houses to satisfy its claims. Thus if the U.S. government was to use force, it "would be less open to criticism if it were done on those grounds than if it appeared to interfere by violence with the judicial process."[44]

In December 1904 portions of the American-European Squadron under command of Rear Admiral Jewell, the American South Atlantic Squadron under the command of Rear Admiral Chadwick, and the American-Caribbean Squadron under the command of Admiral Sigsbee carried out naval maneuvers close to the island of Culebra near Puerto Rico. The feeling in Venezuela was that the assembly of such a large fleet would considerably "strengthen the hands of the United States Government in any action which they may see fit to support the interests of the Asphalt Company."[45] Such an impression was given further credence when Captain Parker arrived in Caracas as the new military atttache at the American Legation in November 1904.[46] Parker, who was expected to remain in Venezuela for a year, lost no time in ascertaining the logistics of deploying U.S. troops in the country. In January 1905, Parker met with Mr. Almond, the general manager of the La Guayra and Caracas Railway, to enquire whether the railway company would be willing to transport up to seven thousand U.S. troops to Caracas.[47] Almond, however, made it perfectly clear to Parker that the railroad would be unable to assist the U.S. government in the event of an American intervention.[48] In spite of this setback Parker continued to tour the country, drawing up plans for a possible landing of troops, while the Venezuelan government pressed ahead with greater need to mount its newly acquired cannons in La Guaira and Puerto Cabello.

When Bowen returned to Venezuela on December 17, 1904, he followed a more conciliatory tone. He hoped to become the "gendarme" of the interests of other countries "and that foreign grievances combined with the trouble of the Asphalt Company might force President Roosevelt to take prompt action to overthrow Castro."[49] Mr. Wiener, the French minister, feared for the future of the FCC. He assisted Bowen by all means in his power to achieve the overthrow. Toward the end of 1904 it was made clear to Bowen that Castro wanted to conclude a general treaty of arbitration with the United States for settling disputes before they escalated into diplomatic problems. Secretary of State Hay felt that such a position was utterly preposterous and could not be taken seriously.[50] In spite of this rejection in January 1905, Castro accepted arbitration on all five U.S. claims, with the asphalt dispute in particular to be settled by international arbitration. Hay suggested that Venezuela pay Bs 5 million annually to all powers as a good starting point.

Most of the decisions made at the State Department on Venezuela at this point were made by Francis Loomis, the undersecretary of state and former minister in Caracas, because the secretary of state was suffering from poor health, which would eventually lead to his death. The basis for the protocol was eagerly awaited in Caracas. However, when it arrived on January 12, 1905, it was signed by Loomis and did not cover the Bs 5 million agreement, nor the claims of other nations, "nor anything except that asphalt case!"[51] The document was couched in such "displeasing terms that President Castro immediately rejected it."[52] It was subsequently learned that the "entire protocol had been written by the attorney of the asphalt company"[53] because the NY&B feared arbitration and thus could not agree with the scheme. Loomis asked Bowen to obtain the withdrawal of Carner, the restoration of the Hamilton concession to the NY&B, and an indemnity to the company for the loss of trade and pitch extracted. Negotiations continued for a time to settle the asphalt case according to Bowen, but the Asphalt Trust sent an agent to Washington "who succeeded absolutely in undermining the influence of Mr. Hay as is shown by his cablegram to President Castro sent just after Mr. Hay addressed his so called 'ultimatum' to Venezuela, and stating in substance that after President Castro had answered the ultimatum the matter would be allowed to drop."[54] Hay was not to blame for the State Department's action, according to Bowen, as "it is now pretty generally known that he was utterly unable to cope with the forces arrayed against him"[55] because of his poor health.

Gustavo Sanabria, the Venezuelan foreign relations minister, was very dissatisfied with the situation because Loomis was now in charge of securing a settlement for a company that had previously prompted his recall "from Venezuela at the request of President Castro."[56] Despite this, Sanabria tried to get Castro to adopt a conciliatory policy because he feared that the United States would use hostile action. Castro, however, would have none of this. He instructed Manuel Urbaneja to draw up a flat refusal to the U.S. government, which both Gustavo Sanabria and Eduardo Blanco, the Education minister, refused to sign. A ministerial crisis ensued, and General Ybarra replaced Sanabria as foreign minister. Ybarra sent the rejection to Bowen.

On February 15 the Federal Court and Cassation rendered its decision on the NY&B's October 5 appeal. It confirmed that the original judge had the authority under the new organic law of the court to order the sequestration of the company's assets. The American government tried on four more occasions to obtain the removal of Carner as the Receiver but with no success. Immediately after the court's decision Castro left Caracas for a round of festivities in the country.

The general mood of the diplomatic corps was reflected by Bax-Ironside when he reported that if the United States decided to "employ force to obtain the consent of the Venezuelan Government for their demands, it is sincerely to be hoped that they will take steps to depose the President"[57] because the continuation of his administration would "mean but a fresh era of crime; and the eventual ruin of the industries of this country."[58] It was felt at this juncture that the United States was thinking of establishing a customs receivership similar to the one in the Dominican Republic. However, Bowen warned the State Department at end of January that if Venezuela was invaded by the United States, then Castro could count on the full support of the country's military establishment and the entire population in repelling the attack. The State Department, however, was not contemplating invading the country. It only sought arbitration of the five U.S. claims. Bowen had therefore overstepped his position and was now conducting diplomacy on his own initiative, convinced that he could arrive at a settlement with Castro. Such action would eventually lead to a dispute that showed the seedier side of American diplomacy at play. It would ultimately lead to Bowen's downfall and leave Loomis severely weakened. There was some sympathy for Venezuela. The *South American Journal* wrote that

> The disputed claim advanced by the American Asphalt Company is even more untenable than that of the French Cable Company. It bears upon it the "bar sinister" of the Standard Oil Trust. This is put forward on behalf of an American Asphalt Company, which appears to be of the same tentaculous description as the famous Standard Oil Trust.[59]

By February 1905, Wright was convinced that Bowen wanted to prevent arbitration from taking place. On several occasions, both in writing and verbally, Wright pointed out that the blockading powers had officially protested in Washington about the amount of their payments. Although Bowen justified his action to the State Department by stating that he was pursuing a policy for peace, he was nevertheless reprimanded by Washington when it became aware of the fact that "pourparless of a nature unauthorized by them were being carried out with the Venezuelan government by their representative"[60] in Caracas. Bowen was forced to apologize, but he defended his behavior by arguing that any action calculated to avoid extreme measures was justifiable.

General Ybarra was so alarmed at Bowen's behavior that he had sent copies of his notes to the Venezuelan minister in Washington to have them confirmed by the State Department. Ybarra was confident that it would be impossible for Bowen to remain at his post under these circumstances. The general impression, supported by certain members of the American colony in Caracas who were associated with the NY&B, was that he was "discredited with his government."[61] Bowen's position worsened on March 23 when *El Monitor*, a small circulation paper, published an article entitled "Venezuelan Money: What the Foreigner Have [*sic*] Carried Off." The paper alleged that Bowen had received a fee of Bs 169,382.72 for his services to the Venezuelan government at The Hague.

When Bowen read *El Monitor*'s article, he immediately tried to see Gustavo Sanabria, the new foreign affairs minister. Bowen turned up at a private residence, where Sanabria was dining, in an extremely agitated mood. Bowen lost his temper completely, waving a copy of *El Monitor* in Sanabria's face and "demanding an instant official apology, the punishment of the Editor and the suppression of the paper."[62] Bowen steadfastly refused to budge until he had received an apology, but Sanabria pointed out to the

American that he had not acted correctly by thrusting himself uninvited into somebody else's home. Bowen brushed aside all such remarks shouting, "You will give me an immediate apology, as demanded, for the conduct of the Venezuelan Gt [*sic*], as you yourself are te [*sic*] publication of this article"[63] adding that he regretted to have "ever served such a set of rascals."[64] Bowen was unsuccessful in his quest, leaving without an apology. Once he calmed down and realized what a diplomatic *faux pas* he had made, Bowen addressed a polite letter to Castro, but he received no reply in return. The government, however, published the breakdown of the fees that were paid to Bowen in the *Official Gazette* of March 6. It was shown that Bowen had received only Bs 26,000 for his services, with the remainder going to the British government in accordance with the protocol. As soon as the correspondence between Bowen and Sanabria and the copy of the report that the finance minister made was published in the *Official Gazette*, the American minister tried to get the diplomatic corps to issue a document that questioned the freedom of the Venezuelan press and requested that no more attacks be permitted against diplomatic representatives in the future. Bowen's intention was to strengthen his own position with the government, but the situation was against him. Bax-Ironside, the British minister, stated at a meeting of diplomats that it was ridiculous to ask for support because the U.S. government had been the first to stop such action during the last thirty years. The British minister then left, while Bowen tried to get a majority of the diplomats present to sign. Most refused, at which point Bowen lost his temper. He berated the assembled crowd and said that he had given them the chance to show that "you will not stand the treatment that has been accorded in past time by the V Gt [*sic*] to the Diplomatic Corps in this country. This opportunity you have now lost, and I shall never get it to you again. The world will now say 'The Diplomatic Corps at Caracas consists of cowards.' "[65] Bowen's fate was sealed at the end of March, when the *Washington Times* criticized him for receiving his fee of $5,000 from the Venezuelan government "in return for blackguarding three other friendly foreign governments, complaining not only of the fact that some obscure Venezuelan sheet should suspect his services of having been worth six times as much as they really were, but also that the money paid him, according to contract, was not sufficient to pay his expenses much less recompense him for services rendered."[66] The *Washington Times* concluded that it was impossible for a U.S. minister to serve the interests of Venezuela even if he had the approval of the U.S. government.

THE ASPHALT QUESTION UNRESOLVED

The Barber asphalt interests defended their corner with every weapon at their disposal, threatening to disgrace Loomis, now undersecretary of state at Washington, with the information that Carner had in his possession about certain business deals that Loomis had been involved with when he was the American minister at Caracas. Carner had been an employee of the NY&B when Loomis was the U.S. minister. Now that the affairs of the company had reached a critical stage, Carner was worried that the Americans would intervene in favour of the NY&B. He warned Loomis that "if he continued to use his influence in favour of the Company in Washington he had sufficient evidence in his possession to show the American public that Mr. Loomis had, at one time, been in the pay of the Company."[67] This threat seemed to have worked because Loomis replied with what Bax-Ironside referred to as an "indiscreet" letter to Carner, informing him that the American government would not intervene in favor of the company and that he would "use every effort not only to restrain them from doing so, but also to endeavour to arrange that the Government should retrace the steps already taken by them in the matter, on the condition that he returns all incriminating documents to him."[68] Bowen also found evidence against Loomis in the Legation's archives, which he forwarded to Secretary of State Hay. The correspondence showed that Carner had bribed Loomis, who was head of the American Legation between 1897 and 1901, paying him Bs 100,000 "to obtain certain concessions from President Castro in favour of the Company"[69] that had been arranged "through the instrumentality of M. Jaurett, at that time Reuter's agent."[70] Other accusations were that Loomis had been successful in "securing the payment of a claim by Venezuela to Lorenzo Mercado, a non-American, without advising the State Department of his actions or interests in the matter,"[71] and had been involved in "an agreement with an American banker, Charles B. Meyers, in which Loomis would use his influence in persuading Venezuela to seek a loan from his bank in return for one-seventh of the profits."[72] Other papers allegedly revealed Loomis' private interests in a mining concession and in a construction project. Bowen's action was clearly directed at saving his own position at the expense of Loomis. This initially proved successful, but in the end both would be forced to leave the service for bringing it into disrepute. Hay gave Bowen the choice of either remaining in the State Department in Washington or accepting the next "best available" post in the diplomatic service. Bowen refused both offers because he wanted to stay in Caracas, something that ultimately led to his downfall, as the U.S. government intended to send somebody else to clear up the mess.

U.S. PRESSURE

The U.S. government was getting impatient with Castro's behavior. It sent a stern note on March 10, 1905, challenging Venezuela's position and warning that if the administration did not agree to an impartial arbitration, so that the injured parties could get a fair hearing, then the United States would be forced to "take such measures as it may find necessary to effect complete redress without resort to arbitration."[73] Furthermore, the United States would be at "liberty to consider, if it is compelled to resort to more vigorous measures, whether those shall include complete indemnification not only for the citizens aggrieved but for any expenses of the Government of the United States which may attend their execution."[74] U.S. intervention now seemed almost certain. Bax-Ironside reported that the "question of American intervention in this country will, I am convinced, eventually become an accomplished fact."[75] The Venezuelan government appeared perplexed at the belligerent mood of the U.S. government because, as far as it was concerned, the Mixed Commission had settled all pending matters between the two countries, and the NY&B and Olcott cases belonged to the ordinary courts of the country. Alejandro Ybarra, the foreign minister, answered Hay's ultimatum in the following manner:

> I believe, with good foundation, that the Venezuelan Government has in reality no pending questions with the Government of the United States, it being an evident fact that, supported by every kind of evidence, that the Venezuelan Government arranged in Washington, by its protocol signed in 1903, the subjects that could be matters for discussion, and that were decided by the Mixed Commission that afterwards met in Caracas.[76]

Although Roosevelt wanted to intervene in Venezuela, there were other more pressing problems. There was the Dominican Republic, the Russo-Japanese War, an agreement over China with the Kaiser and the Moroccan crisis was about to erupt. Roosevelt had to leave the question of Castro, whom he referred to as that "unspeakably villainous little monkey,"[77] for a later date.

Bowen realized that Hay would do nothing against Loomis and was more likely to put a break on his own diplomatic career. Bowen therefore felt that his only chance of getting out of the mess that he had created was to put his case directly to the American public. In March, Bowen supplied Albert Felix Jaurett,[78] the Associated Press representative, on his return to Caracas[79] all "the information at his command in order that it might be published."[80] Jaurett took the evidence against Loomis, which was made public over Carner's head when it was published in the *New York Herald* on April 26, 1905 and widely distributed by the Associated Press. The reports accused Loomis of accepting, among other benefits, a check for $10,000 from the NY&B in consideration for services rendered to the company in his official capacity. The reports also alleged that Loomis brought a valuable claim against the Venezuelan government for a trifling sum and then used his position to collect the full amount. The final accusation was that he had contracted with Meyers (the banker) to settle a claim of $10 million against the Venezuelan government in exchange for about one-seventh of that sum. The following day, Loomis issued an unqualified denial to all three charges, stating that "the only foundation for the first was that in order, when leaving Caracas, to convert Venezuelan money lying to his account at a Bank into United States currency, he had exchanged cheques, at the published United States Government rate, with the Manager of the Asphalt Company."[81] Bowen was thrilled at the way events had turned out because he felt that this would remove the restraining influence of Loomis in reaching a lasting settlement to the problems pending with Venezuela.

The accusations of Bowen against Loomis caused a certain amount of consternation among the diplomatic corps in Washington. At the same time some of the revolutionaries, such as Antonio Paredes, arrived in New York to ascertain whether Loomis and the NY&B could help them financially. The public's reaction in the United States was not very great, but there were demands for a thorough investigation to be conducted by President Roosevelt himself. In Venezuela it was felt that W. H. Taft and Roosevelt would try to save Loomis' skin because he was "the real author of what happened in Panama and here they do not disguise the fact that Mr Roosevelt owes him this great service and that he can not afford to mistreat him."[82] Roosevelt wanted to see Bowen out, which he stated to Henry Cabot Lodge when he wrote that

> The Loomis-Bowen affair is most irritating. From all that appears, Loomis was entirely straight but he was certainly indiscreet and did things which enabled Bowen and the others to make an attack upon him. It is another case of disregarding Socrates' maxim as to the difference between private man, who only has to do what is right, and a public man, who ought so to conduct himself that no one can have an excuse for *saying* that he has not done what is right. At the same time, unless something is shown against Loomis I can not possibly get rid of him, and Bowen will have to be turned out whether Loomis is innocent or not; for it appears clearly that having forwarded the charges to the Department and the Department not having acted upon them, he then procured their publication in the press and is responsible for the entire scandal. Many of his accusations are too preposterous for belief. They in effect include the statement that Loomis has conducted the affairs of the State Department in reference to Venezuela by himself, in defense of the wishes of John Hay and myself. I really think the man is a little hipped.[83]

On April 29, Bowen was instructed to return to Washington to explain his accusations. On May 2, the day after Bowen left Caracas, William Russell, who had previously been in Bogotá, was appointed U.S. minister in Caracas. Castro and his government viewed the departure of Bowen "with great satisfaction."[84] Bowen arrived in New York on May 8, and it was understood that if he furnished a satisfactory explanation of his actions, he would be reinstated into diplomatic service as U.S. minister to Chile. Both Loomis and Bowen, however, left the diplomatic service. R.

Bacon replaced Loomis as undersecretary in September. The fate of the U.S. diplomats was interpreted by Venezuela as the "triumph of Venezuelan diplomacy in spite of the intrigues by the accomplices of the New York and Bermudez Co."[85]

THE UNITED STATES SENDS SPECIAL ENVOY CALHOUN

On May 20, 1905, soon after Bowen's departure from Caracas, the Judge of first instance rejected the NY&B's appeal because the Hamilton contract was bilateral, with mutual benefits therein given and like obligations assumed. The company had limited its activities to asphalt while neglecting to perform its other obligations in the contract, as it had not canalized the rivers. The government agreed that the contract had the character of a lease and that it had performed its side of the bargain, while the lessee had limited itself to only part of its obligations. The NY&B's contract was thus dissolved, and the company was ordered to pay damages that neutral appraisers were to determine. The company appealed on May 26, but the court upheld its decision on August 7, 1905.

At this juncture the United States and Venezuela appeared to be heading for a confrontation that could ultimately involve armed intervention by the Americans. However, Secretary of State Hay, after a long illness, died in June 1905. Elihu Root succeeded him. One of Root's first acts when he arrived at his new post was to review all the documentation on Venezuela. He decided in the end that the best course of action would be to get independent legal advice before the dispute was escalated further. It was decided to appoint Judge William Calhoun as special envoy of the president. Calhoun went to Venezuela to conduct an objective inquiry into the affair for the U.S. government to determine whether American interests were in danger and "how far those having these interests have by their own misdeeds forfeited their right to protection"[86] and "what action, if any, is required."[87] On August 3, 1905, the Venezuelan Congress granted Castro wide-ranging powers to negotiate a solution over the NY&B problem.

Judge Calhoun and William Russell, the new American minister, arrived in Caracas on August 19. Calhoun soon joined the leading club in Caracas and made the acquaintance of business and political leaders "to hear everything that Venezuelans might have to say against his own countrymen."[88] He invited "expressions of opinion from foreign merchants and managers of industrial enterprises, and enquired as to the interest of European nations in this country, showing particular interest with regard to Germany."[89] He also met Castro, but the "levity and lack of dignity"[90] of the president did not make a favorable impression on him. At the end of September, Calhoun completed his investigation in Caracas. He left for New York on October 2, accompanied by Robert Wright, the NY&B's local representative.

THE NY&B AND MATOS

At the instigation of the Venezuelan government the suit against the NY&B for complicity with Matos was transferred to Trinidad and New York to hear the testimony of some of the key witnesses in the affair. This would then be translated and entered in the Venezuelan court as evidence. The prosecution was represented by Rufus Billings Cowing Jr. of Cowing, White & Wait, while the NY&B was represented by Nicoll, Anable and Lindsay. Some seventy witnesses were called to testify, divided equally between the United States and Trinidad. At the start of the trial on October 17, 1905, General Francis V. Greene declared that when he had returned from Europe in 1901, he was surprised to hear that Mack, Sewall, and Andrews had decided to support Matos against Castro. Greene declared at the trial that

> [a] grave error was committed and that proceeding in such a manner was not acting in good faith with the State Department in Washington, which during that time and as is shown by the majority of the messages sent by Secretary Hay to me, had backed the Bermúdez Company, thereby allowing it to continue possession of its assets.[91]

Greene also stated that it would have been impossible for him to ask for State Department support because it would have involved great risk for the company. Greene did not think that Matos could win. He thought that the best solution was to keep pressing the State Department for its help. A few months after this, Greene left the company, while Mack kept a controlling interest in the NY&B. The suit continued for a number of years; a final judgment was rendered on August 12, 1907, against the NY&B, with the company liable for damages of Bs 24 million. This action was quite distinct from the one that resulted in the cancellation of the Hamilton concession. It enabled the government to appropriate all of the company's rights and the rest of their property as partial payment for the enormous damages awarded.

After Calhoun's return to the United States, Root had a full briefing with the judge, who felt that the company had been treated harshly and that all American disputes could be settled amicably. Root decided that all outstanding questions with Venezuela could be settled "without recourse to either of the alternatives contemplated in the despatch of March 10, 1905."[92] Root instructed Russell on October 18, 1905, to see whether the Venezuelan government would enter into negotiations and to ascertain whether they would "meet us halfway in a friendly and practical effort to reach substantial justice without too much regard to technical questions."[93] The definition of halfway was left deliberately vague because it was up to the NY&B to propose a solution, even though the State Department would assist where appropriate. Root sent Clyde Brown, the NY&B's treasurer, to Venezuela toward the end of November to make a final effort to reach a settlement with Castro.

The behavior of both the NY&B and Castro is sordid and indefensible. Although it is hard to have any sympathy for either party, Castro's behavior is probably the worse of the two because he sought to blackmail the company for personal gain in a situation that was untenable and that, had it been accepted, would have been to the detriment of his country. The dispute with the NY&B, however, did not rest here. It would continue to haunt Castro during the rest of his period in office.

NOTES

1. FO 420/226. Bax-Ironside to Lord Lansdowne, 18 June 04.
2. W. Handley, "Our Small South American Trade," *US Monthly Consular Reports* 75: (286), July 1904, pp. 10–12.
3. Acting Vice Consul G. Haggard, "Diplomatic and Consular Reports: Venezuela—Report for the Year 1905 on the Trade of the Consular District of Caracas," (HMSO 1906), *PP* vol. cxxiv, 1907, pp. 911–37.
4. FO 199/275 Corbett to Grey, 12 February 09.
5. William M. Sullivan, "The Rise of Despotism in Venezuela: Cipriano Castro, 1899–1908." PhD. diss., The University of New Mexico, 1974.
6. Sullivan, p. 536.
7. "Cartas de Caracas," *Venezuela: Ecos de una Tiranía*, 3:15, November 1907, pp. 118–19.
8. FO 420/226 Bax-Ironside to Lansdowne, 19 July 04.
9. Sullivan, p. 538.
10. José Rafael Ricart, *El trabajo. Consideraciones sobre las Causas de Fuerza que han Impedido el Desarrollo Útil de Nuestras Industrias y Demostración Sucinta de la Necesidad de Abrir un Paréntesis de Paz, de Garantías y de Protección a la Propiedad y al Trabajo, sin lo Cual el Progreso Patrio Será Imposible*, Caracas, Tip. Americana, 1903.
11. Consul de Lemos, "Diplomatic and Consular Reports: Venezuela—Report for the Year 1905 on the Trade and Commerce of Ciudad Bolívar," (HMSO 1906), *PP*, vol. cxxxiv, 1906, pp. 903–11.
12. "La exposición del General C. Castro en el Congreso," *El Universal*, 30 July 09.
13. Some observers nevertheless felt the need to praise Castro for his economic achievements. Ramón Pérez Meza in a letter to Castro soon after the Revolución Libertadora stated that the *cabito* had organized the "public finances which has generated uninterrupted revenues never achieved by past governments," (AHMSGPRCP Enero 1–10 1908 *Síntesis* of article Ramón Pérez Meza included in letter to Castro, 3.1.08). Public works such as roads, theaters, industry, and commerce flourished under Castro. The following buildings were completed during this period: Teatro Nacional, Palacio Municipal, Palacio de la Hacienda, Escuela Militar

de la Planicie, Plaza de la Republica, the Leporcomio de Cabo Blanco, and the Avenida del Paraiso.

14. William J. Calhoun, "Wrongs to American Citizens in Venezuela," *Senate Document No. 413*, vol. 24, 60 Cong. 1 Sess., September 1907–1908, pp. 161–563.

15. Ibid., p. 195.

16. Ibid., p. 228.

17. Ibid., p. 229.

18. Ibid.

19. FO 420/226 Bax-Ironside to Lansdowne, 23 June 04.

20. CO 295/430 Bax-Ironside to Lansdowne, 12 June 04.

21. CO 295/430 F. H. Villiers (FO) to secretary of state (CO), 11 July 04.

22. FO 420/226 Clifford to Lyttelton, 15 June 04.

23. CO 295/430 Statement by Robert K. Wright, 1 October 04, enclosure in Bax-Ironside to FO, 22 October 04.

24. Carlos Benito Figueredo, *Presidenciales*, Madrid, Establecimiento Tip. de El Liberal, 1908.

25. Calhoun, p. 229.

26. Ibid., p. 262.

27. Ibid.

28. Ibid., pp. 262–63.

29. Ibid.

30. FO 420/226 Bax-Ironside to Lansdowne, 25 July 04.

31. Bowen to secretary of state, 24 July 04, in "Venezuela," *Foreign Relations*, 59th Cong., 1 Sess., Dec 4, 1905 to June 30, 1906, pp. 919–1038.

32. Ibid.

33. CO 295/430 R. Herbert and C. Rivers Wilson to Lansdowne, 8 August 04.

34. CO 295/430 F. H. Villiers (FO) to secretary of state (CO), 30 July 04. A Colonial Office Minute initialled by H.R.C. states that

> The status of the Bermudez Company is very mysterious. Mr. Clifford says that it is a subsidiary Company of the New Trinidad Lake Asphalt Company . . . Mr. Bax Ironside on the contrary, says that the Bermudez Company's Agent was "much surprised" to hear that the Trinidad Company owned the bulk of the Company's stock, and that hitherto *both* Companies have posed as American and considered that there has been a technical transfer of shares for the purpose of enlisting the support of HMG, in view of difficulties anticipated in obtaining the interest of the U.S. Government. If . . . the U.S. Government are supporting the Company we shall probably not receive any pressing demands for the support of HMG, who are only interested to the extent that a blow to the New Trinidad Company would affect the revenue derived by Trinidad from the asphalt royalty. Mr. Bax Ironside has been instructed to "lend such support as he properly can" and has approached the Venezuelan Government. In the circumstances I do not see that we can press the F. O. to take more vigorous action. (CO 295/430, H.R.C. 3 August 04 in Bax-Ironside to Lansdowne, 18 June 04)

35. FO 420/226 Bax-Ironside to Lansdowne, 6 August 04.

36. FO 420/227 Bax-Ironside to Lansdowne, 20 August 04.

37. CO 295/430 Bax-Ironside to Lansdowne, 17 August 04. In April 1904 the Venezuelan government purchased eight Creuzot guns of powerful and heavy caliber, which were originally intended for the Boer Government. In July the German ship *Graecia* arrived in La Guaira with 209 boxes of firearms, 1100 boxes of cartridges, 18 boxes of cannon and accessories, and two guns. The caliber of the

cannons was estimated at 5.9 inches and weighing approximately 7.5 tons. One gun was to be placed at Punta de Guarape, near the eastern side of La Guaira, and the second one placed at El Palomar, on the shore near the baths of Maiquetía. There were two more at Castillo San Agustín.

38. CO 295/430 Bax-Ironside to Lansdowne, 20 August 04.

39. Ibid.

40. Orray Thurber, *Origen del Capital Norteamericano en Venezuela. La Epoca del Asfalto (1884–1907)*, trans. Angel Villasana, Barquisimeto, Editorial Nueva Segovia, 1955, p. 32.

41. Ibid., p. 45.

42. Norman Hutchinson to Mr. Hay, 27 September 04, in Calhoun, p. 196.

43. Thurber, p. 68.

44. FO 420/227 W. I. Penfield, "Report by the Solicitor in the matter of the seizure of the Bermudez Lake," undated.

45. FO 420/228 Bax-Ironside to Lansdowne, 6 December 04.

46. He held a similar position at the U.S. Legation in Bogatá.

47. FO 80/470 Bax-Ironside to Lansdowne, 7 January 05.

48. FO 80/470 Percy C. Wyndham to Lansdowne, 5 April 05.

49. FO 420/232 Bax-Ironside to Lansdowne, 26 December 04.

50. Hay to Bowen, 3 February 05, in Calhoun, p. 201.

51. H. W. Bowen, "Queer Diplomacy with Castro," *North American Review* 184, March 30, 1907, pp. 577–80.

52. Ibid.

53. Ibid.

54. Ibid.

55. Ibid.

56. CO 295/434 Bax-Ironside to Lansdowne, 3 January 05.

57. FO 420/232 Bax-Ironside to Lansdowne, 22 January 05.

58. Ibid.

59. "Venezuela is not always in the wrong" *South American Journal*, 4 November 05.

60. 295/434 Bax-Ironside to Lansdowne, 6 February 05.

61. FO 80/462 Bax-Ironside to Lansdowne, 25 February 05.

62. FO 199/250 Bax-Ironside to Lansdowne, 6 March 05.

63. Ibid.

64. Ibid.

65. Ibid.

66. "H. W. Bowen Again," *Washington Times*, 30 March 05. Bowen's technique, according to the American newspaper was "simple and picturesque to a degree" (ibid.) as it consisted of the following:

> in gathering around him at the close of each day's work, while negotiations were pending, the reporters and correspondents of newspapers to whom Mr. Bowen would communicate, with charming affability, and condescension, how a few hours before he had been compelled to make clear to the representatives of the three effete monarchies what their places were; how, in fact, he had administered to them a few wholesome lessons in international deportment; how he had told them to mind their p's and q's and how they failed before his anger, and how they had humbly apologised for living and promised never, no never, to be bad again. (Ibid.)

67. FO 420/232 Bax-Ironside to Lansdowne, 20 February 05.
68. Ibid.
69. Ibid.
70. Ibid.
71. Hendrickson, Embert J., "The New Venezuelan Controversy: The Relations of the United States and Venezuela, 1904–1914" (PhD diss. University of Minnesota, 1964) p. 65.
72. Ibid.
73. Calhoun, p. 515.
74. Ibid.
75. FO 420/232 Bax-Ironside to Lansdowne, 19 March 05. He further stated that

> Unwillingness on the part of the American Government to bear the responsibility involved may tend to postpone it, but the ninety-four years of independence of Venezuela have sufficed to show that the nation is unfit for self-government. The mixture of races, the generally low moral tone prevalent, the universally unscrupulous standards existing, and the entire absence of honesty and fair dealing exhibited by those who have obtained power by sanguinary revolutions, point a moral which will take effect. The potential wealth of this country, its large size and its propinquity, both to Europe and North America, will necessitate an improvement in its Government. Such an improvement must come from outside, and it may be hoped, at not a very distant date. (Ibid.)

76. Calhoun, p. 516.
77. Hendrickson, Embert J., "Roosevelt's Second Venezuelan Controversy," *Hispanic American Historical Review* 50: 3, Aug. 1970, pp. 482–99, p. 487. p. 487.
78. Jaurett left France after he embezzled funds from the French army. He arrived in Panama. After the collapse of the M. de Lesseps canal in Panama, Jaurett left for Mexico, where he was associated with Count Dupres. After the death of Dupres he married his wife and thus inherited a fortune. He became the agent of the Compagnie Five Little, a French sugar machinery company. Jaurett was also a heavy gambler, losing $45,000 in gambling debts and embezzling up to $60,000 in Mexico.
79. Jaurett was expelled from Venezuela on November 14, 1904, because it was claimed he had misrepresented the political situation of the country. He started a legal action against the Venezuelan government, claiming the sum of $192,460.
80. FO 199/250 P. C. Wyndham to Lansdowne, 14 March 05.
81. FO 199/250 Hugh O'Beirme to Lansdowne, 5 May 05.
82. Carlos B. Figueredo to Castro, 5 May 05, in "El Gobierno de Castro y la New York and Bermudez Company," *BAHM*, vol. 7: 41–42, March–June, 1966, pp. 91–205.
83. T. Roosevelt to H. Cabot Lodge, 24 May 05, in Henry Cabot Lodge, *Selections from the Correspondence of Theodore Roosevelt and Henry Cabot Lodge, 1884–1918*, New York, Charles Scribner's Sons, 1925, vol. 2, p. 124.
84. FO 80/470 Percy C. Wyndham to Lansdowne, 14 May 05.
85. Domingo Castillo to C. Castro, 7 September 05 in "El Gobierno de Castro y la New York and Bermudez Company," *BAHM*, vol. 7: 41–42, March–June 1966, pp. 91–205.
86. Philip C. Jessup, *Elihu Root*, New York, Dodd, Mead & Co., 1938, vol. 1, p. 494.

87. Ibid.
88. FO 420/235 Wyndham to Lansdowne, 5 October 05.
89. Ibid.
90. Ibid.
91. Thurber, p. 29.
92. Calhoun, p. 517.
93. Ibid.

8

Diplomatic Relations Deteriorate

The asphalt dispute, with all its international ramifications, was not the only one that Castro was handling at the time. He was also at loggerheads with the FCC. At the time of Calhoun's arrival in Caracas, it was rumored that the French government was almost ready to intervene in the country but had refrained from doing so because it did not want to "precipitate matters until it has had time to confer with President Roosevelt."[1] There was general dissatisfaction with the poor service that the FCC provided because the link crossing the Dominican Republic meant that "breakages in the line are of frequent occurrence, and long intervals elapse in many cases before the service is restored."[2] In addition, the cable charges were exorbitant, and the general service was insufficient and unsatisfactory because of political unrest. Consequently, on November 3, 1903, Arroyo Parejo, the Attorney General, issued a writ against the FCC that sought compensation for the bad service and requested the annulment of the contract because of the constant breakdowns. On February 25 of the following year, the Tribunal de la Primera Instancia decided against the FCC. The company immediately lodged an appeal. On March 18 the Federal Court and Cassation reversed the lower court's order on payment of costs, but the main legal battle dragged on until May 11, when the Venezuelan government and the FCC agreed that the French company would acquire the cable monopoly for twenty years by paying the government twenty French centimes for every cable sent or received with no other taxes levied. On the same date a further agreement was reached in which the FCC admitted the validity of the previous decree against it. In addition, both parties agreed to renounce their mutual rights or claims, which had been the subject of litigation between them, and the cable company ceded their coastal cable stations to the government.

Such an amicable state of affairs would not last for long because M. Guinterrand, the dismissed manager, would soon be selling the correspondence transmitted during Matos' revolution. M. Quievereaux, the French consul in Caracas, was deeply implicated in the Matos revolution. He had sent telegrams to the rebel leader through the FCC, some of which were in his own handwriting and signed by him. Although Guinterrand told Quievereaux that the original telegrams had been destroyed, copies of the correspondence had been made. One set of copies went to Albert Felix Jaurett, the Reuters foreign correspondent and editor of the *Venezuelan Herald*, in the hope that one day they could be used to both blackmail the French government and extort money from Venezuela. J. E. Sauvage Monet, the former FCC director in Martinique, Haiti, and Brazil, joined the plot soon afterwards.

Quievereaux, who was in Paris at the time, heard that the correspondence could fall into Castro's hands. He was alarmed at the adverse consequences that this would bring to the French government, so he hurried to the Palais D'Orsay where he was told in no uncertain terms that they had always backed the FCC. At the realization that the FCC manager had misused the consular offices, and by so doing directly implicated the French government in the Matos rebellion, Quievereaux sent a mutual friend on May 17, 1904, to see M. Jeramec, president of the company, to explain that his own position was in jeopardy if the company did not use the whole weight of its influence to save the former French consul. Jeramec was unaware of these events because he had been appointed to his position in 1903, but he nevertheless convened a directors' meeting, where the consul's charges were denied. The FCC could do nothing for Quievereaux. This was the last straw for a man who was obviously tormented at the thought that a diplomatic scandal would soon break in which he had unwittingly played a part. That night he committed suicide by gassing himself in his hotel room.[3] A little later the directors tried to secure the silence of Guinterrand, who had worked for the company for fifteen years and was the former manager of the Caracas office. Guinterrand was in Paris readying himself for his new post at Para in Brazil when he was dismissed after Quievereaux's death.

In mid-1904, with Guinterrand now out of the company, he and his fellow conspirators felt that the right moment had arrived to blackmail the French government. Through a Venezuelan intermediary, a former Foreign Minister, they offered the documents for sale to the French Legation in Caracas for Bs 300,000. They said that if they did not receive prompt payment, the documents would be forwarded to Castro, who would publish them and possibly sever relations with France for complicity with the cable company in the Matos rebellion. Wiener, the French Minister, now faced the almost impossible task of extricating France from a difficult position by acquiring the documents, and there was no guarantee that copies had not been made. Wiener refused to be blackmailed, and Guinterrand was arrested in Paris and sent to prison.

At the same time the Franco-Venezuelan Mixed Commission was about to discuss France's Bs 48 million claim against Venezuela. In anticipation of this, Castro started negotiating a loan with the FCC in July 1904 to pay off the French foreign claims, which the Venezuelans thought was closer to Bs 7 million. It was at this critical stage of negotiations that the Matos telegrams were offered to Castro, who readily agreed to acquire them for the sum of Bs 125,000. This placed Castro in a stronger position. He suggested to Wiener at Macuto, a coastal resort close to Caracas, both that the Venezuelan government was not satisfied with the manner in which the FCC transacted its business and that an action was pending against the company for annulment of its contract. Castro stated that he would be willing to "drop the action on condition that the Company constructed a new cable from Martinique to the Venezuelan Coast, and paid in full the whole of the sum which would be due to French claimants under decision of the French Commission, which has not yet commenced sitting."[4] The French government, however, was not willing to be blackmailed. It instructed Wiener that he should have no more personal interviews with Castro. The Venezuelan president was keeping his options open because he was also negotiating with the West India and Panama Telegraph Company for a cable connection with Trinidad.

Castro did not give up his hopes of reaching a settlement. In September 1904, José Antonio Velutini and M. F. Arroyo Parejo arrived in Paris to negotiate a new loan. They were armed with photographic copies of the FCC documents. They hoped to force the French government to come to some arrangement regarding the cable company by underwriting the flotation of a Venezuelan loan. But the French were getting impatient. Wiener pressed Alejandro Ybarra, the foreign affairs minister, in January 1905 for a quick settlement of the dispute because the FCC was in the process of getting a $4,234,127 loan to build an underwater telegraph line to the Far East. The French president, F. Delcasse, feared that the legislative chamber would not approve the bill while problems remained in Venezuela. As far as Castro was concerned there were "no pending questions with France and that the cable controversy would be settled legally in the proper tribunal."[5] However, the French now threatened Venezuela with force, placing two warships at Wiener's disposal at Martinique. The Dutch also joined the French to place more pressure on Castro.

In March 1905 the government won its case against the FCC in its suit over bad service when the federal court ruled against the company. Wiener immediately warned Castro of the ramifications and convinced him that the company needed to maintain its property until it had appealed the decision, because it was likely that France would join the United States in its intervention to help the NY&B. Castro remained optimistic that a new loan of $14,434,524 would be negotiated by M. Cavallini and F. Madueño with French and Italian banks, of which the Banque de Paris et des Pays Bas was the most important. This bank would be partly financed by establishing a monopoly of cigarettes in Venezuela. This attempt to get a loan ended in failure in early July. The Venezuelan government started court action against the FCC, suing for damages on eight charges of complicity with the Matos rebellion. Their main evidence were the telegrams sent by Quievereaux, which Guinterrand had recently acquired. The action against the FCC would proceed simultaneously with the action against the NY&B.

A press campaign and official pressure convinced the French government to recall Wiener. This was a matter of extreme irritation to the Dutch because they were to join in "any demonstrations which might be made by France."[6] A Dutch gunboat cruised in readiness off the Venezuelan coast. This only served to increase Castro's attack on the company's property. On September 4, 1905, Castro ordered the closure of the company's central station in Caracas and all coastal stations with the exception of La Guaira. Desire Brun, the director of the cable company, launched a fierce protest to Diego Bautista Ferrer, the Development Minister, and was promptly expelled from the country on September 6.

The acrimonious feeling against the FCC was not isolated. Most of the large trading houses, such as Blohm, Boulton, and Vollmer, as well as the Banco de Venezuela supported Castro's actions. The chambers of commerce of Caracas and Maracaibo also backed Castro's actions. They complained bitterly about the poor service of the cable company that had adversely affected business. The Maracaibo Chamber of Commerce, in particular, underlined the need for a reliable service as essential, especially when exporting coffee, and "considered the measure adopted by the government as convenient to the general well-being of Commerce and applauds and approves it for the healthy effects derived from its application."[7] The *El Constitucional* newspaper wrote that the demise of the FCC "would end the severe difficulties in which the actual service of its telegraphic line causes to the public and especially commerce."[8]

At the end of September the FCC agreed to the closure of all cable offices with the exception of La Guaira, where an inspector would be posted. One bolivar per word would be charged for all international communications that moved through the La Guaira office. An arrangement was made concerning Porlamar on Margarita Island. This was only a provisional arrangement, pending the arrival in Venezuela of General Valeriano, manager of the national telegraphs and post, and M. Bousquet of the FCC, who would begin negotiations. Valeriano sailed for Venezuela on October 14 after Castro agreed to the terms.

The FCC reached this solution behind the French government's back, which was furious when it found out that the cable company had surrendered to the demands of the Venezuelan government.[9] It appeared that the company had abandoned the main issues that the French government had pursued and which it would not allow to drop. In Caracas, Olivier Taigny, the French Charge d'Affaires, requested an explanation from the Venezuelan government. He received an "insulting" reply that brought the rupture of diplomatic relations a step closer. After the Taigny incident the French reacted by expelling A. Maubourquet, the Venezuelan charge d'affaires in Paris, imposing a boycott on Venezuelan goods, and assembling a fleet in the Caribbean. Castro reacted by retiring all French consuls and recalling all Venezuelan diplomatic representatives from France. In addition, all remaining cable managers were deported.

The United States offered to arbitrate, but Castro refused because he considered the problem not to be a diplomatic one. Jean Jules Jusserand, the French Ambassador to the United States, informed both Roosevelt and Root that France might break off relations with Venezuela. He added that if Castro refused U.S. arbitration, France would have to employ "more telling measures than the mere sending of naval vessels into Venezuelan waters,"[10] temporarily occupy parts of Venezuelan territory, seize customs houses, and have "recourse, in a word, to means which, while having chances of being felt, would avoid bloodshed."[11] A third French gunboat now joined the two already at Fort de France, and two more were placed on alert at Brest, home of the French navy. The United States was content with the French action as long as it received a written pledge that France would not occupy Venezuelan territory on a permanent basis. At the same time the Dutch, who were also experiencing problems with Castro over trade between Curacao and the mainland, were prepared to join with France in any action against Venezuela.

THE FRENCH BACK DOWN

The French government, however, was in a quandary with regards to the FCC and the possible rupture of relations with Venezuela. The French did not want to undertake unilateral action and had been counting on American support, but the United States was now reluctant to move because new evidence had come to light that the NY&B "had largely assisted the rebellion of General Matos."[12] The news, which had come as a "bombshell" to Russell, together with Roosevelt's recent interpretation of the Monroe Doctrine, militated against American mediation. The French did not want to get themselves embroiled in a futile expedition of their own. The worsening political situation in Morocco definitely prevented the French government from taking coercive action against Venezuela. The French shifted their position to doing all in their power to prevent the Venezuela incident from getting out of hand. There was some suspicion among the French that Castro's inexplicable behaviour was due to Germany's support behind the scenes. The political Director at the Ministry of Foreign Affairs informed Reginald Lister, the British ambassador in Paris, that he could not go so far "as accusing her, for we have not caught her in the act . . . but our suspicions are aroused, and the tone of various important organs of the German press has not tended to allay them."[13] This was wholly unjustified because, according to Bax-Ironside, the influence of Germany in Venezuela was "nil,"[14] the same as the US where "such phrases as 'the good offices of the United States' and the 'influence of the United States Ministers' are fallacies and merely create a visible factor in the situation."[15] In December 1905, Castro discussed with Bax-Ironside his problems with the United States and France. The British diplomat expressed a "wish to smooth away the difficulties between G. B. [*sic*] and Venezuela."[16] Nevertheless, the situation was sufficiently serious for the British government to despatch the HMS *Indefatigable* to La Guaira for the protection of the lives and property of British subjects in case the United States or France decided to use force against Venezuela.

Castro kept the pressure up on the FCC, ordering the company to pay taxes of Bs 134,255 in accordance with the December 5, 1905, regulations of the Classifying Board of Municipal Taxes of the Federal District. In December 1905, the American legation tried for the last time to get Venezuela to agree to arbitration by sending a strongly worded note on behalf of France about the FCC to the Venezuelan government. Russell informed Castro that only the efforts of the U.S. government had prevented the use of force by France, which was "now irritated by the character of the successive questions which have been put to her, which she regards as dilatory."[17] But Russell's note had no effect on the Castro government, leaving the French government with no recourse but to break off diplomatic relations on January 9, 1906. The French reserved the right to occupy temporarily the customs houses to secure satisfaction. The following day federal troops occupied the offices of the FCC in La Guaira.

On January 11, 1906, Russell formally informed the Venezuelan government of the rupture of relations with France. The United States would look after French interests in Venezuela and Venezuelan interests in France. On the same day the FCC was disconnected. On January 14, Oliver Taigny boarded the French Mail packet steamer moored at La Guaira without receiving his passport and became "arbitrarily detained on this vessel."[18] He "was informed by the officials at La Guayra [*sic*] that he would not be allowed to land again on Venezuelan soil."[19] The reason for this was that Castro had instructed Eduardo Celis to deny port privileges to French warships. This was highly irregular because Taigny had to return to Caracas to receive his passport and then leave on either a French warship or an English Royal Mail steam packet, which was to leave on January 18. Upon finding that he was unable to leave, Taigny spoke from the ship with the American consul at La Guaira, who was on shore, and explained to him his "predicament."[20] The following day Taigny sent a letter to Luis R de Lorena Ferreira, the Brazilian minister and doyen of the diplomatic corps, protesting in the strongest manner possible the action of the Venezuelan government. However, the letter did not reach the Brazilian diplomat until January 18 "owing to some unaccountable delay"[21] on the part of either the U.S. consul or the U.S. minister in Caracas. However, Russell managed to forward all of Taigny's belongings to the French mail packet steamer, which sailed on January 16.

By the time the diplomatic body became aware of this incident on January 18, Taigny was already sailing for France. However, the diplomatic corps nevertheless agreed unanimously to send a strong protest to General Ybarra, the Venezuelan foreign affairs minister. Ybarra replied that the French minister at the time of the incident was not a diplomat but just an ordinary French citizen because diplomatic relations had been broken. Further protests followed, but General Ybarra maintained that the Taigny incident was not a diplomatic one and should not be discussed by the diplomatic corps because "it would establish a fatal precedent were this Government to accept intervention in the form which it has been offered, seeing that any of the nations at present represented here might find itself tomorrow in a similar position."[22] The French increased pressure by placing its fleet on maneuvers in the Caribbean, creating the impression in Venezuela "that immediate coercive measures against the Government of President Castro were contemplated by the French Government."[23] However, the French were forced to back down, according to M. Rouvier, the French foreign affairs minister, because of the "present state of affairs in Europe in connection with the Morocco question."[24] As a result there was no need for the British to send the HMS *Indefatigable* to La Guaira.

THE STICKY ASPHALT PROBLEM

As the French crisis approached its denouement, Castro and Clyde Brown, the NY&B negotiator, tried to reach an agreement. At the first meeting on November 25, 1905, Castro suggested that a solution could be achieved that involved the company recognizing the decision of the Federal Court to rescind the Hamilton concession, but that a Mixed Commission with lawyers appointed by both the government and the company could be set up to study the validity of its titles "which would also take into consideration the ruling pronounced by the Federal Court in the [La] Felicidad trial and the ruling pronounced by the Federal Court and of Cassation in the trial for the resolution of the Hamilton contract."[25] As we have seen, the Mixed Commission appointed to calculate the cost of the damage the Matos revolution caused had reached the estimate of Bs 42 million. The government felt that the fairest way of distributing the cost would be for each of the parties responsible, Venezuela, the revolutionaries, the NY&B and the FCC, to pay a quarter of this sum. This implied that the company should pay $2.1 million for damages inflicted on the country during the Matos revolution. Castro did not consider the validity of the company's titles as a stumbling block because he had been conferred sufficient powers by Congress on August 3 of that year to negotiate the matter in the broadest terms possible. Castro had deliberately withheld the promulgation of the decree "with the purpose that said regulation could be made in accordance with any new contract entered by the Company."[26] The new contract would therefore entail "all the rights and privileges which the Company desires."[27]

Brown continued to argue that the company had been forced to help the revolutionaries "as a means of defence"[28] because the state had been unable to protect the company's property. He claimed that the NY&B had paid $130,000 to Matos "for the protection of its property during the revolution and for its rights afterwards in case the rebellion had triumphed but without any knowledge or understanding how the money would be used by them."[29] The company therefore could not be blamed for payments that had been made under coercion. The statement that the company had been coerced was utterly false, as was Brown's assertion that during the conflict the company had followed a strict policy of neutrality, "complying with the instructions transmitted by the Company."[30]

At another meeting between Castro and Brown, who this time was accompanied by Russell, the Venezuelan government stressed its anxiety to reach a settlement with the NY&B. The question to be settled now was how much the Bermudez Company could assist toward paying its portion of the settlement,[31] while the granting of new concessions to the NY&B would be cleared up later. The company argued that it was unable to pay Bs 10.5 million, or a quarter of the claim, because it had lost money through the sequestration of its properties, the investment of $500,000 in developing the site, and the cost of $100,000 toward building a refinery at Guanoco in 1900. Moreover, Brown said that the company was not responsible for all of the Matos misdemeanors, calculating that it had only contributed a twentieth of the claims. However, the company, made an attractive counter-proposal. The company would allow the Venezuelan government greater participation in the earnings of the operation by levying a royalty on the asphalt produced, which would secure additional revenues to the government, if Venezuela agreed to waive all its claims for damages in the concession and revolutionary suits and other claims against the company, as well as restore the asphalt property to the NY&B while preventing

Carner from shipping any further cargoes of asphalt. The company would acquiesce in the annulment of the Hamilton contract and would waive all claims against the Venezuelan government for damages and losses incurred by the sequestration of its property. It also offered to pay a royalty of Bs 5 per ton, which would exempt it from any further taxation. The company would also be granted a railway concession over the five miles to the port with the privilege of using local wood for ties, wharves and other purposes. Finally, it would be allowed to import and export barrel stock.[32]

Russell, Wright, and H. Hutchinson had a further talk with Castro, who objected to the Bs 5 per ton royalty because it was not an amount mentioned in the mining code and did not guarantee any additional income to the government. However, Clyde Brown was working on a new proposal under which the company would accept the decision to annul the concession as long as a new and special contract was awarded to the company.[33] In return the company would pay $20,000 annually to the Venezuelan government over the remaining eighty-one years of its concession. The special contract would restore the Hamilton contract to the company, including payment for the asphalt already mined. All import duties on machinery and the import and export of barrel stock would be exonerated, and the company would be given the privilege of cutting timber for wharves and railway ties. The NY&B would also be awarded the land to build its railway, would have the free right of navigation on rivers, would be exempted of all additional taxation, and would be dropped from all suits.[34] By December 1905 it appeared that Castro had accepted Brown's proposal, leaving the revolutionary suit to be settled separately, although subject to proceedings in court and by mutual agreement of the parties involved. Brown was willing to pay the judgment costs if they were less than Bs 200,000 and if two years of the annual tax were waived immediately upon the execution of an agreement. This was also contingent on Castro restricting "shipments of Bermúdez asphalt."[35]

Russell wanted to make the NY&B case a diplomatic matter and advised that "if the presumable intent of the Venezuelan Government is to ship asphalt during these negotiations in order to make a further profit on the company's capital or to extort from the company concessions of greater hardship . . . it will not only be wanton outrage upon the company, but also an act of bad faith towards the Government of the United States."[36] The *South American Journal* wrote in November 1905 that the French and American claims for compensation after the seizure of their properties were untenable because the main objective of the company was to keep the Venezuelan asphalt "from being worked in competition with their monopoly of the article in the United States."[37]

In January 1906 the government answered Brown's proposal by stating that the royalty offer was acceptable, but added that the company did not address the court's verdict nor did it offer to pay for losses and damages incurred on account of the Matos revolution, which the company had financed. The British minister sympathized with Castro. Bax-Ironside reported that the NY&B had funded Matos but that the company did not "offer one 'sou' to the country to which he caused so much loss and damage."[38] Castro was still willing to agree to the proposal, but negotiations foundered when Brown found out that Carner was still shipping asphalt from Guanoco. Negotiations broke down, and Brown sailed for the United States on January 8 "having failed in his efforts to come to an arrangement with President Castro."[39] Castro's agents retained possession "of the valuable Bermúdez Asphalt Lake and continue[d] to work it for the benefit of the President and his associates."[40] The Asphalt company was hit by a defamation suit when Amzi Lorenzo Barber sued the General Asphalt Company for $250,000 in June 1906 because he had been accused in the company's annual report of developing a competing supply of asphalt in Mexico, of conspiring with Castro to take the NY&B's properties away in Venezuela, and of selling his shares secretly in 1900.

The United States now pressed the Venezuelan government to accept its proposal of arbitration on pending claims, but it received the following answer from José de Jesus Paúl, the Foreign Affairs Minister, at the end of February:

> [A]s the cases referred to by your excellency can not be considered as being comprised amongst those which call for diplomatic action, the government of Venezuela would view it with satisfaction if the government of the United States would consider this question as closed, the interested parties always having the right of recourse to the tribunal of justice of the Republic should they deem fit.[41]

The Americans now considered their situation in the country hopeless because the Venezuelan government paid no attention to either the threats or entreaties on the part of Russell, the American Minister in Caracas. Bax-Ironside reported that Castro had shown "scant courtesy and lack of consideration"[42] to Russell toward the end of February 1906. Matters were aggravated further in March when the chief of police of La Guaira walked into the American consulate and "arrested the Consular Clerk."[43]

Under these circumstances in the summer of 1906, Secretary of State Root decided to leave Venezuelan matters to rest until after the Pan-American conference at Rio de Janeiro was over and he returned to Washington. Moreover, the United States was not ready to make its claim stick. Root informed President Roosevelt in early July that although "we have a lot of claims to make . . . I do not think it is wise to press them at this moment, and some of them are not quite in shape to be pressed."[44] Nevertheless, it was felt that the United States would intervene in Venezuela. The British government requested clarification from Root in February 1907 as to their intentions and whether they contemplated taking any action for the settlement of the outstanding claims. The United States was not in a belligerent mood. Root replied that the United States "would probably bring strong diplomatic pressure to bear to induce Venezuela to submit these questions to arbitration, and it might be necessary to lay papers before Congress."[45] It was unlikely, however, that any action would take place during the current session of Congress. Root thought that it "would be difficult to arrive at any settlement as long as President Castro lived, as he was afflicted with megalomania."[46]

On February 29, 1907, Secretary Root requested the Venezuelan government to reconsider the five outstanding American claims and take them to the International Arbitration Court at The Hague. According to a Foreign Office memorandum an examination of the claims suggested that the State Department was under "pressure from private interests of a not unimpeachable character [and] allowed itself to be put in an internationally invidious position of pressing very questionable pecuniary claims on one of the small powers towards whom it is a principle of American foreign policy to play the part of a beneficent if jealous Jehovah."[47] The first claimant was Albert Felix Jaurett, a Frenchman by birth but American by naturalization (although his papers were thought to be fraudulent).[48] Jaurett wanted an indemnification of $25,000 for his expulsion from Venezuela. Jaurett who was described as a French adventurer, was a journalist whose "only residence in the United States was two months in Florida."[49] He had been in the pay of the NY&B during the Matos rebellion and had made himself obnoxious to the Venezuelan government by publishing a series of articles against it. The question was whether it was legal to expel a foreigner under Venezuelan law if the person in question was domiciled in the country, which Jaurett was. The Venezuelan government's position was that Jaurett was not a resident of the country because he was associated with the U.S. Legation even though he was not an American citizen and of no interest to the U.S. government. The Castro administration also felt that the United States had taken up Jaurett's claim because of his intervention in favor of Loomis in the dispute with Bowen.

The second claim stemmed from Fitzgerald's concession and involved the Manoa Company, the Orinoco Company, and the Orinoco Corporation. The claim was whether the companies suffered heavy losses as a result of the action taken against them by the Venezuelan government. According to a Foreign Office memorandum, Fitzgerald's concession comprised ten thousand square miles in the Orinoco delta and was awarded merely as a political move to obtain American protection over the territory that British claims affected. The Venezuelan government was successful because it got President Cleveland of the United States to intervene in opposition to the British claims. However, to get rid of the concession afterward the Venezuelan government resorted to "the Oriental procedure of retracting and reenacting the concession from or to various parties until it had involved the companies to whom the various adventurers sold out in an inextricable tangle of litigation."[50] It was under this condition that the claim was referred to the Mixed Commission in 1903. Umpire Barge, head of the commission, found that the rights of the claimants subsisted in spite of the executive cancellations but that it was up to the Venezuelan courts and not to the commission to decide in whom those rights resided. It was unclear whether such a decision was right or wrong, but Venezuela produced more arguments in support of it than the U.S. government did. The Americans argued that Barge's decision was unjust, inequitable, and a misconception of the powers of the commission as established in the protocol. The Venezuelan government argued that the decision was an arbitral award rendered in due form to which no protest was made at the time and that payments made under it were accepted.

The reason for the United States not contesting the decision was due to Rudolph Dolge, the U.S. consul in Caracas and secretary of the commission, who succeeded in merging the Manoa Company and the Orinoco Company into the Orinoco Corporation. Dolge would manage this company after he resigned his consular post. Castro then awarded parts of the original concession to other parties. The Orinoco Corporation enlisted the help of the U.S. government in its claim over the rights of all the original claimants. The U.S. government came into collision with the award of Barge, who asserted the jurisdiction of the Venezuelan tribunals under the terms of the original contract to rule that these rights had been perfected, which the tribunals had recently done on the grounds of breach of contract. According to the Foreign Office "the whole affair is shady from start to finish and Mr. Bowen was unquestionably right in refusing to touch it though this involved him in a quarrel with Dolge which afterwards cost him heavily in his quarrel with Mr. Loomis."[51]

The third claim was regarding the Orinoco Steam Ship Company, which the United States wanted reopened and resubmitted to a new arbitration. It was argued that the only grounds on which a revision of the arbitral award could take place would be if the case was not in conformity with the Protocol as not being on an absolute basis of equity. It also opened up the whole question as to whether countries should accept arbitral awards. The fourth claim was by the NY&B. The United States wanted arbitration to determine the rights of the company under the Hamilton concession and to establish the losses suffered as a consequence of the alleged denial of justice to the company in civil actions. According to the Foreign Office the NY&B claim confirmed on "every page the biblical warning as to the unpleasant consequences of having anything to do with pitch."[52] The company complained of infringement of its concession and a denial of justice, while the Venezuelan government alleged that the concession was null and void for breach of contractual obligations. Although the company's involvement in the Matos rebellion to some extent vitiated the moral status of the company, this should not have affected the legal rights at stake. The Venezuelan government endeavored to confuse the title by the subsequent grants to other concessionaires, arguing that under a clause in the concession the Venezuelan courts had jurisdiction. However, the U.S. government replied that it was the concession "itself which is in question and that the action of the Venezuelan Government amounts to its cancellation."[53] The United States therefore insisted on arbitration. This was in itself an equitable point of view and not an unjustifiable claim. However, the Matos connection had severely injured its respectability, which was not initially conspicuous. On January 1, 1905, Venezuela offered to sign a general arbitration treaty for all questions of a legal matter. However, the United States instead offered a general treaty. The Asphalt Company's lawyers prepared a draft for special arbitration, which Venezuela rejected.

The fifth claim was the Crichfield one. The U.S. government wanted Venezuela to withdraw its opposition to the alleged rights of the US-Venezuela Company, an asphalt company, to carry on its business in accordance with the terms of Guzman's concession, which George Washington Crichfield had acquired. Alternatively the rights of the company should be determined and the damages fixed by arbitration. The Venezuelan government based their rejection of the claim on the grounds that the concession was not ratified by Congress. The U.S. government maintained that a 1902 Congressional act ratified all executive acts during the provisional presidency of Castro. The case seemed likely to be compromised on the basis of a recognition by Venezuela of the company's rights, but negotiations dragged on in an apparent attempt by Venezuela to confuse title by reconcession. The claim was omitted from the Note of February 28, 1907, but was reinserted in that of June 2, 1907. The company elected to resume the contract and claim damages.

It was odd that the five claims were apparently listed in inverse order of merit. It appeared almost certain that if the claims were referred to arbitration, only a small amount of them would be awarded. If this was to be allowed on the grounds of rejection of the award, as the U.S. government claimed practically in the Orinoco Steam Ship Company's case, the reluctance of the Venezuelan government to arbitrate was excusable. The Venezuelan government asserted that some of the controversies had already been arbitrated and that the Venezuelan courts had dealt with most other important claims. In addition, it argued that no country should be forced to arbitrate property matters that have already been decided by the courts within its own boundaries. Moreover, one or more of the claimants were not U.S. citizens, and some of the U.S. claimants had encouraged revolutionary activity in Venezuela. Finally, Venezuela stated that the claimants were not entitled to the support of the United States because of the perjury and financial trickery that they employed. As a consequence "if these allegations are true and there are many of them indisputable, further pressure in support of these American claims, to say nothing of coercion, would seem impossible."[54] It was felt by the British that Castro's contentions might hold in a country with a good justice system but that "as individuals may have bad reputations, that Venezuela's conduct has long been regarded the world over as disreputable and tyrannical, and that President Castro has used Courts and Government offices to arbitrarily and wrongfully injure American citizens."[55] If the U.S. Congress gave the administration a mandate to press the matter, two forms of coercion were suggested: the traditional demonstration leading up to the seizure of customs houses or a punitive duty of Venezuelan products.

Rudolph Dolge informed the Venezuelan government on April 5, 1905, that the ownership of the concession had been transferred from the Orinoco Company to the Orinoco Corporation, but this was not accepted. On December 13, 1906 the Federal Court and of Cassation denied the validity of the transfer of the concession to the Orinoco Corporation because the contract was between two parties, and one had not told the other of the transfer, thus rendering the contract null and void. A breach of contract had taken place "and the transfer which the Orinoco Corporation alleges did not have the consent of the National Government, a requirement which was fulfilled with the transfer of the Fitzgerald concession to the Manoa and this in turn to the Orinoco Limited."[56]

In response to Root's request of February 28, 1907, for Venezuela to reconsider the claims and take them to the International Arbitration Court at The Hague, Castro stated that he was willing to come to an amicable solution in the case of Crichfield and the US-Venezuela Asphalt Company. However, he added that this was impossible in the case of the Orinoco Corporation, the Orinoco Steam Ship Company and the NY&B because the local courts had already adjudicated. He added that if the verdicts of the Venezuelan-American Mixed Commission, which were favorable to Venezuela, were revised "by reason of the right which she had on her side, there would be no reason then why the rest of the verdicts of the mixed commission *against* [*sic*] Venezuela should not be revised; verdicts claimed by her in several cases to be contrary to law."[57] Secretary Root replied on June 21, 1907, that Castro's answer was "a simple denial of the correctness of the attitude of this Government."[58] He added that "the curt and contemptuous way in which it ignores or dismisses the serious and respectful representations of the United States produces a painful impression of indifference and disrespect."[59] Nevertheless, Secretary Root wanted Russell to press for arbitration of the claims. On August 13, Russell presented a formal proposal for arbitration that Secretary Root had drafted on June 21. On August 20 the Venezuelan government answered that it would only allow arbitration in Crichfield's case.

The Asphalt Trust in the United States was also finding life difficult. In November 1906 a subsidiary was found to have defrauded the municipality of Philadelphia over five years because it had not adequately completed its paving contract. More seriously, the $10 million suit brought by the Venezuelan government against the NY&B for damages in the Matos revolution was finally decided in favor of the plaintiffs on August 7, 1907. The court ordered the company to make an initial payment of Bs 24 million to the government as compensation of damages.[60] A number of experts were appointed to assess the damage in five other areas of dispute, such as the reduction of revenue and the loss of life. When the verdict was handed down, the *South American Journal* wrote that it would be "unpardonable for the State Department to further lend its countenance to the defendant in its controversy with Castro,"[61] and that the support of a "rebellion against the constitutional authorities would be regarded as sufficient ground for the confiscation of the property of the abettors by any Government in the world."[62]

RELATIONS WITH THE NETHERLANDS DETERIORATE

The Netherlands was another country whose citizens had suffered harassment at the hands of Castro. Venezuelan gunboats continuously seized many small craft that flew the Dutch flag, while many sailors from Curacao, just offshore from Venezuela, had been detained in mainland prisons. The surtax on trade from the island was also a thorn in the side of the colonial authorities. Castro believed that the Netherlands were conducting economic warfare against Venezuela when they introduced on July 26, 1901, a law "which depreciated foreign gold and silver coins in her colonies."[63] Moreover, during the Revolución Libertadora the Dutch had allowed the *Ban Righ* to enter Willemstad, and during the "peaceful blockade" foreign ships had docked there fifty-two times. It was also alleged that Castro wanted to annex the island, something that the Dutch government would allow only if the local population approved such a move. It was also thought that both the United States and Germany were willing to purchase Curacao, something that would not suit Castro. It was better to have Dutch neighbors than Americans or Germans, which is what de Vries, Castro's confidential agent in Amsterdam, recommended at the time.

In September 1904 the Dutch Minister Reus, warned the Venezuelan government that the Dutch warship *Kortenaer* would seize indefinitely all Venezuelan warships that were caught illegally detaining Dutch boats sailing between Curacao and the mainland. Castro reacted by immediately demanding that the island's governor be removed for his unfriendly attitude and that all Venezuelan conspirators on the island be expelled. Venezuelan ships, however, continued interfering with Dutch sailing ships from Curacao. Vessels were seized and their crews imprisoned. Reus could not obtain any satisfaction for his complaints. He became so exasperated that after conferring with the Curacao governor, he recommended in March 1905 lifting the ban on the export of arms to the mainland as the only effective way the Dutch could retaliate. He also recommended seizing any Venezuelan gunboats that were caught detaining merchant vessels between Curacao and Venezuela. Reus informed Castro that his government's desire "was to put to an end, in a legitimate but effective manner, to these seizures of Dutch vessels and the imprisonment of their crews by the Venezuelans, which had become intolerable."[64] He added that Dutch warships would patrol the coastline to protect their ships. Dutch Foreign Minister de Weede explained that at this stage they did not intend to take reprisals for past offenses nor to lift the ban on the export of arms to Venezuela, but he stated that any Venezuelan gunboat found inside the three-mile limit would be impounded. De Weede also issued instructions to Dutch ships to detain Venezuelan gunboats only when Dutch cruisers had caught the Venezuelan vessels seizing or interfering with Dutch shipping. In response Castro recalled Domingo Carvajal, the Venezuelan consul, and in October he prohibited foreign consular agents in Willemstad to clear ships heading for the mainland.

On November 15, 1906, Reus submitted an extensive memorandum to the Venezuelan government that detailed the Dutch grievances, which was surprisingly well received. Castro agreed to exchange diplomatic representatives and to rescind the order that prohibited foreign consuls to clear merchant vessels in the Dutch Antilles. More surprisingly was the amendment of January 12, 1907, which lifted the 30 percent transhipment tax on European and American goods that were channeled through the Antilles. However, the dispute with the Netherlands escalated further, leading to the rupture of diplomatic relations in 1908.

NOTES

1. FO 420/235 P. C. Wyndham to Lord Lansdowne, 28 September 05.
2. FO 420/225 Bax-Ironside to Lansdowne, 30 March 04.
3. According to the newspaper reports the Consul.

Prior to going to bed he forgot to turn off the gas ring where he had boiled water for making a cup of tea. This was at least the version given by the newspapers as well as the conclusion reached by the legal-medical expert team. (J. E. Sauvage, "La Compañía Francesa de Cables Telegráficos y la Revolución Venezolana de 1902–03," in Venezuela, *Venezuela y la Compañía Francesa de Cables Submarinos. Ruidoso Proceso. Documentos Publicados en 'El Constitucional*, Caracas, Imprenta Nacional, 1906, p. 105)

4. FO 420/226 Bax-Ironside to Lansdowne, 2 August 04.
5. William M. Sullivan, "The Rise of Despotism in Venezuela: Cipriano Castro, 1899–1908," PhD. diss., The University of New Mexico, 1974, p. 445.
6. FO 420/233 Wyndham to Lansdowne, 26 May 05.
7. *El Constitucional*, "La Justicia de la Restauración," 8 September 06 in Ven-

ezuela, *Venezuela y la Compañía Francesa de Cables Submarinos. Ruidoso Proceso. Documentos Publicados en "El Constitucional,"* Caracas, Imprenta Nacional, 1906, p. 40.

8. Ibid., p. 39.
9. General Valeriano to C. Castro, 30 September 05, in Venezuela, Venezuela y La Compania Francesa, p. 41.
10. Elihu Root to Jean J. Jusserand, 23 December 05, in Hendrickson, "The New Venezuelan Controversy," p. 97, in Sullivan, p. 449–50.
11. Ibid.
12. FO 420/235 Wyndham to Lansdowne, 22 November 05.
13. CO 295/438 Reginald Lister to Sir Edward Grey, 26 January 06.
14. FO 371/163 Bax-Ironside to Grey, 23 March 06.
15. FO 371/164 Bax-Ironside to Grey 23, February 06.
16. FO 371/162 Bax-Ironside to Grey, 3 December 05.
17. Philip C. Jessup, *Elihu Root*, New York, Dodd, Mead & Co., 1938, p. 495.
18. CO 295/438 Bax-Ironside to Grey, 25 January 06.
19. Ibid.
20. Ibid.
21. Ibid.
22. CO 295/438 General Ybarra to Diplomatic Corps, 21 January 06.
23. CO 295/438 Sir Francis Bertie to Grey, 10 March 06.
24. Ibid.
25. AHM Varios 1905–1909 Clyde Brown to William W. Russell, 4 December 05.
26. Ibid.
27. Ibid.
28. Ibid.
29. Ibid.
30. Ibid.
31. Russell to Root, 26 November 05, in William J. Calhoun, "Wrongs to American Citizens in Venezuela" *Senate Document No. 413,* vol. 24, 60 Cong. 1 Sess., 1907–08, pp. 161–563.
32. Clyde Brown to Russell, 4 December 05, in Calhoun.
33. Russell to Root, 10 December 05, in Calhoun, pp. 161–563.
34. Brown to Russell, 12 December 05, in Calhoun, pp. 161–563; and AHM Varios, 1905–1909.
35. Brown to Russell, 23 December 05, in Calhoun, pp. 161–563; and AHM Varios, 1905–1909.
36. Brown to Russell, 23 December 05, in Calhoun.
37. "Venezuela Is Not Always in the Wrong," *SAJ* 4 November 05.
38. A. Ybarra to Russell, 5 January 06, in Calhoun, pp. 161–563.
39. CO 295/438 Bax-Ironside to Grey, 5 January 06.
40. Ibid.
41. Russell to secretary of state, 29 February 08, in Calhoun, pp. 161–563.
42. FO 371/164 Bax-Ironside to Grey, 23 February 06.
43. FO 371/164 Bax-Ironside to Grey, 19 March 06.
44. Jessup, op. cit., p. 497.
45. FO 199/250 Howard to Grey, 5 February 07.
46. Ibid.

47. FO 199/250 George Young, "Memorandum. United States v. Venezuela," undated.
48. Ibid.
49. Ibid.
50. Ibid.
51. Ibid.
52. Ibid.
53. Ibid.
54. Ibid.
55. Ibid.
56. AHMSGPRCP Julio 1–14 1909 "Memorandúm para el Ministro de Fomento," 23 June 09.
57. Venezuelan Foreign Minister to Minister Russell, 23 April 02. U.S. State Department, "'Venezuela,' Papers Relating to the Foreign Relations of the United States of America," *House Document*, No. 1040, Vol. 1, 60th Cong., 2nd Sess., 1908–09, pp. 774–830, No. 385.
58. E. Root to Russell, 21 June, 07. Ibid., No. 90.
59. Ibid.
60. Calhoun, pp. 919–1038; and Jessup, pp. 494–98.
61. *SAJ*, 11 November 05.
62. Ibid.
63. Sullivan, p. 435.
64. CO 295/434 Sir Henry Howard to Lansdowne, 16 May 05.

9

Castro Starts to Lose His Grip

On the domestic political front, Castro also faced a number of extremely difficult moments up to November 24, 1908, when he was forced to go to Berlin to seek a cure for a kidney complaint. At the end of the Matos revolution the country was satiated with war and wanted a strong government that could lead the country out of the morass it had fallen into. Congress appointed Castro provisional president and Gómez first vice president in 1904.

However, the activities of the revolutionaries in the offshore colonial islands of Curacao and Trinidad continued. Julio Paz Rodríguez, the Venezuelan consul (who was later to become editor of *El Eco Restaurador*), informed Henry Moore Johnson, the governor of Trinidad, in March 1905 that the rebels were meeting almost daily on the island and had "converted the asylum offered by the Government of this Colony into an impregnable bulwark from which they attack with impunity my government."[1] Paz Rodríguez wanted the colonial government to make a public declaration that the revolutionaries could not use the island for their opposition activities. However, the British colonial authorities could only impose sanctions against the revolutionaries if peace and order had been disturbed in Venezuela. As this was not the case there were no grounds on which to interfere, which Hugh Clifford, the colonial secretary, pointed out to the Venezuelan government. Moreover, the island's government did not believe that any of the revolutionaries present offered any threat to Castro's government. They claimed that Antonio Paredes, the most conspicuous rebel on the island in 1905, had "no following whatever and that the empty talk in which he freely indulges is not worthy of serious attention."[2]

In New York in April of that year, J. M. Ortega Martínez, Caribe Vidal, and Horacio Ducharme met to discuss ways of co-operating to depose Castro. At the same time, Gregorio Segundo Riera, Mocho Hernández's lieutenant, tried to secure financial assistance from U.S. sources by promising to award American companies liberal concessions once the new government was in power. In spite of these developments many of the exiled *caudillos* returned to the country after a general amnesty was granted in May 1905. However, the peace of the country would be short-lived. In January 1906, Nicolás Rolando, after receiving word that he was about to be arrested, left Ciudad Bolívar for Trinidad. General Alejandro Ducharme, who left the country disguised as a tourist, followed Rolando.

LA ACLAMACIÓN

The relationship between Castro and Gómez began to turn sour after 1903, and it deteriorated significantly in 1906. Gómez's political standing received a significant boost after he brought peace to the country in July 1903, making it difficult for Castro to get rid of him without a plausible explanation. Moreover, both were partners in numerous business ventures that the entrepreneurial Gómez managed. Gómez therefore became a delicate problem for Castro, especially as he started to believe that his hitherto placid *compadre* now harbored the secret ambition of succeeding him at the helm. Castro decided to weaken Gómez, both politically and financially, by calling in a loan that was estimated at between Bs 200,000 and Bs 600,000. Gómez did not have the wherewithal to repay the loan to the government, but he asked his friend General Antonio Pimentel to lend him the funds. The Banco de Venezuela archives show that the government requested the bank to open a special account on October 10, 1905. Three promissory notes of Bs 259,722.67 each, totaling Bs 779,168.01, were signed by Gómez and Antonio Pimentel[3] and deposited. This covered the payment of the outstanding loan plus interest.

In an extraordinary move Castro tried a new tack in 1906, which was to show Gómez how difficult it was to govern by putting him in charge of the government. In so doing, Castro hoped to demonstrate to Gómez that he did not have the necessary skills to administer a country, despite what his advisers were telling him, and thus he would desist in his ambition to succeed Castro. It is difficult to comprehend Castro's motives because Gómez had already been officially in charge of the government during the difficult period of the "peaceful blockade." In addition, it is unlikely that Gómez would have acted against Castro in the absence of a strong, coordinated opposition. Nevertheless, on April 9, Castro retired from the presidency because of his poor health, his hectic lifestyle, and his need for a rest. The following day Castro took José Rafael Revenga, Ramón Tello Mendoza, and Julio Torres Cárdenas, collectively known as the Valenciano doctors, and left on the train for La Victoria, "The Sacred city of the Restoration" as Gumersindo Rivas, the director of *El Constitucional*, described it. A day after arriving in La Victoria, on April 11, Castro left for a tour of western Venezuela. The state presidents received him with great pomp and ceremony, and in spite of the pain he had to endure he continued to give long speeches. The Valenciano doctors considered Castro's political maneuver to be unnecessary and dangerous because it placed too much power in the hands of the vice president. They wanted General Linares Alcántara to take over instead. Interior Minister Julio Torres Cárdenas in particular could not understand Castro's game plan. He confessed to Alcántara, who had an army of four thousand men stationed in Aragua, that he wanted to know "what moved General Castro to undertake such an unnecessary political manoeuvre."[4] Castro's supporters, particularly Tello Mendoza, who was against Gómez because he had taken away "some very juicy income from the slaughterhouse business of Caracas"[5] started the idea of La Aclamación. This would lead to friction between Gómez and Castro because the former felt that the latter had instigated the whole maneuver.

At the instigation of Tello Mendoza, Carlos Bejarano García, the editor of *El Industrial* of La Victoria, the capital of Aragua, wrote an editorial that attacked the government of Gómez and mentioned for the first time the idea of La Aclamación. General Alcántara, the president of Aragua, arrested the journalist because he had been disrespectful to Gómez. Alcántara felt that there was no need for friction between Castro and Gómez. Moreover, if Castro wanted to return to the presidency, there was little doubt that Gómez would agree. A movement for Castro's return, Alcántara reasoned, would only serve to give Gómez more importance than he deserved. However, Castro was sure that Gómez would not move against him even though both José Rosario García and Leopoldo Baptista, Gómez's chief advisers, encouraged the vice president to do so because they thought he would be better for Venezuela than the *cabito*. Castro was so confident of his position that he gave Gómez a list of the people he should appoint as ministers. Castro wanted Lucio Baldó as Secretary General and Lorenzo Carvallo as Governor of Caracas. Castro believed that the game played by the Valenciano doctors, in particular Tello Mendoza, was counterproductive. So at the end of April he travelled to Caracas with Alcántara to put a stop to it.

On Castro's return to Caracas, Lorenzo Carvallo ensured that no official met him at the train station. Only the chauffeur sent by his wife was there to take him to his home at Villa Zoila, where he found to his consternation that there was no police protection for Doña Zoila. Castro soon learned from reports from Manuel Corao and Graciano Castro that there was an anti-Castro campaign in Caracas and that his life was at risk without proper protection. It was clear that Castro was *persona non grata* in certain official circles. Gómez's close entourage was convinced that the cabito had been the inspiration for the article in *El Industrial* and was acting accordingly. Alcántara saw Gómez and convinced him that this was not the case. The vice president later met Castro at Villa Zoila where they discussed the composition of the new cabinet, as this had not been announced. The list of possible ministers that Gómez handed to Castro did not please the president, and it would be a source of friction in the ensuing months that formed the basis of the first serious dispute between Castro and Gómez. When Gómez mentioned Arístides Tellería as the new development minister, Castro became extremely agitated, reminding the vice president that Tellería was an enemy of the "cause" and that during the Revolución Libertadora Gómez had wanted to execute him. Castro realized at this juncture that he could no longer take for granted the loyalty of Gómez. He also realized that he would have to work hard in order to regain the initiative from his *compadre*. Alcántara also saw Castro about certain appointments. He felt that the appointment of Diego Antonio Carvajal as governor of the federal district was not appropriate, especially as he had been a previous enemy of Castro's and would be unable to work with Diego Carnevali Monreal as secretary to the governor. Castro then appointed Luis Mata Illas as governor.

Although it was generally felt that Gómez had his hands tied by Castro, the acting president surprised everybody when he reorganized the cabinet on May 1. He brought in Leopoldo Baptista as interior minister and Arístides Tellería as development minister, fueling a certain amount of amazement and jealousy. Gómez's other appointments were José de Jesus Paúl as foreign minister, Francisco de Sales Pérez as finance minister, Luis Mata Illas as public works minister, Carlos León as education minister, Lucio Baldó as secretary general, and Alejandro Ybarra as governor of Caracas. As a security measure Gómez hid a cache of mauser carbines on Pimentel's estates.

Castro interpreted the appointment of Gómez's own cabinet as a reaction against him. It was also taken by the wider public as a sign that Castro's health was in worse shape than had first been thought, and conspiracies and plots soon hatched. Castro returned to Caracas on May 15 with the belief that he was almost invincible and that he would stay in power forever because Congress and the state presidents were his friends and had been appointed by him. Castro at the country's barracks "had the men he had used in his most recent campaign and General Manuel Salvador Araujo, the hero of Ciudad Bolívar, as his War and Navy Minister."[6] Moreover, all his opponents were either in jail or exiled. There now existed, however, a possible challenge from Gómez, which needed to be dealt with swiftly. It was clear to Castro that the only way he could return to power and put an end to any pretensions that Gómez harbored was by organizing a plebiscite to support his return. The country, according to the exiles, was waiting for Gómez to act. However, the "liberating gesture of Gómez was to fall on his knees before the well-known drunken henchmen and merrily sign the papers presented by the followers of the satrap, with a dagger in one hand and an ironic smile on their faces."[7] Gómez, however, knew the game that Castro was playing and would not fall into the trap of moving too early against his *compadre*.

Castro did not remain in Caracas for the May 23 celebrations, preferring to return to the relative safety of La Victoria, where he had transferred eight thousand mauser carbines and six million rounds of ammunition and from where he could start his campaign to return to public life. On the anniversary of his revolution on May 23, Castro issued a proclamation, *Ofrenda a Mi Patria*, at La Victoria. He painted a picture of himself as a martyr, and he ratified his desire to retire from public life. The following day Gómez, who was advised by José Rosario García, asked Castro to return and take over the presidency because he was unable to deal with the country's political situation. Gómez urged Castro to "take over the government and guide the country in a proper direction."[8] Gómez wanted Castro to return to Caracas as soon as possible because "I am aware of the urgency in calming the excitement which has been produced and if it continued would cause great harm to the Republic."[9] Gómez said that he would then retire from politics "for my family and will then have achieved peacefulness which is my only aspiration."[10] However, Gómez demanded "protection for my friends who are also yours, and who I will demand should give their loyal support to the government as a pressing need for the Cause and the Fatherland."[11] There was no reply from Castro. Gómez threatened to resign from the presidency, and Castro then offered on May 27 "to be at your side, heading your private office in order to immediately proceed to the reorganization of the Republic."[12] While Congress met to discuss Gómez's resignation, he telegraphed Castro. Gómez proposed meeting at Los Teques for a final understanding, but Castro paid no attention. Gómez then threatened to convene Congress for a special session and present his resignation as vice president if Castro did not take charge of the government, but the president felt that Gómez should go ahead and do what he pleased. Nevertheless, the differences were patched up on June 5, when Gómez travelled to La Victoria for a meeting with Castro. Gómez returned to Caracas on June 8 and made several changes to his cabinet. Two of his ministers, Carlos León and Arístides Tellería, resigned from their posts to allow for the reconciliation between Gómez and Castro. Later exiled, León travelled to New York while Tellería left for Havana.[13]

As a result of Castro's May 23 speech, the idea of forming the Juntas de Aclamación gained steam. Two delegates from each state first met in Caracas on June 10 and then proceeded to La Victoria to ask Castro to return to Miraflores. On June 11 the delegates from thirteen states and the federal district of Caracas gathered in La Victoria to form the Asamblea Plebiscitaria. They then presented Castro with the proclamations of the people, requesting his return to the presidency, which would now be for six years after Congress reformed the constitution in 1905. Castro accepted the request and returned to Caracas on July 4, assuming the presidency a day later. Gómez had to accept the result out of political necessity. The exiled press described Gómez's behavior when he handed over power to Castro:

> [T]he vice-president made the hand-over as somebody who is getting rid of something which is heavy with dishonour. In that tribe of idiots, Gómez is the only-begotten with the virtue of the under-privileged and the only man to show geniality, a courageous fighter and of honest civil connections. . . . Without the strength of his arm, the restoration foetus would have been torn apart in the Andes.[14]

Castro's new government was able to come to terms with some of the exiles, allowing Matos to reacquire his embargoed properties in August after paying the treasury Bs 60,000. Castro also returned the confiscated properties of generals J. M. Ortega Martínez and Amabile Solagnie, who were released from prison together with Nicolás Rolando, Francisco Vásquez, Ramón Guerra, Horacio Ducharme and more than one hundred others. The *caudillos* quickly returned to their respective regional power bases to reestablish their political hold. Nicolás Rolando was powerful in the eastern and central parts of the country. Gregorio Segundo Riera went to Coro. Roberto Vargas went to the Llanos. Amabile Solagnie went to Lara. Zoilo Vidal went to Guayana. David Gimón went to Guárico. Francisco Vásquez went to Sucre. Mocho Hernández acted on a national level. The rebels had little intention of remaining inactive, but they decided to bide their time before once again taking up arms against the Castro government. A situation for revolt presented itself sooner than they had anticipated because two months after taking power, Castro suffered a serious illness and left for Macuto. Once again it appeared that the future of his presidency was in the balance. A number of political factions, such as the Alcantaristas, the Gomecistas, and the Castristas were playing for the ultimate prize.

LA CONJURA

The year 1907 was marked by a palace conspiracy, the almost fatal disease of Castro, an abortive insurrection led by General Paredes, and "the gradual exacerbation of the relations with the United States as a result of the persistent refusal of the Venezuelan Government to reopen the question of the American claims."[15] At the beginning of 1907 the revolutionary newspaper published in Paris, *Venezuela. Ecos de una Tiranía,* referred to the pressing need of succession. The paper indicated that Gómez, who was "the direct heir," had broken with the Valencian *camarilla* by indicating that he would be willing to govern with the *caudillos* who took part in the Revolución Libertadora because they were the only honest men left in the country, but they were disliked by the "eunuchs which rule in the regency, and the anguish of the future disaster make them think of a new dauphin."[16] The revolutionaries, however, could not accept Gómez "because it implied acknowledging the legality of Castro."[17] Therefore, they could not sanction his position as heir apparent. The *Venezuela. Ecos de una Tiranía* newspaper was even more scathing toward Alcántara, calling him a "pupil of a seraglio of eunuchs"[18] who "we ignore whether he possesses the childish naivety of imagining whether he can take over the government to perpetuate *Castrismo*."[19]

Gómez was nevertheless beginning to be considered as a serious contender to replace Castro, especially now that the president's health had deteriorated again. Although Vice President Gómez would succeed Castro in the event of his death, it was by no means certain that the Valenciano doctors would allow Gómez to remain in power. The Valencia clique of Torres Cárdenas, Tello Mendoza, Revenga, and Corao felt that "whoever reaches power will need them unavoidably."[20] Gómez therefore started to curry favor from all those whom he felt would support him.

The country's international relations was one important area that needed to be addressed, and Gómez wanted support. In January 1907, Gustavo Sanabria, the former foreign affairs minister, informed the British minister of Gómez's intentions if he came to power, assuring Bax-Ironside that "every effort will be made to place Venezuelan relations with Foreign Powers on a more amicable footing than is now the case, and that General Gómez will make special endeavours to conciliate Great Britain and France."[21] The British, however, had been relatively well treated by Castro. Up to the end of 1906, Bs 8.75 million out of the Bs 9,458,150 of the British claims awarded at the 1903 Mixed Commission had been paid. Gómez also intimated to the U.S. minister that as head of state he would settle all outstanding issues with foreign companies and modify the existing mining laws to attract foreign capital.

At the same time, José Lastre, who had been expelled from Venezuela in 1906, started publishing in San Juan, Puerto Rico, a "genuinely constitutionalist" newspaper called *Gómez Unico*, whose owners "are real friends of the Restoration Cause, upholders of the law and its honest principles."[22] The paper considered Castro to be demented, deranged, and unable to govern. The paper called for Gómez to legally succeed Castro. It praised Gómez as "humble, a democrat, a good friend, loyal and determined, who only gathers praise for his virtues."[23] It also stated that the country demanded the presence of Gómez "in power to counteract the pretension of that circle of innocuous plotters who have accompanied Castro in his dangerous wilfulness in power for over eight years."[24] But Gómez was "blind with that man, who even though he is feeling the effect of the evil poison of the felony of Don Cipriano, does not want to believe the counsel of his friends."[25] The paper added that the main supporters of Castro, "those thieves"[26] such as Torres Cárdenas, Celis, Velutini, Revenga, Tello Mendoza, Alcántara, Cecilio Castro, Carnevali, Delgado Chalbaud, J. J. Briceño, Régulo Olivares, Sarmiento, Jorge Bello, and Uzcátegui were "the chums of that lucky man who is devoured by envy, who is dominated by vengeance, who is blinded by his thirst for power."[27] Gómez could count on the support of the newspaper backers, who remained unknown but who were "friends of action with the country, who will second his rise to power in order to save Venezuela from the fate which the will of a man without morals and respect has plunged the country."[28] It was imperative, the paper stated, that all of Gómez's friends united to bring him to power, so that with him "in power, with his renowned and irreproachable honesty, the government will demonstrate with practical deeds a general development in all spheres."[29] It is unlikely that Gómez had anything to do with this newspaper. It could have been a maneuver to get rid of Castro rather than to bring Gómez to power.

Castro's kidney trouble returned with a vengeance in February 1907. The president had to undergo a difficult operation. Some medical experts believed that he would probably not wake up from the operating table, while others only gave even odds that he would recover satisfactorily. With the possible demise of Castro the political fighting intensified. Two clear groups developed that had first come to light during La Aclamación: the Valenciano-caraqueño doctors and the supporters of Gómez. Gómez, who was described at the time by Bax-Ironside as a "particular villainous looking cut throat,"[30] was clearly going to defend his position, using force if necessary. There were two conspiracies during this period, which was known as La Conjura. Gómez and all the Andino generals and colonels who were annoyed at Castro and opposed the Valencia clique headed one plot. The old Revolución Libertadora *caudillos*, who were organizing a new invasion overseas and had the support of a number of conspirators in the interior of the country, headed the other faction. Antonio Paredes was one of the most important people in this second conspiracy. Gómez's support came mainly from the Tachirense soldiers he had stationed outside Caracas; certain large landowners; and certain large trading houses which were increasingly disgruntled at the way the country was being governed, and so gave him political and monetary support. General Santiago Briceño Ayesterán offered to raise five thousand soldiers in Lara to support Gómez, while other Tachirenses also rallied around him. Gómez also enlisted the help of Doña Zoila, Castro's wife. The *New York Herald* wrote in January 1907 that Gómez would ensure peace in the event of Castro's demise, that he had the support of Castro's enemies abroad, and that if "Mr. Gómez is called to the Presidency . . . he would insure the exact fulfilment of obligations to foreign nations, and that he would cultivate friendly relations with other countries and try to attract foreign capital and immigration."[31]

On the other side, the Valenciano doctors were equally determined to remain in power. José Rafael Revenga, Castro's Secretary General, and Julio Torres Cárdenas, the Interior minister, assumed increasingly important roles. They were adamant that if Castro died, they would prevent Gómez from taking over. Eliseo Sarmiento, José Antonio Velutini, and Román Delgado Chalbaud, head of the country's tiny navy, were also opposed to Gómez. There was a press campaign in *El Porvenir* and *El Combate* that called for Gómez's resignation. As his operation drew closer Castro placed government troops on alert in Maracay and La Guaira, ordering Eliseo Sarmiento, the Carabobo commander in arms, to be prepared for an uprising in his barracks. The order went out to Román Delgado Chalbaud to place his small navy on alert at Puerto Cabello. Castro reinforced Maracay's battalions with four thousand mauser carbines and one million rounds of ammunition.

To ensure political success, both political groups needed the support of Linares Alcántara, the powerful Aragua *caudillo* who remained undecided as to whom he should support. It was important for each side to win him over because of his large army. Linares Alcántara, the son of Francisco Linares Alcántara, one of Guzmán Blanco's presidents, was the first Venezuelan to graduate from the West Point Military Academy. He had first made contact with Castro through Diego Castillo, the Venezuelan consul in Cúcuta, who took kindly to him because he thought he was a man with great military potential. When Castro visited Caracas in 1898, Alcántara's home was the only one where the *cabito* was received. Castro asked Alcántara to join the 1899 rebellion, but he refused because of his pledged support to Andrade. Nevertheless, after he achieved power in 1899, Castro appointed Alcántara *Jefe Expedicionario* and then president of Aragua, where his family had a loyal following of five thousand men known as the "cabezones"[32] of Aragua.

Alcántara at this stage would not support Gómez, something he made clear to Colmenares Pacheco when they met in La Victoria. Although Colmenares Pacheco argued that the cause would continue with Gómez, Alcántara was noncommittal, stating that all state presidents had a particular duty to follow. Gómez's advisers were surprised and alarmed by such a rebuttal. They feared that their approach to Alcántara would reach Castro's ears in Macuto. The only solution was for Gómez to travel to the seaside resort and explain to his *compadre* as best he could his intentions. Alcántara was also undecided as to whether he would support the Valenciano doctors because of his own desire to succeed Castro. Alcántara thought that it was the right time to strike but Angel Carnevali Monreal convinced him not to go against the convalescing president. Alcántara informed Briceño Núñez, the conspirators' commissioner, that he would not take up arms against Castro because he owed his allegiance to him, and in the event of his death would go against Gómez. To secure Alcántara's loyalty, Castro appointed him head of the army and had Delgado Chalbaud and Eliseo Sarmiento report to him. Alcántara discussed the possibility of toppling Castro with the two pro-Castro supporters, but they reached an agreement that became known as the "Pacto de la Cabrera," which was that they would take over the government if Castro was to fall severely ill. Delgado Chalbaud, who controlled the navy, would take Sarmientos' troops to La Guaira while Alcántara's troops would reach Caracas by train from Maracay where they were billeted.

PAREDES INVADES

There is little doubt that the government was in disarray because Castro was ill. The exiles took advantage of the situation to mount their own bid for power. At the same time Gómez and his supporters felt that their time had come to take over the presidency. While building up their hidden arsenal in Trinidad the exiles had been preparing their invasion of Venezuela. In October 1906, Sir H. M. Jackson, the governor of Trinidad, was informed by Villegas Pulido, the Venezuelan consul, that a consignment of fifty revolvers, two thousand cartridges, and fifty machetes were expected to arrive on the island, while a further shipment of one thousand rifles and seven hundred thousand cartridges would arrive in November from New York. All the arms were intended for Antonio Paredes' uprising. The Venezuelan government wanted the colonial authorities to prohibit the transfer of the arms from the customs house to the rebels, but the island authorities refused, alleging that this would hamper trade. In the past, when the Venezuelan government had requested the introduction of measures that prevented the possibility of arms and ammunition being exported to Venezuela, the colonial authorities had agreed to consider these requests if the Venezuelans removed or mitigated the 30 percent surtax that was imposed on trade between the two countries. As Venezuela had refused to consider such a measure, Sir H. M. Jackson was not "inclined to give something for nothing, at the request of a Consular Officer, the advantages which his Government has declined to negotiate for with His Majesty's Minister at Caracas."[33] The governor therefore replied to Villegas Pulido that unless he received proof that the arms were intended for "warlike purposes,"[34] he could not interfere with the legitimate trade between the two countries. Jackson further stated that once it was established that the arms were for the rebels, then special precautions would be taken.

Although Villegas Pulido was convinced that the arms were for the rebels and informed the colonial authorities of his view, nothing transpired until early January, when the police received information that a further shipment of revolvers had been cleared "by a man known to be on friendly terms with the Venezuelan revolutionary party, and that recruiting was going on and an expedition being prepared for an early start."[35] The police were also informed that a number of men were leaving that evening from a pier two miles from Port of Spain. Upon hearing this news the governor published a Gazette Extraordinary calling attention to Sections 11 and 12 of the Foreign Enlistment Act, warning any locals of the consequences if they were to join the rebels. This would prove to be a great blow to the revolutionaries because recruitment stopped immediately. That evening the pier was watched while the police patrolled the bay. Three boats were spotted at the pier, manned by men who were placing arms on the boats, "but as soon as the search light of the launch was turned on them, they disembarked and dispersed."[36] The following morning one of the men went to the police and confessed that he and the others "had been recruited for work in Venezuela by a Venezuelan whom he did not know, but whom his followers addressed as 'General.' "[37] The police were further informed that Paredes "was very indignant at the actions of this Government, which he considered had no right to interfere to protect President Castro's Government."[38] Paredes intended to use a steamer to pick up small groups of men who were located at different islands at the entrance to the Gulf of Paria. On January 13 the HMS *Indefatigable*, at the request of the island's governor, arrived from Barbados to patrol the entrance of the Gulf of Paria. However, it did not encounter a rebel ship after two nights, and so it departed for Kingston, Jamaica, on January 16. On February 4, Paredes invaded Venezuela near Barrancas in the Uracoa region, taking arms from the customs house "after a short exchange of fire and left towards Uracoa, probably with the intention of attacking Maturín."[39]

On February 9, 1907, Castro had an operation for a fistula of the urinary tract[40] (an opening from the urethra or bladder to the perineum) at his residence in Macuto. A team of doctors headed by José Rafael Revenga, and which included Pablo Acosta Ortiz, David Lobo, José Antonio Baldó, and Adolfo Bueno performed the operation. The makeshift operating theatre was surrounded by soldiers with orders to kill the surgeons if Castro did not wake up. During the operation Castro ceased breathing; in spite of the threat to their lives, Dr. Acosta Ortiz stopped using chloroform. Although Castro responded and started to breathe again, the surgeons did not continue with the operation, and they sutured the wound. Castro was later informed by his doctors that he would have to have surgery abroad.

While Castro was convalescing from his operation, he received news on February 13 that Paredes had been captured at El Rosario, near Morichal Largo. Castro ordered General Luis Varela to "give immediate orders to shoot Paredes and his officers. Advise me of receipt and fulfilment."[41] According to Rafael Gandeca, General Varela handed him a letter to deliver to Jesús García, which contained the order to kill Paredes. H. Torrelles carried out the order on February 15 on the steamer *Socorro* on the Orinoco River. The body was thrown overboard together with seventeen other officers who had also been shot dead. Pedro Mata recovered the body of Paredes, who had been shot twice, from the Orinoco and buried it on his estate.[42]

At the time the regime was divided into two factions: those who wanted a coup and those who were willing to protect the constitutional rights. Both parties disliked Gómez, who was perceived as more of a hindrance than an asset to their plans. Gómez wanted an end to the conspiracy because he needed the support of the conspirators both at home and abroad to reach the presidency. On February 20, a few days after Paredes' death, a fly sheet appeared in La Guaira that accused Castro of murder and of expropriating money from the treasury. It stated that

> Venezuela cries for this new shame launched against its haughty forehead by the criminals. Wretched ill-treatment! There are still more than sufficient worthy offspring, courageous and unselfish citizens, honourable men who have never yielded to the restoration, and have never served it, others who were scorned and later abandoned its poisonous ranks because of all its ignominy, and they will seek revenge and redeem you. Mother, Venezuela, you will be rehabilitated.[43]

This is the first time that the theme of *rehabilitación* appears, which would be subsequently used by Gómez in his December 1908 coup. There was a certain amount of confidence in the Gómez camp that he would soon become president, which was illustrated by the senseless murder of Luis Mata Illas,[44] the recently appointed governor of Caracas. On January 27, Eustoquio Gómez and Isaías Nieto started drinking heavily in the bars of Caracas. As they got more inebriated they started shouting "Viva Gómez." Upon hearing about the unruly behavior, Gómez ordered Mata Illas to detain Eustoquio, whose consumption of liquor had "induced a madness to all those present at the bar"[45] culminating when "suddenly a number of revolver shots against the ceiling and the floor were made in order to make the women who worked there jump."[46] Mata Illas tried to reason with Eustoquio, but it was difficult to persuade him to leave the bar. Just as the governor was about to depart, Rafael de la Cova shouted "police," at which point it appears as though everybody opened fire, fatally wounding Mata Illas. Dr. Antonio Miguel Letterón examined the body at the Hospital Vargas, where it was found to have "various wounds caused by different calibre bullets."[47] The cause of death was "the large haemorrhage which followed the wound made at the convex side of the liver."[48] Although the death of Mata Illas was not premeditated, it did not endear Gómez to Castro. Eustoquio Gómez, Isaías Nieto, and Milton Martínez were detained for the murder of the Caracas governor.

CASTRO RECOVERS

Once Castro recovered sufficiently from his surgery toward the end of February, he was able to go on the attack. He wanted to ascertain for himself what was really happening in the country. He threatened to send to prison anybody who did not tell him the truth because, as he wrote to Leopoldo Torres, "this means peace for the Republic, the tranquillity of the families and general social well-being"[49] because "you know that it is necessary to amputate when one tries to save a body which has a gangrenous limb, as up to now science and civilization have been unable to discover another method."[50] At this time Gómez found it expedient to make a trip to the interior of the country. Upon his return to Caracas he slept in a different house every evening because he feared for his life. The reasoning was that as first vice president Gómez would succeed Castro in the event of the latter's death, and the Castrista group would want to get rid of him. Gómez later described an assassination attempt by the Valenciano doctors. This occurred when Gómez was invited by General Félix Galavís to go to the La Vaquera estate, where he found Carnevali, Celis and others. He also saw a peasant ploughing with two bullocks. Gómez thought instinctively that this was an assassin, and he approached him with his hand on his gun to inquire about his ploughing technique. The man was shaking like a leaf and was unable to go through with the assassination. Gómez then confronted the men in the house. Celis stated later, "gentlemen, I am withdrawing from the conspiracy as we can not beat Gómez."[51]

Gómez redoubled his efforts to win Doña Zoila's confidence, so that she would convince her husband that he was not about to double-cross his *compadre*. Gómez also spoke openly about the need for Castro to remain alive because he was the only person who could guarantee peace, as "his death would be an immense setback for Venezuela and his followers, especially the Tachirenses, and that he, as his best friend, would feel like an orphan without his support."[52]

Castro's health continued to concern his physician. Many of his closest allies believed that he would soon die. Doña Zoila clearly shared this view and, fearing for her husband's health, increased her efforts to get Castro to go abroad for an operation. Doña Zoila reasoned that Castro had a sufficiently close group of friends, headed by Gómez, who had shown their complete loyalty to the *cabito* and would look after his interests. José Ignacio Cárdenas, Castro's agent in Europe, was instructed to find a suitable surgeon and clinic for the president's operation. Cárdenas convinced Castro of the need to go to Europe, recommending a clinic in Berlin.

It appeared, especially to Doña Zoila, whose influence grew in direct relationship to her husband's illness, that Gómez was the only guarantee that Castro had of retaining power. As a result of Castro's illness Doña Zoila was perceived, especially by the exiled revolutionaries, to have taken over the running of the government. It was widely rumored that Doña Zoila

> had ordered three thousand soldiers from the Andes because she only has faith in her fellow countrymen, less romantic than her spouse and as she is not unaware that Cipriano Castro is hated in the whole Republic, the kind lady inundated the capital with half-savage henchmen, with faces that recall the prehistoric statues of the ancient idols of Mauritania, and as a strong lady within that circle of iron, debates, growls and puts her oar into everything . . . She has relegated Vice-President Gómez—that an adverse destiny has lead him to occupy each year a more ridiculous role—to a third level; no minister dares to make a decision without prior approval, and even the august sick-man lives listening to her reprimands. This does not mean that the lady does not possess honesty and a good reputation.[53]

There were two groups that wanted to eliminate Gómez from political life. There was the Valencia doctors, and there was a second group that was composed of Delgado Chalbaud, Eliseo Sarmiento, and Graciano Castro. Both parties wooed Alcántara. However, as Blanco Fombona wrote, Alcántara was "a player who aspires to win without taking risks."[54] Eliseo Sarmiento, who commanded the Valencia garrison, and Delgado Chalbaud, who was head of the Venezuelan navy, were itching to stage a coup. However, the notion that they should wait until after Castro's death prevailed. To neutralize Alcántara as a possible threat, Gómez suggested that he join a political alliance that he was forming with all his Tachirense friends to support Castro, because there was a strong possibility of the exiles mounting another revolution. Alcántara went to Macuto, to visit the convalescing Castro, and was confronted by the rumor that he had been organizing a political alliance to take over the government. Although Alcántara protested his innocence, Castro suspected him. The Valencian doctors later left the country.

Fearful that Alcántara would turn against him, Castro appointed him president of Bolívar state, a remote part of the country that was far away from Alcántara's political power base in Aragua. Later, when Castro resumed the presidency, he averted a civil war because he started to remove many Alcanteristas from office and, for good measure, ordered a battalion in Maracay to guard Gómez. Castro, having recovered somewhat from his illness, spoke with Gómez on March 1, 1907, for four hours, during which he "formalized the rapprochement that had been begun by the benevolent efforts of Zoila Castro."[55] Gómez was in a strong position. He had weakened Alcántara and, with the support of Leopoldo Baptista, "who was encamped at Carora, Lara, with 6,000 men,"[56] gained "complete control over the garrisons and ammunition supplies of Caracas."[57] A ministerial crisis was expected in April, but when Gómez went to Villa Ignacia where Castro was staying in Macuto, he went straight into the president's bedroom without having to announce his arrival, "which proves that between them they have good intelligence."[58] The reorganization of the army took place and all the "appointments for the head of the first and second battalions made lately have fallen on individuals who are clearly Gomecistas."[59]

On June 13, Castro forced the entire cabinet to resign after he discovered that an overdraft of Bs 7.7 million had been built up at the Banco de Venezuela and that "four million bolivars had been misappropriated from the Public Works Ministry."[60] José Rafael Revenga, the surgeon who had operated on Castro, was out of the cabinet and appointed consul in Rome. Governor Angel Carnevali Monreal, who had replaced Mata Illas, was also removed for pilfering Bs 213,271 from municipal receipts. Gustavo Sanabria replaced him. Castro also introduced new government reforms by establishing, on August 2, state juntas "to receive and distribute all funds for local government and six days later named a new Cabinet."[61] Castro also appointed new state presidents because he found certain states to be lacking in loyalty, honesty, and political circumspection. Castro did not allow Gómez to resign as first vice president. Gómez's conduct during the murder of Mata Illas was irreproachable. He attended the funeral and did not interfere in the arrest of his cousin Eustoquio.

José de Jesús Paúl, the newly appointed foreign affairs minister, saw Bax-Ironside in May 1907 and expressed succinctly the fears that many of Castro's supporters were having about the government. He stated that the *cabito* had no chance of recovering from his illness and that he remained "stubborn and difficult, nay impossible to manage; it was as useful to enter into a discussion with him as to talk to a stone wall. I quote the Minister's own words."[62]

Although Castro was now out of medical danger, his popularity was certainly waning. The general view was that at some stage he would have to leave the presidency because his administration was leading the country down a very uncertain route, the outcome of which was further political unrest and economic chaos. However, apart from the abortive Paredes rebellion, the exiled revolutionaries did not seem to pose a threat to the government at the beginning of 1907. Arístides Tellería, Munchi Leyba, and Miguel Bethencourt met regularly at a place called Librería in Curacao. Since his arrival in March on the island, Tellería had declared his admiration for Gómez.[63] Later, Namias de Crasto spoke with Cornet, Riera's father-in-law, who stated that Cornet had said that "if Castro and Riera reach an understanding then there is no revolution that is worth anything."[64] When Leopoldo Baptista had been in Curacao, he had seen Riera but "did not want any type of involvement."[65] In April of that year Mocho Hernández was in London. By the middle of 1907 the rumors of an impending revolution decreased. Castro was not surprised at this "because the revolutionaries in Venezuela can be compared with the bogeyman which the house servants use to frighten the goats. Those who want to breach the peace do not count with chiefs who can fight, nor with people who will follow them, nor with arms with which to fight."[66]

CASTRO'S LUCK RUNS OUT

In 1907, Castro had narrowly escaped both dying from a fistula complaint and being deposed from the presidency. Castro's political judgement, let alone the moral issue, in the Paredes affair was questionable, and the increasing monopolies that he awarded himself and his cronies were strangling the economy. The deteriorating economic conditions led the government, on November 11 of that year, to increase by 10 percent the tariffs levied on the sale of rice, corn, wheat, beans, and lentils. There was also a 25 percent increase on the sale of common bottles, sterilized milk, soda, crystal, and felt hats. Castro's rationale behind the increase was to "give greater protection to the national development of agriculture and industry."[67] Castro continued to monopolize all the commercial activity of the country for himself and his close associates, including Gómez. Castro's personal fortune, according to *Venezuela. Ecos de Una Tiranía*, was based on the following monopolies: cattle, tobacco, alcohol, salt, postage and the mint. He also owned the Puerto Cabello lighthouse, the Coro railway line, most of the shares in the Táchira railway, the bonds of the Puerto Cabello harbor, and the exclusive navigation rights for the Zulia River, Lake Maracaibo, and the Orinoco river. Castro also held a stake in the Caracas Tramway Company, the Caracas Brewery, the light and gas companies of Caracas, the asphalt deposits at Bermúdez and Zulia, the telephone company, the lighthouse and tramway of Carúpano, and the port of Maracaibo. He also owned wheat and maize-milling plants, oil concessions, a paper factory, and the best houses in Caracas, Valencia, and La Victoria. Castro had also acquired the following estates, with the purchase price given in parentheses: La Candelaria (Bs 200,000), El Banco (Bs 150,000), and the Mariana stables (Bs 250,000). Castro, however, was punctual at paying the government's foreign debts and the considerable sums borrowed from the Banco de Venezuela to finance the war against Matos were "honourably and promptly paid."[68]

Political opposition grew stronger because of the worsening economic conditions. Most of the defeated *caudillos* of the Revolución Libertadora who had returned from exile after the May 1905 general amnesty now began to prepare for Castro's downfall. Toward the end of 1907, reports reached the government that there was an increase in political activity among the revolutionaries and that they had the possibility of arming themselves. One can trace the beginning of the end of Castro's administration to this period, when the excesses of his rule and his tempestuous whims alienated hitherto staunch supporters of his regime. What was not certain was whether Gómez would end up in Miraflores. Clearly, the removal of

Castro would leave Gómez as the constitutional successor, but most people did not consider him to be a serious contender. Many of the regional *caudillos* remained abroad, waiting for the right moment to launch their revolutionary bids. By the end of 1907, Doña Zoila had completely reconciled her differences with Gómez because he offered the best guarantee that her wealth would be safeguarded in the event of her husband's death. According to *Venezuela. Ecos de una Tiranía*, Doña Zoila "only forgets the most essential: the hatred which her friends inspire. It is not the 'Restoration' as the current regime calls the country but 'Devastation.' "[69]

Gómez had a number of advantages in his quest for power. In spite of what contemporary accounts said of him, he had displayed courage and military skill while defeating the strong regional *caudillos* during the Revolucion Libertadora. He had also shown considerable political skill in maintaining his position as the regime's second strongest man, especially during La Aclamación and La Conjura. His dexterous, acute political touch allowed him to step through a political minefield. He managed to keep his position while others, such as Linares Alcántara, had been banished to distant regions. Gómez was also the constitutional successor. Possibly most important of all, he controlled a relatively large army from Táchira, which he made sure was loyal to him by feeding and paying the soldiers well for work on his various estates that were dotted around Aragua and Carabobo. Gómez therefore emerged from La Conjura stronger politically. He entered, possibly for the first time, into the national political equation as a force to be reckoned with.

The fear of foreign intervention was always present among certain government officials. It was only five years since the country had experienced the "peaceful blockade." There appeared the threat of a repeat performance now that France had broken off relations, and there seemed no way of solving the American question or, for that matter, the Dutch grievances. With the United States becoming more aggressive and impatient over its claims, the fear among certain circles close to the government was that Venezuela could come under direct U.S. influence, possibly becoming a sort of American protectorate. The fate of Cuba was a lesson that some in Caracas took very seriously. They did not want to witness the same thing in Venezuela. Consequently, José de Jesús Paúl assured the British minister in May 1907 that with the demise of Castro, the new government of Gómez, which would be formed in accordance with the constitution, would considerably improve foreign relations. He added that he hoped the new government "would be welcomed by the Great Powers."[70]

NOTES

1. CO 295/432 Julio Paz Rodríguez to Henry Moore Johnson, 14 March 05.
2. CO 295/432 Johnson to P.C.H. Wyndham, undated.
3. Almost two years later, on July 16, 1907, the finance minister informed the

Banco de Venezuela that they should receive from Pimentel and Gómez the sum of Bs 400,000 to be deposited in the *cuenta especial* and that it should also accept another promissory note signed by Pimentel and Gómez for Bs 400,000, which would expire on March 31, 1908. This would be exchanged for the three promissory notes totalling Bs 779,000. The Bs 400,000 promissory note was cancelled on January 2, 1908. On July 4, 1907, Gómez deposited Bs 500,000 in Banco de Venezuela. On July 14, 1908, he deposited Bs 300,000 for a grand total of Bs 800,000. (Tomás Polanco Alcántara, *Juan Vicente Gómez. Aproximación a una biografía* Caracas, Academia Nacional de Historia, 1990.)

4. Francisco Segundo Alcántara, *La Aclamación* (1906), *La Conjura* (1907), *La Reacción* (1908), Caracas, Ediciones Librería Europa, 1958, p. 20.

5. Ibid.

6. Pablo Emilio Fernández, *Gómez el Rehabilitador*, Caracas, Jaime Villegas Editor, 1956, p. 160.

7. "La Aclamación del Terror," *Venezuela. Ecos de una Tiranía*, vol. 2:1, September 1906, p. 82.

8. Gómez to Castro, 24 May 06 in Victoriano Márquez Bustillos, *Semblanza del General Juan Vicente Gómez*, Caracas, Lit. del Comercio, 1919, p. 116–17.

9. Ibid.

10. Ibid.

11. Ibid.

12. Castro to Gómez, 27 May 06, in Elías Pino Iturrieta, *Castro, Epistolario Presidencial*, Caracas, UCV, 1974, p. 164.

13. During his exile Tellería was closely associated with Rolando and Mocho Hernández's plot against Castro.

14. Blas M. España, "Castro y Gómez," *Venezuela. Ecos de una Tiranía*, vol. 2:1, September 1906, pp. 85–86, p. 86.

15. FO 199/275 Corbett to Grey, 2 December 09.

16. "En Expectativa," *Venezuela. Ecos de una Tiranía*, vol. 3: 12, February 1907, p. 89.

17. Ibid.

18. Ibid., p. 90.

19. Ibid., emphasis added.

20. Ibid.

21. FO 371/162 Bax-Ironside to Grey, 17 January 07.

22. *Gómez Unico*, vol. 1, 2:6, 1907.

23. *Gómez Unico*, vol. 1, 2:5, 1907.

24. Ibid.

25. Ibid.

26. Ibid.

27. Ibid.

28. Ibid.

29. Ibid.

30. FO 371/164 Bax-Ironside to Cartwright, 2 February 06.

31. "Venezuela Wants No Revolution," *New York Herald*, 4 January 07, reprinted in *SAJ*, Vol. lxii, 1907.

32. A *cabezón* is a name given to a very fierce cockerel.

33. CO 295/440 Sir H. M. Jackson to Earl of Elgin, 12 January 07.

34. Ibid.
35. Ibid.
36. Ibid.
37. Ibid.
38. Ibid.
39. *El Luchador*, 16 February 07, in FO 199/230 C. H. de Lemos to FO, 18.2.07.
40. Most writers attribute the removal of kidney stones as the reason for the operation.
41. U.S. Department of State (DS) 831.001C27/9 Biggs to Secretary of State, 19 January 13. Cipriano Castro to General L. Varela (Ciudad Bolivar), Macuto, 13 February 07.
42. The official version of Paredes' death was that after his capture on February 13 at El Rosario, he tried to escape. In the ensuing gun battle he was shot dead with several officers. Among government casualties: Ensign Ricardo F. Prato, Sgt. Nicolás Acosta, and Private Antonio Medesa. In April 1907, Héctor Paredes from Berlin accused Castro of the murder of his brother, but this was dismissed by the court because of lack of evidence on March 10, 1908. Manuel Paredes, another brother, started a court action in the Federal Court of Cassation in 1909 against Castro for the murder of Antonio Paredes. It was the same accusation as Héctor Paredes, but this time Manuel Paredes was able to obtain the appropriate documentation of what happened to his brother. The court admitted the action and proceeded to question witnesses, but during the court's hearing one of the judges noticed that the code word used was "orebel," whereas in the copy it was "orebee." As no such word exists, the nearest being "oreble," most of the judges were of the opinion that it did not make much difference to the result, which was the telegram sent by Castro to General Luis Varela ordering the assassination of Paredes. Nine days later, on March 19, the court decided that

> there is enough evidence against General Cipriano Castro for the homicide against the person of General Antonio Paredes, with the result that the suspension of General Cipriano Castro as president of the Republic of Venezuela by the Court's decision of 17 February because of the criminal charge started by the Attorney General still stands and because the process refers to a common criminal act the records of the case are forwarded to the Judge of First Instance in the Criminal for the pursuit of the trial. (Ramón J. Velásquez, *La Caída del Liberalismo*, Caracas, Ediciones Centauro, 1991, p. 366)

43. Archivo de Manuel Landaeta Rosales (AMLR), Tomo 5, "Revoluciones en Venezuela 1901–08", Muchos Venezolanos Honrados, "El Crimen del Aportadero," *La Guaira*, 20 February 07, p. 12.
44. Mata Illas treated Gómez when he was wounded in Cumaná during the Revolución Libertadora.
45. Ramón David León, *El Brujo de la Mulera*, Caracas, Fondo Editorial Común, 1976, p. 154.
46. Ibid.
47. Ibid., p. 153.
48. Manual María Galavís, *Alegatos. Defensa del General Eustoquio Gómez ante el Juzgado de Primera Instancia en lo Criminal de la Sección Occidental del Distrito Federal*, Caracas, n. p., 1908, p. 16.
49. Castro to Leopoldo Torres, 28 February 06, in Pino Iturrieta, p. 153.

50. Ibid.
51. Fernández, *Gomez el Rehabilitador*, pp. 168–69.
52. Ibid., p. 170.
53. "La Regencia," *Venezuela. Ecos de una Tiranía*, vol. 3:15, November 1907, p. 113.
54. R. Blanco Fombona, *Camino de Imperfección. Diario de Mi Vida, 1906–1914*, Madrid, Editorial Madrid, 1933, p. 62.
55. William M. Sullivan, "The Rise of Despotism in Venezuela, Cipriano Castro, 1899–1908," PhD. diss., The University of New Mexico, 1974, p. 595.
56. Ibid.
57. Ibid.
58. AHM Documentos 1900–1929, Luis N. Power to M. Namias de Crasto, 10 April 07.
59. Ibid.
60. Sullivan, p. 599. Castro managed to repay the Banco de Venezuela in full by the time he left for Germany in October 1908. (FO 199/295 Corbett to Grey, 12 February 09.)
61. Sullivan, p. 600.
62. CO 295/443 Bax-Ironside to Grey, 9 May 07.
63. AHM Documentos 1900–1929 M. Namias de Crasto to C. Castro, 10 March 07.
64. Ibid.
65. Ibid.
66. Castro to José Lares, 6 June 07, in Pino Iturrieta, p. 168.
67. *Gaceta Oficial*, 14 November 07.
68. FO 199/275 Corbett to Grey, 12 February 09.
69. "Le Memorial Diplomatique," reprinted in *Venezuela. Ecos de una Tiranía*, vol. 3:16, November 1907, p. 116.
70. CO 295/443 Bax-Ironside to Grey, 9 May 07.

10

Castro's World Collapses

The beginning of 1908, Castro's last year as president, did not augur well for him. The reports that Castro received from the various states clearly indicated that the ravages of civil conflict had taken their toll, inflicting a great deal of hardship on the country. Moreover, the economic conditions in Venezuela during the last years of the Castro administration deteriorated because of depressed coffee prices and the president's poor health, which had increased commercial uncertainty. In addition, government interference and drought in the western part of the country reduced trading activity. Low coffee prices particularly affected Táchira. Many Tachirenses abandoned their coffee plantations and migrated to the center of the country. General Velasco Bustamante, the governor of San Cristóbal, reported that the state was "extremely poor owing to the dreadful coffee harvest of last year, the previous struggles and so many other causes that do not escape your attention."[1] Velasco Bustamante wanted a further Bs 2,000 per month from the administration to distribute among government supporters. However, far from ameliorating the plight of the Andes, on March 23, 1908, Castro decreed that all goods bound for Mérida, Trujillo, Táchira, and Colombia had to go through the ports of Santa Bárbara, La Ceiba, and Encontrados. The Gran Ferrocarril del Táchira, in which Castro held stock, serviced all these ports. The decree depressed Táchira's economy even further and increased political opposition.

Zulia also went through a period of economic depression after being struck by a plague of locusts in 1907 and by a drought in 1908. Moreover, the rupture of diplomatic relations between Venezuela and The Netherlands in 1908 meant that many small businessmen in Zulia faced financial ruin. Several hundred merchants who depended on the trade with Curacao, Aruba, and Bonaire were also hit. General José Ignacio Lares, the president of Zulia, referred to the poor economic state of the region and the floating population of over five thousand in Maracaibo who were out of work.[2] Other parts of the country suffered a similar fate to that of Táchira and Zulia.

The Castro administration reacted by awarding more monopolies to its supporters. On March 8, 1907, Juan Otañez Mauco was awarded the sole monopoly to export cattle, but public indignation was so great that the measure was rescinded on July 31. During the same period Sullivan writes that "Gómez, Leopoldo Baptista, Antonio Pimentel, and M. S. Araujo cornered a sector of the national tobacco market at about the same time that General Castro's brother Carmelo and other favourites were named state liquor superintendents."[3] On June 30 of the same year, Alfonso Martínez Sánchez was awarded a twenty-five-year monopoly to manufacture and sell paper products without having to pay federal or local taxes.

REVOLUTIONARY ACTIVITY BY THE EXILES

The situation for the exiles at the end of 1907 changed significantly. John Meehan, Castro's secret agent in the United States, reported in November that Ortega Martínez was actively preparing in New York an expedition against Castro, meeting frequently with "the general manager and others of a large ammunition and arms house."[4] Ortega Martínez, who was living in New York City, had placed a large order with Francis Bannerman at 501 Broadway for eight thousand rifles and proper ammunition, later adding another two thousand rifles, a number of field guns, and cartridges. The start of the revolution was delayed, however, because the rebels in Venezuela were waiting for General Vidal to arrive from Trinidad[5] and because Bannerman insisted on full payment before delivery, something that Ortega Martínez could not afford to do. Instead, he offered to pay for half the consignment in cash with the rest to follow afterward.

Certain exiles were scathing in their criticism of these efforts. The revolutionary newspaper *Venezuela. Ecos de una Tiranía* wrote toward the end of 1907 that the rebels were not listening to the "people's rage that foreshadows the storm"[6] because they were divided and were waiting for Gómez to take over to minimize the efforts of the exiles. The paper stated that this was not a solution because Gómez, with his "insatiable thirst for gold"[7] was the "major factor of the monopolies which have ruined the country, they can not nor should they deceive those who want a change of leaders, regime and of principles."[8] The paper further stated that there was no difference between Gómez and Castro because they were "Siamese twins who form one single body, and in spite of different temperaments, they possess the same spirit."[9]

At the beginning of 1908 a number of rich exiles had gathered in Paris, including Manuel Antonio Matos, General Corao, Torres Cárdenas, and Manuel Revenga. Corao was the wealthiest of the group residing at the royal suite of the Hotel Scribe, "furnished with 17th century armchairs and consoles and which also counts amongst its curiosities a silver salver used by archdukes, dukes and American potentates."[10] Corao was a keen horse trainer who had won the Grand Prix at Longchamp. He lived an extremely luxurious lifestyle, regularly receiving at ten each morning his "masseur, chiropodist and hairdresser"[11] who "tortured his swarthy anatomy,"[12] while "a famous actress shows him Paris, worldly and rich away from the majority of the Venezuelans, and a young Tachirense, a dentistry student, José María Cárdenas, acts as his interpreter and secretary."[13] Mocho Hernández was the busiest rebel in Paris, preparing his revolution with the help of the NY&B and ordering General Corao in January 1908 to distribute Bs 12,000 among his supporters in Trinidad in order to keep them happy.[14] Gómez sent out feelers to Mocho Hernández to establish what support he could expect for his coup from the Nacionalistas. Mocho Hernández was surprised at this overture because a go-between had already initiated negotiations to bring the two men closer together. Concluding that the unnamed go-between felt that an agreement between Gómez and Mocho Hernández would frustrate his own plans, Mocho Hernández informed General Parra in Curacao that he was quite happy for Gómez or any other personality to join him "in order to free the Fatherland of Castro by avoiding the disaster of a war."[15] In Curacao, the talk among the revolutionaries was for a united front, with Miguel Bethencourt and Salomón Senior, "the latter an agent of General Ramón Ayala who also represented Arístides Tellería,"[16] having several meetings with General Riera, a Mochista, to work out details. But as Namias de Crasto, Castro's agent on the island, reported, this was difficult to achieve. Armando Rolando, Nicolás' brother, continued the preparations for the revolution in Genoa. Initially, it had been thought that the yacht *Elizabeth* in Genoa had been fitted out for an expedition against Castro, but there was uncertainty about this as the ship's transfer papers remained with the German consul and hence it could not leave port.

ROLANDO ESCAPES FROM VENEZUELA

In February, Armando Rolando reached Paris, where Corao, Torres Cárdenas, and Revenga wanted Mocho Hernández to recognize Nicolás Rolando as the undisputed leader of the revolution. However, the Nacionalista leader was doubtful "given the character and reach that his aspirations entertain"[17] and felt that the venture would only serve to "further consolidate Castro's hold and make it more difficult to obtain the means to overthrow him."[18] According to Velutini, Corao and Torres Cárdenas were "deeply at odds with each other,"[19] feeling that it would be extremely difficult to organize a strong opposition against Castro "because among these men there is deep anarchy and each believes that he can be the leader."[20] Other revolutionaries were also doubtful of the whole venture. In New York, General Emilio Fernández felt that any revolution without the support of Gómez would fail because all the revolutionaries were "a band of charlatans."[21] Mocho Hernández preferred to wait for further news before committing himself fully. In Curacao, General Riera continued to seek funds for the revolution in return for promising liberal concessions if successful.[22] Meanwhile, the situation was further complicated by the arrival of a number of Venezuelan refugees in Curacao who were known to be plotting against Castro. The sailing vessel *Rosita* had left Maracaibo for Curacao with a number of suspected persons, and the Venezuelan government was demanding its return and the extradition of General Rolando. However, the Dutch colonial authorities did not comply. The Venezuelan government was further enraged when it received "the Dutch Minister's note reflecting on the conduct of the Venezuelan Consul."[23] Castro ordered the expulsion of Mr. de Reus, but this was "rescinded on the urgent entreaty of the Minister of Foreign Affairs and Finance."[24]

Nicolás Rolando, who was the last *caudillo* to be defeated by Gómez in the Revolución Libertadora posed the greatest political threat to the Castro regime because over the next few months he managed to unify most of the exiled factions. Héctor Paredes arrived at Barbados in the early part of the year, informing the rebels on the island that all was fixed and ready in Europe for Rolando's revolution. Nicolás Rolando had planned to take up arms in his native Anzoátegui on March 1. However, General Velutini[25] who felt that the *caudillo* had exaggerated his role in the Revolución Libertadora because "our own errors in the East allowed Rolando to shine,"[26] informed the authorities of the revolutionary plot because "it would be a complete fiasco if Rolando committed such madness as to start an uprising, and such a fate would fall on anybody who dared to start a rebellion against General Castro."[27] Consequently, P. J. Adrian was sent to capture Rolando in February 1908, but Rolando escaped from Barcelona to Margarita Island. Pedro Ducharme and his men in Guiría and in the surrounding coastal regions were not so lucky. They were captured and sent to the San Carlos fort outside Maracaibo. On February 14, Rolando left Juangriego on Margarita Island for Blanquilla. From there he proceeded on February 16 to Macanao, arriving two days later at Santa Fe and reaching Bonaire on February 18. After a rest, Rolando arrived in Curacao on February 23, where he reached agreement with his backers and many of the other exiled groups on the island. The feeling among the revolutionaries on Curacao was almost unanimous in wanting the United States to intervene to get rid of Castro. However, Rolando, who had the backing of the Valenciano doctors, received an offer of Bs 250,000 *fuertes* "for the expenses of the revolution."[28] Rolando negotiated with Bethencourt, Leyba, Riera, Peñaloza, and Tellería, managing to reach an agreement with the latter two. The Mochistas were excluded because the price for their support was too high. Riera demanded five states, which Rolando found exorbitant as "the East and the Andes had already been taken."[29] Rolando could offer at most two or three states, something that Leopoldo Landaeta, the Venezuelan consul, felt would be unacceptable to the Mochistas because "despite the hints that have been given to Riera on this island, it is not felt that he has sufficient support to assume the leadership."[30]

Although Rolando had achieved some semblance of unity among the exiled revolutionaries, there were still many who were not prepared to recognize his leadership. It was necessary to find some common ground under which all the forces could unite to defeat Castro because the leader "will not have sufficient authority unless he is appointed by the united revolutionary party to explain to those who confuse Venezuela with Castro, that Venezuela is us and that the legendary soul of the Fatherland vibrates and lives in us."[31] The revolutionaries in Paris who published *Venezuela. Ecos de una Tiranía* urged all other revolutionaries to join forces with Rolando, stating that

> The party of the revolution is today more powerful than ever: General Nicolás Rolando, after his audacious and daring escape, full of danger, unites abroad the prestige of his name with that of an admirable group of patriots who deserve all praise, who as exiles have saved the honour of the Republic and constitute the permanent terror of the satrap. Let us join together under a single banner to achieve the same ideal that we all have; let us recognise at the appropriate moment a sole leader and march to war convinced that by toppling from power the vilest person who prostitutes the office, we will build a far reaching political system which will rid forever from the Fatherland's sky any future conquering eagles.[32]

In New York, Ortega Martínez, Alejandro Ducharme, Horacio Ducharme, and Caribe Vidal were still preparing their own revolution, which was understood to be financed by the Asphalt Trust. As soon as Eloy Escobar Llamozas (who had previously sold asphalt to Grell & Co.)[33] was appointed *Depositario* of Guanoco, General Andrews, president of the Asphalt Trust, went to Trinidad to try to bribe him. Guanoco was a good base from which to start a revolution because of its easy access to Trinidad.[34]

In early March, Armando left Paris for New York, where he met his brother Nicolás. Once in New York, Armando advised his brother Nicolás that he should follow his own instincts and those of Velutini to support

Gómez instead of fighting Castro. Nicolás rejected the notion and left immediately for Trinidad, reaching the British colony on March 27[35] to continue his preparations. Armando travelled to Barcelona in May with a letter from his brother proposing that Velutini join Nicolás in the fight against Castro.[36] The following month Nicolás was joined by Alejandro Ducharme, who had left La Guaira under the false name of John Lessueur and reached Bonaire on April 9 before proceeding to Curacao.[37] He later travelled with Baltázar Vallenilla Lanz, Rolando's secretary, to Trinidad.[38]

The international problems that Castro encountered also served to encourage the view among the revolutionaries that his end was near. Rolando was now practically commuting between Trinidad and New York, preparing his revolution. In May reports reached Castro that Román Delgado Chalbaud, head of the Venezuelan navy, was implicated in a revolutionary plot, something that he strenuously denied. The list of alleged plotters compiled by J. Bolet included Leopoldo Baptista, Generals Silverio, Gabaldón, Acosta, Eudoro López, and Manuel Guruceaga, businessmen Pedro Ramírez Tirado, Francisco Burguillos, E. Borjas León, and Guillermo Muir. Delgado Chalbaud forwarded this list to Castro.[39] The news of these plots did not go unheeded. Suspected persons were arrested, exiled or imprisoned, and "all available posts have been given to Andinos."[40] Sir Vincent Corbett reported that even Gómez "would not be sorry to shake off the yoke of his despotic master."[41]

At the end of May, Rolando was in Trinidad, but he had to return almost immediately to New York because his son was about to undergo an operation. This situation offered good cover for discussions with the NY&B. The intermediary between Rolando and the NY&B was Rudolph Dolge, who had inspired the press attacks against Castro and Venezuela in the United States. During his brief stay in New York, Dolge "had been negotiating with General Rolando and has stated publicly that he has secured the cache of arms to overthrow the present government."[42] By this time the United States had severed relations with Venezuela. The American government was not going to take any action until after its own presidential elections. Moreover, the NY&B had failed to get the Senate Foreign Relations Committee to condemn Castro. Roberto Henderson offered the revolutionaries "the sum of Two Hundred Thousand Dollars (sic) through Luis Iglesias (sic), an employee of the trading house of American Trade Company (sic) and involved in the Matos revolution."[43] General Zoilo Vidal—"El Caribe"—and Ortega Martínez had the support of Crichfield, another of the U.S. claimants.[44] In Trinidad a *tertulia* composed of Baltázar Vallenilla Lanz, General Alejandro Ducharme, Zoilo Vidal, and Carlos Domínquez Olavarría, the "interpreter of the New York and Bermúdez Co,"[45] met at the home of Miguel Barceló, the Venezuelan consul and a cousin of Simón Barceló. In May, General Peñaloza was busy organizing an invasion force in Colombia. In June, Rolando made a last effort to secure Mocho Hernández's support, then went back to Trinidad. He planned to launch his revolution in early July simultaneously with Peñaloza in the west. The Nacionalistas were seeking U.S. assistance in return for some very liberal concessions in Venezuela.[46] At this stage all the revolutionaries except for Mocho Hernández, Ortega Martínez, and Guzmán Álvarez accepted Rolando as their leader.[47] His operational base was in the Llanos, but most of his loyal supporters were in Urica (Rondones), Santa Rosa (Clemente Pino), and Cantaura (Armandito Fernández).[48] Further reports stated that Rolando would invade through Conoma and Arapito "to gather strength in the 'Silleta' and open a front."[49]

In June, Castro became sufficiently worried about the revolutionaries. He ordered "all possible political dissidents arrested, increased the size and strength of his army and placed heavy military patrols in all suspected districts."[50] However, Rolando's invasion, was postponed, ostensibly because of his son's poor health, who was very ill in New York and had to undergo a dangerous operation. Although Rolando promised to be back in late July, he remained indefinitely in New York, much to the chagrin of his supporters. In September, Rolando had to postpone his return trip to Trinidad once again because "the surgeons who operated on the child advised that he should stay another month in New York in order to be sure of a successful outcome."[51] The Rolandistas interpreted this as meaning that their leader was still negotiating with his backers.[52] Rolando was now expected on October 6 or by mid-October at the latest because the revolution was scheduled to start on November 1 "under the system of guerrillas."[53] The rumors in New York in late October were that Castro would be murdered during Christmas.[54] Meanwhile, Peñaloza was busy organizing his revolution from the west.

Manuel Dávila Blanco, Castro's agent in Trinidad, had taken all precaution to detain Rolando "on his arrival in Grenada,"[55] but by mid-October the rebel's supporters in Trinidad were becoming impatient. At the end of October, Castro was alerted from Bogotá that a massive revolution was being planned against the government, with the invasion through "Curacao or the Goagira and from Cúcuta, but the strongest group will pass through Goagira[*sic*]."[56] Rolando continued negotiating in the United States while his supporters waited for him in Trinidad. After long, protracted talks the revolutionaries on the British colonial island met on November 5 to elect a revolutionary junta with Rolando as their leader. Their plan was to assassinate Castro during Christmas.[57] However, the political situation in Venezuela changed radically a few weeks later with Castro's departure from the country on November 24 to seek a cure for his urinary complaint in Germany. Many of the revolutionaries now stepped back to digest what the new situation would entail. José Antonio Velutini advised Armando Rolando of the following:

I will repeat what I told you here: that as Vice-President I am not allowed to enter into any revolutionary pacts; that in all my long political life I have tried to prevent being judged inconsequential and much less a traitor; that Castro's trip, Gómez's rise to power and the international complications were events that should lead Nicolás to tread carefully and I finished by expressing to you that I was willing, as a token of my friendship, to lend you funds for the needs of your family during that time, an offer which I reiterate today and which you can take up at your convenience.[58]

Velutini added the following:

I want to be useful to Nicolás as a personal friend but I can not agree to support a revolutionary plan either directly or indirectly. My official position ties my hands as long as Castro, who has been ungrateful and disloyal, is in power; today, when Gómez, who has looked after me, starts what appears to all as a Liberal administration by decreeing the freedom of the political prisoners and inviting all Venezuelans to offer a patriotic solution to the internal political difficulties and the international conflicts, what motivation do I have to stop pursuing the behaviour I have adopted so far?[59]

BRITISH ASSETS UNDER ATTACK

The attack on foreign assets continued unabated. Now that French and American property had been dealt with, Castro turned his attention to British interests in Venezuela. To some of the foreign observers in the country it appeared as though Castro wanted to get rid of all the foreign legations to confiscate the property of their citizens. According to Sir Vincent Corbett, the British minister, Castro from the very beginning of his rule had "exhibited a marked anti-foreign bias and a complete disregard of the rights of foreign subjects."[60] It appeared that the one distinct, clear policy of the Venezuelan government was to eliminate foreign investment in the country to guarantee "his countrymen, and incidentally to himself, the free development of the national resources untrammelled by foreign interference."[61]

For example, in July 1904, Castro made an offer of Bs 1 million for The Central Railway line to A. Cherry, the manager, informing him that if the company did not accept, then "steps would eventually be taken by the Government to dispossess the Company on the grounds of non-fulfilment of the terms of their contract."[62] As a result, all through 1907 the spare parts belonging to The Central Railway were detained at the La Guaira port in an undisguised attempt to blackmail an already starving enterprise. Castro had also threatened other assets financed by British capital, such as the Puerto Cabello-Valencia Railway, The Barquisimeto-Tucacas Railway, The Caracas Tram & Telephone Co., and he contemplated seizing the La Guaira Harbour Corporation.[63] On January 10, 1908, Castro cancelled the concession held by The Venezuelan Match Company, a British company, and three days later he cancelled the concession held by another British firm, The Venezuelan Salt Company. Sir Vincent Corbett, the British minister, felt that if the British government did not react to the "flagrantly illegal proceeding,"[64] it would only encourage Castro to continue to harass other British companies with impunity.

BUILDING BRIDGES TO THE FRENCH

In January 1908, José Gil Fortoul, the Venezuelan minister in Berlin, spent time in Paris exploring the possibility of reaching an "equitable settlement" (*arreglo equitativo*) with the French. Gil Fortoul understood equitable settlement to mean that "we skip over the incident that caused the rupture and that friendly relations would continue as before."[65] Under such conditions it was felt that a new treaty could be signed in which past differences were forgotten. The question of the FCC was easily solved because the company desperately wanted a new contract. In March, Gil Fortoul met with M. Conty, the South American Director of the French Foreign Ministry, to decide when relations between the two countries would be renewed. It was agreed that the French would drop any grievance or complaint they had over the Taigny incident.[66] The French did not consider the FCC "as a diplomatic question."[67] Gil Fortoul informed Castro that "the Company could raise the problem with us as a personal matter, independently from the diplomatic route, because the French government wants diplomatic relations to be re-established without having to go back to past incidents."[68] Gil Fortoul understood that France was willing to renew diplomatic relations without alluding to the initial reasons for the rupture, which would be of great advantage to the Venezuelan government now that it was having so many troubles with other foreign powers. France demanded in return that any claims made after 1903 be submitted to the Mixed Commission for settlement, which included the "responsibility of the Venezuelan government in the annulment of the cable's privilege and the responsibility of the French government in the Matos revolution."[69] The French insisted on arbitration by a Mixed Commission in Caracas for their claims after 1903. This was acceptable to the Venezuelan government because the claims were small, and they were confident of winning.[70] Venezuela would also be able to contract any company to establish a cable link, although Gil Fortoul felt that the FCC was the best company because the government could acquire the coastal stations and a line between Puerto Cabello and La Vela in return for the administration contributing toward the costs of the cable from La Guaira to Fort de France.[71] Castro wanted to establish a direct telegraphic link with Britain, but the British government was opposed to a link until an arrangement had been arrived at with the FCC, because the Venezuelan government could use this as a powerful lever and "play off the British against the French commercial interests in very much the same way as has sometimes been successfully adopted by Eastern Rulers."[72]

In May 1908, J. E. Sauvage Monet informed Castro that the FCC problem was almost solved and that he was available for employment.[73] The problem was funding. The FCC needed at least $192,460 for the La Guaira-Fort de France link. The company proposed two ways to finance the line. A government loan could be raised that was guaranteed by Venezuela, or equity finance could be used by establishing a new company. The FCC accepted Madueño's idea of raising capital for the cable company by a bond issue, but a guarantor was needed for the construction of the telegraphic line from La Guaira to Fort de France, "and in the case of these bankers being responsible people, the Company's tax expert would talk to them about the new share structure of the Company and other details in the business."[74] If the French government allowed Madueño's bond issue to proceed, then everything would be fine. Madueño was able to persuade some of the leading European banks that he was acting on behalf of the Venezuelan government. Madueño left for Venezuela with an FCC agent on July 31 to discuss the terms of the issue with Castro.[75] However, this became more complicated for his bankers when the United States broke off diplomatic relations with Venezuela in June.

If the issue failed, the FCC was willing to reach a separate agreement with the Venezuelan government, and they would send a commission to Caracas once the basis of the agreement was known. The suggestion was to lease the coastal network to the government with the proposed La Vela-Puerto Cabello line *in lieu* of the government's claims. In return the FCC would reopen the route through Santo Domingo. Alternatively, the government would acquire the coastal network and the proposed La Vela-Puerto Cabello line for $192,460 which would be used to fund the building of the La Guaira-Fort de France line.[76] On June 5, Paúl informed Gil Fortoul that it would be appropriate to send a commissioner from the cable company to settle the dispute, but the company wanted to know the basis for an agreement before sending a representative. The situation, however, was about to explode in Gil Fortoul's face because Madueño's plan was an intricate fraud that was closely related to the new cigarette and banking contracts, which Castro was about to award. The plan called for the participating banks, the "Swiss Bank for Foreign Trade" and the "Banco di Roma" to deposit funds in the Deutsche Bank of Berlin. The funds would only be released once the Venezuelan government had accepted certain modifications to the cigarette and banking contracts. Under such conditions it was clear that no bank would accept the deposit because it would expose them "to the disagreeable consequences of any divergence between the bankers and the government over the rights of each one over the deposits."[77]

Gil Fortoul was still waiting for an answer to the FCC proposal when Madueño's fraud was discovered. Gil Fortoul was blamed for assisting Madueño. He was suspended as Venezuelan minister in Berlin because of the incompetent manner in which he had handled the FCC affair and for getting the fraud mixed up with the cable company settlement.[78] In his defense Gil Fortoul argued that he had never given Madueño an open letter to act and that the idea of a special contract with the FCC was one that Castro had approved three years earlier. Gil Fortoul pointed out that this had been only one of a number of alternatives that he had proposed. Nicolás Veloz Goiticoa replaced Gil Fortoul in August as Venezuelan minister in Berlin, the same month in which the government won its action against the FCC. Paúl wrote to Castro that

> the Company was found guilty, with the sentence containing the declaration on the responsibility of the French government for the action of M. Quievereaux sent to you. I have not forgotten the bet you made on what you would do when you received this telegram, and I am vividly saddened to be so far away from you because I will be unable to accompany you in a toast for your health and the success of the claim which the sentence allows.[79]

FOREIGN RELATIONS WORSEN

During this period Venezuelan gunboats continued harassing foreign ships. The Dutch schooner *Penelope*, proceeding under the Dutch flag and sent by the controller of import-export transit duties at Aruba, was stopped at sea by a Venezuelan ship. The schooner and its five crew members were taken to Adicora and later transferred to Coro, where they remained detained at the Castillo San Antonio from March 13 to April 4. The Dutch ship *La Justicia*, which belonged to an Aruban merchant, was also detained in the same manner.[80] A number of other ships were also stopped. Castro placed more pressure on colonial trade on February 19, 1908, when a decree was issued that prohibited foreign ships from the colonial islands from entering Venezuelan ports. This meant that stevedores from the colonies could not work on European or American merchant ships going to Venezuela, depriving a large percentage of Curacao's mainly Black population of twenty-seven thousand of their main source of employment. This compounded the trouble facing Curacao, which was going through a deep recession because salt production was on the decline while "phosphate exports had diminished, and a serious drought in 1908 lowered fifty cents per day stevedore wages and ten cents per day hat worker wages to a new level of poverty."[81] To further complicate matters at the end of February, Dr. R. Gómez Peraza declared that La Guaira was infested with bubonic plague. The result was that trade between the colonial islands and the Venezuelan port was temporarily halted, creating not only further unemployment but also a shortage of food for the colony.

The main fear of foreign intervention at this stage, however, was what sort of action the United States would take to enforce its claims. Paúl, at the weekly reception meetings he had with Sir Vincent, spoke with "great bitterness of the unfriendly attitude of the American Government which seems, he said, to be doing everything in their power to exasperate that of Venezuela."[82] Paúl confessed to Sir Vincent, that he could only suppose that the U.S. government wanted to pick a fight with Venezuela and establish a blockade. The arrival of the USS *Tacona* on March 18, 1908, in La Guaira to pick up the legation's mail caused the local population to panic. They thought that it was the beginning of a U.S. naval demonstration against the government. More importantly, among certain government officials the *Tacona*'s visit was interpreted as an ultimatum from the U.S. government because William Russell, the U.S. minister, had received unsatisfactory answers to his notes on U.S. claims. On April 5, Paúl became less anxious because Russell assured him that the *Tacona*'s visit was "without political significance"[83] and that the presentation of the Venezuelan Papers to the U.S. Congress had caused little excitement. Russell repeated the same message to Sir Vincent and stated that he had "received no new instructions from Washington"[84] because "the Venezuelan Papers had not yet been considered by the Senate, and he had no reason to suppose that the situation was in any way different from what it had been at any time these last six months."[85]

Despite these assurances, Venezuelan public opinion was firmly rooted in the belief that the United States would intervene. The *El Tiempo* newspaper reported on April 12 that "public opinion is increasingly worrying about the motives of the United States, which using the pretext of defending its own interests under the Monroe Doctrine, wants to interfere in our internal politics."[86] These sentiments were also repeated in the international press. The *Daily Telegraph* of London reported that Roosevelt was "utterly sick of Venezuela's procrastination in yielding to the American claims and keenly resents the taunting attitude of the Venezuelan government."[87] The paper added that the United States was planning to "send a naval and military force against President Castro."[88] The rumors of U.S. government intervention originated in reports from the American commercial community in Venezuela, which professed to have reliable sources of information "that action is imminent."[89] The exiles fanned these rumors to scare Castro.

BUBONIC PLAGUE

Because of the outbreak of bubonic plague, or "pernicious fever of the coast"[90] according to Sir Vincent Corbett, in La Guaira toward the end of February 1908, Castro imposed a rigid quarantine. This virtually cut off the port from the rest of the world. S. W. Knaggs, the acting governor of Trinidad, immediately issued a proclamation that declared Venezuela to be an infested place and established regulations that applied to vessels, passengers, and cargo arriving from La Guaira or from any other place that was felt to be infested so that proper supervision could be exercised during the plague infection. Castro retaliated to Trinidad's alleged closure of Port of Spain and San Fernando to Venezuelan shipping by issuing a decree on April 28 "prohibiting all commercial intercourse between Venezuela and Trinidad."[91] The customs houses at Ciudad Bolívar and other eastern Venezuelan ports were transferred to Carúpano and San Cristóbal. Passenger traffic was also stopped between the two countries. Venezuela was basically going to "boycott the British colony"[92] to the detriment of trade with the colony. The small Venezuelan agricultural producers who sold their produce in Trinidad suffered. Their market was now closed and they were not able to "supply [themselves] with the necessaries of life."[93]

Castro's action was triggered by the suspicion that Trinidad was a hotbed of political intrigue and plots against him, and therefore "the question is primarily not a commercial but a political and personal one."[94] Castro was therefore ready to place every sort of hindrance to communication between Trinidad and the mainland. Castro's actions, according to Sir Vincent had an effective impact. There were many exiles on the island scheming his downfall, so he "succeeded not only in defeating their plans but in establishing his authority or a basis which to all appearance is more secure now that it has ever been."[95]

An analogous situation was also happening in Curacao, which would have far-reaching effects on Castro and the country's political life. In May the Dutch colonial authorities did not allow the *Gloria* to anchor because the vessel came from Guanta, "a place close to the infected port of La Guaira[96] and, in the opinion of the competent authority, was in an exceedingly filthy condition."[97] As soon as Castro became aware of this situation he issued the Decree of May 14, ordering that goods should now be "transhipped through the Custom House at Puerto Cabello instead of Curacao, which is, the regular port of transhipment"[98] because the authorities of the Dutch Antilles had imposed a quarantine on ships arriving from noninfected Venezuelan ports. The new decree meant that ships loading coffee at Maracaibo, for instance, for transhipment in Curacao to Europe were refused clearance. Castro's decree was calculated to deal a "paralysing blow to the trade of that island."[99] Commerce with Venezuela was very important for the colony's well-being. No less than 280 Dutch vessels entered Venezuelan ports between 1905 and 1906, compared with 136 British ships and 106 American ships during the same period. On May 19 another decree was issued "by which the traffic between Venezuelan ports and the Netherlands Antilles was suspended for smaller ships, including all the Curacao schooners, without regard to the tonnage, so that the Curacao sailing ship trade is now at an almost complete standstill."[100] The ostensible reason for the presidential action was that Castro believed that these measures would compel oceangoing vessels to touch at Venezuelan ports, which would "thus reap all the profits of direct communication with Europe."[101] But the real reason, as with Trinidad, was political. Curacao was the scene of intense negotiations among the various factions of the exiled *caudillos*. In addition, the exports of arms and ammunition, though prohibited officially, continued illegally and the "demand for General Rolando's extradition and the surrender of a sailing boat '*Rosita*' which left Maracaibo for Curacao with refugees have not been favourably received by the Dutch Minister."[102]

The decrees to close trade between Curacao and Trinidad and the port of La Guaira "practically put an end to the foreign trade of the country."[103] This had an immediate, direct impact on the Venezuelan economy and the government's revenues, leading to a practically empty exchequer. Trinidad complained bitterly about Castro's behavior, but the British government took no steps save for an exchange of Notes, to have the decision reversed. The quarantine regulations could be easily dealt with, according to Sir Vincent, if the Venezuelan government could inspire confidence in the way affairs were managed at La Guaira and other Venezuelan ports, "but such methods as refusing to allow a ship to clear because her bill of health was endorsed and throwing into gaol an unfortunate doctor who had reported a case of suspicious sickness were hardly likely to inspire confidence abroad."[104] Although Paúl admitted that there was some truth in this, matters did not improve when bubonic plague was declared in Trinidad on June 10 and communications between the island and Venezuela were suspended. They were only reopened on October 17 when the Venezuelan government received official assurances from Trinidad that the island was free from plague.

U.S.-VENEZUELAN RELATIONS ON A COLLISION COURSE

The strained relations between Venezuela and the United States were due to the position taken over the five outstanding American claims. The most important one was that pertaining to the NY&C. Judge Calhoun, Roosevelt's special commissioner, examined the claims in detail and concluded that Venezuela had not acted to deny justice to American citizens and that no party was to blame wholly for the affair. Therefore, it appeared at the beginning of 1908 that U.S.-Venezuelan diplomatic relations had just about reached their nadir. Although the United States had contemplated intervening militarily in Venezuela in defense of the American claimants during 1905/06, the moment had not been propitious. In December 1907, President Roosevelt turned his attention once again to Venezuela. He sent a special message to Congress about the difficulties that had arisen between the Venezuelan government and the United States, especially with the NY&B. Roosevelt wanted Congress to grant him the authority to use any "efforts which may best serve the purpose to compel Venezuela to submit this particular question to an International Tribunal and pending the result all shipments from the Bermúdez Lake to cease."[105] Senator Henry Cabot Lodge entered a resolution in the U.S. Senate for Roosevelt to submit the correspondence between the two countries on the pending controversies in order for Congress to debate and decide on future action. During this time, Calhoun's report and the correspondence that related to the Venezuelan question were published to prepare public opinion for a possible American intervention in the near future.[106] Nicolás Veloz Goiticoa, Venezuela's charge d'affaires in Washington, welcomed the move. He reasoned that once the documents entered the public domain the U.S. government would be forced by public opinion to abandon its coercive designs on Venezuela. However, the US design, as Russell later confessed to an official at the British embassy in Washington, was to save face rather than to "obtain a mandate for further action."[107]

In January 1908 the United States requested Venezuela to submit any of the five claims to arbitration.[108] Paúl interpreted this move as a triumph for Venezuela's foreign policy and as a face-saving device of the U.S. government. He informed Castro that the American offer was to "obtain a result that would place at a safe and discreet distance our national pride and decorum, aspiring that the winner will allow an honourable capitulation."[109] Lord Bryce, the British ambassador to Washington, also felt that this was a face-saving device, reporting that it was a way of "extricating the State Department from a position of some difficulty,"[110] because although it was annoyed at the "shifty and crusty"[111] behavior of Castro, it had no "great zeal on behalf of the claimants mentioned."[112] The Venezuelan government was prepared to negotiate on two of the claims but not in the case of the NY&B company or the other two that it felt involved unscrupulous speculators.

AMBROSE H. CARNER

Since the NY&B had been stripped of its concession in 1904, Carner had been exploiting the asphalt from the same concession. Production increased considerably and costs declined, as can be seen from Table 10.1. Under Carner's administration between 1904 and 1907, the Guanoco operation generated an operating profit of Bs 754, 000. This is detailed in Table 10.2. It should be noted that Carner's selling price of Bs 25 per ton was much lower than the prevailing market price in New York, which was closer to Bs 40 per ton. One of the main reasons for the lower price was that the Trust would not deal with any company that purchased Guanoco

Table 10.1
NY&B Guanoco Production and Costs, 1904–1907

Year	Production (tons)	Costs (Bs)	Costs Per ton (Bs)
1904–Jan 1905	8,000	217,000	27.00
1905	24,000	570,000	23.75
1906	29,000	550,000	19.00
1907	40,000	600,000	15.00

Source: AHMSGPRCP Julio 1–15 1908, Alfred Scharffenorth, *Informes sobre las Minas de Asfalto de Guanoco*, 1.7.08.

asphalt. So Carner could only sell to one group who "naturally need to have complete security of obtaining the amount of asphalt that they need to honour their contracts with the various municipalities or companies, because this guarantee only allows them to purchase the Guanoco asphalt."[113] The buyers therefore demanded a lower price because "these people not only want the necessary guarantees but also a price advantage that will reward the risk they are taking."[114] In August 1908 it was reported that the Asphalt Trust was trying to get the United States to impose an import tax on the Guanoco asphalt, making it less competitive. According to Alfredo Scharffenorth, who had represented the NY&B in Caracas in 1891, more Guanoco asphalt could be exported to the European market. It was felt then that higher prices could be achieved for the high-quality Guanoco asphalt "if it were not for the rumors which the Asphalt trust, the former owner of the Guanoco mines, continues to circulate."[115] At the prevailing market price it was estimated that a profit of between Bs 15 to Bs 20 per ton could be generated, assuming production of forty thousand tons, to give an annual profit of Bs 600,000, which could be invested in better equipment to increase production to one hundred thousand tons, leading to total operating profits of Bs 2 million. The cost of production in Guanoco, however, was higher than in Trinidad because working conditions were more difficult.

The Venezuelan government felt that Barber was purchasing Guanoco asphalt cheaply, but there were few outlets for it. Even though production had increased significantly since 1904, it was difficult to see how much more could be done. The concession was being run on a shoestring budget, and the equipment was in an awful state of disrepair.[116] There was little or no new investment to generate profit, which Eliseo Vivas Pérez, the government's administrator, brought to the attention of Castro. When the government took over the works in 1904, the asphalt operation was already in bad shape. The nine-kilometer railway that linked Guanoco with the pitch lake was in a bad state of repair. Sleepers were rotting away, and

Table 10.2
Operating Profit at Guanoco, 1904–1907 (Bs)

Revenue	
Production over 3 years of 100,000 tons at Bs 25 per ton sold to Carner for his agents in New York	2,520,000
Other revenue for business (shops, etc.)	171,000
Total Revenue	2,691,000
Total Production Costs	1,937,000
Operating Profit	754,000

Source: AHMSGPRCP Julio 1–15 1908, Alfred Scharffenorth, *Informes sobre las Minas de Asfalto de Guanoco*, 1.7.08.

the embankment hidden by scrub and in part covered by water from the high tides. Buildings, machinery and locomotives, all the tools in the depot and other production materials, especially the rail tracks to the mine, were extremely worn out and scarce and the pier was dangerous to use because it was rotten and could not cope with the weight of a fully loaded train.[117]

Since 1904 only essential repairs had taken place on the equipment to keep production going. The port was falling down. The railway line had been extended from the lake to the offices using new rails, which were placed on the old sleepers, and using old bolts, "wasting the benefit of using new rails, with the result that the line was in bad condition."[118] There were no spare parts for repairs and tools. The rolling stock, which had been badly maintained since 1901, was rusting away and breaking down continuously. The result was that "it will not [be] too long before the Guanoco establishment is just one junk yard of useless machinery and tools, a monument to the incompetence and maladministration of Vivas Pérez."[119] The living conditions for the laborers were also bad. The workers complained about their food, that their pay had been altered, and that the company shop had overcharged them. They were paid at the end of the month, but they wanted to be paid every two weeks. According to Captain Dunn of the *Enfield*, a supply boat to the asphalt lake, the Vivas Pérez administration "using front-men and other means, speculates with gambling dens in which brawls and other pastimes are a frequent occurrence."[120] There was a brothel "where the fallen women, who Vivas Pérez has brought from the poor sectors of La Guaira, meet."[121] Because of the intense heat the men worked completely nude "in view of innocent women and children who walk on the street, and the forces of order, even after repeated complaints, do not apply the common law of decency to compel them to cover their nakedness."[122] Vivas Pérez was also helping himself to part of the payroll.

Supplies were difficult to get, "especially fresh meat for the provision of the boat, and not because there is any scarcity but because the boat was singled out, demanding payment in advance at the rate of twenty cents per pound of meat, when the price to the general public was twelve and half cents."[123] This became more critical in December, when Vivas Pérez stated that over 3,000 tons of meat had been loaded when only 2,760 tons had been taken aboard. Captain Dunn was unable to obtain other supplies because Vivas Pérez held the monopoly of fresh meat in the area, and "only the Civil Chief in Guanoco, an intimate ally, can slaughter an animal."[124] J. Figueroa, on an inspection visit, reported in August 1908 that the wages paid to the workers were lower than they had been in 1904, without overtime pay, and that living conditions had deteriorated substantially.[125] In spite of these conditions the Venezuelan government was anxious to increase its revenues from this source. In February 1908, Carner offered to pay Bs 4 per ton of asphalt in taxes, stating that he could sell fifty thousand tons annually. The offer was conveyed to Castro by Andrés Vigas, who recommended accepting it.[126]

The trouble between Vivas Pérez and Carner started when the former stole the payroll and the Trinidadian workforce declared themselves on strike. Through Carner's intervention the problem was solved, but the delivery of asphalt was desperately slow because of inefficient government administration. Carner estimated that each delayed day meant that he lost $150. Therefore, he wanted to take over the administration of the asphalt lake to ensure that delivery dates were kept. Vivas Pérez accused Carner of blocking his own efforts to increase production, but the American reiterated his belief that he had a greater vested interest in getting all the asphalt out on time and on a regular basis. Carner had placed at Vivas Pérez's disposal all his equipment and offices at Trinidad. In addition, Carner had deposited funds in advance for buying asphalt and had opened credit facilities at New York. On June 5, Carner paid the balance of what the company owed in taxes to the court and requested that "the account be settled as agreed."[127]

In April 1908 the Venezuelan government and Barber's asphalt company engaged the lobbying services of John Foster at $5,000 per year to argue Venezuela's position to Congress, Root, and Roosevelt. Foster started by initiating a vigorous press campaign that showed the fairness of Venezuela's position against the NY&B. In April, Veloz Goiticoa stated that by Foster defending his own interests he was also defending Venezuela's. In addition, "an extensive press campaign in the country in our favour has been started and soon many articles will appear showing the fairness"[128] with which Castro defended Venezuela's interests. On April 21, the day before the Senate Foreign Relations Committee, headed by Senator S. M. Cullom, met to discuss the Venezuelan question, Foster sent a memorandum to the Senate commission suggesting that Congress allow Venezuelan-U.S. affairs to be settled by Root "with whom I have been conferring."[129] Carner was sure that with Foster's help the U.S. Congress would not debate in full the Venezuelan question. He believed that by December his agent would have managed to get the question dropped for good from U.S. foreign policy.

It was not only the Venezuelan government that used lobbyists in its pursuit to influence a favorable outcome. The Orinoco Company also lobbied the Senate committee for arbitration through the law firm of Ralston, Siddons and Baxter, who concluded on behalf of the company that they had "reason to *doubt* if we could find in Venezuela counsel who would dare *vigorously* prosecute such of our claims as are predicated upon the arbitrary and illegal acts of the present National Executive."[130]

Foster's campaign in favor of Castro, which portrayed him as acting within the law "and that none of the five claims put forward are of a nature entitling them to demand the intervention of the United States Government"[131] paid off. The American government on the whole did not have sufficient grounds to intervene because it might risk "a long and bloody campaign, destroy a valuable trade, and spread fear and hatred throughout South America."[132] It was felt in commercial circles in the United States that any coercive action against Venezuela would lead to a decline in trade between the two countries, allowing other nations to fill the vacuum. This was what had occurred during the "peaceful blockade." If the United States invaded, Castro would fight to the end. There were also natural barriers to an invasion and the threat of disease for any occupation force. *The Nation* warned that if Roosevelt "ever seriously takes in hand the spanking of Castro, he would be forced either to keep his forces on his ships, or to pay a heavy price for his temerity"[133] because public opinion was against the use of force.[134] Roosevelt was keenly aware that he could not get the American people "to take the least interest in Castro."[135] He concluded that if "I started to deal with him as he deserves, the enormous majority of my countrymen would be so out of sympathy with me as if I undertook personally to run down and chastise some small street urchin who yelled some epithet of derision at me while I was driving."[136] In addition, the Republicans did not want to give the Democrats a strong issue to fight over during the forthcoming presidential campaign. The latter consideration became the most important, putting an end, for the time being at least, to any coercive measures against Venezuela that Roosevelt's government might have entertained. It soon became apparent that the Senate was also not interested and that "it is quite evident that forcible measures would merely react on the Administration"[137] because of the involvement of the Asphalt Company with the Matos revolution. In May 1908, Carner informed Castro that "we are absolutely sure of achieving that Venezuelan matters will not be discussed by the U.S. Congress during the current session."[138] The Senate Foreign Relations Committee soon afterward decided to postpone the debate to an extraordinary session of Congress, but no firm decision would be made until the new Congress convened after the presidential elections in November. On May 30 the 60th Congress ended its first session without recommending action on Venezuela. Secretary Root believed that Castro would destroy himself in Venezuela.

In view of Venezuela's refusal to settle the U.S. claims through arbitration at The Hague and Roosevelt's judgment "that justice is not to be obtained in the Venezuelan Courts,"[139] it was felt that there was no need to maintain a presence in Caracas. So on June 20, a few days after Taft secured the Democratic presidential nomination, the U.S. government closed its legation in Caracas. The move came as a surprise to everyone, including Jacob Sleeper, the charge d'affaires, who left with the military attache on June 25 on the U.S. gunboat *USS Marietta*. The State Department played down the withdrawal of Sleeper, stating that it did not mean a rupture of diplomatic relations, but that it was unnecessary to man a post where their presence was of no public service and at great personal risk in view of the outbreak of plague. Russell, the previous U.S. minister in Caracas, confessed to a British official in Washington that "his departure from Caracas had no more momentous motive than the wish to obtain a more congenial post."[140] The affairs of the United States would be handled by Luis de Lorena Ferreira, the Brazilian charge d'affaires. The move, however, signaled a change of tactics on the part of the U.S. government, which was no longer inclined to give much importance to the NY&B claim "but to base their future action more especially on the claim of the Manoan Company, which is legally stronger and which has an important political interest as the establishment of the original concession would amount to the creation of an important American 'sphere of influence' in the Orinoco valley."[141]

The Venezuelan government took at face value the reasons for the departure of Sleeper and did not appear to be unduly worried. The government did not expect the United States to make any further moves until after the presidential elections. The Venezuelans also closed their legation in Washington. In early July, Castro was confident of his position with respect to the United States. A regimental band played "The Star-Spangled Banner" on July 4 outside the closed American legation in Caracas, demonstrating to all that Venezuela did not have a quarrel with the United States. Moreover, Castro now held the conviction that the German Kaiser would come to the aid of Venezuela in any confrontation with the "yankee peril." Veloz Goiticoa was moved to Berlin to replace the disgraced Gil Fortoul because the Venezuelan government wanted to establish cordial relations with Germany, whose Kaiser was "a bloke like me,"[142] according to Castro. The popularity of the Germans, according to Sir Vincent, was in the public's belief that only Germany was capable of standing up to the Monroe Doctrine. The United States was detested in the country, and this was "in no way confined to the adherents of the present government."[143]

DUTCH SEVER DIPLOMATIC RELATIONS

With the withdrawal of the United States, a total of three countries now had severed relations with Venezuela: France, Colombia, and the United States. A fourth would soon follow because The Netherlands was getting impatient at the treatment of its citizens and property. A number of Notes had been exchanged between M. Reus, the Dutch charge d'affaires, and the Venezuelan government. The Dutch severely criticized the conduct of the Venezuelan consul in Curacao because he had incorrectly stated "that quarantine was imposed on arrivals from non-infested ports, as well as the generally 'tactless' attitude of that official, and suggesting that he was not fitted to discharge the duties of his post."[144] Reus also pointed out that the establishment of an embargo on legitimate trade "was a direct encouragement to 'illicit' trade."[145] In the early part of June, Reus further complained to the Venezuelan government about Roberto López, the Venezuelan consul in Curacao, for refusing to dispatch the Dutch steamer *Christiansted* on May 20 because it did not pay the 30 percent surtax on its cargo. However, the consul was not at fault because he had to get permission from the Venezuelan government to dispatch small ships. The problem did not lie with López, who had no problem in processing their papers, but with the Venezuelan government in Caracas. Reus felt that relations between Curacao and Venezuela had reached such a low point that it was time to "introduce a change, which would lead to a discriminatory and arbitrary treatment of the Dutch colonial interests, similar to the one imposed without any motive during the last few weeks by the Government of the Republic and which can not be accepted as a normal state of being."[146] Reus wanted an explanation for the hostile behavior of the Venezuelan government toward the Dutch Antilles. He claimed that the government had imposed "the measures now in operation against the trade and navigation of a neighbouring Dutch colony,"[147] which were incompatible with "friendly relations."[148]

José de Jesús Paúl answered Reus on June 10, stating that his government's intentions were not meant to be hostile toward the Dutch. He added that the incident with the *Christiansted* was correct on López's part. He explained that Reus had misunderstood the transhipment procedure, which was only allowed under Venezuelan law if the ship to which the merchandise was to be transferred had not arrived in port. Paúl explained that under such circumstances the 30 percent surtax was waived, but such a situation was open to abuse, especially now that plague had been declared in La Guaira. Paúl further stated that oceangoing liners destined for La Guaira used this pretext and discharged their goods in Curacao, incurring the 30 percent surtax because Cristobal Colón, Carúpano, and Puerto Cabello were the only ports under the decrees of April 22 and May 14 that were cleared for "the transfer of export and import of merchandise and products."[149] Such measures were not inspired by any hostility toward Holland, Paúl said, but had been applied to channel foreign trade "in its own territory, with their own resources, avoiding if possible the problems and inconveniences that harm our national interests and which is brought to our attention by the inspectors who warn us of the tremendous damage inflicted by the clandestine trade, as you know full well."[150]

The Venezuelan government's reply to the Dutch memorandum was deemed offensive by the Dutch, who attributed the misunderstanding between the two countries to Reus's "own gross-grained character and not the fault of his Government"[151] and further accused the Dutch charge d'affaires of being influenced by Venezuelan revolutionaries who encouraged illicit arms trafficking. After more than forty-eight hours without a reply from Reus, José de Jesús Paúl reported to Castro that he thought the Dutch charge d'affaires had suffered "a general paralysis to his thinking faculties."[152] Paúl notified the British and Dutch legations that the government's refund of the 30 percent surtax for May, which was Bs 275,065.87, was ready for collection at the Banco de Venezuela. This was surprising when account is taken of the "damage caused by the interruption of traffic in La Guaira."[153]

The original personal disagreement between Reus and Castro was caused by a mistranslation by the Venezuelan Foreign Ministry of the expression *un mauvais reve*, which the Dutch diplomat had used in a Note written in French to the Venezuelan government. The phrase had been translated as *espiritu malodeto*, which Castro understood to mean that he was the "evil spirit." When Reus saw Paúl on the subject of the Venezuelan consul in Curacao, "he at once detected a grave mistranslation of an important phrase."[154] It appeared that he had written that the " 'interruption of commercial relations was like a bad dream' and that this was mistranslated as 'the interruption of commercial relations due to malignant inspiration.' "[155] According to Corbett this mistranslation was offensive because the only application of the phrase could be to Castro, hence the strongly worded Note sent to Reus. Upon discovering the mistranslation Reus urged the Venezuelan Foreign Ministry to explain to Castro the error and to amend the original Note, but no member of the Venezuelan cabinet would inform Castro. Reus in desperation offered to withdraw his Note if matters could be smoothed over between the two countries, but this only caused Castro to send him an offensive reply.

It was while Reus was seeking an audience with Castro that his letter to the *Fijdschrift der Vereeniging Hou en Trouw* was forwarded by Mr. Loscher, Blanco Fombona's brother-in-law,[156] to the Venezuelan government. Although Reus had anticipated the rupture of diplomatic relations, he never expected it to be due to a letter published in Amsterdam. The letter, dated April 9, 1908, appeared in the April issue of the trade publication *Hou en Trouw* and was a report on the business conditions in Venezuela. According to Reus, he had written it at the instructions of the government. The letter was "to give the Association in question every information in his power."[157] In the letter Reus openly criticized the Venezuelan government and its economic policy by stating that Castro had almost ruined the country because of the creation of monopolies, "which are later annulled by the use of all sorts of astute pretexts."[158] Sir Vincent agreed with most of the contents of the letter, reporting that "as far as the substance of his letter is concerned its truth is indisputable."[159] Reus later explained in an interview that the letter "was simply intended for their private information"[160] but had been published without his knowledge, approval, or permission, which was a "case of incomprehensible and irresponsible indiscretion."[161] The editor of the *Hou en Trouw* at the beginning of August called on Mr. van Swinderen at the Dutch Foreign Office, who explained that most letters were closely vetted before publication but by some accident the Reus letter had "not been submitted to him and had, to his great regret, appeared in the *Hou en Trouw* in its original form."[162] Reus had not been commissioned to write the letter and therefore "was in no way to be blamed in regard to this letter."[163] After the meeting the minister accused the Association of "having acted with a rashness and an unjustifiable want of knowledge of human nature and of business which puts to shame the recommendations respecting the association furnished at the time of the Minister's predecessor by authoritative persons."[164]

The harassment of Dutch shipping continued. On the night of June 12, two Dutch sloops sailing from Aruba to Curacao, the *Carmelita* and the *Marion*, were fired upon at sea and stopped by a Venezuelan gunboat. They were first taken to Adicora and then to La Vela de Coro, where the ships and their crew were detained for two days. The sloops were later released, but not before the captains were forced to sign affidavits testifying to the nonviolent treatment by the Venezuelan gunboat. Tension between Curacao and Venezuela further increased on June 14, when Castro ordered that all the transhipment of goods would take place at Puerto Cabello instead of Curacao because of the amount of smuggling that was allegedly taking place on the Dutch island. Castro's move was not unpopular because within Venezuela there was a feeling that Curacao was getting too big for its own boots. José Ignacio Lares, the president of Zulia, wanted to see the demise of the Dutch colony as a trading center and the establishment of a free port on the Venezuelan islands of Las Aves or Orchila.[165]

The Dutch retaliated by closing the colony to all Venezuelan ships. The dispute caused a severe recession in the Dutch Antilles because the islands' main occupation was trade with Venezuela and was "as if our ports were blocked by Venezuela."[166] Some of the blame for the escalation in tension between the Dutch colonies and Venezuela was due to the Dutch colonial authorities, who did not foster good relations with their large neighbor. In June 1908, for example, reports reached Caracas that revolutionary activity was increasing in Curacao. Roberto López, the Venezuelan consul, informed Castro that Miguel Bethencourt, Agustín Díaz Bethencourt, and Rafael Rodríguez were in constant communication with Peñaloza,[167] who was planning to invade Venezuela from Colombia. The Dutch authorities refused to deport the Venezuelan revolutionaries from Curacao, much to the chagrin of the Venezuelan government, which in turn refused to answer Reus's complaints about aggression committed on Dutch shipping.

The Venezuelan and Dutch governments were now on a collision course. The Venezuelans had a very good reason for wanting Reus recalled because of his indiscreet letter in the *Hou en Trouw*. Matters came to a head on July 20, when Reus was formally requested to leave the country. Reus had to bear most of the brunt of the mounting tension for his frank portrayal of the business conditions in Venezuela, which was not meant for public consumption. Secretary General Hannema at the Dutch Foreign Office assured the British ambassador that the Reus letter had never "been approved by Government despite the assurances by Reus."[168] The sentiment in the Netherlands was against Reus. The Dutch liberal newspaper *Valderland* stated that he was the "cause of the offensive action of President Castro."[169] The Amsterdam newspaper *Handelstalad* wrote that the correspondence was "certainly not a prudent letter for a Minister Resident to write concerning a country to which he is accredited."[170] Although it was recognized that Castro had the right to expel Reus, he did not conform to diplomatic procedure and should have complained directly to the Netherlands government about their representative. The *Gelderland*, a Dutch cruiser, arrived a week later on July 28 to pick up Reus. The Venezuelans complained that it had refused to salute when entering the port. It was generally acknowledged that Reus had "rendered an ill service to his Government."[171] On September 12 he was honorably relieved of his duties as Netherlands consul general in Caracas with personal rank of Minister Resident and was placed on the inactive list.

In September the Dutch government reviewed the Venezuelan grievances against it. It did not consider Castro's complaint of the nonsalute of the flag by the *Gelderland* to be valid since the warship did not have to salute, according to international etiquette, if it revisited the same port within a year. However, in dealing with the Reus letter and the treatment of the consul in Curacao the Dutch "acknowledge that Venezuela is on the whole in the right."[172] The whole question now therefore turned on the attitude of Venezuela toward Curacao. The Dutch grievances against Venezuela were the way Reus was expelled from the country, which was considered of minor importance, the detention by Venezuelan gunboats of Dutch ships, and most importantly the attitude adopted against Curacao because the colony faced economic ruin if the May 14 decree was not rescinded.

The announcement of the rupture of relations between The Netherlands and Venezuela was greeted in Curacao with a great wave of anti-Venezuelan sentiment. At Willemstad on the evening of July 25, a crowd surrounded the house of R. F. Gramcko y García, a Venezuelan who had published an article in *El Avisador* that was later reprinted as a leaflet and widely distributed on the island. Entitled "Siluetas Curazoleñas—El 5 de Julio," it defended the Venezuelan government. Some three hundred people surrounded Gramcko y García's home, demanding that he come out. Gramcko y García said that they wanted "to kill me."[173] While the police watched passively the mob broke into the house, knocking down the main door with axes. Soon afterward the mob reached the bedroom where Gramcko y García, his mother, and his sister were hiding.[174] The Venezuelan consul was then forced to sign a written retraction of certain offensive statements contained in the leaflet. He then had to appear on the building's balcony to ask the crowd for their forgiveness. His family was then "compelled to play the Dutch National Anthem, while several Venezuelans who had been expelled from their country shouted 'Down with Castro!' 'Long Live Queen Wilhelmina.' "[175] The following day Mr. Zeppenfeld, the attorney general, saw him to ask whether his article had been inspired by Roberto López, the Venezuelan consul. Gramcko y García vehemently denied this. At around noon a large crowd demonstrated before the Venezuelan consulate and then surrounded the German consulate where López, who by all accounts was disliked by the locals for his "insolent and overbearing conduct,"[176] had taken refuge. The crowd stoned the consulate to knock down the Venezuelan shield, but it was unable to accomplish this. A witness reported that an American by the name of Dugan provided a ladder to take the shield down, which was then thrown into the Schaloo canal.

The main instigators of these demonstrators were some of the Venezuelans living on the island who opposed the Castro government such as Arturo, Julio, and Enrique Leiva and the Maduros, who were "members of the Colonial Council, the others in the retinue were from the trading houses, but there were no blacks."[177] In addition, "no inquiry was made by the authorities because among them were two employees who had violated the home of Mrs. Gramko [*sic*] which was presided by the Commander of the Police."[178] López, his family, and Gramcko y García's family were forced to flee the island, arriving at La Guaira on the American steamer *Maracaibo*.

In Holland, public opinion felt that the Dutch government should follow a policy of restraint. Queen Wilhelmina was reported to be "much averse to war."[179] The Chamber of Commerce of Curacao in August addressed a petition to the Queen of the Netherlands "protesting against President Castro's action and justifying the measures taken by the Colony in regard to plague in Venezuela."[180] The *South American Journal* also reported a prescient view that a revolution against Castro in Venezuela "may save all trouble, without the help of a Dutch intervention."[181] On August 1, a Dutch warship with a course set for La Guaira was spotted from the El Vigia fort. Because the ship belonged to an unfriendly nation, Santiago Briceño Ayesterán, the head of the La Guaira port, consulted Paúl, who advised that the ship should be received. However, Castro countermanded the order, stating that "the Dutch warship should not be allowed to dock and should drop anchor away from the port. It should not be received and not allowed to take provisions, and should remain incommunicado."[182] The order arrived too late, and Briceño made his health inspection of the ship. Paúl later denied that Briceño had sought his advice over this matter. A further dispute arose over of the ship *Zulia*, which arrived at La Guaira two days later. Briceño again consulted his supervisors and was given clearance to inspect the ship. When Castro became aware of this, he reacted violently. Briceño tendered his resignation because he felt that the president had acted in an arbitrary manner. Nevertheless, on August 17, Briceño, a former president of the Lara state, accompanied Castro on a tour of the country. They were warmly received when they arrived at Barquisimeto.

The Dutch inquired whether the United States would object to any coercive measures against Venezuela. The United States responded that it did not mind as long as any territorial occupation was not permanent.[183] What the Dutch were proposing to do in Venezuela was not considered to be against the Monroe Doctrine because The Netherlands was not "hostile nor a major power and consequently not a threat to American interests in the Caribbean."[184] The Dutch government was moving inextricably closer to a confrontation with Venezuela.

With the *Gelderland* already on station in the Caribbean, the battleship *Jacob van Heemskerch* sailed on August 11 for the West Indies while the armored cruisers *Holland* and *Utrecht* were prepared for duty in the tropics. On August 18 the Dutch cabinet agreed not to escalate the confrontation further but decided that the two cruisers and the armored ship *Friesland*, commanded by Cohen Stuart (the former Minister of Marine), would depart for the Caribbean at the end of August. In addition, arms were shipped to Aruba for the population to defend themselves in case of a Venezuelan raid. The general feeling was that the Dutch government was planning to intervene in Venezuela with the help of the United States, because The Netherlands lacked the resources to maintain a naval blockade on its own and a short-lived one would not serve any useful purpose. Although Reus at his press conference of August 26 stated that such a suggestion was "pure invention,"[185] he had confided to Corbett at the end of July that The Netherlands was considering a naval demonstration against Venezuela.

On August 20, Paúl sent a Second Note to the Dutch government stating that the expulsion of Reus should not affect the good relations between Holland and Venezuela. Paúl added that the failure of the *Gelderland* to salute the Venezuelan flag and the attack on the Venezuelan consul at Curacao rendered it impossible for the Venezuelan government to maintain friendly relations with the Dutch government so long as no satisfactory apologies were given to these insults. The Netherlands did not want war with Venezuela, as Dutch Foreign Minister Van Swinderen explained to Sir H. Howard, the British Ambassador at The Hague. The Dutch replied to the First Note sent by Paúl on July 20 in the most polite and conciliatory tones, agreeing with the Venezuelan grievances over Reus and the treatment of the Venezuelan consul at Curacao. However, the Dutch maintained that the May 14 decree had to be rescinded to reopen friendly relations. The Dutch added that if this did not happen, then the Dutch-Venezuelan Protocol of August 20, 1894, which guaranteed that Dutch authorities would prevent any subversive acts against Venezuela from originating in their colonies, would be considered null and void.

VENEZUELA BECOMES MORE ISOLATED

Venezuela entered the last quarter of 1908 more isolated than ever. There was the threat of an American, French, or Dutch invasion. Castro's own support within the country was beginning to wane. This was notable during the Independence Day celebrations on July 5 when "there was no cheering and many of the bystanders did not even raise their hats as His Excellency passed."[186] Sir Vincent Corbett, the newly appointed British Minister, had only just arrived in the country. He undertook a tour of several cities of Venezuela at the end of September to gauge public support for Castro. Sir Vincent found that the sentiment against Castro's government "which is so conspicuous among the industrial classes of the capital, is generally reflected in the opinion of the same classes throughout the country."[187] The educated, commercial, and landowning classes favored revolution. Most of the officials were unhappy with Castro because of inflation and the decline in economic activity, but Sir Vincent was surprised to find that the majority of the population was indifferent to which kind of government was in power because they had not "yet attained the degree of civilization which might prompt them to take an interest in political or constitutional questions."[188] The British diplomat also found that the population in the provinces was poor but not living under what he qualified as misery. On the contrary, he stated that they were on the whole "cheery and smiling, and the children well-liking."[189] There was, however, little doubt that the richer classes preferred a change of government. Sir Vincent concluded that the government's policies were having a disastrous effect on the prosperity and development of the country, but the effects were felt "only by a comparatively small section of the community; the great majority of the people are content to leave things as they are lest a worse fate befall them."[190] Finally Sir Vincent felt that Castro would remain in power "at least as long as he preserves his mental and physical faculties unimpaired."[191] However, if the Dutch took coercive measures unilaterally or with the help of the United States, the prescient Sir Vincent felt that a new factor would be introduced, "the effect of which is wholly impossible to forecast."[192]

On August 2, Castro introduced new government reforms that established state *juntas* to receive and distribute all funds for local government. Six days later he named a new cabinet. Castro also appointed new state presidents because he found that the old ones lacked honesty and political circumspection. Soon afterward Castro left on a seven-week tour of the country, but the "fatigues incident on an uninterrupted round of festivities seem to have proved too much for the President's health."[193] He returned to Caracas on September 24 in a near state of collapse, which for days afterward was so bad that some feared for his life. It became apparent to Castro that his medical problem could not be solved in Venezuela because no physician was brave enough to perform an operation on him. During the first half of 1908, Castro recovered partially. However, his health began to deteriorate by late summer, and his illness was compounded by his tour of the country. Fearing for his life, Doña Zoila increased her efforts to get her husband to go abroad for an operation. She felt that Castro had a close group of friends, headed by Gómez, who would look after his interests. Castro did not want to risk leaving Venezuela however, and so José Ignacio Cárdenas was entrusted to secure the services of Dr. Israel, a top kidney specialist in Berlin, to travel to Venezuela by offering him Bs 250,000.[194] However, Cárdenas intentionally failed to convince Israel to make the journey to Venezuela, Velásquez believes, because as a supporter of Gómez he wanted to get Castro out of the country. So he urged the president to travel to the Berlin clinic. Castro had no option but to go because there was nobody in Venezuela who was capable of operating on him. Castro had nearly died the previous year, so he thought it was preferable to take the risk of leaving the country rather than die on the operating table. Castro felt that the trip would be too short for any of his officials to try to oust him.[195]

IMPENDING INVASION

The reports of an impending invasion of the country intensified during the last three months of 1908. In Trinidad the exiles were waiting for Rolando's arrival. It was now openly known that the revolutionaries had ample financial backing, although Rolando had been unable to enlist the help of the United States. He was informed by both Secretary of State Root and Mr. Bacon that the U.S. government "could not support a revolutionary movement in Venezuela."[196] The Dutch were also cognizant of the revolutionaries' plans. From Bogotá an unsigned telegram arrived on October 11 stating that "I am positively aware that a formidable revolution is being organised against your government, with an invasion taking place through Curacao, La Guaira and Cúcuta, with the strongest group passing through La Guaira."[197] However, to the consternation of the revolutionaries on the island, Rolando did not arrive in Trinidad in October. He was now expected to arrive in Grenada at the end of the month, when the authorities could detain him.[198]

Castro started to take these reports seriously, ordering all barracks to inspect and clean their arms in readiness for action. Velasco Bustamente reported in early November that "work is underway on the composition of arms, construction of new boxes for the rounds of ammunition."[199] It also served as cover for Castro's own preparations for his trip to Europe. Having strengthened the country's garrison, Castro also appointed General Pedro María Cárdenas, his trusted friend, as governor of Caracas, and General Maximiano Casanova, the military commander of Caracas, as head of the central states army. The warden of La Rotunda prison and the commanders of the principal barracks were all loyal to Castro. To maintain contact with Venezuela and prevent Gómez or any body else from staging a coup, a secret committee was established that consisted of R. Garbiras Guzmán, Castro's Secretary General, Finance Minister Arnoldo Morales, Interior Minister Rafael López Baralt, Development Minister Jesus María Herrera Irigoyén, the heads of the post and telegraph administration, the governor of Caracas, and a few others. The committee would communicate with Castro in a private cipher and receive orders directly from him.[200] Castro's orders before he left for Europe were succinct and directed at Gómez. If his *compadre* "attempted to act contrary to orders he was to be deposed and the Minister of Interior, Dr. López Baralt, was to assume the Acting Presidency."[201] Castro added that the German trading houses headed by Blohm & Co., which had extended a letter of credit worth $70,975 for Castro's expenses, would oppose any new government.

THE DUTCH INCREASE THEIR PRESSURE

The Netherlands were demanding that the May 14 decree be rescinded by November 1, something that Paúl was urging Castro to accept because if the Dutch did not receive a satisfactory answer, they were "determined to have recourse to energetic measures,"[202] as it was euphemistically termed. Castro's action had no doubt been arbitrary, vexatious, and unfriendly, and the complaints of the Dutch were well founded. However, Corbett argued that it did not seem that even all the injuries together were "sufficient grounds to justify the employment of the active coercive measures which it is popularly pretended that the Netherlands Government is preparing against this country."[203] The economic situation of Curacao was becoming acute, and the possibility of the island becoming part of the United States was openly discussed. If The Netherlands wanted to retain their Caribbean colonies, it needed to take action against Castro. The Venezuelan president, who was now very ill, treated "the whole question of his relations with the Dutch as an unimportant matter which need cause nobody any anxiety."[204] Castro did not heed Paúl's advice. On October 12 he rejected the Dutch Second Note that wanted a repeal of the May 14 decree. Castro stated that the Dutch freely admitted that "the Government of Venezuela have the perfect right to issue, with a view to Venezuela's own interests, the decrees and resolutions which are here concerned, this lying within the sphere of the internal affairs of Venezuela."[205]

Castro was sure that the Dutch question would not get out of hand because Curacao was a burden and expense to Holland. He believed that the Dutch would cede it to Venezuela. Paúl was doubtful that the Dutch wanted to cede Curacao. However, if they did contemplate such action, he thought that it would be to the United States and not to Venezuela. However, Castro was confident because he knew "what I am about; Germany would never allow that."[206] As the Dutch Note admitted that Reus had acted indiscriminately and also took the blame for the consul's attack at Curacao, Castro concluded that there seemed "to be no reason why a friendly discussion of the other point at issue should not lead to a satisfactory understanding."[207] He therefore proposed that the Dutch government appoint a properly accredited commissioner to negotiate with the Venezuelan government. Negotiations led nowhere. The Dutch foreign minister announced on November 10 in the Second Chamber of the States General that because of the failure of Venezuela to repeal its May 14 decree, the Dutch government considered itself "released from the obligations of the Protocol of 1894, and that the prohibition to export arms to Venezuela was to be temporarily suspended."[208] This move was clearly designed to increase the freedom to maneuver for the revolutionaries on the islands. Rolando took immediate advantage and shipped 130 boxes of arms and ammunition.[209] It was a worrying escalation for those who had to defend Venezuela's coastline. José Rafael Gabaldón wrote to Secretary General R. Garbiras Guzmán from Puerto Cabello that "in Curacao there is free trade of arms to our ports, which has increased my vigilance because it is extremely easy for the rebels to take them to our coasts, which if truth be told, are not well guarded."[210] The Dutch government reasoned wrongly that Castro would react to this new development. De Swinderen, the Dutch Foreign Minister, waited for the effect that "the free exportation of arms from Curacao to Venezuela and the removal of control over the movements of revolutionaries would produce on the President."[211] Castro countered the Dutch threat by announcing that he would annex the island.

On November 25, the day after Castro departed for Europe, the Dutch government rejected Venezuela's proposal outright, stating that if there were to be friendly relations between the two countries, then the May 14 decree was "incompatible therewith even if it be the exercise of his sovereign right."[212] The rejection was a formal denunciation of the protocol. As long as the May 14 decree was in place there could be no negotiations. The Dutch, however, acknowledged that it was within Venezuela's right to impose a restriction on trade with Curacao if it so desired. The rejection was not seen as a real threat but a bluff by the Dutch. The British ambassador to The Hague commented that it "would thus appear that the despatch of the principal vessels of the Dutch Navy to the West Indian waters was an attempt at 'bluff' which has lamentably failed."[213] The Dutch government had not handled the situation properly, and it received adverse comments in the press.

GÓMEZ PREPARES HIS COUP

Castro may have been deaf to the reports of a large uprising against him, but Gómez was not. He continued his plans for his own coup. This was not only motivated out of high political ideals but by self-preservation. There was little doubt that if the exiled revolutionaries toppled Castro, there would be no place for the "brujo de La Mulera," as he was known, in any new administration. Of course, this also applied to the other pro-Castro supporters. They would either have to rebel themselves or go into exile, which was not an appealing prospect at any time. The view that Castro, whose unpredictable moods had made Venezuela the pariah of the Americas and brought economic depression to the country, was the main obstacle to peace gained ground. Consequently, it was necessary to get rid of Castro to start rebuilding some sort of institutional framework, both externally and internally, within which Venezuela could operate. Gómez as vice president was the natural successor. Because of his large standing army and his undoubted military skills and courage, he posed a considerable obstacle to the plans of the exiles if he was not taken into account. Gómez wanted as many people as possible supporting him, as that would clearly make his task easier. It was thus natural for both parties to come together to work for the demise of Castro. Many who joined Gómez at this juncture felt that he could be manipulated and that his political acumen was simplistic and naive. Once Castro was out of the way, it was reasoned, Gómez would be easy to neutralize. Many people assumed that the middle-aged cattle trader would probably return to his old commercial activities in Táchira. The country would then be returned to its natural rulers and proper heirs after the disastrous Tachirense experiment. Gómez, who clearly had his own supporters, was thus perceived as a short-term nuisance who would soon be dispensed with and of no long-lasting effect. Leopoldo

Baptista, a close adviser who had his own political agenda, described this feeling succinctly when he stated that once he had assumed power, Gómez was "a problem of one semester."[214]

Gómez's idea was to set one group against another and thus "take advantage of the distrust of the Yellow Liberals towards the Nationalists as well as that which exists between the Easterners against the Andeans, to flatter all in secret and alert General Peñaloza of the possible manoeuvres of the Nationalists and to put Doctor and General Roberto Vargas on guard against the Yellows of the Cabinet, it was a work of patience and astuteness."[215] Many of those who joined Gómez now would not last very long in government.

In July 1908, Gómez won the support of a number of important erstwhile opponents, such as Linares Alcántara, the president of the Bolívar state who had four thousand men at his disposal in his native Aragua, Delgado Chalbaud, the head of the small Venezuelan navy, and Eliseo Sarmiento. To have Linares Alcántara's and his own soldiers billeted in Caracas, Gómez placed Graciliano Jaimes in the Mamey barracks, Olegario Salas Padrón in the San Mauricio barracks, and Ramón Párraga in the San Carlos barracks. Santiago Briceño Ayesterán, Pedro Murillo, and Régulo Olivares also joined Gómez at this time. In addition, Gómez commanded the overwhelming support of the enlisted men, especially those from Táchira.

It was expected that the exiled revolutionaries would invade Venezuela during late summer or early autumn, but for various reasons this did not occur. Some authors, such as Velásquez, have attributed this lack of activity to the role played by Doña Irma Gómez de Martínez, Gómez's sister. It is alleged that Doña Irma travelled secretly to Trinidad to inform the rebels that Castro would soon be overthrown and that a new government would welcome them back.[216] This seems highly implausible, however, as the government's spy network would have found out about it and put an end to the political aspirations of the increasingly untrustworthy vice president. Moreover, in the event of Castro's spies discovering Doña Irma, the revolutionaries themselves would have denounced the treason to serve their own purposes. Although the trip was secret, this author still believes that some sort of detection would have happened because of the smallness of the island and the amount of gossip that took place. Moreover, the rebels in later years would have alluded or written about this peculiar incident, but there is no documentary evidence that Doña Irma's trip took place in any of the archives examined by this author or in contemporary accounts.

Gómez, as Sullivan points out, was behaving with great political acumen. His enemies in the country were rendered impotent in the aftermath of the 1907 conspiracy. There was also the general apathy and weariness after the abortive Paredes revolt in Oriente. Other authors, such as Fuenmayor, state that Gómez entered into secret pacts with Castro's enemies overseas after the Revolución Libertadora, and that at the time of his coup "he already had contracted serious commitments, and had signed secret pacts, through agents and special commissioners, with all the exiled Venezuelans, either from Yellow Liberalism or from the Nationalist Mochismo."[217] It was understood that the exiles in "New York, in the Antilles and Europe, had joined to support Gómez when he decided to topple Castro."[218] There is no documentary evidence of such a pact. Moreover, it was the very possibility of an invasion by Rolando that precipitated Gómez's coup in December rather than leaving it for the original date in January. Gómez was preparing his own coup without the need of the exiles. Félix Galavís, who since the western campaign of the Revolución Libertadora had established close links with Gómez, undertook important missions "to ensure the support in favour of the various army commanders in the centre of the Republic."[219] General José María Cárdenas, the head of the Táchira army and married to Gómez's daughter Flor, was on the side of his father-in-law.

CASTRO LEAVES VENEZUELA

Venezuelan politics changed completely with the departure of Castro from the country toward the end of November, opening the way for a possible settlement of its differences with the foreign powers and bringing a new dawn to Venezuelan politics. It is not known when Castro finally made up his mind to leave, but toward the middle of November he prepared for his trip to Europe on the *Guadaloupe*. The diplomatic corps was informed of his departure on November 20. On the same day the Banco de Venezuela was ordered to forward $7,698 for Castro's arrival in Paris and to allow him unlimited credit while he was in Europe.[220] On November 23, Gómez was appointed provisional president. Castro ordered the rest of the cabinet to "surround him and give him your support in his discharge of his elevated mission as if he were me, and you will have fulfilled your duty."[221] Castro was convinced that he left a country "on the road to achieve real prosperity and greatness owing to its strict compliance of its commitments, by its well-balanced budget and by the solid peace which the Nation enjoys, and which is up to you to conserve so that it can last for ever."[222]

On November 24, Castro travelled to La Guaira to leave for Dr. Israel's clinic in Berlin.[223] At 11:00 A.M., Castro boarded the *Guadaloupe*. The ship departed at 3:30 P.M., arriving in Carúpano the following day. Castro disembarked in order for the *jefe civil* of Carúpano to send his *Alocución* to General Herrera, the president of the state. Castro returned at dusk to the ship, which departed that night for Trinidad, arriving a day later on November 26. Castro could not land at Port of Spain because the ship came from an area of plague, so the Venezuelan consul came by launch to greet Castro and see whether the president had any last-minute orders for

Caracas. The ship left for Martinique, where it took coal aboard, and then left on November 28 for Point-a-Pitre, Guadaloupe. After a voyage of two weeks across the Atlantic Ocean, the ship docked at Santander on December 9, where the governor of the province welcomed Castro on behalf of the Spanish government. King Alfonso XIII sent a greetings telegram. A number of Venezuelan consuls in Europe and Carmelo Castro were waiting in Santander to welcome Castro. Consul General Rísquez headed the group, which also included Carlos Hahn, consul at Genoa, Segundo Mendoza, consul at Liverpool, and Diógenes Escalante, the consul at Santander. The following day Castro disembarked at Pauillac in France, where M. Gont of the Quai d'Orsay detailed the conditions for his stay in France because the country had severed diplomatic relations with Venezuela. Castro then boarded a train for Bordeaux, where he checked into the Hotel de France. Later he declared at a press conference that Holland would not attack Venezuela. Contemporary reports described Castro as looking "surprisingly well, his face betraying no sign either of fatigue or physical suffering."[224] The following day, December 11, he arrived in Paris and checked into the Hotel Palais D'Orsay. While in Paris he heard rumors that "Gómez was going to betray me, that I will not be able to return to my country, but I have full confidence in my guiding star . . . always a winner, never defeated."[225] Castro, the "Napoleon of the Andes" as he was referred to by some newspapers, finally arrived in Berlin on December 14. He stayed at the Hotel Europa and hired a fleet of ten large cars for his entourage.[226]

The departure of Castro for Europe because of health reasons had a resounding effect on the plans of the political exiles. It also accelerated Gómez's own plans for a coup. The country was now more isolated than ever, drifting from one crisis to another with the threat of foreign intervention growing stronger by the day.

NOTES

1. AHMSGPRCP Enero 1–10 1908 G. Velasco to C. Castro, 10 January 08.
2. AHMSGPRCP Enero 11–20 1908 Jose Ignacio Lares to Castro 16 January 08.
3. William M. Sullivan, "The Rise of Despotism in Venezuela: Cipriano Castro, 1899–1902," PhD. diss., The University of New Mexico, 1974, pp. 581–82.
4. AHMSGPRCP Unclassified, John G. Meehan (Secret Service Bureau & Confidential Enquiry Office) to Jacob Pimentel, New York, 27 November 07.
5. AHMSGPR CP Enero 21–31 1908 Alfredo Núñez to Castro 31 January 08.
6. "La Revolución" *Venezuela. Ecos de una Tiranía*, vol. 3:16, December 1907, p. 121.
7. Ibid.
8. Ibid.
9. Ibid.

10. Laureano Vallenilla Lanz, *Escrito de Memoria*, Caracas, Ediciones Garrido, 1957, p. 21.
11. Ibid.
12. Ibid.
13. Ibid.
14. AHMSGPRCP Enero 11–20 1908 Alcántara to Castro, 11 January 08.
15. AJMH Vol. 55 J. M. Hernández to General Rafael Parra, 15 January 08.
16. AHMSGPRCP Enero 11–20 1908 Namias de Crasto to Castro, 18 January 08.
17. AJMH Vol. 55 Hernández to R. Parra, 9 March 08.
18. AJMH Vol. 55 Hernández to Hermocrates Parra, 10 March 08.
19. AHMSGPRCP Feb 14–29 1908 J. A. Velutini to Julio (C. Velutini), 25 February 08.
20. Ibid.
21. AHMSGPRCP Enero 11–20 1908 N Crasto to Castro, 18 January 08.
22. Elias H. Cheney to R. Bacon, 22 June 08, in Julius Enhert Hendrickson, "The New Venezuelan Controversy: The Relations of the U.S. and Venezuela, 1904–1914," PhD. diss., The University of Minnesota, 1964, p. 166n.
23. FO 199/215 Corbett to Grey, 18 June 08.
24. Ibid.
25. AJMH Vol. 55 Mocho Hernández to Dr. Hermocrates Parra, 10 March 08.
26. AHMSGPRCP Feb 14–29 1908 J. A. Velutini to Julio (C. Velutini), 25 February 08.
27. Ibid.
28. AJMH Vol. 55 Hernández to Rafael Parra, 9 March 08; Hernández to Hermocrates Parra, 10 March 08.
29. AHMSGPRCP Marzo 1–15 1908 Leopoldo Landaeta to Castro, 1 March 08.
30. Ibid.
31. "Sursum Corda," *Venezuela. Ecos de una Tiranía*, vol. 4:20, June 1908, p. 153.
32. "Union," *Venezuela. Ecos de una Tiranía*, vol. 4:19, April 1908, p. 145.
33. AHMSGPRCP Julio 16–31 1908 Juvenal Anzola to Internal Affairs Minister, 22 July 08. According to *Venezuela. Ecos de una Tiranía* Castro

> has been the agent of North American speculators with whom he exploits today the Bermúdez Lake, against other speculators who have grown accustomed during long years to harvest ministers and judges; he knows that the Franco-Venezuelan problem and other European and American political problems have held back France from seeking redress for Castro's excessive ignorance and alcoholism. (*Venezuela. Ecos de una Tiranía*, Vol. 2:1, September 1906, p. 84)

34. AHMSGPRCP Marzo 1–15 1908 Julio Paz Rodríguez, Memorandúm, 12 March 08.
35. AHM SGPRCP Marzo 16–31 1908. "Itinerario de Rolando."
36. AHMSGPRCP Marzo 22–31 1930 Simón Barceló to Gómez, 24 March 30.
37. AHMSGPRCP Abril 1–11 1908 Roberto López to Castro, 11 April 08.
38. AHMSGPRCP Abril 12–30 1908 C. Blanchi to Castro, 27 April 08.

39. AHMSGPRCP Ago. 1–14 1908 R. Delgado Chalbaud to Castro, 4 August 08.

40. FO 199/233 Corbett to Grey, 7 May 08.

41. Ibid.

42. AHMSGPRCP Ago. 15–31 1908 T. R. to José de Jesus Paúl, 18 August 08.

43. AHMSGPRCP Julio 1–15 1908 (sic) Gonzalo Febres Cordero to Castro, 4 October 08.

44. AHMSGPRCP Oct 14–31 1908 P. L. Whitaker to R. Garbiras Guzmán, 22 October 08.

45. AHMSGPRCP Ago. 1–14 1908 M. Dávila Blanco to Castro, 11 August 08.

46. The Paris revolutionary newspaper *Venezuela. Ecos de una Tiranía* stated that

> The revolution gathers in its bosom the most prestigious military men, the most honest, the richest, most popular men, it has the backing of popular opinion; it can also count on the putrefaction with which the tyranny is slowly sinking, it has it all if it wanted it but it remains impotent with its arms crossed as a sphinx. . . . Blind ambition destroys the work of national regeneration. The revolutionary leaders have not managed to unite in order to appoint a Chieftain, who in the name of the oppressed Fatherland will lead the armed fight against despotism, taking away this Revolution its great moral and material force that such a union would beget. ("Sursum-Corda," *Venezuela. Ecos de una Tiranía*, Vol. 4, 20 June 1908, p. 153)

47. AHMSGPRCP Julio 16–31 1908 J. M. Sarmiento Barrios to Castro, July 1908.

48. AHMSGPRCP Junio 1–15 1908 P. Giuseppi-Monagas to Castro, 10 June 08.

49. AHMSGPRCP Julio 16–31 1908 Plácido Campo to Castro, 27 July 08.

50. Sullivan, p. 614.

51. AHMSGPRCP Sept 1–30 1908 M. Dávila Blanco to Castro, 30 September 08.

52. Ibid.

53. Ibid.

54. AHMSGPRCP Oct 14–31 1908 P. L. Whitaker to R. Garbiras Guzmán, 22 October 08.

55. AHMSGPRCP Oct 14–31 Dávila Blanco to Castro, 19 October 08.

56. AHMSGPRCP Oct 1–13 1908 Telegram, 11 October 08.

57. AHM SGPRCP Oct 14–31 1908 Whitaker to Garbiras Guzmán, 22 October 08.

58. AHM SGPR CP Marzo 22–31 1930 (sic) José Antonio Velutini to Armando Rolando, 25 December 08.

59. Ibid.

60. FO 199/275 Corbett to Grey, 12 February 09.

61. Ibid.

62. FO 420/226 O. Bax-Ironside to Lord Lansdowne, 22 July 04.

63. Sir Vincent Corbett writes that

> The combined detention throughout the year at the custom house at La Guaira of the goods belonging to the Central Railway (a bona fide British undertaking) in defiance of the express

stipulations of their contract, was an undisguised attempt to blackmail an already starving enterprise. Moreover, General Castro was at no pains to conceal his intention of laying predatory hands on other British concerns; he personally threatened in more or less distinct terms the Managers of the Puerto Cabello-Valencia Railway and the Barquisimeto-Tucacas Railway (both of which are British), as well as the Caracas Tram and Telephone Companies (which are Venezuelan companies financed by British capital and under British management). He also, I am sure, contemplated the seizure of the La Guaira Harbour Corporation (which is purely British). I cannot doubt that had the ex-President's health been speared and unless His Majesty's Government had forcibly intervened, there would not in a year or two have remained a single British enterprise in Venezuela. (FO 199/275 Corbett to Grey, 12 February 09.)

64. FO 199/274 Corbett to Grey, 12 February 09.
65. AHMSGPRCP Enero 11–20 1908 José Gil Fortoul to Castro, 14 January 08.
66. AHMSGPRCP Ago 1–14 1908 Fortoul to Castro, 6 August 08.
67. AHMSGPRCP Marzo 1–15 1908 Fortoul to Castro, 1 March 08.
68. AHMSGPRCP Marzo 1–15 1908 Fortoul to Castro, 14 March 08.
69. AHMSGPRCP Ago 1–14 1908 Fortoul to Castro, 6 August 08.
70. AHMSGPRCP Julio 16–31 1908 Fortoul to Castro, 30 June 08.
71. AHMSGPRCP Marzo 1–15 1908 Fortoul to Castro, 14 March 08.
72. CO 295/447 Corbett to Grey, 6 May 08.
73. AHMSGPRCP May 1–15 1908 J. E. Sauvage to Castro 14 May 08.
74. AHMSGPRCP Julio 16–31 1908 Fortoul to Castro, 20 July 08.
75. AHMSGPRCP Junio 1–15 1908 Fortoul to Castro, 8 June 08.
76. AHMSGPRCP Julio 16–31 1908 Fortoul to Castro, 20 July 08.
77. Ibid.
78. In a personal letter, Paúl stated that the reason for the suspension was for not having "followed properly your instructions on the French matter," (AHMSGPRCP Ago 1–14 1908 Fortoul to Castro, 6 August 08) and for having allowed "the interference of Madueño in the cable matter, mixing it with the cigarette, and bank business." (Ibid).
79. AHM SGPRCP Ago 15–31 1908 Paúl to Castro, 24 August 08.
80. FO 199/215 Howard to Grey, 4 August 08.
81. Sullivan, p. 604.
82. FO 199/250 Corbett to Grey, 6 April 08.
83. Ibid.
84. Ibid.
85. Ibid.
86. FO 371/791 "La Actitud de los Estados Unidos," *El Tiempo*, 12 April 08.
87. "Defiant Venezuela," *Daily Telegraph*, 9 April 08.
88. Ibid.
89. FO 199/250 Corbett to Grey, 6 April 08.
90. Ibid.
91. CO 295/445 S. W. Knaggs to secretary of state for the colonies, 9 May 08.
92. CO 295/447 Corbett to Grey, 30 September 08.
93. CO 295/445 Knaggs to Corbett, 20 August 08.
94. CO 295/447 Corbett to Grey, 30 September 08.
95. Ibid.

96. Guanta is some four hundred miles away from La Guaira.

97. FO 199/215 Howard to Grey, 4 August 08, Enclosure, Trans. "The Netherlands and Venezuela," 3 July 08.

98. FO 199/215 Corbett to Grey, 18 June 08, MinRelInt, *Memoria*, 1908, Doc. 35, p. 129.

99. FO 199/275 Corbett to Grey, 12 February 09.

100. FO 199/215 Howard to Grey, 4 August 08.

101. CO 295/447 Corbett to Grey, 4 June 08.

102. Ibid.

103. FO 199/233 and FO 420/249 Corbett to Grey, 4 June 08.

104. FO 199/250 Corbett to Grey, 6 April 08.

105. CO 295/443 Bax-Ironside to Sir Edward Grey, 10 December 07.

106. U.S. Congress, *U.S. Congressional Record*, vol. 42 3, 60 Cong., 1 Sess., 1907, pp. 2518.

107. FO 199/250 Bryce to Grey, 29 June 08.

108. The five claims that the United States wanted to send to the International Court of Arbitration at The Hague were the following: (1) Jaurett (2) Manoa Orinoco and Orinoco Corporation (3) Orinoco Steamship (4) the NY&B (5) Crichfield.

109. AHMSGPRCP Feb 14–29 1908 Paúl to Castro, 24 February 08.

110. FO 199/250 Bryce to Grey, 1 April 08.

111. Ibid.

112. Ibid.

113. AHMSGPRCP Julio 1–15 1908 Alfred Scharffenorth, "Informes Sobre las Minas de Asfalto de Guanoco," 1 July 08.

114. Ibid.

115. Ibid.

116. AHM SGPRCP Junio 1–15 1908, Eliseo Vivas Pérez to Castro, 3 June 08.

117. AHMSGPRCP Julio 1–15 1908 Alfred Scharffenorth, "Informes Sobre las Minas de Asfalto de Guanoco," 1 July 08.

118. AHMSGPRCP Dic 14–23 1908 Trans. Alfred Lynch to Andrés J. Vigas, 16 December 08.

119. Ibid.

120. Ibid.

121. Ibid.

122. Ibid.

123. Ibid.

124. Ibid.

125. AHMSGPRCP Ago 15–31 1908 J. Figueroa to Castro, 22 August 08.

126. AHMSGPRCP Feb 14–29 1908 Vigas to Castro, 14 February 08.

127. AHMSGPRCP Junio 1–15 1908 Paúl to Castro, 10 June 08.

128. AHMSGPRCP Abril 12–30 1908 N. Veloz Goiticoa to Castro, 17 April 08.

129. AHMSGPRCP Abril 12–30 1908 A. H. Carner to Castro, 29 April 08.

130. cf. U.S. Senate, Jackson Harvey Ralston, *Venezuelan Claims. Letter of Messrs Ralston & Siddons and George N. Baxter to Hon. S. M. Cullom, Chairman of the Committee on Foreign Relations of the Senate of the United States*, April 28 1908, Washington, USGPO, 1908.

131. FO 199/250 Corbett to Grey, 4 May 08.

132. "Spanking Castro," *The Nation*, vol. 86:2235, 30 April 08, pp. 390–91.
133. Ibid.
134. AHMSGPRCP Abril 20–30 1908 Veloz Goiticoa to Castro, 24 April 08.
135. Sullivan, p. 614.
136. Ibid.
137. Root to Whitelaw Reid, 22 May 08, in Hendrickson, p. 156.
138. AHMSGPRCP Mayo 1–15 1908 A. H. Carner to Castro, 6 May 08.
139. FO 199/233 Corbett to Grey, 27 June 08.
140. FO 199/250 Bryce to Grey, 29 June 08.
141. FO 199/250 Corbett to Grey, 21 June 08.
142. FO 420/249 Howard to Grey, 10 August 08.
143. FO 371/569 Corbett to Grey, 27 June 08.
144. FO 199/215 Corbett to Grey, 18 June 08.
145. Ibid.
146. AHMSGPRCP Junio 1–15 1908 Trans. J. H. de Reus to Foreign Affairs Minister, 6 June 08.
147. Ibid.
148. Ibid.
149. AHMSGPRCP Junio 1–15 1908 Foreign Affairs Minister to J. H. de Reus, 10.6.08.
150. AHMSGPRCP Junio 1–15 1908 Foreign Affairs Minister to Reus, 10 June 08.
151. FO 199/215 Corbett to Grey, 18 June 08.
152. AHMSGPRCP Junio 16–30 1908 Paúl to Castro, 17 June 08.
153. Ibid.
154. FO 199/215 Corbett to Grey, 21 June 08.
155. Ibid.
156. R. Blanco Fombona, *Camino de Imperfección. Diario de Mi Vida, 1906–1914*, Madrid, Editorial Madrid, 1933, p.121.
157. FO 199/215 Corbett to Grey, 22 July 08.
158. MinRelExt., *Memoria*, 1909, p. 504. According to Blanco Fombona, Reus was referred to as the "fifth evangelist" in Caracas because, according to the *Caraqueños*, "he has spoken the gospel; that is to say the truth." Blanco Fombona, p. 120.
159. FO 199/215 Corbett to Grey, 22 July 08.
160. FO 199/215 Howard to Grey, 26 August 08, trans. Nieuwe Courant, "Mr de Reus interviewed," 26 August 08.
161. Ibid.
162. FO 199/215 Howard to Grey, 6 August 08.
163. Ibid.
164. FO 199/215 Lord Acton to Grey, 4 November 08, Enclosure No. 2, Minister for Foreign Affairs to Hou En Trouw Association, 13 August 08.
165. AHMSGPRCP Ago 1–14 1908 José Ignacio Lares to Castro, 3 August 08.
166. FO 199/215 Howard to Grey, 4 August 08, Enclosure, "The Netherlands and Venezuela," 3 July 08.
167. AHMSGPRCP Junio 16–30 1908 Roberto López to Castro, 28 June 08.
168. FO 199/215 Howard to Grey, 31 July 08.
169. FO 199/215 Howard to Grey, 25 July 08.
170. FO 199/215 Howard to Grey, 24 July 08.

171. FO 199/215 Howard to Grey, 25 July 08.

172. FO 199/215 Howard to Grey, 8 September 08.

173. AHMSGPRCP Julio 16–31 1908 R. F. Gramcko y García to Castro, 29 July 08.

174. Ibid.

175. FO 199/215 Howard to Grey, 28 July 08.

176. FO 199/215 Corbett to Grey, 30 July 08.

177. AHMSGPRCP Ago 15–31 1908 López to Castro, 20 August 08.

178. Ibid.

179. SAJ, 22 August 08.

180. FO 199/215 Howard to Grey, 4 August 08.

181. SAJ, 22 August 08.

182. Santiago Briceño Ayesterán *Memorias de Su Vida Militar y Política*, Caracas, Tip. América, 1948, p. 355.

183. FO 199/215. *The Netherlands Orange Book*, 1908. On August 1 the Dutch inquired whether the United States "would object to coercive measures in Venezuela should the national honour of Netherlands require them." (U.S. Minister to Secretary of State, The Hague, 1 August 08 in U.S. Department of State, "Papers relating to the Foreign Relations of the United States of America," *Venezuela*, 61 Cong. 2 Sess., 1909–1910, vol.1, p. 631) The reply from the United States was swift, stating that the American government "should not feel at liberty to object to measures of the character described in the minister's question not involving occupation of territory either permanent or of such a character as to threaten permanency." (Secretary of State to U.S. Minister at The Hague, 2 August 08, in U.S. Department of State, "Papers Relating to the Foreign Relations of the United States of America," *Venezuela*, 61 Cong. 2 Sess., 1909–1910, vol. 1, p. 632).

184. Hendrickson, p. 176.

185. FO 199/215 Howard to Grey, 26 September 08, trans. Nieuwe Courant, "Mr de Reus interviewed," 26 August 08.

186. FO 199/233 Corbett to Grey, 5 July 08.

187. FO 199/233 Corbett to Grey, 3 October 08.

188. Ibid.

189. Ibid.

190. Ibid.

191. Ibid.

192. Ibid.

193. FO 199/233 Corbett to Grey, 29 September 08.

194. Equivalent to $1.2 million in 1999 prices. There was another curious explanation advanced and taken seriously, which was that Castro left the country to extricate himself from the impasse that he had got the country into. The reasoning behind this view was that Dr. Israel, after examining Castro at his clinic, did not feel that there was any need for surgery. (FO 199/215 Acton to Grey, 23 December 08.) This is highly unlikely because Castro was operated by Dr. Israel, and it seems wholly improbable and out of character that he would shirk from his duties.

195. Francisco Segundo Alcántara, *La Aclamación* (1906), *la Conjura* (1907) *y la Reacción* (1908), Caracas, Ediciones Librería Europa, 1958, p. 59.

196. AHM SGPRCP Sept 1–30 1908, *The Mirror* (Trinidad newspaper) "Plan to Upset Castro If Dutch Act in Venezuela," 18 September 08.

197. AHMSGPRCP Oct 1–13 1908 Telegram, Bogota, 11 October 08.
198. AHMSGPRCP Oct 14–31 1908 Blanco to Castro, 19 October 08.
199. AHM SGPRCP Nov 1–15 1908 J. Velasco Bustamante to Castro, 7 November 08.
200. FO 371/791 Corbett to Grey, 19 December 08.
201. FO 199/233 Corbett to Grey, 25 December 08. According to Segundo Alcántara, Castro thought that "his captains would surround Gómez because he had ordered it and who would abandon him as soon as he had requested it and decided to leave without giving instructions on the matter without thinking that Gómez in the presidency could remove and persecute his political enemies, in particular general Alcántara." (Segundo Alcántara, p. 59)
202. FO 199/215 Corbett to Grey, 27 September 08.
203. FO 199/215 Corbett to Grey, 17 November 08.
204. FO 199/215 Corbett to Grey, 17 October 08.
205. FO 199/215 Trans. Paúl to The Netherlands Foreign Affairs Minister, 12 October 08.
206. FO 420/249 Corbett to Grey, 12 December 08.
207. FO 199/215 Corbett to Grey, 17 October 08.
208. CO 295/447 Acton to Grey, 10 November 08.
209. AHMSGPRCP Enero 9–19 1909 Miguel Bethencourt to Gómez, 16 January 09.
210. AHMSGPRCP Nov 1–15 1908 José R. Gabaldón to R. Garbiras Guzmán, 11 November 08.
211. CO 295/447 Acton to Grey, 12 November 08.
212. FO 199/215 Acton to Grey, 1 December 08.
213. Ibid.
214. Ramón J. Velásquez, "Aspectos de le Evolución Política de Venezuela en su Útimo Medio Siglo," in *Venezuela Moderna, Medio Siglo de Historia 1926–1976*, Caracas, Fundación Eugenio Mendoza, 1976, pp. 3–385.
215. Ibid. This is confirmed by Sir Vincent Corbett, Blanco Fombona, Ramón J. Velásquez and Angel María Nuñez, "Los Secretarios de Gómez," *BAHM* Abril–Sept 1968, pp. 13–29.
216. Vallenilla Lanz, p. 27; Sullivan, p. 615.
217. Juan Bautista Fuenmayor, *Historia de la Venezuela Política Contemporánea, 1899–1969*, Caracas, Talleres Tip. Miguel Angel Garcíae Hijos, 1975, p. 192.
218. Ibid.
219. Pablo Emilio Fernández, *Gómez el Rehabilitador*, Caracas, Jaime Villegas Editor, 1956, p. 176.
220. This facility was cancelled on January 5, 1909.
221. C. Castro "Alocución," 23 November 08, in MinRelInt., *Memoria*, 1908, p. 17.
222. Ibid.
223. Pedro María Morantes (Pio Gil), *Diario Intimo y Otros Temas*, Caracas, Ediciones de la Presidencia de la República, 1965.
224. "President Castro in France," *The Times*, 11 December 08.
225. Vallenilla Lanz, p. 23.
226. *The Times*, 10–15 December 08.

11

A New Government in Venezuela

Castro's surprising decision to leave Venezuela changed the political picture of the country. Some of Castro's enemies, such as General Corao, placed themselves immediately at Gómez's disposal. The Venezuelan exiles in Paris firmly believed that the president's departure had averted a U.S. invasion of the country to oust him from power, saving "momentarily the shame of the republic."[1] More importantly, Rolando and his followers now had second thoughts about their revolutionary plans. Simon Barceló, secretary to General Velutini, disclosed some years later that Armando Rolando, the brother of Nicolás, heard the news of Castro's departure and felt that the most prudent course of action was to "seek out Velutini, whose clear vision he knew was formed from past experience, handing him the letter from Nicolás that he had since May and in which he proposed a rapprochement in order to fight against Castro."[2] The most sensible course of action, which Armando recommended in Barcelona, was "as Velutini indicated, to acknowledge your [Gómez's] authority."[3]

On the day of Castro's departure for Europe the university students demonstrated against him, giving their "support to General Gómez and lashes out against the tyrant who for nine long years has suppressed all human rights, including those of his closest supporters and General Gómez, who at a solemn occasion was referred to as 'The Saviour of the Saviour.' "[4] The police dispersed the group but during the ensuing days the students returned to the streets and burned an effigy of Castro. More importantly, powerful interests within Venezuela were also calling on Gómez to save the country from the chaos and economic ruin that Castro's administration had brought. The army looked for leadership from Gómez, and the people, according to Sir Vincent Corbett, were like sheep "ready to stampede, if they are given a lead, in any direction."[5] Briceño Ayesterán, an eyewitness to the events, notes in his memoirs that as soon as Gómez took over "one could start to feel signs of a reaction that was instigated by important members of national politics and almost all connected to the government, with the purpose of forcing Gómez to ignore the legitimate authority of his boss and friend."[6] According to José Ignacio Lares, the president of Zulia, there were strong rumors in Maracaibo of revolutionary activity in Colombia, where a large invasion force of "Rangelistas, Mochistas, Pañalozistas and Rolandistas"[7] were all united and ready to invade. However, the exiled revolutionaries, such as Rolando, Riera, Mocho Hernández, Ortega Martínez and Peñaloza, all supported Gómez once he took over from Castro.

When news reached Arístides Tellería in Curacao of Castro's departure for Europe, Nicolás Rolando and Oscar Larrazabal, who represented Mocho Hernández, visited him to seek advice "over the importance of this matter and the attitude which General Gómez would adopt."[8] Tellería was sure that the country would support Gómez given the unpopularity of Castro, but Rolando had his doubts. Larrazabal agreed with Rolando and transmitted his news to Mocho Hernández in Paris. Rolando and his followers were also having second thoughts because they were losing financial support from the "moneyed adversaries of General Castro both in Venezuela and abroad,"[9] who "see a better chance in obtaining their object by working on the vanity or patriotic feeling of General Gómez than by subsidizing filibustering expeditions from Curacao, or up the Orinoco."[10] On November 28, Sir Vincent Corbett reported that he had "not the smallest doubt that already powerful influences are being brought to bear on General Gómez to convince him that the salvation of the country—to say nothing of his own material interests . . . demand that he should assume power in his own name, and decree the end of the Castro regime."[11] It became clear that the best option for the revolutionaries who did not have sufficient financial backing was to urge Gómez to take over from Castro. Rolando drafted a letter with Tellería and Mocho Hernández to Gómez "expressing the need of a change of regime in the country which would guarantee the rights and freedom of the people in the exercise of all its legal functions, without onerous restrictions to its decency and to national progress."[12] In addition, factions of the old Liberal party now began to acknowledge Gómez as a true Liberal. It was clear to some observers such as Corbett that the "chances of a revolutionary movement from the outside may, therefore, for the present be considered negligible."[13]

PREPARATIONS FOR THE COUP

The new Gómez government was fearful that the Dutch would actively encourage and support the Venezuelan revolutionaries in Curacao. Gómez continued Castro's orders of maintaining the country's garrisons on a state of alert and readiness for combat because of a possible Dutch retaliation or Venezuelan revolutionary threat. José María García, the president of Falcón, reported on December 4 that he had organized the squads of men that Gómez had ordered.[14] Similarly, Carlos Liscano, the president of Lara, reported on December 7 that the two companies of men that Gómez had ordered were ready.[15]

As soon as Gómez became acting president he redoubled his efforts with Paúl and Baptista to start his coup. Paúl continued in his post as foreign affairs minister, while Gómez appointed Baptista, a lawyer by profession who had travelled and studied in Europe and was a cultivated and intelligent man, as his secretary general. Baptista "has latterly kept studiously aloof from politics and declined to associate himself with Castro's absolutist regime."[16] Gómez's inner circle of advisers apart from Baptista and Paúl were Juan Pietri, Francisco Linares Alcántara, Aquiles Iturbe, José Rosario García, Carlos Jiménez Rebolledo, Félix Galavís, and José María Cárdenas (married to Flor, Gómez's sister, and head of the *Tachirense* army). The moving spirit behind the Reacción, as this period is known, was Leopoldo Baptista, who enjoyed the utter confidence of Gómez and, according to the British minister, would "resign his claims to the Presidency in favour of Dr. Baptista's candidature in return for certain privileges and favours in connection with the cattle-rearing and export business"[17] because he recognized his own "incompetence to rule."[18] Gómez was seen by some as a figurehead and a stalking horse for an attack on Castro. Nobody took him to be a serious political figure.

On Castro's side there was a determined band of loyal supporters, the interest of a much larger group of officeholders and military commanders, and the formidable Blohm & Co., the largest trading house in the country. Gómez's fiercest opponents were Jesús María Herrera Irigoyén, Arnaldo Morales, the warden of La Rotunda, and the commanders of the main Caracas barracks; as well as the German commercial houses, especially Blohm. It soon became evident to Gómez that a section of the cabinet would only take orders from Castro, "and unless a radical change was affected it would be impossible to carry on the Government with reasonable efficiency."[19] The situation was becoming more critical. There was widespread hatred of Castro, especially among the better classes. However, the situation was not expected to be ripe for action until the new year. Thus patience was the key word for Gómez.

THE DUTCH QUESTION RETURNS

The Dutch government's bluff of sending a large part of its navy to the Caribbean had failed, with the result that "negotiations [are in] a complete deadlock, and the futility of the Government's diplomacy is adversely commented on in the press."[20] Gómez, Baptista, and Paúl met on November 25 at the Casa Amarilla to consider the Dutch Question, the rupture of diplomatic relations with the United States, France, and Colombia, the bad feeling created by the 30 percent surtax against Trinidad, and the threat of an invasion by Venezuelan exiles. According to Paúl, Gómez stated that his hands were tied because Castro had left his friends in key government and military positions, but he agreed that something had to be done and that they should try to reverse Castro's disastrous foreign policy. Gómez at this early stage was constrained from taking any positive action because of his weak position. Gómez had to wait until he could muster sufficient strength among the military commanders before taking any action. In the meantime, Gómez continued implementing Castro's policy in the light of mounting opposition. For example, a proposed public meeting at the Plaza Bolívar, the capital's main square, to acclaim Gómez and no doubt abuse Castro was cancelled because the provisional president felt such support was premature. Gómez was therefore able to inform Castro on November 29 that it was "all quiet in the country, and that the small incidents in the East have disappeared, only on the side of the border with Colombia does it appear that preparations are increasing."[21] It was also rumored that Nicolás Rolando had acquired financial backing from the NY&B and that he would invade Venezuela on January 10, 1909.[22] Several editors of minor newspapers were imprisoned for printing anti-Castro editorials, and a number of students "were arrested for making anti-liberal [*sic*] Restoration speeches during a popular demonstration for returning exile Dr. Carlos León."[23]

Gómez's political platform rested partly on the abolition of the innumerable monopolies, including the 30 percent surtax on goods imported from the Dutch and British West Indies, the annulment or reduction of a number of Castro's decrees on customs duties, the restoration of peace to the country, and the reestablishment of diplomatic relations with Colombia, the United States, France, and The Netherlands. The abolition of the 30 percent surtax was especially appealing to the British and Dutch governments because the establishment of free competition would clash directly with the monopoly interests of the German trading houses, especially Blohm. An influential German delegation approached Gómez privately to urge him not to yield to the advice of his ministers who recommended the revocation of certain of Castro's decrees, especially the November 17, 1907, which raised the duty of various dry goods. The delegation offered the provisional president a "substantial bribe if he would accede to their position, or in other words if he would maintain General Castro's financial policy."[24] Gómez listened to the delegation but did not commit himself. There were more pressing problems that he had to face, such as the Dutch question.

Gómez's preparations to stage his coup progressed well, and more revolutionaries came over to his side. Arístides Tellería announced that General Colmenares Pacheco, Gómez's brother-in-law, and Leopoldo Baptista the secretary general, were his friends and that he would therefore support Gómez.[25] Leopoldo Baptista had previously secured the support of Caracciolo Parra Picón in Timotes, Trujillo state, in order for the latter to persuade Amador Uzcátegui and José Ignacio Lares, the presidents of Mérida and Zulia respectively, to support Gómez. Trino Baptista, the brother of Leopoldo and the president of Trujillo state, already supported the coup against Castro.[26] Factions of the old Liberal party, effectively driven underground after their crushing defeat by Castro and Gómez during the Revolución Libertadora, began to acknowledge Gómez as a true Liberal. For instance, H. Sarría rejoiced at seeing in Gómez "a Liberal so loyal to his principles like you reach the Capitol; Venezuela and the Liberal party, which will soon support you, pin their hopes on you and I congratulate you as I have no doubt that your magnanimity and ideals will save the Republic."[27]

By early December more revolutionaries had come over to support Gómez. Ortega Martínez, Peñaloza, and Riera arrived in Caracas. Rolando, Mocho Hernández, and Arístides Tellería wrote to express the need for a change in the leadership of the country, which would guarantee the rights and liberties of the people.[28] Gómez welcomed this because his intention on assuming the presidency was to conciliate "public aspirations with my public duties, endeavouring to establish a regime with constitutional guarantees in accordance with our institutions."[29] Moreover, he wanted "for each Venezuelan the effectiveness of his rights without this aspiration being a concession or favour, but only the imposition of the law."[30]

Venezuela's international situation was becoming more critical by the day. The Netherlands amassed its warships at Curacao in preparation to take action. The U.S. government was clearly waiting for a suitable moment to make its influence felt. It became apparent to the Dutch government after its bluff was called that it would need to escalate its pressure to have any effect on the new government of Venezuela. The Dutch cabinet meeting on December 1 was to decide whether coercive action should be taken against the country. The Dutch cabinet debated whether to bombard Puerto Cabello and La Guaira, but it concluded that it would do more damage to foreign merchants than to Venezuela because of the 1907 protocol that "if Holland should institute a rigid blockade on Venezuelan ports, or seize Venezuelan custom houses, there would be loud outcries from debtholders abroad, as well as from the American merchants who buy Venezuelan coffee and cocoa."[31] The Dutch believed that Castro was unlikely to return and that both Gómez and Paúl would greatly facilitate negotiations because they were "disposed to be friendly."[32] The Dutch decided to mount a naval demonstration, but the blockade of Venezuelan ports would not take place "before the result of the demonstration and also of President Castro's visit to Europe is known."[33] The United States reiterated its view that it did not oppose any coercive action by Holland against Venezuela as long as it was confined to a blockade or other maritime measures. Mr. Beaupre, the U.S. charge d'affaires, confirmed this for the Dutch Foreign Minister van Swinderen.[34] It was clear that the Dutch cabinet was divided as to what course of action should be taken because the meeting was a tense one that lasted nine hours. A wait-and-see attitude was eventually adopted because the Queen was against war.

DUTCH WARSHIPS OFF VENEZUELA

On the morning of December 2, three Dutch warships took up their stations at Puerto Cabello, La Guaira, and at the entrance to Lake Maracaibo, cruising backward and forward between Puerto Cabello, Coro, La Guaira, and Higuerote. The warships did not interfere with trade, but Pompilio Quintero warned Gómez that "if the political events were to become more complicated then it is vital to look closer at Zamora as the enemy's centre of operations."[35] Quintero felt that the San Carlos fort at the entrance to Lake Maracaibo should be reinforced. At an emergency cabinet meeting that morning Paúl expressed the views of Gómez and most of his colleagues when he argued that the May 14 decree should be suspended and that Venezuela should enter into negotiations with the Dutch government for the settlement of the dispute. One stalwart Castrista, however, attacked Paúl and accused him of "trying to reverse the policy of his Master, General Castro."[36] However, the foreign minister countered by stating that as long as Castro was in the country "he had dutifully obliged his orders, but now that the General was absent from the country a new situation had arisen and the Council of Ministers was responsible for the maintenance of the national interests and were justified in modifying his policy if those interests required it."[37]

However, there was a growing feeling that Gómez should seize the opportunity and overthrow Castro using the popular support that he undoubtedly commanded. R. Blanco Fombona, who for four months was the governor of Territorio Federal Amazonas in 1905, was closely involved in the events leading up to Castro's eventual overthrow and writes in his diary that the movement against Castro's government started on December 4. Blanco Fombona and his group feared that Gómez would not go ahead with this plot in the same way that he had failed to capitalize during La Aclamación, when Castro withdrew to La Victoria and Gómez urged him to come back. Blanco Fombona's plan was for a public demonstration against Holland that would get the crowd to go to the presidential palace to urge the government to overthrow Castro. Blanco Fombona wanted to "stake one's all; not only to make speeches at Bolívar's statue and against Holland, but also to lead the people to the presidential palace and to get the head of the Executive involved morally with our words and our own civic protest."[38]

However, Gómez appeared immovable, which Blanco Fombona blamed on cowardice. He wrote that the situation had reached an impasse, and the opposition was worried "that Gómez will betray and put an end to it,"[39] while Gómez was afraid that "Castro's friends will gang him."[40] Blanco Fombona argued that Gómez had already betrayed Castro but was frightened that he would be lynched by "the military friends of Castro."[41] It was therefore necessary to abandon Gómez and call for "free elections and let the country decide its destiny."[42] Baptista and the rest of the government wanted to "explain away Gómez's treason with the appearance that this was the result of national coercion,"[43] and that the country in general "wishes sincerely to manifest its antipathy, its hatred towards the misgovernment of Castro and its pretensions to perpetuate itself in power."[44] The demonstration was planned for December 5, but the government did not allow it.

Gómez was becoming impatient with the number of Castristas in government, but Baptista advised that because Castro would not return until February there was no need to worry. Castro's friends were pressuring other cabinet officials to keep him in power, especially those who had gained from Castro's monopolies and from the large trading houses such as Blohm & Co and Boulton.[45] The only member of the cabinet who was strongly anti-Castro was Paúl, the foreign minister. Baptista also needed time for his own coup against Gómez. Baptista could easily organize a popular demonstration against Castro, but he did not want to do it, preferring to win over people such as Linares Alcántara, the president of Bolívar.

After the Dutch escalated their action the political situation inexorably moved toward some sort of denouement. At this stage the plotters still feared the reaction of Castro and his followers in the country. To make doubly sure of succeeding, the inner circle debated Paúl's suggestion of requesting help from foreign powers, including the United States, to defend their coup. They planned to ask each country to send a gunboat to La Guaira, and Gómez sanctioned this move. Paúl discussed these matters and how best to accelerate the coup with Blanco Fombona on December 8, who was shocked by what he heard.[46] The young Venezuelan writer tried in vain to convince Paúl of the error of his judgment in calling on foreign powers for assistance, but the foreign minister insisted that the plotters on their own would be unable to protect themselves. Blanco Fombona reasoned that the best way to defend the coup would be to deploy some five hundred to one thousand men under the command of Oscar, his brother, to repair the streets near Caracas. So when the plotters were ready, they could attack the barracks in the capital city. After the meeting Blanco Fombona immediately saw Baptista about the plan, who answered that Paúl's plans would not take effect.

THE DUTCH ENTER VENEZUELAN TERRITORIAL WATERS

The Dutch escalated their action further. On December 10, Dutch warships entered Venezuelan territorial waters. They arrived at Cumarebo and Los Taques, where they inspected the registers of the merchant schooners *Carmen Josefa* and *Victoria*. On the same day General Jorge Bello, commander of the San Carlos fort, requested reinforcements. A Dutch warship that had been taking soundings at the Bar of Maracaibo decided, in a deliberate act of provocation, to start firing practice three thousand meters away from the fort. Bello feared that the two squads he had to guard five hundred prisoners would rebel. The warship did not interfere with trade, which José Ignacio Lares, the president of Zulia, reported on December 11.[47]

At the cabinet meeting on December 11, Paúl argued for a speedy solution with Holland. At the session Gómez presented Bello's telegram as proof for the need to take action, but the cabinet refused to act until Castro returned, agreeing that Bello should not open fire and thus provoke a bombardment "because the Dutch would get tired with using up powder in salvoes and would leave with its musical orchestra for another place."[48] It was decided to send a Note of protest against the violation of Venezuelan territorial waters. Paúl stated to Sir Vincent Corbett that the Dutch action was a gross violation of territorial sovereignty that had been manifestly carried out with a deliberate purpose, which involved not only the violation of Venezuela's sovereignty but also "of the Law of Nations, as the Government of Holland has neither notified the establishment of a blockade in regular and effective form nor made any declaration of war."[49] The Dutch action seemed odd because it was difficult "to understand what the Dutch are doing or propose to do,"[50] with their ships cruising the Venezuelan coastline, occasionally holding up and examining "Venezuelan sailing boats, but those have hitherto been released at once and ordinary international commerce is not interfered with."[51] However, Venezuela's small navy did not venture out of port.

Gómez's coup was originally planned for early January, but the worsening Dutch situation brought the date forward. There were now definite signs that a coup was being prepared. On December 11, Gómez cancelled all public engagements. The cabinet reduced Castro's Bs 8-million letter of credit with the Banco de Venezuela and cancelled the construction of a triumphal arch in Caracas that extolled the virtues of Castro's revolution because the money was needed elsewhere. Gómez also released certain important political prisoners from Mérida and Trujillo who were held at the San Carlos fort in Zulia. Taking advantage of the threatened Dutch invasion, Gómez strengthened his own military position both in Caracas and in the rest of the country. Some two thousand new recruits were brought into Caracas to offset the strength of Pedro María Cárdenas, the governor of Caracas, with loyal Gomecista officers positioned in the key garrisons of the capital, ready to spring into action when needed. The state presidents who supported Gómez were alerted to the impending coup.

By December 12 well-informed people generally knew that Gómez had "now definitely thrown in his lot with the party of the Reacción as it is now called, which has for its object to render General Castro's return to power impossible."[52] On that same date Interior Minister Rafael López Baralt wrote to all state presidents to inform them of the events leading up to the Dutch naval demonstration. He stated that Venezuela had proposed to send a confidential agent to negotiate a settlement, but the Dutch had instead rescinded the 1894 agreement "without any declaration, invading with its squadron our territorial waters and at the same time inspecting our own naval vessels."[53] López Baralt added that the Dutch had "violated the sacred earth of the fatherland and the Nation will know how to comply with its duty. There are no divergent political opinions that would tear apart its soul, consequently the effort of all united Venezuelans will correspond to the noble and legitimate cause of defending the nation, which the current government of the republic supports."[54] The worst came later in the day when the Dutch cruiser *Gelderland* captured the Venezuelan gunboat *Alexis*, threatening to sink it if the captain did not surrender. The captain finally relented, and the ship's crew was put ashore at Puerto Cabello. Later the Venezuelan gunboat *23 de Mayo* was also captured. Both ships were towed to Curacao. The Dutch government immediately issued a statement stating that the capture of the ship was the "beginning of a policy of reprisals and captures adopted by the Dutch government after it had assured itself that such action would be in conformity with international law."[55] It was made perfectly clear that these measures were against Castro and not the people of Venezuela, with the sole intention of guaranteeing "that there shall be no further molestation of Dutch ships in regard to which President Castro had failed to make any reassuring statement as to the future."[56] The Dutch reprisals against Venezuela appeared to *The Nation* to "make the 'hostilities' appear less like opera-bouffe."[57] The Dutch government explained "that their act does not mean war; that these harmless vessels, with their rusty rifles, have merely been borrowed for a short time as a reprisal in order to compel Venezuela to pay attention to just demands."[58]

The Dutch seizures of Venezuelan gunboats, however, was the catalyst that instigated Gómez's coup by contributing to an internal crisis, which forced the conspirators "to show their hands earlier than they desired."[59] The country was now defenseless. It was at the mercy of the Dutch warships, of the planned invasion by Venezuelan exiles, and of the possible internal uprisings by officers who did not support Gómez. Paúl immediately sent Notes to the diplomatic corps that vigorously protested against the violation of Venezuelan territorial rights by Holland. Venezuela could not protect foreign citizens "not because of a domestic disturbance but owing to the hostility of a foreign naval force."[60] Some of Paúl's cabinet colleagues decided that they did not want to do anything that would displease Castro. So they agreed to consult him by telegraph to ascertain his views.

Leopoldo Baptista encouraged students, such as Manuel Briceño Rabello from Trujillo, to demonstrate in the streets of Caracas after the news of the Dutch naval demonstration reached the capital. At an emergency cabinet meeting it was decided to offer the interior ministry post to Linares Alcántara because this would mean that his troops would be neutralized at the beginning of the coup. At the same meeting it was agreed that Baptista would become Gómez's secretary general and Paúl would be sent overseas as minister plenipotentiary to settle the country's disputes with the European powers. Others who would form part of Gómez's first cabinet included Francisco González Guinán, Rafael María Carabaño, Aquiles Iturbe and Régulo Olivares.

Linares Alcántara left Ciudad Bolívar for Caracas, arriving in La Guaira on Saturday, December 12, just as the crisis began. He was greeted by Eloy González—a representative of Garbiras Guzmán, Castro's last secretary general—who warned him not to trust Gómez "and who would probably try to raise the Castrista flag taking advantage of the confused moments in which the country is living through."[61] However, Linares Alcántara argued that Castro had abandoned his friends when he left the government in the hands of Gómez "with the nucleus so weakened that the rest were left no other alternative but to weather the storm until the situation is clearer."[62] He added that he had no loyalty for the former president. Linares Alcántara then boarded the train to Caracas where he was met by Leopoldo Baptista, who drove him to see Gómez. Both men embraced warmly. Gómez explained that now that Castro was out of the picture there were no obstacles between them. They agreed to meet the following day at 8 A.M., but at 7:00 A.M. Baptista telephoned to postpone the meeting for 2:00 P.M. The plotters wanted to commit Linares Alcántara to their cause by staging his attendance at an anti-Castro rally that was being planned. Notice was given to the students to organize a patriotic demonstration at the Plaza Bolívar later that afternoon. According to Sir Vincent Corbett, neither Paúl, Baptista, nor the rest of the cabinet realized what was going to happen. The first to arrive at the capital's main square were the students. By 3:00 P.M., it was full of people "at the beginning not many of the populace were present with only 'decent people' as we tend to call the bourgeoisie and those who work in liberal professions."[63] The Casa Amarilla by this time was "crowded with an assemblage of the distinguished persons of the capital."[64] At 2:00 P.M., Gómez welcomed Linares Alcántara, but moments later Baptista interrupted them to state that a protest march had started in the Plaza Bolívar. A little after 4:00 P.M., Gómez drove to the Plaza Bolívar "wreathed in smiles, and was received with frantic cheers."[65] He entered the government building and shortly afterward appeared on the balcony, flanked by Paúl and Baptista. Patriotic speeches by Dr. Toro, the former consul in Trinidad, and by a student were delivered from the steps of the Bolívar statue. The speeches called on the people to support Gómez and put an end to the current tyranny. Later Castro's portrait was burned. Paúl gave a speech on Dutch aggression and urged the nation to rally around Gómez. Leopoldo Baptista advised Paúl to continue referring to Holland, but the crowd only jeered when Paúl alluded again to the Dutch insult to the national honor. The mob demanded the release of the political prisoners and that government monopolies be abolished. The crowd also wanted to hear Gómez speak, but he refused. It was left to Paúl to exhort "the people to trust General Gómez to solve the difficult problems confronting Venezuela and praying them to help him to bear the burden of responsibility."[66] Suddenly, Juan Pietri took hold of Gómez's arm "and shouts: Long live Gómez! Down with the Tyrant!"[67] Gómez immediately left the balcony and toured the town with Baptista, Linares Alcántara, and others. Gómez knew that "he governed with the support of public opinion and that he had in the newspapers the expression of that support."[68]

R. Blanco Fombona, Elias Torres, Andrés Sánchez, and Juan Pietri, "promoters of the disturbances"[69] as some observers referred to them, then led the mob on a rampage, seeking to destroy the most potent symbols of the former regime. By late afternoon the mob assembled before the office of *El Constitucional*, which resulted in "a pitched battle with the staff of the newspaper."[70] The mob stormed the offices of the newspaper. One person died and several more were wounded when a number of shots were fired. The police arrived soon afterward and restored order. The mob dispersed and took "Pietri in triumph to his home,"[71] where more speeches were made. Pietri was exhausted by the events of the day and had to ask Blanco Fombona to take the mob away from his house. Blanco Fombona became the unofficial leader "of that mob of people."[72] There were more speeches at San Francisco and El Panteón. The mob continued to swarm around the city, breaking "as many busts and portraits of Castro that we could find."[73] They wanted to attack the house of Rivas' mistress, but Blanco Fombona opposed it because "it was cowardice to leave *El Constitucional*, because it was defended by men and then to go and attack defenceless women."[74] Others wanted to ransack Tello Mendoza's home. Instead, they returned to the Plaza Bolívar where Blanco Fombona made another speech, at the end of which he was carried on their shoulders "against my will and took me around the square, suffocating, mauled, half-dead with tiredness."[75] Blanco Fombona was finally able to escape "the crowd which hailed me with the absurd shouts of: Long live the people's brains! Long live the great democrat and other silly things."[76] Similar events took place in other cities. In Maracaibo, for instance, more than five thousand demonstrated against the Dutch. In Coro a theater was filled to capacity with demonstrators. According to official figures the demonstrations during December 13 in Caracas resulted in two deaths and three wounded people.[77]

Late on the afternoon of December 13 a cabinet meeting was hurriedly convened to consider what to do against the Dutch aggression. The cabinet decided that it constituted an invasion of Venezuelan territory, and the "national sovereignty is threatened and the territorial integrity, honour and dignity of the Fatherland are in danger."[78] Foreign Affairs Minister Paúl, Finance Minister Arnoldo Morales, and Development Minister J. M. Herrera Irigoyen (two of Castro's staunchest supporters in the cabinet), offered to tender their resignations. General Pedro María Cárdenas, governor of the Federal District, also offered his resignation unless he was allowed to take the measures he considered necessary for restoring law and order in the capital. Cárdenas resignation was not accepted. In the evening the government suspended constitutional guarantees in the Federal District and imposed martial law, which was later extended to the rest of the country. The government issued a decree that conferred extraordinary powers on Gómez and placed the country in a state of defense in preparation for further Dutch action. Sir Vincent interpreted the special powers conferred on Gómez as a "coup d'etat aimed at General Castro, rather than the Dutch."[79]

Martial law allowed Gómez to call upon the states to cooperate in the defense of Venezuelan territory and Venezuelan institutions, to collect taxes in advance, to arrest, imprison, or expel from the country people considered dangerous to the state, to abolish civil rights, to change the place of residence of the government, and to execute people who acted hostile to its national defense. The real object of the exercise, according to Corbett, was to "finally supersede General Castro and put an extinguisher on his pretension to continue to issue orders in spite of his absence from the country and his formal surrender of power."[80] Sir Vincent reported the proclamation of martial law by Gómez "may have for its object the checking of irresponsible revolutionary movements, just as well as the necessity to meet the external situation brought about by the action of the Dutch warships."[81] It would be of considerable help in fostering Gómez's coup plans.

The following day, December 14, the mob sacked the publishing house of *Editorial Cosmos* and destroyed the *Lavandería Venezolana*, both of which were owned by Gumersindo Rivas, at an estimated loss of Bs 40,000.[82] The crowd also destroyed a drugs warehouse that was owned by the Dutchman Henrique Thielen, the son-in-law of Ramón Tello Mendoza, and then proceeded to sack Tello Mendoza's chemist shops. In the afternoon the Cigarrería Nacional and another chemist shop that Henrique Thielen owned were saved when troops managed to restore law and order. It was estimated that the total losses amounted to between Bs 200,000 and Bs 300,000.[83] Rumors soon spread that "the nearby towns had armed themselves and were marching towards Caracas."[84]

The country was now virtually paralyzed and under the martial control of Gómez and his army. However, with the country appearing to descend into anarchy the secret committee appointed by Castro decided to arrest Gómez and his supporters, but they "lacked the courage at the critical moment."[85] That same evening Pedro María Cárdenas detained Bernabé Planas, Juan Pietri, Vicente Emilio Velutini, and Elias Torres. They were accused of initiating the ransacking of Henrique Thielen's property and Gumersindo Rivas' *El Constitucional* and *Lavandería Venezolana*. Blanco Fombona managed to evade being arrested by hiding from the authorities. He was scornful of Gómez's leadership, feeling that there were two groups in the government: "the Castrista and other reactionaries."[86] He felt that Gómez was "compromising with everybody, fooling the whole world. He is not the man which the moment demands."[87]

U.S. REACTION

When news of the capture of the *Alexis* reached Washington, members of the Senate Committee on Foreign Relations declared that Castro was about to get "his long-deserved spanking."[88] The news was not unexpected because the Dutch had previously consulted with the United States about the whole maneuver. The American government's attitude was one of "strict neutrality, unless foreign commerce or foreign interests are seriously interfered with—a contingency which is not considered probable."[89] The *Nieuwe Courant*, an Amsterdam newspaper, on December 14 published an "elaborate and probably inspired expose"[90] of the conflict, concluding that the seizure of the *Alexis* was a "legitimate act of reprisal . . . justified by the failure of the negotiations conducted with so much patience by the Netherlands Government."[91] Depriving Venezuela of its warships would make it more difficult for the government to put down a rebellion. Thus, either the government of Gómez would repeal the May 14 decree, or the revolutionaries would be successful in deposing Castro. The newspaper added that an act of reprisal was not an act of war, but it could be recognized by another party as a *casus belli*. Holland was exposing itself to the risk of a declaration of war by Venezuela. However, because the Puerto Cabello guns did not fire when the *Gelderland* was within range, it was thought that Gómez intended to "submit to the inevitable."[92]

On December 14, Rafael María Carabaño met with Santiago Briceño Ayesterán, who commanded part of the army and had five thousand men at his disposal, to inquire whether he would join the plotters, as many of the former Castrista political figures "and all the leaders who formed part of the Libertadora revolution"[93] were backing Gómez. However, Briceño Ayesterán refused to join the conspiracy. Carabaño returned the following day to offer him the Public Works Ministry, but he refused again because he was not a man "who is only looking for a position but a man of principles."[94] That same day, however, Briceño Ayesterán informed Pedro María Cárdenas, Garbiras Guzmán, and Rafael López Baralt of the impending coup. As a result the Castristas started to take preventative measures. General Maximiano Casanova placed the Batallón Urdaneta under Governor Pedro María Cárdenas. The troops that had been deployed in the center of Caracas to deal with the riots were ordered back to barracks, with the commanders only taking orders from Cárdenas or Casanova. When this reached Gómez's ears, he decided to seize power.

When the cabinet agreed to confer special powers on General Gómez, Paúl informed the diplomatic corps of the acting president's intention of restoring the country to normalcy. Gómez had almost complete military control of the country, but he still feared Castro's reaction. Paúl was unduly nervous of the possibility of an anti-Gómez reaction, especially in the provinces. This appeared to be paranoia, but as Corbett charitably explained, "allowance must be made for the nervousness of a man who for weeks past had been working literally night and day in imminent peril of his life in hatching a treasonable conspiracy"[95] that if unsuccessful would mean many long years of penury as an exile, imprisonment in chains, or death. Paúl therefore reasoned that because there was no guarantee that Gómez would succeed in his venture, to safeguard the success of the coup it was legitimate to seek the support of foreign powers in the Dutch situation. Paúl felt that if foreign moral support could be achieved, then the revolution would succeed. He felt that given Holland's belligerent attitude, Venezuela could not protect itself or the interests of other countries because many people would not respect or accept Gómez's authority as the new leader of the country. The presence of foreign, neutral warships would prevent this from happening and give a strong warning to anybody who resisted the Gómez coup. Paúl used the example of the 1903 "peaceful blockade" by Germany, Britain, and Italy to argue that if an American warship had been at La Guaira, then a German warship would not have been allowed to block the entry of a Red 'D' Line ship at any Venezuelan port, and the blockade would have been stillborn. He believed that the presence of foreign gunboats from friendly nations would forestall any reaction in favor of Castro and would give the Gómez government added legitimacy. Paúl did not want the foreign powers to intervene in the "internal politics of the country nor to support in any way a political plan."[96] Paúl's sole motivation was for the foreign powers to protect their interests because the government was unable to do so because of Holland's attitude, "this being one practical situation in international law where it is justified to have neutral naval vessels as a countervailing force against the hostile act [of] the squadron that blockades the coasts of a country."[97] Sir Vincent Corbett writes that the coup plotters at the time

> believed it to be of vital importance to themselves to secure the moral support of foreign powers. They hoped, as the result of their conciliatory declarations to see the war-ships of all nations speeding to La Guaira to salute General Gómez's accession to power, and to overawe by their presence the disaffected elements in the country. Things, however, went a good deal more smoothly than they anticipated, the necessity for foreign moral support disappeared, and there upon their consuming anxiety to be on friendly terms with the world at large sensibly diminished.[98]

With this in mind Paúl saw a number of foreign representatives on December 14. Paúl first saw Luis de Lorena Ferreira, the Brazilian minister who was in charge of American and French interests in the country. Paúl informed him that because foreign interests were at risk, it would be desirable for a U.S. warship to be in Venezuelan territorial waters, especially as Gómez was about to "carry out a radical change in the foreign affairs policy adopted by General Castro in order to resolve in a friendly manner the pending differences with foreign countries."[99] Paúl continued to explain that both had witnessed the type of chaos that Venezuela could drift into, especially as Castro's supporters had "in their hands powerful elements of resistance."[100] The United States had also to consider "the state in which our coasts and ports are after the attitude adopted by the Dutch navy has rendered useless our protection and defenses because of the blockade by its coastguards and a consequent lack of communication."[101]

Paúl also saw Sir Vincent Corbett on December 14 and made the same request for the British government to send a warship to protect its citizens and property because the present government was unable to do so due to the internal situation. Sir Vincent replied that he appreciated enormously "the attitude of General Gómez and the interest shown by the government in protecting foreigners and their assets,"[102] but he did not think that foreign interests in the country were in any danger. Paúl then inquired whether any British warships were planning to sail to Venezuela because the "presence of a British ship would be very agreeable as affording a moral support to the Government of General Gómez."[103] Corbett informed the British government of Paúl's request, but no action was taken. The next morning, December 15, Paúl saw Count Aldriovandi, the Italian minister, and repeated his request, which was also turned down. The only country that took Paúl's plea seriously, was the United States, which was looking for just such an opportunity to press for a solution to its inflated American claims. Paúl would later be accused of wanting to set up an American protectorate, but this was untrue because he requested the help of other powers.

THE AMERICANS ACT

After the meeting with Paúl, Luis de Lorena Ferreira telegraphed the State Department to inform them that the Venezuelan foreign affairs minister requested to "make it known [to] American Government wish [of] President Gómez to settle satisfactorily all international questions. Thinks convenient presence American warship to Guaira in prevision [*sic*] of events."[104] The United States seized the psychological moment because it would get them out of the impasse they were in with Castro. The request for help by the Gómez camp was just the excuse the United States was looking for because Roosevelt wanted to intervene in the country in the same way that he had done in Cuba, Santo Domingo, and Panama. He could not do so, as he explained to William Bayard Hale of the *New York Times*, because he was unable to wake "our people so that they would back a reasonable and intelligent foreign policy which would put a stop to crying disorders at our very doors."[105] Secretary of State Root had also battled against the desire by some in the State Department to "bulldoze Venezuela,"[106] preferring to follow a more patient approach. Although he felt sorry for the Venezuelan people who allowed themselves to be governed by such "an irresponsible tyrant"[107] as Castro and had suffered the consequences, he believed that it was "only through suffering that they can ever reach the stage of true self-government and true liberty."[108] Root hoped that the awful "experience through which Venezuela is now passing will lead to an effective reaction and the inauguration of a permanently better state of things."[109] The United States therefore reacted swiftly to Paúl's request. Roosevelt advised Secretary of State Root to "send a first-class man down there in order to be on the ground before the trouble takes place."[110] William Buchanan, the man who had masterminded the secession of Panama from Colombia in 1901 and who was the first U.S. minister to that country,[111] was appointed to the task. The United States interpreted Paúl's message as meaning that the Venezuelans wanted to settle the five American claims, which would "naturally involve the acceptance of the proposal of the United States for the arbitration of the pending claims and the disavowal of the discourtesies referred to in the instructions to the American Charge."[112] It was clear to the United States that the purpose of the new government was to "revoke the policy followed by President Castro"[113] as Root stated when he announced on December 17 that he was sending Special Envoy Buchanan to Venezuela. The U.S. government's attitude toward the Venezuelan revolution would be "benevolent," and it would not interfere.

Paúl was later blamed for allowing the Americans to enter Venezuela with such a large force, but his defense was that the telegram had been written by the Brazilian diplomat without allowing him to check the wording. Lorena used the phrase "as a precaution of events," which Paúl felt could give rise to "elated spirits or driven by a personal agenda, have supposed that those events and that precaution is related to an American intervention in our domestic politics."[114] According to Paúl this was not only slanderous, but untrue because he sought the help of several other foreign diplomats. Paúl would later blame González Guinán, who replaced him as foreign minister after the coup, for misinterpreting him. It was González Guinán who on December 28, in answer to Lorena's December 27 letter that was sent three days after Paúl left for Europe, stated that

> I have given a report of your above mentioned note (the one which has the cablegram from Mr. Lorena) to Mr. General Gómez, Acting President of the Republic, and he has expressed his wishes to reach an amicable and fair solution with the American government over the pending matters, and with this in mind he is delighted with the arrival of High Commissioner Mr. Buchanan, who can clearly start his important work on assessing the Venezuelan government.[115]

Although the action of the Dutch navy off the coast of Venezuela was viewed with consternation by some in The Netherlands, Count Limburg Stirum, *Chef de Cabinet* of The Netherlands, felt that "the seizure of the Venezuelan police vessels was a step taken by way of reprisal"[116] and that "the present action of the Dutch Government was taken with the countenance of the United States"[117] and was not "intended to seize any of the Customs Houses which would prejudice the interest of neutrals."[118] The Dutch at this stage realized that their policies were not producing the desired results. They conceded that "the restoration of peaceful mutual relations was in the interest both of Holland and Venezuela."[119] Consequently, Baron Seckerdorff, the German minister who was looking after Dutch affairs in Venezuela, was instructed to inform the government that The Netherlands was willing to settle its differences if the May 14 decree were repealed. The Venezuelan government was willing to consider the decree a dead letter until further notice. The Dutch were content to reach an agreement as long as the Venezuelan government met the following conditions: that the Venezuelan measures would carry the same weight as if the decree had been withdrawn and that said measures should be explicitly notified to the colonial government of Curacao. The Dutch were also willing to stop their naval demonstration and to regard themselves as bound by the 1894 protocol, and hence renew the prohibition of arms exports. The Dutch government also agreed to meet the Venezuelan plenipotentiary if the May 14 decree were repealed.[120] Gómez, Paúl, and Baptista met the German minister on December 17. Gómez assured Baron Seckerdorff that he wanted an amicable solution "but that internal political complications made it difficult for him to take the necessary measures at once and asked for a delay of two or three days."[121] In Holland the Committee for the Promotion of Peace with Venezuelan had been formed. On December 19 a notice appeared in all Dutch newspapers that urged the Dutch government to accept the Venezuelan suggestion to send a special commissioner for peace.

THE PLOT GAINS STEAM

It is hard to imagine how chaotic the political situation of the country was at this stage when nobody was sure who could be trusted. On December 15, José Rosario García asked Linares Alcántara to accompany him to see Gómez. Garbiras Guzmán had informed García that Linares Alcántara was fomenting a "yellow revolution,"[122] but Guzmán also informed Gómez that this was a ploy "to distance him from the Castrista group, which was still dangerous, in order to find a door through which to slip pass."[123] All the key leaders like Sarmiento, Delgado Chalbaud, and Emilio Rivas had gone over to Gómez, who was also popular with the general population. However, the German trading houses, in particular *Blohm & Co.*, were in favor "of General Castro and hostile to General Gómez."[124]

The political situation deteriorated. The pro-Castro cabinet resigned on December 17 to give themselves more flexibility. Soon afterward Caracas was electrified with the knowledge that change was imminent because if Gómez did not act now, there was little doubt that General Pedro María Cárdenas would take him prisoner. The Urdaneta battalion quartered at the San Carlos and Mamey barracks were commanded by Maximiano Casanova (stationed at San Carlos), Juan de Dios Angulo (stationed at Mamey), and an illegitimate half brother of Castro. They refused to obey Gómez's orders and only answered to Pedro María Cárdenas.

Blanco Fombona and the men his brother Oscar could muster were ready to strike on December 20 because they preferred "to die in the camps, fighting and not to fall into that rats' nest to be decapitated by the barbarous crowd or at least drag chains while Castro and his hired assassins so desire."[125] Blanco Fombona wrote in his diary on December 18 that some argued that it would be difficult to fight "against the barbarous Andean system"[126] of both Castro and Gómez, but if they did not and Castro returned, "will he not be a Caligula? And if Gómez manages to consolidate his rule, will he not be another Castro? With our complacency we will lose our liberty and civilization."[127]

It was now a question of who would move first. The secret committee that Castro had set up before his departure waited for orders from Berlin to spring into action. Gómez continued his military preparations, positioning troops and their equipment into key areas. On December 18, two companies from Barquisimeto took up their positions in Maracay, a key city from which to fight a rearguard attack if necessary. In addition, arms and ammunition from the national armory and the Federal District armory were distributed to Gómez's supporters.[128] General Ilario Lázaro from the Federal District received six rifle slings and six leather pouches. The Miranda battalion received 192 rifle slings, 192 leather pouches, 192 cartridge belts, 192 belts, 192 blankets, and 192 sandals; and the Guaicaipuro battalion received 188 rifle slings, 188 leather pouches, and 188 belts. In addition, the Miranda battalion received from the 13 de Abril Battalion 192 mauser carbines, and 5,760 rounds of ammunition from the San Mauricio barracks. The national armory also provided General Ilario Lázaro with six mauser carbines, six bayonets and 150 rounds of ammunition, the Miranda battalion with 192 bayonets, and the Guaicaipuro battalion with 188 mauser carbines and 188 bayonets with 5,640 rounds of ammunition.[129] Loyal troops were also deployed in Coro and Maracaibo. Gómez also brought two thousand new recruits into Caracas to offset the strength of Governor Cárdenas.

The country was virtually paralyzed under the martial control of Gómez and his army, and defenseless against the Dutch threats. It seemed that if something were not done soon, a period of anarchy would ensue. Moreover, the administrative order that Castro created had broken down. There was a widespread revulsion to the monopolies that had been granted, which had led to economic depression. On December 18, Rafael José Velazco reported that the exiled revolutionaries were "the next to move."[130] Gómez therefore needed to move quickly because the revolutionaries were on his doorstep and the Dutch had taken away the Venezuelan navy, his most effective troop carriers. Moreover, the Dutch at any time could invade and take the side of the revolutionaries. Thus it was necessary to pull the rug out from under the revolutionaries by making peace with the Dutch and the exiles. According to the *Times*, General Pedro María Cárdenas, Torres Cárdenas, the commanders of three battalions, and Castro's secret committee met at the home of R. Garbiras Guzmán, Castro's last secretary general, on the evening of December 18 to plot the downfall of Gómez.[131] It was agreed both that Gómez had to be replaced by Rafael López Baralt as acting president and that Arnoldo Morales should distribute funds among the conspirators.

The pro-Castro *junta* naturally telegraphed the news to Castro, who is alleged to have wired back from Berlin in a coded message that they "should strike down the Serpent of sedition beginning at the head, and punish the people of Caracas."[132] The telegram, intercepted by the director of telegraphs, was interpreted by Pedro María Cárdenas to mean that Gómez, Paul, and Baptista should either be arrested or eliminated. Considerable controversy surrounds this telegram because the original was never discovered. Most historians, including Velásquez and Picón Salas, suggest that the telegram was fabricated by José Rosario García and Baptista to convince Gómez to act. The evidence for this is rather superficial and relies on its rustic or telluric phraseology, which is closer to Gómez than Castro, "more rural than provincial"[133] as Velásquez writes, and is from somebody who "talks about sowing and animal husbandry and who has found a philosophy and method for politics in the teachings of nature."[134] Contemporaries close to the events in Venezuela also cast doubts on the authenticity of the telegram. Blanco Fombona described it as "an enormous and absurd hoax."[135] Moreover, he was convinced at the time that nobody in Caracas believed "in such a conspiracy and in such silly phrases and sent by telegraph."[136] Further evidence that shows that Castro could not have been able to send such a telegram was that on December 18, the day when Castro was supposed to have sent it, he was interned at Israel's clinic. However, on December 18 Castro still had all his intellectual faculties and was quite capable of sending orders back to Venezuela, especially as he was keeping a close watch on events. Based on the evidence it would appear that the conspiracy was hatched at the initiative of the pro-Castro faction in the cabinet and could conceivably have been a coup against Castro as well.

The arguments about the missing telegram are deceptively persuasive, but communication between Castro and his secret committee was almost continuous up to the time of the coup. Therefore, it is not unlikely that he could have issued orders for the disposal of his old crony. The wording of the telegram may have been different, and a copy of the telegram could have been secured from the Berlin office of the cable company. Moreover, as the country was cut off from the rest of the world because of its dispute with the FCC, telegrams from Europe were sent to Trinidad, where Benavides Ponce would forward them by boat to Cristóbal Colón[137] to have them retransmitted to Caracas. According to Guzmán Calderón, the chief of the telegraph station at Cristóbal Colón who was very friendly with Manuel Felipe Torres, Castro's illegitimate son, between December 13 and 19 he received from the Caracas office two cablegrams in cipher that were signed and addressed to the consul in Trinidad. The former collector of customs at Cristóbal Colón, L. Niemtschik, later stated that the telegraph office of Caracas had ordered Guzmán Calderón to request a boat to send an urgent telegram to the consul of Venezuela in Trinidad. Guzmán Calderón forwarded the received telegram in a sealed envelope for the consul.[138] Guzmán Calderón also stated that the telegram containing the order to kill Gómez was one of a number of ciphered cablegrams that he received during this period from the Venezuelan consul in Trinidad to transmit to Caracas. Gómez was aware that the secret committee had been receiving telegrams from Castro and that it was more than likely that they would try to do something against him. The relevance of the authenticity of the telegram takes a secondary place when it is noted that the secret committee had tried to move against Gómez almost a week before.

Whether it was caused by the alleged Castro telegram or by the deteriorating political situation itself, the pro-Castro supporters were now planning the easiest way to get rid of Gómez and his supporters. Many pro-Castro officers left their posts for secret nightly meetings to plan the best way of keeping Castro in power. It was decided that the pro-Castro ministers would meet with their military supporters early on Saturday, December 19, to put an end to Gómez's ambition of taking power. When Gómez became aware of the intentions of the secret committee, his mind was made up for him because he had no other option but to launch his bid for the presidency. After receiving proof that his life was in danger on December 18, Gómez felt that it was the right time to move. He ordered the cabinet and General Cárdenas to resign. General Félix Galavís was ordered to have La Sagrada, the presidential guard of honor of three hundred men, ready to move early the next morning. General Graciliano Jaimes was ordered to be ready for a meeting the following morning with the people who would form the cabinet. In Valencia, González Guinán received an urgent message on December 18 to leave for Caracas immediately.

GÓMEZ TAKES OVER

At 5:30 A.M. on December 19, Gómez left his house in El Paraiso for the Mamey barracks. He was guarded by La Sagrada and travelled with Leopoldo Baptista, Manuel Salvador Araujo, Félix Galavís, Juan Pietri, Aquiles Iturbe, and Jimenez Rebolledo. Linares Alcántara was shaving when he was interrupted by Rafael María Carabaño, who rushed into the bathroom shouting that"in the street there was an unusual movement of 'sagrados.' "[139] At the same time Gómez telephoned Linares Alcántara to meet him at the Casa Amarilla. Gómez then headed for the Casa Amarilla while his commanders moved on the various barracks of the city. The Mamey barracks were taken by Graciliano Jaimes without any difficulty because Juan de Dios Angulo, the commanding officer, was not at his post and was arrested upon his return. At the San Carlos barracks General Maximiano Casanova, after a brief exchange of fire, surrendered to General Eliseo Sarmiento. Lorenzo Carvallo secured the control of the Cuartel de San Mauricio and the police force.

When Gómez arrived at the Casa Amarilla he found Pedro María Cárdenas waiting for him. Cárdenas was in a defiant mood and maintained that there was no plot to assassinate Gómez. Gómez seized him by the shoulders and shaking him roughly told him "So this is what you traitors thought! But I have discovered all and I have trapped all."[140] Cárdenas tried to use his revolver, but Gómez held his arms while a guard disarmed him. Cárdenas was then taken away to prison despite his demands for an explanation.[141] When Garbiras Guzmán and Rafael López Baralt arrived, they were arrested and sent to La Rotunda prison, where seventy-pound shackles were attached to their ankles. Arnaldo Morales, the former finance minister, was also jailed "for handing out money to the conspirators to assassinate Gómez."[142] In the afternoon Briceño Ayesterán joined his former colleagues at La Rotunda. Briceño Ayesterán urged Leopoldo Baptista to release him because he had not plotted against Gómez's life. He complained "energetically against such infamy, and I would not know how to pardon anybody who would stain his name with such thoughts, as there have been no assassins in my family."[143] At a trial in 1909, Briceño Ayesterán's name was not included among those accused of plotting to assassinate Gómez. He was released on March 9 of that year.

Although the engineers behind the coup were Paúl and Baptista, with the latter providing "the brains of the movement [and] expected to play an increasingly prominent part in the future,"[144] it was doubtful, as Sir Vincent Corbett writes, that they would have succeeded had it not been for the "efficient and wholehearted support of General Gómez without whom the movement would have been doomed to failure."[145] It was Gómez's personal courage and heroism, Sir Vincent believed, that had "turned the scale on Saturday morning: and he acted alone."[146] If Gómez faltered or had failed to hold the support of a body of troops, then Sir Vincent had no doubt that he "would have been murdered and a Military terrorism established to hold the government until the return of General Castro."[147] The revolution came "within an ace of failure"[148] because without Gómez's prompt action he would have been murdered by pro-Castro supporters on December 19. This was "only thwarted at the last moment by the prompt decision with which it was met, and the admirable coolness and courage shown by the General himself."[149]

ALL QUIET IN CARACAS

Early that morning the news of Gómez's coup spread like wildfire around Caracas. People streamed out of their homes and headed for the Plaza Bolívar and the Casa Amarilla, where they found Gómez "receiving well-wishers and the hurrahs of many of the people who were around at that time of day."[150] A certain amount of alarm spread among the plotters later during the day when news reached Caracas from Berlin that Castro had been given a popular and official welcome. Rumors circulated that he would return escorted by warships that were purchased from the German government. Sir Vincent writes that

> It was this news—demonstrably absurd though it was—that encouraged the Castroist Camarilla to determine on attempting a counter coup d'etat, and if necessary assassinating General Gómez. The plan miscarried; but, that it came within an ace of success I attribute without hesitation to the fact that the conspirators believed that if they succeeded in establishing a Provisional Government, they would have

the support of Germany and they knew it would be welcomed by the German colony here.[151]

In spite of this, there was remarkably little resistance to Gómez's coup. A few skirmishes took place in Cristóbal Colón and in San Antonio de Maturín in eastern Venezuela. In Cristóbal Colón on December 28, Manuel Felipe Torres, the illegitimate son of Castro, refused to hand over certain provisions to General Evaristo Parra because he alleged that they belonged to him. Torres promptly shot Parra through the forehead and wounded Eloy Añez in the left arm. Torres then went to the barracks and made the men mutiny, ordering the death of the officers. In Táchira, General Pedro Murillo secured control of the state by arresting the head of the telegraph office, while General Celestino Castro, the president of the state, was allowed to escape to Colombia "for reasons that you will understand."[152] In Carúpano, Elbano Mibelli, Pedro Alcántara Leal, and Olegario Salas took temporary control of the town on December 27. In San Antonio de Maturin the *jefe civil* captured Basilio Acevedo, José Aristimuño Coll, and Francisco González, who intended to take up arms on December 29. Further investigation revealed, however, that the affair was only "a lack of respect for the local authority"[153] and had been satisfactorily resolved.

Among Castro's state presidents only Luciano Mendible at Guárico took up arms, rather belatedly on December 29. He claimed that Gómez had betrayed the people with his promises of freedom when he had tried to turn the country into "a feudal state at the almost exclusive service of a regionalism that has been exploiting the country with a shamelessness that makes the promises and pronouncements made by General Juan Vicente Gómez improbable and impossible."[154] Mendible's efforts were badly timed because he placed himself under the command of Nicolás Rolando, "the only chieftain who inspires us with total confidence because of his background as a patriot, for his efforts that are a sacrifice and for his genuine liberal ideas."[155] Rolando was at the time travelling to Venezuela to join Gómez's new government. Not surprisingly, Mendible's uprising was short-lived. On January 5 he was captured with forty-five thousand rounds of ammunition and three hundred and twenty mauser carbines.[156]

Gómez's coup was a well-executed maneuver in which he tried to plan for all eventualities to the extent that his supporters shamefully tried to enlist the help of foreign powers with disastrous consequences. A sad, and dishonorable chapter in Venezuelan history ended on December 19. However, the new government of Gómez paid dearly for Castro's excesses.

NOTES

1. "Actitud de Holanda," *Venezuela. Ecos de una Tiranía*, vol. 4: 24, November 1908, pp. 186.

2. AHMSGPRCP Marzo 22–31 1930 Simón Barceló to Gómez, 24 March 30. Simón Barceló, who was General Velutini's private secretary for more than twenty-two years, wrote to Gómez in 1930 that "Armando Rolando was always a cautious politician and an important factor in the distancing of Rolando from Velutini."

3. AHMSGPRCP Marzo 22–31 1930 Simón Barceló to Gómez, 24 March 30.

4. Manuel Landaeta Rosales, "Rasgos Biográficos del General J. V. Gómez," in *Venezuela Conjuración 1909*, pp. 397–403.

5. FO 371/571 Sir Vincent Corbett to Sir Edward Grey, 28 November 08.

6. Santiago Briceño Ayesterán, *Memorias de Su Vida Militar*, Caracas, Tip. América, 1948, p. 362.

7. AHM SGPRCP Nov 16–30 1908 José Ignacio Lares to Gómez, 27 November 08.

8. Arístides Tellería, *Mi Actuación en la Vida Pública*, Havana, Fernández & Cia, 1950.

9. FO 371/571 Corbett to Grey, 28 November 08.

10. Ibid.

11. Ibid.

12. Tellería, p. 254–55.

13. FO 199/233 Corbett to Grey, 28 November 08.

14. AHMSGPRCP Dic 1–14 1908 M. García to Gómez, 4 December 08.

15. AHMSGPRCP Dic 1–14 1908 Carlos Liscano to Gómez, 7 December 08.

16. FO 199/233 Corbett to Grey, 25 November 08.

17. FO 199/233 Corbett to Grey, 12 December 08.

18. Ibid.

19. FO 199/233 Corbett to Grey, 25 December 08.

20. FO 199/215 Acton to Grey, 1 December 08.

21. AHM COP 100 Gómez to Castro, 29 November 08.

22. AHM SGPRCP Feb 1–14 1909 Guillermo Wenzel to Gómez, 3 February 09.

23. William M. Sullivan, "The Rise of Despotism in Venezuela: Cipriano Castro, 1899–1908" Ph.D. diss., The University of New Mexico, 1974, p. 618.

24. FO 199/213 Corbett to Grey, 21 January 09.

25. AHM SGPRCP Dic 14–23 1908 Arístides Tellería to Gómez, 13 December 08.

26. Domingo Alberto Rangel, *Gómez: El Amo del Poder*, Valencia: Editores Vadell Hnos., 1975.

27. AHMSGPRCP Nov 1–15 1909 H. Sarria to Gómez, 5 December 08.

28. Tellería, p. 254–55; and AHMSGPRCP Dic 14–23 1908 Tellería to Gómez, 13 December 08.

29. Juan Vicente Gómez, "Alocución," MinRelInt, *Memoria 1908*, 20 December 08, pp. 291.

30. Gómez "Alocución," MinRelInt, *Memoria 1908*, 20 December 08.

31. "The Dutch and Venezuela," *The Nation*, 17 December 08, p. 595.

32. CO 295/447, paraphrase from Teleg. No. 13 from Lord Acton, 5 December 08.

33. Ibid.

34. U.S. Charge d'Affaires to Foreign Minister at The Hague, 01 December 08,

U.S. Department of State, "Papers Relating to the Foreign Relations of the United States of America," *Venezuela*, 61 Cong 2 Sess., 1909–10, pp. 609–35, vol. 1, p. 634.

35. AHMSGPRCP Dic 1–14 1908 Pompilio Quintero to Gómez, 5 December 08.

36. FO 199/215 Corbett to Grey, 2 December 08.

37. Ibid.

38. R. Blanco Fombona, *Camino de Imperfección. Diario de Mi Vida, 1906–1914*, Madrid, Editorial Madrid, 1933, p. 134.

39. Ibid., p. 133.

40. Ibid.

41. Ibid.

42. Ibid.

43. Ibid.

44. Ibid.

45. FO 199/233 Corbett to Grey, 12 December 08.

46. Blanco Fombona writes that

> Paúl is terrifying, telling me that with the approval, more with the advice of Gómez, that he will call on the Powers, including the terrible United States, to support the reactionary movement with their armed ships in La Guaira. (Blanco Fombona, p. 137)

47. AHMSGPRCP Dic 1–14 1908 Lares to Gómez, 11 December 08.

48. José de Jesús Paúl, *El Doctor José de Jesús Paúl a Sus Compatriotas* (Paris: Imprentia de Lagny, 1909) p.8.

49. FO 199/215 Corbett to Grey, 11 December 08, trans. Enclosure, Paúl to Corbett, 11 December 08.

50. FO 199/215 Corbett to Grey, 12 December 08.

51. Ibid.

52. Ibid.

53. R. López Baralt to Presidente del Zulia, 12 December 08, MinRelInt, *Memoria, 1908*, pp. 230–31.

54. Ibid., pp. 231–32.

55. "Holland and Venezuela," *The Times* 15 December 08.

56. Ibid.

57. "The Dutch and Venezuela," *The Nation* 17 December 08, p. 595.

58. Ibid.

59. FO 199/233 Corbett to Grey, 12 December 08.

60. Ibid.

61. Francisco Segundo Alcántara, *La Aclamación* (1906), *La Conjura* (1907) *La Reacción* (1908), Caracas, Ediciónes Librería Europa, 1958, p. 60.

62. Alcántara, p. 60–61.

63. Blanco Fombona, p. 139.

64. "Holland and Venezuela," *The Times*, 15 December 08.

65. FO 199/215 Corbett to Grey, 13 December 08.

66. "Holland and Venezuela," 15 December 08.

67. Carlos Emilio Fernández, *Hombres y Sucesos de Mi Tierra, 1909–1935*, 2d ed., Madrid, Talleres del Sagrado Corazón, 1969, p. 40. Blanco Fombona writes that

> What we want, everybody shouted, is the fall of Cipriano Castro. At last, doctor Juan Pietri stepped on the balcony where Gómez was standing and grabbed the vice president's arm and

together with his own arms started waving to the crowd, while letting out a stentorian shout: "Death to Castro." Gómez left the balcony immediately. (Blanco Fombona, p. 140)

68. Pedro Luis Blanco Peñalver, *López Contreras ante la Historia*, Caracas, Tip. Garrido, 1957.
69. AHM Documentos F. Smidey to J. M. Smidey, 17 December 08.
70. "Holland and Venezuela," 15 December 08.
71. Blanco Fombona, p. 140.
72. Ibid.
73. Ibid., p. 140–41.
74. Ibid.
75. Ibid.
76. Ibid.
77. R. López Baralt to Presidente de Estado, 14 December 08, MinRelInt, *Memoria 1908*, Doc 52 pp. 282.
78. "Holland and Venezuela," *SAJ*, vol. 65: 25, 19 December 08, p. 698.
79. FO 371/571 Corbett to Grey, 13 December 08.
80. Ibid.
81. FO 199/215 Acton to Grey, 17 December 08.
82. "Los Primeros 30 Días del Gobierno de Gómez," BAHM, vol. 1:5 March–April 1960, pp. 133–261; Don José Borda to Ramírez, 15 December 08, p. 150.
83. Ibid.
84. Blanco Fombona, p. 141.
85. FO 371/791 Corbett to Grey, 19 December 08.
86. Blanco Fombona, p. 141.
87. Blanco Fombona further states that "we will have to fight him. My revolutionary brothers are also in hiding." (ibid.)
88. "Holland and Venezuela," *The Times* 15 December 08.
89. Ibid.
90. FO 199/215 Acton to Grey, 15 December 08.
91. Ibid.
92. Ibid.
93. Briceño Ayesterán, p. 362.
94. Ibid.
95. FO 199/221 Corbett to Grey, 13 June 09.
96. FO 199/221 Paúl to Corbett, 18 June 09.
97. Ibid.
98. CO 295/454 Corbett to Grey, 22 March 09.
99. FO 199/221 Paúl to Corbett, 18 June 09.
100. Ibid. The contents of the letter were verified by Sir Vincent himself in a letter sent to Paúl on July 14, 1909, in which he confirms that "taken as a whole, your account of the conversation referred to agrees very closely with my own recollection of the same."
101. Ibid.
102. Ibid.
103. FO 199/233 Corbett to Grey, 15 December 08.
104. U.S. Department of State, "Papers Relating to the Foreign Relations of the

United States of America," *Venezuela*, 61 Cong 2 Sess., 1909–10, vol. 1, pp. 609–35. The Spanish text is as follows:

Reacción contra General Castro iniciada. Ministro Exterior me requirió hoy pedir hacer constar Gobierno Americano voluntad Presidente Gómez ultimar satisfactoriamente todas las cuestiones internacionales. Halla conveniente presencia nave de guerra americana La Guaira previsión acontecimientos. Hizo identica comunicación otras legaciones. Luis R. de Lorena Ferreira to Francisco González Guinán. (MinRelExt, *Libro Amarillo*, 1909)

105. Roosevelt to William Bayard Hale, 3 December 08, in Philip C. Jessup, *Elihu Root*, New York, Dodd, Mead & Co., 1938, p. 497.
106. Root to M. W. Stryker, 30 November 08, in Jessup, p. 498.
107. Ibid.
108. Ibid.
109. Ibid.
110. Roosevelt to Root, 17 December 08, in Hendrickson, p. 184.
111. E. Robert Bacon and James Brown Scott, eds., *Addresses on International Subjects by Elihu Root*, Cambridge, Harvard University Press, 1916, p. 176.
112. E Root to W. I. Buchanan, 21 December 08 in U.S. Department of State, "Papers Relating to the Foreign Relations of the United States of America," *Venezuela*, House Doctor 101, vol. 1, 1909, 61st Cong., 2 Sess., 1909–1910, pp. 609–35.
113. Paúl, *El Doctor José de Jesús Paúl a Sus Compatriotas*, Paris, Imprenta de Lagny, 1909, p. 14.
114. Ibid., p. 13–14.
115. Ibid., p. 15. In a letter sent to Gómez in July 1909, Paúl categorically takes all the blame for American warships. He writes to Gómez the following:

I will for my part, when calm returns the serenity and impartiality of the mind that all matters require, shed light on a matter which I take full responsibility, as it is or could have been, so that your Government will not appear as it is has been alleged to have promoted a foreign intervention for your maintenance and consolidation of power. (Paúl to Gómez, 6 July 09, p. 22)

116. FO 199/215 Acton to Grey, 18 December 08.
117. Ibid.
118. Ibid.
119. Ibid.
120. FO 199/215 Acton to Grey, 13 January 09.
121. FO 199/215 Corbett to Grey, 18 December 08.
122. Alcántara, p. 65.
123. Ibid.
124. FO 371/571 Corbett to Acton, 17 December 08.
125. Blanco Fombona, pp. 142–43.
126. Ibid.
127. Ibid.
128. AHMSGPRCP Dic 14–23 1908 Ministro de Guerra y Marina to Gómez, 18 December 08.
129. Ibid.
130. AHMSGPRCP Teleg Dic 9–18 1908 Rafael José Velazco to Gómez, 18 December 08.

131. "New Cabinet in Venezuela," *The Times*, 23 December 08.

132. FO 199/233 Corbett to Grey, 25 December 08. The Spanish note was "la culebra se mata por la cabeza."

133. Ramón J. Velásquez, *La Caida del Liberalismo Amarillo: Tiempo y Diana de Antonio Parades*. Caracas, Ediciones Venezuela, 1960, p. 364.

134. Ibid.

135. Blanco Fombona, p. 143.

136. Ibid.

137. Also known as Macuro.

138. U.S. archive DS 831.001C27/12 Trans. "Criminal Proceedings against General Cipriano Castro and others, to whom is imputed the crime of attempted assassination of General Juan Vicente Gómez, 1909."

139. Alcántara, p. 65.

140. Pablo Emilio Fernández, *Gómez el Rehabilitador*, Caracas, Jaime Villegas Editor, 1956, p. 181.

141. In 1911, Cárdenas met Castro in Paris, who was still in shock at what his *compadre* had done. Castro confided in Cárdenas, stating that "knowing for twenty-four years, dealing with him for twenty-four years and hoodwinked over twenty-four years." (Nemesio Parada, *De Ocumare a Miraflores*, Caracas, BATT 1975, p. 108.)

142. AHM SGPR Teleg Dic 26–28 1908 Phelps to Associated Press, 26 December 08.

143. Briceño Ayesterán, p. 364.

144. FO 199/233 Corbett to Grey, 25 December 08.

145. Ibid.

146. Ibid.

147. Ibid.

148. FO 199/213 Corbett to Grey, 21 January 09.

149. FO 199/233 Corbett to Grey, 25 December 08.

150. Blanco Fombona, p. 143.

151. FO 199/213 Corbett to Grey, 21 January 09.

152. Murillo to Gómez, 24 December 08, in Venezuela, *Conjuración Contra la Vida del General Juan Gómez, Presidente de Venezuela y Sus Consecuercras*, Caracas, Imprenta Hacrosal, 1909, p. 161.

153. Carlos Herrera to Interior Minister, 2 January 09, MinRelInt, *Memoria 1908* p. 333.

154. Luciano Mendible, *30 Años de Lucha. Documentos para la Vida Pública del Dr. Luciano Mendible, 1908–1940*, N.P. 1941, p. 5–6.

155. Ibid., p. 6.

156. Julio Rodríguez Silva to F. L. Alcántara, 11 January 09, MinRelInt, *Memoria 1908* p. 351.

12

La Rehabilitación

The collapse of law and order, the rupture of diplomatic relations with four countries, and the monopolistic economic policy pursued by his predecessor were used by Gómez to justify his coup to the country. Gómez saw his role as rehabilitating the country from these ills, hence his revolution was called La Rehabilitación. "Peace, union and work" was the regime's most enduring motto. Upon assuming power Gómez promised the "immediate extinction of absolutism as a form of government"[1] and the establishment of a "genuinely democratic regime."[2] To achieve this, Gómez formed a government that represented a broad consensus of opinion, which included three former Castro ministers. The new cabinet was composed, as had been expected, of Francisco Linares Alcántara as interior minister, González Guinán as foreign affairs minister, Régulo Olivares as minister of war and navy, Rafael María Carabaño as development minister, Jesús Muñoz Tébar as finance minister, Roberto Vargas as public works minister, and Samuel Dario Maldonado as education minister. Aquiles Iturbe was named governor of Caracas. Gómez was careful to give his new cabinet the character of a wholly national government without a dominant faction. Gómez's intention was to achieve a broad consensus of opinion under his power, something that would characterize his rule up to 1913. On December 20, Gómez issued an *alocución* in which he indicated clearly the aims of his government, which was to "conciliate popular aspirations with my public duties, endeavouring to establish a regime with all the guarantees which are appropriate for our institutions"[3] without such an aspiration being a "concession or favour but a clear imposition of the law."[4] Gómez promised that his government would

> make effective the constitutional guarantees, stimulate liberty within the context of law and order, respect the State's sovereignty, shelter industry from dubious schemes, seek a decorous and peaceful solution to the country's international disputes, to live a harmonious and peaceful life allowing only the law to rule in its unquestionable sovereignty.[5]

Although certain prominent Castristas had been imprisoned because of their conspiracy to murder Gómez, all other political prisoners were set free. The exiles were allowed to return home. These measures were quickly instituted. For example, on December 24, José Ignacio Lares, the president of Zulia, informed Gómez that all political prisoners had been released.[6] In Curacao all political exiles were repatriated on December 23. Riera, Tellería, and Hermán Leyba arrived in La Guaira five days later. The new government of Gómez abolished the monopolies on cigarettes and explosives, and the management of the Salt Monopoly was put into the hands of Bank of Venezuela. The question of The Caracas Tramway Company was settled, and goods for The Central Railway were released from La Guaira. In Curacao, Tellería received an answer to his letter of December 9 when Gómez informed him of the December 19 events and requested him to state "very specially to Ayala, Rolando and Hernández that his strongest desire was that they should return immediately to the country and that they should inform all the other Venezuelans living abroad for political reasons, that the doors of the fatherland were open to all."[7]

On December 21, Linares Alcántara, the new interior minister, gave further details of Gómez's plan to reorganize the country with the "wise precepts of the constitution and that the law will be from now on the only constant norm of any official initiative."[8] Linares Alcántara also called for unity and extended a welcoming hand to the exiles. The state budgets were restored to their full amount. Moreover, the state government used any surplus revenue to stimulate local economic development. The municipalities recovered whatever economic resources and privileges they had held previously so that they could become the "cornerstone of the Republic's building."[9] The government also promised to study with "special interest all economic matters affected by illegal privileges"[10] to stimulate industrial and agricultural development. Most people interpreted this as meaning that the pernicious monopolies would be abolished. This later became a source of friction between the Mochistas and the government. Mocho Hernández in his adherence manifesto praised Gómez for liberating the country "from the heavy weight of the monopolies with which the insane exploiters had depleted the sources of national wealth."[11] The government also studied how to stimulate the development of agriculture and industry. The new administration also worked closely with the financial community to increase the creditworthiness of the country.[12] The first step taken in this direction was to stop the threat of a Dutch invasion, while a further stimulus to industry was to make credit cheaper to obtain. The government also encouraged closer commercial ties with Venezuela's trading partners.

Gómez's economic plans were very ambitious given the backwardness of the country's economic infrastructure and of Venezuela's reputation in the major money markets. To secure peace and stability in the ensuing years he would have to maintain a delicate neutrality between the various political factions that were already claiming him as their true leader. He would also have to stimulate the economic development of the country to a degree that had not been achieved previously. Gómez was aware of the economic constraints that operated in the country and the influence that the German trading houses had on the economy. It was therefore necessary to stimulate the development of a source of revenue that was independent from traditional political considerations. Consequently, from the outset of his rule Gómez encouraged the establishment of a healthy, thriving mining industry. There was nothing new in this idea. Past rulers had also pinned their hopes on large mining revenues. What was novel in Gómez's case was that he achieved this independent source of income with the advent of the oil industry in the 1920s. Gómez stated that during his first year as president:

> I secured internal peace by reimposing all civil rights to all Venezuelans and to the political prisoners and to those in exile by a pardon if it was necessary; I declared an amnesty for those involved in the coup of December 19; I abolished the privileges and other measures which restricted the freedom of commerce and industry and, at the same time, while defending the country, reached an amicable and decorous solution to the difficulties, which had been distorted by alarmists or sanctimonious people who together with attributing depressing intentions against our nationality by traditionally friendly nations, came to doubt the clear and manifest intention of the government and people of Venezuela to maintain the sovereignty of Venezuela free of foreign insult and damage.[13]

Although the government's plan was basically a national plan with no political allegiances in mind, many people interpreted it to be "inspired in the purest Liberalism"[14] because "commerce and industry will be reborn to an active life owing to the defeat of the black monster of monopoly."[15] However, as Velásquez writes, "everything remained unchanged the same Congress, the same Courts, the same Councillors, the same State Presidents. The only changes were Cipriano Castro, two or three members of his entourage and some of his family."[16]

Part of Gómez's grand plan was to reestablish diplomatic relations with the United States, The Netherlands, France, and Colombia. To do this, Paúl was appointed Special Envoy to Germany, the United Kingdom, and Italy.[17]

On December 21, commercial links between Colombia and Venezuela were reestablished with the opening of the Zulia River for the transportation of commercial goods from Maracaibo to Colombia. The new government immediately complied with the requests that the Dutch made just prior to the coup. The government suspended the May 14 Decree on December 20 and agreed to negotiate for a new, permanent arrangement with The Netherlands. The Dutch government, however, agreed to meet Venezuela's plenipotentiary minister only if the May 14 Decree were repealed completely. The British felt that this was the appropriate time to press for the suspension of the April 28 Decree. Consequently, on January 2, 1909, Gómez rescinded the decrees of May 14 and April 28, which had suspended trade between Curacao and Trinidad with Venezuela. The May 14 Decree was withdrawn on January 6, allowing Paúl to start negotiations with the Dutch government. A protocol between Venezuela and The Netherlands was signed on April 19, 1909, which was hoped would pave the way for the reestablishment of diplomatic relations. It was agreed that Venezuela would accord the Dutch colony the same abatement in the future as the British or the other colonies in the Antilles. Venezuela would also pay Bs 20,000 compensation for the seizure of five Dutch merchant men in 1908. Holland, in return, would dispatch a special envoy to Caracas and restore the country's vessels.

Gómez's national recovery plan received the wholehearted approval of the country and the political exiles. General Manuel Antonio Matos, the leader of the Revolución Libertadora, declared from Nice, in an interview given to Honore Tourniere of the *Petit Nicois*, that the new cabinet revealed a "complete reconciliation among all important political elements in the country."[18] Matos felt that the government's plan "is supported by a solid base which allows the development of nascent industries"[19] and placed himself at Gómez's disposal. Mocho Hernández from Paris also congratulated Gómez. Generals Corao and José Antonio Velutini advised Rolando in New York to "support General Gómez without reservation,"[20] and "to lend your contingent to a situation that starts with a Liberal cabinet, the freedom of prisoners and with the invitation to all Venezuelans for a satisfactory solution to the domestic difficulties and to the external conflicts."[21] Velutini further advised that with Castro out of the way, "the men of goodwill have to strengthen the peace that we all need so much."[22]

Rolando, who was advised by Melville E. Stowe, felt that Gómez faced two political problems. First, he would encounter internal difficulties with a possible pro-Castro reaction. Secondly, he would face international complications.[23] Nevertheless, most of the exiled *caudillos* on their return to Caracas published statements of their allegiance to Gómez and his new government. They also published their manifestos, which were later reprinted in *Venezuela. Conjuración 1909*.[24] All of them welcomed the dawning of a new age in which liberty and the rule of law would be respected.

They thanked Gómez for deliverance. Mocho Hernández called for unity. He said that he was willing to work with the new government "to achieve that patriotic goal of confraternity which is imposing itself today in all its imperiousness to save the nation and reestablish the Republic."[25] Mocho Hernández returned to Caracas with only one aim in mind, which was to "raise Venezuela from the prostration that the tyranny left her . . . to form again a Fatherland free, prosperous and happy."[26] Carlos Angel Garbiras, another political exile, urged the formation of a "party of government"[27] to "cement the peace in an unshakeable way and later substitute the rifle for the vote, in order for everybody to hoist their own flag of convictions."[28] The idea was for the old *caudillos* and political parties to embrace Gómez, the "modest man and patriot that reintegrated us to civilization."[29] Both Mocho Hernández and Rolando ignored Garbiras' suggestion for a "party of government."[30] Despite these assurances José Ignacio Cárdenas from Paris warned Gómez of Rolando and Mocho Hernández's real intentions of taking power away from him. Cárdenas said that he was aware that the former "is not going to Venezuela in good faith"[31] because "he considers himself indispensable and is going to create a base for his personal ambitions with the trust you accord him."[32] Thus before leaving New York for Venezuela, Rolando sent instructions to his supporters in Paris and to José Gil Fortoul and Laureano Vallenilla Lanz, who "formed part of the committee and *continue their links with Rolando*"[33] to make their revolutionary preparations. In Paris the feeling about Mocho Hernández's return was that he "is not going as a patriot to join up with you once he has proclaimed himself head of the party. And he is determined he will do whatever it takes to achieve his crazy goal. It is also thought that Rolando will go against you."[34]

Gómez was able to stay in power legally after 1908 because Castro was tried for ordering his murder and that of Antonio Paredes in 1907. On January 9, 1909, the Federal Court and of Cassation admitted the writ. On January 17 the court declared "that there was cause for a trial and consequently suspended General Cipriano Castro from his duties as President of the Republic."[35] The government based its case on the intercepted Castro telegram that called for "the snake to be killed by the head." Gómez thus resolved his problem "of staying in power for the remainder of the period without any need for a coup d'etat, the dissolution of Congress or Councils, without confronting the problem of legitimacy."[36] On January 26, Governor Aquiles Iturbe forwarded to Francisco Linares Alcántara, the interior minister, the papers relating to Castro's telegram. Linares Alcantára sent the affidavit to the attorney general to start legal action. The file was then forwarded to the Criminal Tribunal of the First Instance of the western district of the federal district. However, on April 19 a general amnesty was granted to all people who were arrested for disorderly conduct because of the events of December 13, 14, and 19. Thus the interior minister brought to a close "the legal process initiated against Castro . . . once the relevant writ was issued by the respective judge."[37]

BUCHANAN ARRIVES IN VENEZUELA

The only country that responded to Paúl's request for moral support for the revolution was the United States, which seized the moment and dispatched a small flotilla to Venezuela to reactivate their five outstanding claims. The arrival of a strong American naval presence and the subsequent demands by the United States developed into Gómez's first political crisis. However, the naval presence in the short term served to consolidate indirectly his power. On the day of Gómez's coup the cruiser USS *Des Moines* and the gunboat USS *Dolphin* were ordered to proceed from the Haitian capital of Port-au-Prince to La Guaira. On December 21 the USS *Maine* sailed for Venezuela from Hampton Roads, Virginia. The following day Special Commissioner William Buchanan set sail on the USS *North Carolina* for Caracas. The relatively large naval presence was sent because the commissioner was empowered to resume diplomatic relations and to get the new Gómez government to accept arbitration on the U.S. claims. It was not deemed necessary for Buchanan to "complete definitely the signing and submission to arbitration of the pending claim, but it will be sufficient if you receive from the Government of President Gómez an explicit statement committing Venezuela to arbitration of those claims."[38] It was confidently expected that Buchanan would be back in Washington by January 12 of the following year.

Gómez agreed to settle the U.S. claims on December 21 because of his "sincere desire to bring about a reestablishment of friendly relations with the United States."[39] This was very satisfying news to Secretary of State Root, who felt that his policy of patience in the pursuit of the American claims had paid off. Root wrote to Andrew Carnegie on Christmas Eve that "to have success gained in the way of peaceable settlement without any bulldozing in this most difficult case is extremely satisfying."[40] because using force against Castro would have helped him, "while if let alone Castro by following his methods would soon destroy himself and that then we would get a peaceable settlement."[41] According to the Venezuelan government's agent in Washington, code-named Fabriles, Secretary Root was "anxious for any type of arrangement during the current administration in order to save FACE (*sic*)."[42] Fabriles informed Carner that Buchanan "has instructions from Secretary Root to conciliate Venezuela"[43] by proposing arbitration in the Dolge and NY&B claims, but the agent advised that the country "should retain its position in all eventuality ADACTIO (sic) pending decision."[44] Secretary Root, however, wanted Buchanan to get the Venezuelans to agree to arbitration of all five claims.

The settlement of the U.S. claims, especially that of the NY&B, was of great importance to the company operating the Guanoco asphalt deposits. Late in December, A. L. Barke advised Carner to go to Caracas and "advise firmly his friends that they can adopt a firm attitude towards PARABOLE (sic)—that is to say that the Bermúdez claim is *res adjudicata*, and that it would go against the honour and dignity of Venezuela to agree to arbitration in the matter."[45] Other interested parties wanted to take over the running of the asphalt lake from Barber. According to Barke, Charles H. Flint reached an agreement with either Rolando or Ortega Martínez to get the asphalt business for himself. In the past Flint had done $10,000 worth of business in Caracas with Ortega Martínez.[46] Barke, however, did not think that Rolando was a suitable business partner because of his connection with the NY&B during the Matos revolution.[47]

On Christmas Day, Commander Thomas Washington of the USS *Dolphin*,[48] which had set sail from the naval base of Guántanamo in Cuba, became the first American warship to arrive in Venezuela. The arrival of Washington was viewed as a courtesy call, almost as one of solidarity between the American people and Venezuela. Leopoldo Baptista wired the state presidents that the U.S. ship's trip was "on a special mission to present to our President the American people's sincerest friendship."[49] Captain Washington and four officers spent Christmas Day at Mr. Brewer's[50] the house in Caracas. The following day the American officers had a meeting with Gómez and his newly appointed cabinet at Miraflores. A band played the American national anthem, and Gómez conferred with them for fifteen minutes with Linares Alcántara acting as interpreter. At the meeting Gómez expressed his "sincerest wishes that relations with your Nation will be established as soon as possible, as cordial as they have always been and the belief that your visit to our country is the start of our desire to renew our friendship."[51] The government welcomed "with special pleasure such manifestations, attributing to them exceptional importance, because they constitute the first step towards the rehabilitation of our diplomacy in the civilised world."[52] Gómez emerged from the meeting smiling and "satisfied with the interview."[53] The entire cabinet proceeded to the U.S. legation.

The general goodwill afforded to Commander Washington soon evaporated, however, when three other U.S. warships arrived on December 26. The USS *Maine*, with Admiral Arnold, and the USS *North Carolina* (1,500 tons of displacement with a crew of 850 and 42 canons) under the command of Captain Marisell, carrying Special Commissioner Buchanan and W. T. S. Doyle, the head of the Latin American division of the State Department and who would act as Buchanan's secretary on the ship, arrived first. Buchanan's trip was meant to be conciliatory because Root did not want the other Latin American countries to think that they were taking advantage of Venezuela's weak position. The *North Carolina* returned immediately to the United States, and Buchanan transferred to the *Maine*. Later on the same day the USS *New* arrived from Guantánamo base in Cuba with provisions.

Upon his arrival Buchanan expected to find "the country in the throes of civil strife and to be called upon to exert his mediatory influence in favour of the new Administration."[54] It therefore came as a surprise to him to find that Gómez was not only firmly established in Caracas but that his rule had been widely accepted, making any need for foreign moral support superfluous. Soon after arriving Doyle travelled to Caracas ahead of Buchanan to make the necessary arrangements. It soon became clear to the Venezuelan government that Buchanan's intention was not to seek arbitration of the claims as they had been informed, but to pressure Gómez into settling the five American claims to the detriment of the country. It was clear from the beginning that diplomatic relations with the United States would only be renewed once the five claims had been settled satisfactorily. Moreover, Buchanan soon started to volunteer his advice "in other matters in which the United States [was] not directly interested,"[55] arousing a "very perceptible feeling of antagonism."[56] Although, Buchanan soon desisted in his efforts to counsel the new government and concentrated instead on his mission, the damage had been done, reinforcing "a feeling of jealousy of American aggression under cover of the Monroe Doctrine."[57] By New Year's Eve, Gómez had "manifested a desire to reach an equitable and just arrangement of matters pending with the United States."[58] On December 31, Buchanan formally presented Root's instructions to Francisco González Guinán, the new Foreign Affairs Minister, which committed Venezuela to arbitration of the five claims.

Buchanan was initially optimistic that an early settlement was possible, reporting that Venezuela had agreed to arbitration of the Orinoco Steamship Company claim and that it would settle the Jaurett claim with a small indemnity. The potential areas of disagreement were over the court decisions in the cases of the NY&B and the Orinoco Company. In each case the Federal Court and of Cassation of the country had rendered a decision, and the Venezuelan government argued that "the submission of these cases upon their merits would imply disrespect to the judgements of its courts."[59] The Venezuelan government was willing to submit the cases to arbitration if it was ruled that there had been a denial of justice in the local courts. However, Root argued that proof of such treatment would only serve to "cast aspersions on the new Government"[60] and suggested instead for the whole procedure to be arbitrated "without the examination of the judicial proceedings of Venezuela."[61] This move was unacceptable to the Venezuelan government, which stuck to its original proposals. On March 18, 1908, the Federal Court and of Cassation upheld the view that the Fitzgerald concession was null and void, so that "as the grantees of that contract would agree that it was resolved owing to a lack of fulfilment with their obligations."[62] It was while this trial was taking place that the Venezuelan government granted further concessions within the area that was under dispute. The United States decided to support the claims of a new company, the Orinoco Corporation, that had inherited the Fitzgerald concession through its acquisition of the Orinoco Company. The United States asked the Venezuelan government on February 28, 1907, to submit the claims to arbitration. The Venezuelan government argued that the acceptance by the American government of the first payment after the 1903 Mixed Commission had decided on the American claims meant that the United States had tacitly accepted the court's decision that the Fitzgerald concession was not valid. The U.S. government countered that it supported all the claims of the companies because the decision during the arbitration proceedings had favored the companies and the Orinoco Corporation, which had acquired the old concession. This was a change of policy for the U.S. government in the case of the Orinoco Corporation, because up to 1908 it did not recognize that the company had any legitimate rights in Venezuela.

In 1909 the United States asked that the matter be taken again to arbitration, which the Venezuelan government was against. Venezuela argued that the Orinoco Corporation did not exist legally because the government's first payment under the Mixed Commission agreement for the American government to distribute among the claimants included the Manoa Company and not the Orinoco Corporation. In March 1907 the United States had raised the problem of compensation of the Manoa Company, but under the new guise of the Orinoco Corporation, which had acquired the company's rights. The Venezuelan foreign minister sent a Note to Russell on July 24 of that year that said that the Orinoco Corporation "was unknown at the time of its claim and of its examination and decision."[63] The Orinoco Corporation claimed to be the holder of rights that Barge had declared null and void, and it was now also claiming for matters that had occurred after the award of 1903. Thus the Venezuelan government denied the Orinoco Corporation's legal entity in the claims it was making. In addition, the transfer of the assets from the Orinoco Company to the Orinoco Corporation had not received government approval. The Venezuelan government only became aware of the transfer on April 5, 1905, when Rudolph Dolge informed the development minister. The company was aware that the government had not given its approval to the transfer. On February 2, 1907, it sent a protest note to the American Legation in which it stated that the original concessionaire had the right to transfer its rights "without restrictions or liens of any kind."[64] This had no legal basis. The clause that the company used was not valid because the "Fitzgerald contract established a legal link between the contractor and Venezuela: a link which because it was undertaken between two parties cannot be terminated by the will of one of the parties which agreed to form it."[65] In addition, there was the Federal Court and of Cassation decision of December 13, 1906, that denied the Orinoco Corporation's right to hold the Fitzgerald concession. In spite of the Venezuelan government's strong legal case against the companies, the Gómez administration succumbed to U.S. pressure and signed the González Guinán-Buchanan Protocol on February 13, 1909, to submit "the pending differences between the two nations"[66] to arbitration at the Permanent Court at The Hague.

The González Guinán-Buchanan Protocol recognized the Orinoco Corporation as the legitimate holder of the Fitzgerald concession, which placed Venezuela at a disadvantage because "it not only recognises the legal party to seek the revision of the Barge finding and the decision of the Federal Court and of Cassation but also allows it to claim for damages that are alleged to have been caused after the date of the finding."[67] The González Guinán-Buchanan Protocol did not examine the legal position of the Orinoco Corporation as holder of Fitzgerald's concession and the 1903 arbitration decision. Instead, the document said that "it is between Venezuela and the Government of the United States as representative of that Company, which is clearly recognised, purely and simply, its previously denied character of being a grantee of the Fitzgerald contract."[68] As in all cases, the Orinoco Corporation's claim could not be the subject of an international claim unless there had been a miscarriage of justice. However, because the transfer of the concession to the Orinoco Corporation had not been approved by the government, it was deduced that the decision as to "whether Venezuela was obliged not to give its consent to that transfer should have been previously submitted as a discussion point to the Arbiters."[69] Moreover, the protocol did not take into account the damages or losses that Venezuela incurred for the nonfulfillment of the contract. Instead the protocol asked the court to examine whether the decision by Barge on April 12, 1904, had been wrongly awarded. This move had no legal basis because arbitration was binding, and hence there was no room for challenging a decision. In addition, the protocol asked the court to decide on the Federal Court and of Cassation's ruling of March 18, 1908, on the company. The legal counsel for the minister of development argued that such a move would be dishonorable to the country, as it would mean that Venezuela was not a sovereign state because the rulings of the courts "cannot be revised by any power in the world while it remains a sovereign and independent state."[70] Moreover, the counsel argued that "there might be in the decision a denegation of justice and in such a case they can claim damages caused but can never agree to a redetermination of the rights and obligations of sentences already dictated."[71] The Protocol wanted both that the sentence of the first tribunal be revised and that "it should be declared whether an injustice has taken place in the acts of any of the authorities of the Government of Venezuela: such a move, once the direct method had failed to obtain the desired result, would open an indirect way of obtaining a revision of the decision by the Super-Arbiter Barge."[72] Barge had judged all the company's claims, with the result that "if it was determined that certain authorities in Venezuela committed a notorious injustice, the Republic would be obliged to indemnify damages that Barge had decided did not exist."[73] Moreover, the protocol wanted to examine the impact that the decision by the Federal Court and of Cassation of March 18, 1908, had on the company's business. The protocol asked whether the Fitzgerald concession was still valid and, if so, what the rights and obligations of both the company and the government were. If the arbitration decided that there was no miscarriage of justice and declared the Fitzgerald concession valid, then it would indirectly revoke the Federal Court and of Cassation's decision, and the Arbitral Court would be contradicting itself. The pact under letter C of the Protocol was worse still because

> By it, not only is the Arbitrator of the International Tribunal allowed to fix "the rights and obligations of the Government of Venezuela on one hand, and those of the claiming company on the other" in the case of the Fitzgerald contract being declared valid but also it was not foreseen that because it was dealing in concessions in our own land, his integrity is at risk if the United States would argue later the doctrine that they have sustained with our Chancellory that claims made by United States citizens using the diplomatic service cease being the property of the claimants and become the property of the United States.[74]

The development minister's adviser concluded that if Congress approved the protocol, it would constitute "a precedent with fatal consequences for the country. Consequently, a transaction with the Orinoco Corporation, would, if it remained valid, be a validation of the contract and would give cause for the precedent to be set."[75] In the Crichfield claim, both the government and the company submitted their terms for a settlement. Buchanan recommended the Venezuelan government's proposal, but the company refused and Root instructed the special commissioner to seek arbitration. The NY&B claim also proved difficult to solve because Venezuela reaffirmed its right to discipline the company for supporting the Matos revolution.

Now that the immediate internal political crisis was over and the new Venezuelan government no longer needed the moral support of foreign powers to protect them against the return of Castro, the Gómez administration proved less easy to deal with than was expected from their early promises. Far from being inclined to allow all questions of injuries to foreigners that were alleged to have been inflicted by the unconstitutional or illegal actions of Castro, the new government started showing a distinct tendency to use legal technicalities to maintain their negotiating position. By January, Buchanan was worried that no settlement would be reached and that the initiative that the United States held would be lost. An Italian representative would soon arrive, and the differences with France and The Netherlands had to be sorted out. In addition, the hazards facing the new government meant that a period of instability would inevitably ensue. Buchanan thus proposed to sign a protocol that provided for the three unresolved claims to be submitted to the International Court of Arbitration at The Hague if a solution had not been reached within four months. González Guinán, however, continued to express the view that "an arbitration tribunal would not consider the Bermúdez or Orinoco Corporation cases except under denial of justice."[76] The Venezuelans appeared uncooperative because they did not want to cast doubt on the country's legal system, as this would set a precedent that would lead to other claims.

By the end of January, Buchanan's mood of optimism and confidence had changed. He was ready to give up and return to Washington, where talks would continue. The United States, however, would only resume diplomatic relations with Venezuela once the five claims had been settled. Negotiations dragged on until February because there was a great degree of resistance to fall into line with the American way of thinking. Public opposition to the protocol was rife, and Congress, Gómez, and his followers all showed "a no less hearty detestation of foreign dictation."[77] At the beginning of February, Buchanan and González Guinán prepared a draft protocol and submitted it to the cabinet, which rejected it because "it was so worded as to cast doubt on the purity of Venezuelan Justice."[78] The crux of the matter was to find a formula under which the Orinoco Steam Shipping Company's claims and the NY&B's claims, which had already been adjudicated by the Federal Court and of Cassation, could be reexamined outside the country without wounding national dignity. A compromise was finally reached. The State Department accepted the Venezuelan position "upon the denial of justice decision as preparatory to arbitration in the Bermudez & [*sic*] Orinoco Corporation cases, while the Venezuelan Government adopted a more lenient attitude toward the former and agreed to a representative of Barge's decision in the latter case."[79]

This decision prompted the NY&B to accept the Venezuelan terms, paving the way for a protocol to be signed on February 13. Under the González Guinán-Buchanan Protocol the claims pertaining to the Orinoco Steam Ship Company, the Orinoco Corporation, and Crichfield would be submitted to arbitration only if after five months the parties had been unable to reach an agreement with the Venezuelan government. In the Crichfield claim, the Venezuelan government initially offered to extend the concession to settle the claim. However, because of financial difficulties that prevented the company from working the concession, on August 21, 1909, it accepted the offer from the Venezuelan government of $475,000 to be paid in eight equal installments to regain possession of the concession. The same initial offer was made to the Orinoco Corporation, but it also settled by accepting the government's offer of paying $385,000 in eight equal installments to regain possession of its concession. The Orinoco Steam Ship Company's claim was taken to the International Court of Arbitration at The Hague.

On February 13, 1909, agreements were reached concerning the Jaurett claim and the NY&B claim. In the former claim, the French-born American citizen was compensated for his treatment under Castro with Bs 3,000. In the case of the NY&B, the company accepted and recognized its involvement in the Revolución Libertadora and agreed to pay the government compensation of $300,000. The company retained its concession and equipment. The company also agreed to sell asphalt to the government to be used in public works at a 25 percent discount below the prevailing market price. In addition, the company agreed to pay a tax of Bs 4 per ton of asphalt exported per year and a surface tax of Bs 2 per hectare per year.

The settlement of these claims opened the way for the renewal of diplomatic relations between the two countries. On March 20, William Russell was officially received in Caracas as the new U.S. minister. On May 2, Pedro Ezequiel Rojas took his post as Venezuela's minister in Washington. The protocols, however, caused great bitterness and resentment in the country. The cabinet only accepted the agreement after the original document had been substantially changed. In addition, Gómez placed a great deal of pressure on them to accept it.[80] It was felt that González Guinán had surrendered the country to foreign interests and that "Venezuela was heading to join Panama and become an American protectorate."[81]

It was difficult to criticize Gómez directly because of his military power. So the wrath of Congress fell on the hapless Paúl, who was out of the country and could not defend himself. Paúl found himself isolated politically. None of his erstwhile conspirators was willing to defend him. During its first session in 1909, Congress severely censured Paúl for his action during the December crisis and for his subsequent diplomatic efforts. Deputy Chapellín called on Congress to protest against the action that had brought American warships to Venezuela in December, which had given "the appearance of the Venezuelan people taking the first step towards an oppressive protectorate."[82] Chapellín urged the legislative body not to ratify the American protocol because if they did, "we can consider as closed our tribunals which deal with foreign matters and we will have crushed our National Sovereignty in one of its powers which is the judicial."[83] In addition, Chapellín was not too happy with the NY&B's protocol because "Venezuela does not receive the fine for indemnification of damages which had been imposed on said Company but only a very reduced sum."[84] Alarmed at this intense popular feeling against the American protocol, Gómez adopted a "pseudo-constitutional attitude leaving responsibility for all measures to Congress."[85] Gómez's position, according to Sir Vincent Corbett, was shaken. During the months of February and March the "public and the press began to clamour against any further concessions to the pretensions of foreign powers."[86] The *El Tiempo* newspaper, wrote that the public increasingly felt that U.S. policy was not to uphold the Monroe Doctrine but to intervene directly in the internal affairs of the country.[87]

It took a considerable amount of time before all the U.S. claims were finally settled. The Arbitral Tribunal had been appointed to decide whether the first decision against the Orinoco Steam Ship Company, which was given on February 22, 1904, was null and void, and if so to reopen the case. The previous decision was the result of an agreement between Venezuela and the United States on February 17, 1903, when the Mixed Commission was appointed to decide on all unsettled American claims. The final decision was to be given by an umpire appointed by the Queen of The Netherlands in the event of a disagreement among the commissioners. The United States disputed the validity of the award on the grounds that Umpire Barge had deviated from the terms of the proceedings by taking into account technical considerations instead of arriving at his decision on the basis of absolute equity. The tribunal to which both parties agreed to submit this point recognized the principle of revision, thereby securing a moral victory for the United States. However, the aggregate value of the claims allowed, $53,867, was less than 4 percent of the total amount in dispute of $1,401,539. The award established that "whereas an Arbitral decision should be accepted without reserve, both in the interests of peace and no revisory jurisdiction having been instituted, yet application may be made for such revision by agreement between the parties."[88] On October 1, 1910, the Orinoco Steam Ship Company's claim was finally settled when The Hague tribunal rendered its decision on whether Barge's original decision was invalid and, if so, to decide the case on its merit. A. Bernaert and Gonzalo de Quesada, both nominees of the tribunal, found that although the decision was nominally binding, in this instance there had been an "excessive exercise of jurisdiction and an essential error in judgment"[89] that justified a review. It was decided not to review all four items but only those in which an error was manifest. The tribunal in its reexamination adopted Barge's classification of the four claims that the company made: (1) $1,209,701.04 (2) $19,000 (3) $147,638.79 (4) $25,000. The court considered the largest claim, the one for damages and destruction to the company's exclusive concession, and held that Barge's

> ruling on the question of the exclusiveness of the concession was based on his appreciation of the facts and interpretation of the documents, matters clearly within his competence, and was not subject to revision by the Tribunal, whose duty was not to say if the case had been well or ill judged but whether the award was to be annulled. In reality, the court had simply answered again the preliminary question by declining to hold Barge's award void.[90]

The next claim of $19,000 was over unpaid expenses due under the May 10, 1900, Decree. Barge had relied on the Calvo clause in the contract to declare the claim invalid. The tribunal ruled, however, that Venezuela, through its agreements in 1903 and 1909, renounced invoking the Calvo clause. The court awarded the sum to the U.S. company. On the third claim, the tribunal allowed $1,053 plus $25,845.20 and $769.22 to be taken into account with the rest of the claim to be void. On the final claim of legal fees the tribunal allowed $7,000 to be paid with interest on the sum of $64,412.59 instead of the $28,234.93 that Barge had previously awarded. With total interest payments, Venezuela had to pay $92,637.52 on December 25, 1910. This was the first case in which an Arbitral Tribunal annulled a previous decision. The *New York Times* reported that the "disposition of this case in a manner favourable to the contentions of the United States completely vindicates the attitude of the State Department with respect to Venezuelan claims arising out of Castro's rule, all five such claims having been determined in a manner satisfactory to the American Government."[91] The outcome of this in Venezuela was for the government to modify the Calvo clause to the Monroe Doctrine. In November 1912 an executive decree declared that "an appeal by a foreigner to his own country or to an international tribunal for assistance may be entertained only after the alien has attempted to bring his action against the nation and when, either in the procedure or in the decision or the same, he has been the victim of notorious injustice."[92]

Gómez's government was further criticized for its handling of the negotiations that involved the renewal of diplomatic relations with The Netherlands and France. It was felt that Paúl, Venezuela's special envoy, had bungled the negotiations because he had mistakenly advised that the French would only review diplomatic relations once an agreement between the French Cable Company and the Venezuelan government had been reached. In spite of this an agreement was reached on May 13. The Venezuelan government annulled the Bs 24 million fine imposed in 1906, and the company obtained a twenty-five-year lease to handle all external telegraphic communication. The government retained the coastal telegraphic line. However, the French also demanded that the other outstanding French claims be adjudicated by a Mixed Commission. The negotiations finally broke down in December 1909. The manner in which these claims were to be submitted kept both countries apart until 1913, when diplomatic relations were reestablished.

Similarly, The Netherlands demanded that Venezuela recognize the claims of its Dutch citizens, in particular that of Henrique Thielen, who suffered damages to his properties in Caracas during the December disturbances, before it would renew diplomatic relations. The April 19, 1909, Dutch-Venezuela Protocol ceased to be effective in June of that year. The Dutch Foreign Minister van Swinderen declined to have any further official relations with Paúl, the Venezuelan envoy, if Gómez persisted in maintaining that the protocol had to be ratified by Congress. Van Swinderen wanted a definite reply to the question of ratification before the baptism of Princess

Juliana took place because Paúl had already been invited to it and to the dinner at court afterward. Upon hearing this, Paúl took offence and did not attend the ceremonies. Gómez informed van Swinderen that he himself had ratified the protocol but that it had to be submitted to Congress for approval. Van Swinderen then informed Gómez that Paúl had repeatedly assured him, verbally and in writing, that the protocol would not be submitted to Congress and that "all further relations with that gentleman were impossible."[93] This led to the "official announcement of his having exceeded his instructions in his negotiations both with the Netherlands and French Governments."[94] It would take another decade for relations to be formalized between the two countries. On May 11, 1920, a treaty was concluded. On January 15, 1921, diplomatic relations were reestablished with The Netherlands.

After intense pressure from Gómez, Congress reluctantly ratified the American protocol in September 1909, but it retaliated by not approving the protocol that Paúl signed with The Netherlands. Gómez cancelled Paúl's appointment as Special Envoy to the various courts of Europe because of action in Congress, which censured Paúl for asking foreign governments in December 1908 about "the advisability of dispatching warships to La Guaira, to afford moral support to the Government of General Gómez."[95] Congress accused Paúl of compromising the national sovereignty. Sir Vincent Corbett did not believe that the former foreign affairs minister was any better or worse than his countrymen in terms of corruptibility, but "in ability, experience and knowledge of the world he is vastly their superior."[96] Corbett added that

> His request for warships may not have been very judicious, but [it] is obviously childish to speak of it as derogatory in any serious degree of the sovereign position of the State. I told him at the time[97] that I thought he was unduly nervous as to the possibility of an anti-Gómez movement in the provinces, which was what he then feared, but allowance must be made for the nervousness of a man who for weeks past had been working literally night and day in imminent peril of his life in hatching a treasonable conspiracy, the failure of which would have meant for him at the best exile and penury and at the worst imprisonment in chains or death.[98]

Sir Vincent was appalled that Gómez and Baptista would be willing to sacrifice Paúl "for the chance of obtaining a little cheap popularity with the Chambers"[99] because the "success of the Revolution and their own positions are due"[100] to him. At the time Congress did not mention that the United States was the only power that answered Paúl's request, but it was an open secret that Paúl's disgrace was "intended as a demonstration against the United States."[101] Paúl served as a convenient scapegoat for Congress to blame because there was little political reason for censuring

Gómez, whose actions until then indicated that he was committed to the establishment of a genuinely democratic government. Congress would be free for the first time to function without "being trapped by power."[102] Senator Arístides Tellería, in his speech that opened the first session of Congress after the December 19 coup, stated that the country was about to enter the "dawning of a new era."[103]

As all this was happening Castro was being operated upon in Berlin. Castro never returned to Venezuela. He remained a political exile, living mainly in San Juan, Puerto Rico, until his death in 1924. Gómez did not repeat the mistakes of his predecessor and mentor. He maintained cordial relations with foreign powers and with the foreign companies that would soon enter the country in search of oil. But more importantly, Gómez knew a great deal about the country and the regional *caudillos* who featured so prominently in politics during the nine years he spent at the side of Castro as vice president. Armed with this knowledge and his own political instinct he remained in power until his death in December 1935.

NOTES

1. "Mensaje que el General Juan Vicente Gómez, Presidente de la República Presenta al Congreso Nacional en 1909," *Gaceta Official*, 38, no. 10,708, 31 May 09, pp. 31323–8.
2. Ibid.
3. Juan Vicente Gómez "Alocución," 20 December 08, Minrelint, *Memoria 1908*, pp. 291–2.
4. Ibid.
5. Ibid.
6. AHM SGPRCP Dic 24–31 1908 José Ignacio Lares to Gómez, 24 December 08.
7. Arístides Tellería, *Mi Actuación en la Vida Pública*, Havana, P. Hernández & Cia., 1950.
8. "Linares Alcántara to All State Presidents," 21 December 08, *Conjuración* 1909 pp. 10–12.
9. Ibid.
10. Ibid., pp. 11–12.
11. "Manifiesto del General José Manuel Hernández, Caracas, 4 February 09," *Conjuración* 1909 pp. 425–28.
12. "Linares Alcántara to All State Presidents," p. 12.
13. "Presidente de la República, Mensaje que el General Juan Vicente Gómez, Presidente de la República Presenta al Congreso Nacional en 1909," *Gaceta Oficial*, pp. 31323–8.
14. AHMSGPRCP Enero 9–19 1909 Carlos A. Martínez, "Renacimiento," Loose Sheet, 16 January 09.
15. Ibid.
16. Ramón J. Velásquez, *La Caida del Liberalismo Amarillo. Tiempo y Drama de Antonio Paredes*, Caracas, Ediciones Venezuela, 1960, p. 364.
17. It was suggested that Paúl's appointment as special envoy was made by the

German minister, Baron Von Seckendorff. Corbett viewed this as "another instance of unwarranted foreign interference in the domestic concern of the country" (FO 199/221 Corbett to Grey, 13 June 09).

18. "Una Interview con Matos," *Conjuración 1909*, pp. 417–20.

19. Ibid., p. 419.

20. AHMSGPR Teleg Dic 26–28 1908 José Antonio Vicentini to Gómez, 27 December 08.

21. AHMSGPRCP Marzo 22–31 1930 (sic) Velutini to Nicolás Rolando, 25 December 08.

22. Ibid.

23. AHMSGPRCP Dic 24–31 1908 Melville E. Stowe to Rolando, 26 December 08.

24. For example, General Gregorio Segundo Riera, General J. M. Ortega Martínez, General Juan Pablo Peñaloza, General Nicolás Rolando, and General José Manuel Hernández all published manifestos.

25. "Manifiesto del General José Manuel Hernández, Caracas, 4 February 09," *Conjuración 1909* pp. 425–28.

26. Ibid., pp. 427–28.

27. Carlos Angel Garbiras to José Manuel Hernández, Caracas, 7 February 09, *Conjuración 1909* p. 429.

28. Ibid.

29. Ibid., p. 428.

30. Ibid.

31. AHMSGPRCP Marzo 9–19 1909 (sic) Cárdenas to Gómez, 16 February 09.

32. Ibid.

33. Ibid.

34. AHMSGPRCP Marzo 1–8 1909 Cárdenas to Gómez, 8 March 09.

35. Velásquez, p. 364.

36. Ibid.

37. Juan Bautista Fuenmayor, *Historia de la Venezuela Política Contemporánea 1899–1969*, Caracas, Talleres Tip. de Miguel Angel García e Hijo, 1975, vol. 1, 1975, p. 198.

38. U.S. Department of State, "Papers Relating to the Foreign Relations of the United States of America," "Venezuela" *House Document 101*, vol. 1, 1909, 61 Cong 2 Sess, 1909–10, pp. 609–35, Secretary of State E. Root to Special Commissioner Buchanan 21 December 08.

39. Brown to Secretary of State, 22 December 08, in Edward Gerald Duffy, "Politics of Expediency: Diplomatic Relations between the United States and Venezuela during the Juan Vicente Gómez Era," PhD. diss., Pennsylvania State University, 1969, p. 70.

40. Root to Andrew Carnegie, 24 December 08, in Philip C. Jessup, *Elihu Root*, New York, Dodd, Mead & Co., 1938, p. 499.

41. Ibid.

42. AHMSGPRCP Dic 24–31 1908 Telegram to A. H. Carner, 24 December 08. Words in all caps are code names.

43. AHMSGPRCP Dic 24–31 1908 trans. Telegram to Carner, 23 December 08.

44. Ibid.
45. AHMSGPRCP Dic 24–31 1908 trans. A. L. Barke to Carner, 26 December 08.
46. Ibid.
47. Ibid.
48. One thousand seven hundred tons with six canons and a crew of 170.
49. AHM SGPR Teleg. Dic 26–28 1908 J. J. Briceño to L. Baptista, 26 December 08.
50. He was in charge of the U.S. archives at the Legation.
51. "Linares Alcántara to All State Presidents, 26 December 08, MinRelInt, *Memoria 1909*, p. 323.
52. Ibid.
53. AHMSGPR Teleg Dic 26–28 1908 Phelps to Associated Press, 26 December 08.
54. FO 199/250 Corbett to Grey, 24 February 09.
55. Ibid.
56. Ibid.
57. Ibid.
58. Duffy, p. 70–71.
59. Hendrickson, "The New Venezuelan Controversy: The Relations of the U.S. and Venezuela, 1904–1914," Ph.D. diss., The University of Minnesota, 1964, p. 201.
60. Ibid.
61. Ibid.
62. AHMSGPRCP Julio 1–14 1909 "Memorandúm Para el Ministro de Fomento," 23 June 09.
63. *Libro Amarillo*, MinRelExt, 1907, p. 112.
64. AHM Unclassified 'Informe al Ministro de Fomento,' Unsigned, 23 June 09.
65. Ibid.
66. Ibid.
67. Ibid.
68. Ibid.
69. Ibid.
70. Ibid.
71. Ibid.
72. Ibid.
73. Ibid.
74. Ibid.
75. Ibid.
76. Hendrickson, p. 207.
77. FO 371/792 Corbett to Grey, 23 January 09.
78. FO 199/250 Corbett to Grey, 7 February 09.
79. Hendrickson, p. 209.
80. FO 199/250 Corbett to Grey, 24 February 09.
81. Ibid.
82. *DDCS* 1 (9) 9 June 09, p. 54.
83. Ibid., p. 55.

84. Ibid.
85. FO 420/251 Corbett to Grey, 25 April 09.
86. Ibid.
87. "La Actitud de los Estados Unidos," *El Tiempo*, 12 April 09.
88. FO 199/250 Acton to Grey, 25 October 10.
89. Hendrickson, p. 212.
90. Hendrickson, p. 227.
91. AHM SGPRCP Nov 1–14 1910, "Hague Court Holds To New Principle," *New York Times*, 31 October 10.
92. Hendrickson, p. 250.
93. FO 199/215 Count H. Bentinck to Grey, 23 June 09.
94. Ibid.
95. FO 199/221 Corbett to Grey, 13 June 09.
96. Ibid.
97. At Sir Vincent Corbett's house on December 15.
98. FO 199/221 Corbett to Grey, 13 June 09.
99. Ibid.
100. Ibid.
101. Ibid.
102. Venezuela, Congreso Nacional, *Discurso Pronunciado por el General Arístides Tellería, Presidente del Senado de los Estados Unidos de Venezuela—al Inaugurar las Sesiones Constitucionales de 1909*, Caracas, Tip. Americana, 1909, p. 4.
103. Ibid, p. 5.

Conclusion

The ascension of Castro and his *compadre* Gómez to the presidency in 1899 was a considerable success for a group of men with little or no experience in government. In the past there had been countless such local rebellions, which ended as soon as they started. What is clearly outstanding about Castro and his followers is that they were able to achieve power and maintain themselves in government while prospering in an alien environment without having an initially strong political base. Moreover, the appearance of the men from the Andes changed the political landscape of the country forever because it altered the political equilibrium that Guzmán Blanco and his Liberal supporters had developed between the commercial bourgeoisie and the local regional *caudillos*. The result was that local chieftains increasingly perceived their position to be in jeopardy and would later rebel against Castro. Mocho Hernández was the first to go against him. Others, such as Matos, felt at the beginning of the regime that Castro was manageable. Such a conclusion did not seem inappropriate because the rebels from Táchira arrived in power by default. They took over when there was a power vacuum created by the internal bickering of the Liberal party. It is to the credit of Castro and his followers that they were able to adjust quickly to national politics and dominate the country to such an extent that this small band of men would rule Venezuela for the next forty-five years.

Although Castro's administration started the political integration of the country by weakening the regional military chieftains while modernizing the structure of administration, the regime can be characterized as being buffeted by a series of political crises, both internal and external, that eventually served to bring it down. Soon after arriving in power Castro caused Colombia to break off diplomatic relations in 1901. Immediately afterward, he had to deal with the country's worst civil war. In December 1901, under the leadership of Castro's erstwhile friends who had been instrumental in getting him to the presidency in 1899, Manuel Antonio Matos launched his ill-fated Revolución Libertadora. The rebellion grouped together most of the strong regional *caudillos* who had prospered under the old Guzmán Blanco regime. At the outset of the Revolución Libertadora, Gómez was appointed the head of the expeditionary force assembled to crush the rebels. It was during this revolution that Gómez showed his true military capacity. After several skirmishes and combats he was seriously wounded in Carúpano on May 6, 1902, while fighting against Nicolás Rolando. Gómez was then appointed acting president from July 5, 1902, to March 20, 1903, and was instrumental in bringing much needed arms and ammunition against all odds to the besieged government troops of Castro at La Victoria, who then defeated the Matos army in central Venezuela. In the middle of this revolution the Allied powers of the United Kingdom, Germany, and later Italy, blockaded Venezuelan ports in December 1902 to force the government to honor its outstanding foreign claims. The "peaceful blockade," as it was known, indirectly helped Castro to defeat the rebels because it took the impetus out of the Matos revolution. The rebels were forced to side with Castro against foreign powers for the duration of the blockade. At the end of the blockade, when it was agreed that the claims would be sent to arbitration, the rebellion continued, but it was difficult for the rebels to recover the initiative. The government had the upper hand, and Gómez pacified the country in July 1903 when he defeated Nicolás Rolando in Ciudad Bolívar. Gómez had saved the government from the country's biggest civil war. He was now recognized as the regime's ablest military man after Castro, who from now on perceived his *compadre* as a potential political threat. The international repercussions of the "peaceful blockade" would soon be felt. It also had a fundamental impact on U.S.-Caribbean relations, leading to the formulation of Roosevelt's Corollary to the Monroe Doctrine, which was that the American government would assist the countries of the Caribbean to manage their financial affairs to avoid European intervention.

The referral to the International Court of Arbitration at The Hague to determine whether the blockading powers should have preference over nonblockading claimants foreshadowed, according to W. L. Penfield, solicitor of the United States, the triumph of force on the American continent by asserting the rights of intervention. The pattern of American policy in the Caribbean was now set for the first decades of the twentieth century. This played an important role in influencing certain political events in Venezuela.

The Venezuelan blockade and the settlements thereafter meant that if a state that used armed force to collect claims was to have a preferred position in any debt settlement, intervention would inevitably become more frequent. There would always be the possibility that a punitive expedition would lead to a permanent occupation of territory, or that the intervening power would meddle in the internal affairs of the country in a way that would give it political control. The Anglo-German blockade of Venezuela reinforced the U.S. policy that was established during the presidency of Teddy Roosevelt. The American government started to interpret the Monroe Doctrine as *carte blanche* to interfere in the internal affairs of the Caribbean states. Fenton has argued that the "peaceful blockade" of Venezuela was a way of testing the "validity of the Monroe Doctrine."[1] It was, however, more a way of refining a concept that up to then had not been fully tested. After all, the amount of capital invested in Venezuela was largely European, and the United States held only a minuscule amount. In 1903, Bax-Ironside calculated that the United Kingdom had a total investment of $60 million, Germany of $40 million, France of $30 million, while the American exposure was "extremely moderate."[2] There were only seven U.S. citizens in Caracas, "most of whom are either men of straw or adventurers."[3] The Americans' action in the "peaceful blockade" was seen as a way of strengthening the role of the United States in Latin America. In February 1903, W. H. Dunwater wrote that

> Now that the Monroe Doctrine had through their action in Venezuela received the virtuous sanction of both Great Britain and Germany, and the implicit approval of the other Powers, it becomes only a question of time that the United States should gradually assume charge of the South American republics. In those circumstances it is interesting to enquire how the smaller States will like the process, and how they are for the present disposed towards the nation whom destiny seems to have designed as their future masters.[4]

In December 1903, Castro suggested forming an International Congress of all Pan-American states to debate any differences that may arise among them or between the subcontinent and Europe. The only way out for the United States was to ensure that European powers did not meddle in the affairs of Latin America. This would first be seen in the Dominican Republic a few years after the "peaceful blockade" and would later become known as Roosevelt's Corollary to the Monroe Doctrine: The US, in order to prevent European intervention in the region, would assist the countries of the Caribbean in their financial management in order to prevent any disorder that would ultimately lead to European intervention. Munro has argued that Roosevelt's Corollary was a result of his determination to ensure that the United States be recognized as a great power and that it conduct itself as one. The policy prohibited the use of force for the recovery of contract debts claimed from the government of one country by the government of another as being due to the latter's nationals, unless the debtor state refused or neglected an offer of arbitration or otherwise prevented a compromise, or after arbitration it refused to submit to the award. The resolution barring military intervention except in special cases was signed by thirty-nine countries, including the United States, at the Second Hague Conference of 1907.[5]

Gómez, who appeared to most observers to be a naive businessman with little social impact, was a political enigma. Gómez played a minor role in the affairs of Táchira in the 1880s and 1890s, and it is likely that he would have remained a regional businessman had Castro not invited him to join the 1899 rebellion. Gómez's innate commercial and political talents were put to good use by Castro. Gómez's sense of survival also ensured that he would remain in government and ultimately topple his *compadre*. Most contemporary reports seen by this author paint a picture of Gómez as a person who would be unable to govern without the assistance of Castro. Yet his behavior as vice president throughout most of the Castro years shows that he had a delicate political touch and was able to move skillfully within the political cauldron of Caracas without suffering any real setbacks. After early 1905, Gómez was portrayed as part of the opposition to Castro from within the government ranks. In 1907 he was perceived as a real threat during La Conjura, yet Castro remained confident that he would not move against him during his absence in Germany. Clearly, Gómez was not as politically naive as portrayed in contemporary accounts, and he was able to learn fast. When Gómez arrived in Caracas in October 1899, his military experience was limited, yet within two years he had pursued and defeated the country's strongest regional *caudillos*, eventually cleansing the country of all opposition by defeating Nicolàs Rolando in Ciudad Bolívar after a three-day siege on July 21, 1903. Gómez returned in triumph to La Guaira on August 3, and received from Castro the title of *El Salvador del Salvador*, while Congress named him *El Pacificador de Venezuela*, and declared July 21 a national holiday that would be celebrated as the *Día de la Paz*. From then on Gómez's military skill would go unquestioned, acknowledged by friend and foe alike as the regime's ablest military man after Castro. Some contemporary writers stated that he was the epitome of "valour, loyalty and honour at its highest level."[6] For the first time since his arrival in Caracas with Castro, Gómez's popularity soared, which would stand him in good stead during the ensuing years. The Revolución Libertadora allowed Gómez to get to know the country much better than most *caudillos* because he crisscrossed it ceaselessly over a period of twenty-four months. Gómez also came to know the strengths and weaknesses of the *caudillos* relatively well. Although Gómez was the natural successor to Castro, there were many people, including the *cabito*, who did not want to see him as president. Gómez himself did not give any outward signs that he wanted to govern, leading Castro and his closest allies to underestimate this shrewd businessman from the Andes.

The Castro administration has been characterized as a nationalist one. Sir Vincent Corbett described Castro as standing for "the national independence and the opposition to the menace of foreign encroachment, especially on the part of the United States."[7] However, it would be wrong to give such a view much merit because Castro's nationalism stemmed from a wish to accumulate as much money for himself and his cronies than from a real desire to defend the interests of the country. It should be noted that his behavior was seen as a natural reward for governing the country. Soon after their arrival in Caracas his close supporters awarded themselves lucrative monopoly contracts that covered most aspects of the country's commercial life. Castro also distributed monopolies and exclusive trading privileges to local companies in which he and his cronies had a vested interest. Castro was too ignorant of the economic effects this policy would have on the general welfare of the country. Under such conditions the economic prosperity of Venezuela could not grow but would instead "inevitably tend to impoverish the general public and, not only render impossible the healthy accumulation of national capital, but actually impair the taxable capacity of the nation."[8] What is true, however, is that from the beginning of his rule Castro exhibited a marked antiforeign bias and a complete disregard of the rights of foreign subjects. Castro felt that foreign investments in a weak, underdeveloped country would invariably lead to foreign interference. He had witnessed "on every side of him the weaker States yielding up their independence before stronger nations clamorous to bear the 'white man's burden.' "[9] The clear, distinct feature of Castro's treatment of foreign companies was the determination to eliminate them, because then he would have "the free development of the national resources untrammeled by foreign interference."[10] Despite Castro's policy of "Venezuela for the Venezuelans"[11] the government was punctual in settling the 1903 claims. For example, Bax-Ironside in his *Annual Report* for 1906 stated that up to then, $1.75 million had been repaid of the 1903 British award of $1,861,630.[12] Castro also repaid promptly the considerable sums borrowed from Venezuelan banks to finance the fight against the Matos revolution, inspired by "the desire to keep his credit intact for the great day when he would bring into play all his resources and make a definite bid for the leadership of Latin America."[13]

Castro believed that he was building the "permanent welfare and independence of his country,"[14] and that his policies, which were mere rhetoric, were in the best interests of Venezuela. This view is only true if no distinction is made between Castro's own welfare and that of Venezuela. The real intention behind Castro's rhetoric was to enrich himself at the expense of the country and the foreign companies that operated within it. The clear motivation for cancelling the NY&B's concession, for instance, was for pecuniary reasons rather than for any defense of Venezuela's national interests. The same was true for some of the other foreign companies operating in the country. It was clearly wrong for the NY&B to support a revolution against the government of Venezuela, but they were defending their interests in a country where the rule of law did not seem to function. It is reasonable to think that had the NY&B and the other companies involved with Matos's revolution agreed to Castro's requests, the country's foreign policy would have been different.

Venezuela would pay dearly for Castro's behavior. The new government of Gómez in 1909 had to renegotiate foreign claims that had already been settled amicably in 1903. It is doubtful whether the extreme action of certain countries would have arisen if Castro had not acted in such a cavalier fashion against the interests of the United States or any of the other countries that subsequently severed relations, because most of them did not have a strong case against Venezuela. If Castro had not acted in such a contradictory and megalomaniac manner, he would have received greater sympathy from foreign governments. It is clear from contemporary newspaper accounts from the United States, the United Kingdom, and The Netherlands that the problems of Venezuela were reported in this manner because the behavior of the foreign powers left much to be desired. Castro's disastrous foreign policy was a key factor in his success at staying in power, especially during the 1901–1902 civil war. However, it would ultimately be his undoing because the Dutch crisis of December 1908 precipitated Gómez's coup, which brought to power another Tachirense who would remain in charge until he died in his sleep twenty-seven years later on December 17, 1935.

NOTES

1. P. F. Fenton, "Diplomatic Relations of the United States and Venezuela, 1880–1915," *HAHR*, vol. 8:3, August 1928, pp. 330–57.
2. FO 199/173 Draft, Bax-Ironside to Foreign Office, 23 December 03.
3. Ibid. For further reading on U.S. foreign policy at the time see the following: Dexter Perkins, *The United States and the Caribbean*, Oxford, Oxford University Press, 1947; Dexter Perkins, *The Monroe Doctrine, 1867–1907*, Baltimore; The John Hopkins University Press, 1937; Bradford Perkins, *The Great Rapprochement: England and the United States, 1895–1914*, London, Victor Gollancz Ltd., 1969; Theodore Roosevelt, *The Works of Theodore Roosevelt*, vol. 15 (State Papers as Governor and President, 1899–1909) New York, Charles Scribner's Sons, 1926; Scott Nearing and Joseph Freeman, *La Diplomacia del Dólar*, Mexico, Sociedad de Edición y Librería Franco-Alemana S. A. 1927; Selig Adler, "Bryan & Wilsonian Caribbean Penetration," *HAHR*, vol. 20, May 1940, pp. 198–226; John A. S. Grenville and George Berkely Young, *Politics, Strategy and American Diplomacy—Studies in Foreign Policy, 1873–1917*, New Haven and London, Yale University Press, 1966.

4. FO 80/458 W. H. Dunwater, "The Two Americas—South's Feeling towards the North," no date.

5. James W. Angell, *Financial Foreign Policy of the United States: A Report on the Second International Conference in the State and Economic Life*, London, May 29–June 2, 1933, New York, The Council on Foreign Relations, 1933, p. 65.

6. Estebán D. González, *La Obra de Castro y los Hombres de Castro*, La Guaira, Tip. La Equitativa, 1904, p. 13.

7. FO 371/793 Corbett to Grey, 10 February 09.

8. FO 199/275 Corbett to Grey, 12 February 09.

9. FO 371/793 Corbett to Grey, 10 February 09.

10. FO 199/275 Corbett to Grey, 12 February 09.

11. FO 80/362 Bax-Ironside to Grey, 31 January 07.

12. Ibid.

13. FO 371/793 Corbett to Grey, 10 February 09.

14. Ibid.

Bibliography

SECONDARY SOURCES

Books

Acosta Matute, Petro Antonio, *Comercio Internacional de Venezuela, 1830–1831, 1899–1900, 1913–1952* (Caracas: Mimeo, 1956).

Adriani, Alberto, *Labor Venezolanista* (Caracas: Tip. La Nación, 1937).

Aguilera, Delfín A., *Venezuela 1900* (Caracas: Ediciones del Congreso de la República, 1974).

Alamo Ibarra, Roberto, *Resúmenes Estadísticos del Comercio Exterior de los Estados Unidos de Venezuela Correspondiente al Lapso de 1908–1928 y el Primer Semestre de 1929* (Caracas: Lit. y Tip. Casa de Especialidades, 1930).

Alarico Gómez, Carlos, *La Amarga Experiencia (El Bloqueo de 1902)* (Caracas: Ministerio de Educación, 1983).

Alcántara, Francisco Segundo, *La Aclamación* (1906), *La Conjura* (1907), *La Reacción* (1908) (Caracas: Ediciones Librería Europa, 1958).

Alvárez, Pedro J., *La Higiene Social en Venezuela (Contribución a un estudio)* (Caracas: Tip. Agencia Musical, 1943).

Andara, J. L. *En Defensa de la Causa Liberal* (Curacao: n.p., 1903).

———., *La Evolución Social y Política de Venezuela* (Curacao: Imprenta de A. Bethencourt e Hijos, 1904).

———., *De Política e Historia* (Curacao: n.p., 1904).

Andrade, Ignacio, *?Porqué Triunfó la Revolución Restauradora? Memorias y Exposición a los Venezolanos de los Sucesos 1898–1899* (Caracas: Ediciones Garrido, 1955).

Angell, James W., *Financial Foreign Policy of the United States, a Report on the*

Second International Conference in the State and Economic Life, London May 29–June 2 1933 (New York: The Council on Foreign Relations, 1933).

Anzola, Juvenal, *Ciudades y Pasajes* (Caracas: Empresa El Cojo, 1907).

———., *Por la Patria y el Hogar* (Caracas: Empresa El Cojo, 1911).

———., *De Caracas a San Cristóbal* (Caracas: Empresa El Cojo, 1913).

Arcaya, Pedro Manuel, *Estudios sobre Personajes y Hechos de la Historia Venezolana* (Caracas: Tip. Cosmos, 1911).

———., *Estudios de Sociología Venezolana* (Madrid: Editorial América, 1917).

———., *Nuevas Orientaciones de Historia Política* (Washington D.C.: n.p., 1924).

———., *Memorias del Doctor Pedro Manuel Arcaya* (Madrid: Talleres del Instituto Geográfico y Catastral, 1963).

Arcila Faría, Eduardo, *MOP. Centenario del Ministerio de Obras Públicas. Influencia de éste Ministerio en el Desarrollo; 1874–1974* (Caracas: Talleres Italgráfica, 1974).

Arellano, Angel María, *Mis Memorias. Vidas y Paisajes del Campo Táchirense* (Caracas: BATT, 1973).

Arellano Moreno, A., *Guía de Historia de Venezuela, 1492–1945* (Caracas: Ediciones Edime, 1955).

———., *Mirador de Historia Política de Venezuela* (Caracas: Imp. Nacional, 1967).

Bacon, Robert E. and James Brown Scott, eds., *Addresses on International Subjects by Elihu Root* 2 vols. (Cambridge: Harvard University Press, 1916).

Baker, Henry D., *Trinidad and Venezuela—Asphalt Lakes* (Port of Spain, Trinidad: Franklin's Electric Printery, 1924).

Baldó, Lucio, (ed.), *The Oil Industry in Venezuela* (New York: C. S. Hammond & Co., 1924).

Balestrini, César, *Economía Minera y Petrolera* (Caracas: UCV, 1959).

Baptista, Octavio, *Venezuela, Su Historia y Sus Métodos de Gobierno* (Guadalajara: Talleres Linotipográficos Gráfica, 1942).

Bates, Lindon, *The Path of the Conquistadores. Trinidad and Venezuela Guiana* (London: Methuen & Co. Ltd., 1912).

Beebe, Mary Blair, and Charles William Beebe, *Our Search for Wilderness* (London: Constable & Co. Ltd., 1910).

Bello Rodríguez, Zoilo, *Archivo Político* (Caracas: Ediciones de la Secretaría de la Presidencia y del Ministerio de Defensa, 1979).

Benet, F., *Guía Comercial e Venezuela* 2 vols. (Caracas: n.p. 1929).

Benítez, Cristóbal, *Los Partidos Políticos en Venezuela* (Caracas: Editorial Patria, 1930).

———., *Sociología Política* (Caracas: Cooperativa de Artes Gráficas, 1938).

Besson, Juan, *La Influencia del Descubrimiento del Lago de Maracaibo en los Destinos de Venezuela* (Caracas: Empresa El Cojo, 1949).

———., *Historia del Estado Zulia* 5 vols. (Maracaibo: Editorial Hermanos Belloso Rossell, 1951).

Bingham, Hiram, *The Journal of an Expedition across Venezuela and Colombia, 1906–1907* (New Haven: The Yale Publishing Association, 1933).

Blanck S., Juan, *Los Desterrados* (Valencia: Imp. El Radical, 1909).

Blanco Fombona, R., *El Hombre de Hierro* (Caracas: Tip. Americana, 1907).

———., *Judas Capitolino* (Paris: Chartres, 1912).

———., *Diario de Mi Vida, 1904–1905.* (Madrid: Compañía Ibero-Americana de Publicaciones C. A. Renacimiento, 1929).

———., *La Bella y la Fiera* (Madrid: Compañía Ibero-Americana de Publicaciones C. A. Renacimiento, 1931).

———., *Camino de Imperfección. Diario de Mi Vida, 1906–1914* (Madrid: Editorial Madrid, 1933).

———., *Diarios de Mi Vida* (Caracas: Monte Avila Editores, 1975).

Bowen, Herbert Wolcott, *Recollections, Diplomatic and Undiplomatic* (New York: Hitchcock, 1926).

Bracamonte, Rafael, *El General Gómez y el XIX de Diciembre* (Caracas: Lit. y Tip. del Comercio, 1916).

Brandt, Carlos, *Bajo la Tiranía de Cipriano Castro. Su Desgraciada Actitud durante el Bombardeo y el Bloqueo de 1902* (Caracas: Editorial Elite, 1952).

Briceño Ayesterán, Santiago, *Memorias de Su Vida Militar y Política* (Caracas: Tip. América, 1948).

Brito Figueroa, Federico, *Venezuela Siglo XX* (Havana: Casa de las Américas, 1967).

Burgraaf, Winfield J., *The Venezuelan Armed Forces in Politics, 1935–1959* (Columbia: University of Missouri Press, 1972).

Calcaño Herrera, Julio, *Bosquejo Histórico de la Revolución Libertadora, 1902–1903* (Caracas: Lit. del Comercio, 1944).

Campo, Juan, *Comercio Exterior de Venezuela. Análisis Estadístico y Arancelario de Importación y Exportación. Diversos Aspectos de la Economía Nacional* (Caracas: Editorial Elite, 1939).

Capriles Méndez, Ruth, *Los Negocios de Román Delgado Chalbaud* (Caracas, Biblioteca de la Academia Nacional de la Historia, 1991).

Carpenter, Frank G., *South America. Social, Industrial and Political* (Akron: The Saalfield Publishing Co., 1900).

Carreño, Eduardo, *Trayectoria de una Vida Ilustre* (Caracas: Ed. Elite, 1944).

Carrera Damas, Germán, *Consideraciones sobre los límites Históricos del Liberalismo en Venezuela* (Caracas: Imprenta Universitaria, 1959).

Carrillo Batalla, Tomás Enrique, *Moneda, Crédito y Banca en Venezuela* (Caracas: Banco Central de Venezuela, 1964).

Cartay, Rafael, *Historia Económica de Venezuela, 1830–1900* (Caracas: Vadell Editores, 1988).

Castellanos, Rafael Ramón, *Rufino Blanco y sus Coterráneos* (Bogotá: n.p., 1970).

Castillo, Domingo B., *Memorias de Mano Lobo. Sucesos y Relatos de la Época Final de la Influencia Guzmancista* (Caracas: Ed. Garrido, 1956).

Castro, Cipriano, *Comentarios a los Mensajes del General Cipriano Castro. Homenaje de Justicia al Restaurador de Venezuela. Editoriales de "Patria y Castro" de Calabozo* (Caracas, Imprenta Nacional, 1905).

———., *La Verdad Histórica* 2d ed. (Caracas, Tip Garrido, 1942).

Contreras Serrano, J. N. *Cipriano Castro. Gobernador del Táchira (1888–1899)* (Caracas: BATT, 1997).

Cordero Velásquez, Luis, *El General J. V. Gómez en Anécdotas* (Caracas: Urbina & Fuentes Editores Asociados, 1983).

Crichfield, G. W., *American Supremacy. The Rise and Progress of the South Amer-*

ican Republics and Their Relations to the United States under the Monroe Doctrine 2 vols., (New York: Brentano's 1908).

Croes, Hemy, *El Movimiento Obrero Venezolano, Elementos para Su Historia* (Caracas: Ediciones Movimiento Obrero, 1973).

Curtis, W. E., *Venezuela. A Land Where It Is Always Summer* (London: Osfood McIlvaine & Co., 1896).

Dalton, Leonard V., *Venezuela* 4th ed. (London: T. Fisher Unwin Ltd., 1925).

Davis, R. H., *Three Gringos in Venezuela and Central America* (New York: n.p., 1896).

Delgado Palacios, G., *Contribución al Estudio del Café en Venezuela* (Caracas: Publicaciones de la Junta Central de Aclimitación y Perfeccionamiento Industrial, Tip. El Cojo, 1895).

De Nogales Méndez, Rafael, *Verdades* (Caracas: n.p., 1909).

Domínici, Pedro César, *El Mono Trágico (Réplica a un Farsante)* (Paris: L. Duc & Cie Imprimeurs, 1909).

Domínici, Pedro José, *Un Sátrapa. Notas sobre una Tiranía*, (Paris: n.p., 1901).

Drago, Luis M., *La República de Argentina y el Caso de Venezuela* (Caracas: OCI, 1976).

Dugdale, E. T. S., *German Diplomatic Documents, 1871–1914*, 3 vols. (New York: Barnes & Noble Inc., 1930).

Escobar Salom, Ramón, *Evolución Política de Venezuela* (Caracas: Monte Avila Editores, 1975).

Ewell, Judith, *Venezuela, a century of change* (London: C. Hurst & Co., 1984).

Fergusson, Erna, *Venezuela* (New York: Alfred A. Knopf, 1939).

Fernández, Carlos Emilio, *Hombres y Sucesos de Mi Tierra, 1909–1935* 2d ed. (Madrid: Talleres del Sagrado Corazón, 1969).

Fernández, Pablo Emilio, *Gómez el Rehabilitador* (Caracas: Jaime Villegas Editor, 1956).

Figueredo, Carlos Benito, *Presidenciales* (Madrid: Establecimiento Tip de El Liberal, 1908).

Fuenmayor, Juan Bautista, *Historia de la Venezuela Política Contemporánea, 1899–1969* 3 vols. (Caracas: Talleres Tip. de Miguel Angel García e Hijo, 1975).

FUNRES, *Documentos Británicos Relacionados con el Bloqueo de las Costas Venezolanas* (Caracas: FUNRES, 1982).

Galavís, Manuel María, *Alegatos. Defensa del General Eustoquio Gómez ante el Juzgado de Primera Instancia en lo Criminal de la Sección Occidental del Distrito Federal* (Caracas: n.p., 1908).

Gallegos Ortiz, Rafael, *La Historia Política de Venezuela, de Cipriano Castro a Pérez Jiménez* (Caracas: Imp. Universitaria, 1960).

García Gil, Pedro, *Cuarenta y Cinco Años de Uniforme. Memorias 1901–1945* (Caracas: Editorial Bolívar, 1947).

García Villasmil, Martín, *Escuelas para Formación de Oficiales del Ejército. Orden y Evolución de la Escuela Militar* (Caracas: Oficina Técnica Mindefensa, 1964).

———., *40 Años de Evolución en las Fuerzas Armadas* (Caracas: n.p., 1965).

Gerstl, Otto, *Memorias e Historias* (Caracas: Fundación John Boulton, 1967).

Gil Fortoul, José, *El Hombre y la Historia* (Paris: Libreria de Garnier Hermanos, 1896).

———., *De Hoy para Mañana* (Caracas: Imprenta Nacional, 1916).

———., *Historia Constitucional de Venezuela* 5th ed. (Caracas: Ediciones Sales, 1964).

Gilmore, Robert, *Caudillism and Militarism in Venezuela, 1810–1910* (Athens, Ohio: Ohio State University Press, 1964).

González, César, *Vieja Gente del Táchira. Crónica Genealógica* (Caracas: Imprenta de la Guardia Nacional Fuerte Tiuna, 1975).

González, Estebán D., *La Obra de Castro y los Hombres de Castro* (La Guaira: Tip. La Equitativa, 1904).

González Baquero, R., *Análisis del Proceso Histórico de la Educación Urbana (1870–1932) y de la Educación Rural (1932–1957) en Venezuela* (Caracas: UCV, 1962).

González Chacón, Simón, *El Imperio del Desorden. Realidad Política* (Caracas: Tip. del Comercio, 1899).

González Escorihuela, Ramón, *Las Ideas Políticas en el Táchira de los Años 70 del Siglo XIX a la Segunda Década del Siglo XX* (Caracas: BATT, 1994).

Gooch, G. P., and H. Temperley, *British Documents on the Origins of the War* 2 vols. (London: HMSO, 1928).

Grenville, John A. S., and George Berkely Young, *Politics, Strategy and American Diplomacy—Studies in Foreign Policy, 1873–1917* (New Haven: Yale University Press, 1966).

Guardia, Hugo N., *Recopilación de Estadística Cafetera* (Caracas: Publicaciones del Instituto Nacional del Café, 1943).

Guédez, Juan Jacobo, *Del Pretérito. Editoriales de "El Estado" durante las Conjuras de 1907 a 1908. Constitucionalidad o Dictadura* (Caracas: Editorial Venezuela, 1931).

Guerrero, Emilio Constantino, *Campaña Heróica. Estudio Histórico-Militar de la Campaña Dirigida en Venezuela por el General Cipriano Castro, Como Jefe de la Revolución Liberal Restauradora en 1899* (Caracas: J. M. Herrera Irigoyén y Cia., 1903).

Harwich, Nikita V., *Formación y Crisis de un Sistema Financiero Nacional. Banco y Estado en Venezuela (1830–1940)* (Caracas: Fondo Editorial Buria, 1986).

———., *Asfalto y Revolución: La New York and Bermúdez Company* (Caracas: Monte Avila Editores, 1992).

———., ed., *Inversiones Extranjeras en Venezuela Siglo XIX* (Caracas: Academia Nacional de Ciencias Economicas, 1992).

Hernández, José Manuel, *Ante la Historia. El General José Manuel Hernández, Jefe del Partido Liberal Nacionalista al General Cipriano Castro, Presidente de los Estados Unidos de Venezuela* (Philadelphia: n.p., 1904).

Herwig, Holger H., *Germany's Vision of Empire in Venezuela, 1871–1914* (Princeton: Princeton University Press, 1986).

Hill, Howard C., *Roosevelt and the Caribbean* (Chicago: The University of Chicago Press, 1927).

Hood, Miriam, *Diplomacia con Cañones, 1895–1905* (Caracas: Ediciones de la Presidencia, 1975).

Jahn, Alfredo, *El Desarrollo de las Vias de Comunicación en Venezuela* (Caracas: Lit. y Tip. Mercantil, 1926).

———., *El Estado Zulia. Esbozo Histórico-Geográfico* (Caracas: Lit. y Tip. Vargas, 1927).

Jessup, Philip C., *Elihu Root* 2 vols., (New York: Dodd, Mead & Co., 1938).

Jiménez Arraiz, *Del Vivac* (Cumaná: Imprenta Mila de la Roca, 1904).

Laclé, Antonio, *Las Guerras Internas de Venezuela y Como han Perjudicado Su Población* (Caracas: Lit. y Tip. Taller Gráfico, 1932).

Lecuna, Vicente, *La Revolución de Queipa* (Caracas: Ed. Garrido, 1954)

León Carlos, *Autonomías de los Nuevos Estados* (Caracas: Imprenta Federación, 1898).

———., *Autonomías. Narración Histórica al Partido Liberal* (Caracas: n.p., 1900).

León, Ramón David, *Hombres y Sucesos de Venezuela (La República desde José Antonio Páez hasta Rómulo Gallegos)* (Caracas: Tip. Americana, 1952).

Levine, Daniel H., *Conflict and Change in Venezuela* (Cambridge: Harvard University Press, 1973).

Linares, José Antonio, *El General Juan Vicente Gómez y las Obras Públicas en Venezuela, 19 de Diciembre de 1908–4 de Agosto de 1913* (Caracas: Lit. y Tip. del Comercio, 1916).

Lock, C. G. Wornford, *Coffee: Its Culture and Commerce in All Countries* (London: E & F. N. Spoon, 1888).

Lodge, Henry Cabot, *Selections from the Correspondence of Theodore Roosevelt and Henry Cabot Lodge, 1884–1918* (New York: Charles Scribner's Sons, 1925).

López, José Eliseo, *La Expansión Demográfica de Venezuela* (Mérida: Universidad de los Andes, 1963).

López Contreas, E., *Páginas para la Historia Militar de Venezuela* (Caracas: Editorial Las Novedades, 1945).

———., *El Presidente Cipriano Castro* (Caracas: n.p., 1983).

López de Sagrado y Bru, José, *Gobernantes de Maracaibo, 1499–1952* (Maracaibo: Cámara de Comercio de Maracaibo, 1952).

Maldonado, Gerónimo, *Cuestión Social* (Maracaibo: Imp. Americana, 1909).

———., *Patria* (Maracaibo: Imp. Americana, 1909).

Mariñas Otero, Luis, *Las Constituciones de Venezuela* (Madrid: Ediciones Cultura Hispánica, 1965).

Márquez Cairos, Fernando, *Vienen los Andinos* (Caracas: Ediciones Orinoco, 1956).

Martin, Percy F., *Through Five Republics (of South America)* (London: William Heineman, 1905).

Martínez, Carlos A., *Renacimiento* (San Juan de los Morros, Puerto Rico: n.p., 1909).

Martínez Sánchez, Antonio, *Nuestras contiendas civiles* (Caracas: Tip. Garrido, 1949).

Márquez Bustillos, V., *Semblanza del General Juan Vicente Gómez* (Caracas: Lit. y Tip. del Comercio, 1919).

Matos, M. A., *Apuntes sobre la Revolución Libertadora* (Curacao: n.p., 1903).

———., *Recuerdos* (Caracas: Empresa El Cojo, 1927).

Matos Boscán, José V., *Necesidad de Industrializar a Venezuela* (Caracas: Ed. Sur América, 1932).

Mendible, Luciano, *30 Años de Lucha. Documentos Para la Vida Pública del Dr. Luciano Mendible, 1908–1940* (Caracas: n.p., 1941).

Mills, Dorothy, *The Country of the Orinoco* (London: Hutchinson & Co., 1931).

Modesto Gallegos, Manuel, *Anales Contemporáneo. Memorias del General Modesto Gallegos* (Caracas: Tip. Casa de Especialidades, 1926).

Montilla, José Abel, *Fermín Entrena. Un Venezolano del Noventa Nueve* (Buenos Aires: Imprenta López, 1944).

Morales, Carlos, *Daños Provenientes de la Revolución Libertadora. Juicio Seguido por el Señor Carlos Vicente Echevarría contra el General Manuel Antonio Matos* (Caracas: Lit. del Comercio, 1918).

Morantes, Pedro María, *El Cabito* (Caracas: BATT, 1971).

Morantes, Pedro María (Pio Gil) *Diario Intimo y Otros Temas* (Caracas: Ediciones de la Presidencia de la Republica, 1965).

Moros, Eulogio, *Por Justicia* (La Asunción: Tip. Popular-Modiano, 1909).

Muñoz, Arturo Guillermo, *El Táchira Fronterizo. El Aislamiento Regional y la Integración Nacional en el Caso de Los Andes* (Caracas: BATT, 1985).

Munro, D. G., *Intervention and Dollar Diplomacy in the Caribbean, 1900–1921* (Princeton: Princeton University Press, 1964).

———., *The Latin American Republics*, 3d ed. (London: George G. Harrap & Co Ltd., 1961).

Murillo-Chacón, Augusto, *Ecos del Recuerdo. La Vida Tachirense a Comienzos del Siglo XX* (Caracas: BATT, 1969).

Natera Wanderlinder, Felipe, *A la Memoria de Destacado Hombre Público Doctor y General Luis Mata Illas al Cumplirse 59 Años de Su Trágica y Alevosa Muerte* (Caracas: Ministerio de Fomento, 1966).

Navas, Juan Vicente, *Vida Política y militar del Yaracuy, 1855–1945* (Caracas: Biblioteca de Autores y Temas Yaracuyanos, 1962).

Nearing, Scott and Joseph Freeman, *La Diplomacia del Dólar* 2d ed. (Mexico: Sociedad de Edición y Librería Franco-Alemana S.A. 1927).

Nesbitt, L. M., *Desolate Marches. Travels in the Orinoco LLanos of Venezuela* (London: Jonathan Cape, 1935).

Núñez, Enrique Bernardo, *El Hombre de la Levita Gris (Los Años de la Restauración Liberal)* (Caracas: Ediciones Elite, 1953).

———., *Bajo el Samán* (Caracas: Tip. Vargas, 1963).

Núñez, Hilarios, *Constitucionalidad o Dictadura* (Caracas: Tip. Americana, 1909).

Orsi de Monbello, G., *Venezuela y Sus Riquezas* (Caracas: Imprenta de la Patria, 1890).

Pacheco, Emilio, *De Castro a López Contreras* (Caracas: Domingo and Fuentes, 1984).

Parada, Nemesio, *El Táchira de Mi Infancia y Juventud* (Caracas: BATT, 1966).

———., *Vísperas y Comienzos de la Revolución de Cipriano Castro* (Caracas: n.p., 1968).

———., *De Ocumare a Miraflores* (Caracas: BATT, 1975).

Paredes, Antonio, *Como Llegó Cipriano Castro al Poder* 2d ed. (Caracas: Ediciones Garrido, 1954).

Paredes Urdaneta, Rafael, *Los Andinos antes de la Invasión de los Sesenta* (Caracas: Mimeo, 1969).

Parra Aranguren, Fernando Ignacio, *Antecentes del Derecho del Trabajo en Venezuela, 1830–1928* (Maracaibo: Universidad del Zulia, 1965).

Parra León, Miguel, *Problemas de Transporte* (Caracas: Editorial Sur América, 1930).

Parra Márquez, Héctor, *Presidentes de Venezuela* (Caracas: n.p., 1954).

Paúl, José de Jesús, *El Doctor José de Jesús Paúl a Sus Compatriotas* (Paris: Imprenta de Lagny, 1909).

Perera, Ambrosio, *Historia Orgánica de Venezuela* (Caracas: Editorial Venezuela, 1943).

Pérez Vila, Manuel, *Fuentes para la Historia de Venezuela en el Siglo XX* (Caracas: Italgráfica, 1964).

Perkins, Bradford, *The Great Rapprochement: England and the United States, 1895–1914* (London: Victor Gollancz Ltd., 1969).

Perkins, Dexter, *The Monroe Doctrine, 1867–1907* (Baltimore: The Johns Hopkins University Press, 1937).

———., *The United States and the Caribbean* (Oxford: Oxford University Press, 1947).

———., *The Evolution of American Foreign Policy* (Oxford: Oxford University Press, 1948).

Picón Salas, Mariano, *Los Días de Cipriano Castro* (Caracas: Ediciones Garrido, 1953).

———., *Las Nieves de Antañó. Pequeñas Añoranza de Mérida* (Maracaibo: Universidad del Zulia, 1958).

———., *Venezuela Independiente, 1810–1960* (Caracas: Fundación Eugenio Mendoza, 1962).

Pino Iturrieta, Elías, *Castro, Epistolario Presidencial* (Caracas: UCV, 1974).

Pringle, Henry F., *Theodore Roosevelt: A Biography* (London: Jonathan Cape Ltd., 1931).

Rangel, Domingo Alberto, *Los Andinos en el Poder* (Caracas: n.p., 1964).

Ricart, José Rafael, *El Trabajo. Consideraciones sobre las Causas de Fuerza Mayor que han Impedido el Desarrollo de Nuestras Industrias y Demonstración Suscinta de la Necesidad de Abrir un Paréntesis de Paz, de Garantías y de Protección a la Propiedad y al Trabajo, sin lo Cual el Progreso Patrio Será Imposible* (Caracas: Tip. Americana, 1903).

Rios, Pompeyo, *Desarrollo Económico de Venezuela. Desde 1830 hasta 1920* (Caracas: Imp. Universitaria, 1964).

Rippy, J. Fred., *British Investments in Latin America, 1822–1949* (Minneapolis: University of Minnesota, 1959).

Rodríguez, Manuel Alfredo, *El Capitolio de Caracas. Un Siglo de Historia de Venezuela* (Caracas: Ediciones del Congreso de la República, 1974).

Roldán Oliarte, Estebán, *El General Juan Vicente Gómez. Venezuela de Cerca* (México: Imprenta Mundial, 1933).

Roosevelt, Nicholas, *Venezuela's Place in the Sun. Modernizing a Pioneering Country* (New York: Round Table Press Inc., 1940).

Roosevelt, Theodore, *The Works of Theodore Roosevelt. The State Papers as Governor and President* 15 vols. (New York: Charles Scribner's Sons, 1926).

Rosales, Rafael María, *Imagen Cultural del Táchira* (Mérida: Colección de la Corporación de los Andes, undated).

Salas, Federico, *El Clamor de un Pueblo. Estudios Económicos* 2 vols., (Maracaibo: n.p., 1911).

Salazar Martínez, Francisco, *Tiempo de Compadres. De Cipriano Castro a Juan Vicente Gómez* (Caracas: Librería Piñango, 1972).

Sánchez, Juan, *Narración Histórica al Partido Liberal. Aclaratoria a Mis Compatriotas* (Caracas: n.p., undated).

Salcedo Bastardo, J. L., *Historia Fundamental de Venezuela* (Caracas: UCV, 1970).

Sánchez Pacheco, Ciro, *Los Andinos* (Caracas: Ediciones Garrido, 1968).

Schael, Guillermo José, *Apuntes para la Historia. El Automóvil en Venezuela* (Caracas: Gráficas Edición de Arte, 1969).

Scruggs, William L., *The Colombian and Venezuelan Republics* (Boston: Little, Brown & Co., 1905).

Siso, Carlos, *La Formación del Pueblo Venezolano* 2 vols. (Madrid: Editorial García Enciso, 1953).

———., *El Concepto de la Historia en Laureano Vallenilla Lanz* (Caracas: UCV, 1966).

———., *Castro y Gómez. Importancia de la Hegemonía Andina* (Caracas: Editorial Arte, 1985).

Steiner, Zara, *The Foreign Office and the Foreign Policy, 1898–1914* (Cambridge: Cambridge University Press, 1941).

Sullivan, William M., *Bibliografía Comentada de la Era de Cipriano Castro, 1899–1908* (Caracas: BATT, 1977).

Tello Mendoza, R., *Ligeros Rasgos Biográficos del General Juan Vicente Gómez* (Caracas: Tip. Universal, 1904).

Thayer, William Roscoe, *The Life and Letters of John Hay* 2 vols. (London: Constable & Co. Ltd., 1915).

Thurber, Orray E., *The Venezuelan Question; Castro and the Asphalt Trust from Official Records* (New York: n.p., 1907).

Ukers, William H., *Disgregación e Integración. Ensayo sobre la Formación de la Nacionalidad Venezolana* (Caracas: Tip. Universal, 1930).

———., *All About Coffee* 2d ed. (New York: The Tea and Coffee Trade Journal Company, 1935).

Vallenilla Lanz, Laureano, *Cesarismo Democrático. Estudios sobre las Bases Sociológicas de la Constitución Efectiva de Venezuela* 3rd ed. (Caracas: Tip. Garrido, 1952).

———., *Críticas de Sinceridad y Exactitud* (Caracas: Ediciones Garrido, 1956).

———., *Obras Completas* (Caracas: Universidad Santa María, 1983).

Vallenilla Lanz, Laureano (Hijo), *Escrito de Memoria* (Caracas: Ediciones Garrido, 1957).

Velásquez, Ramón J., *La Caida del Liberalismo Amarillo. Tiempo y Drama de Antonio Paredes* (Caracas: Ediciones Venezuela, 1960).

———., *Los Pasos de los Héroes* 2d ed. (Caracas: Ediciones Centauro, 1981).

———., *Memorias de Venezuela. Cipriano Castro—Juan Vicente Gómez, 1899–1935* vol. 4 (Caracas: Ediciones Centauro, 1991).

Veloz, Ramón, *Economía y Finanzas de Venezuela. Desde 1830 hasta 1944* (Caracas: Impresores Unidos, 1945).

Vetencourt, Roberto, *Tiempo de Caudillos* (Caracas: Italgráfica, 1994).

Willis, Captain, *The Cruise of the "Ban Righ" or How I became a Pirate* (London: Brooks Bros. Co., 1902).

Articles

Alamo, Francisco de P., "Un Cafetero que No Necesita Sombra," *Boletín del Ministerio de Fomento* 1:3 (1920) 113–14.

Alamo Ibarra, Roberto, "La Agricultura y la Ganadería en Venezuela," *Proceedings of the Eighth American Scientific Congress* 5 (1940) 41–44.

Batalla Carrillo, Tomás Enrique, "El Desarrollo del Sector Manufacturero de la Economía Venezolana," *Boletín Bibliográfico* 3:17 (January-June 1962).

Beebe, C. W. and M. B. Beebe, "In the Wilderness," *Harpers Monthly Magazine* 118:709 (1909) 836–48.

Bonsal, Stephen, "Castro: A Latin American type," *North American Review* 176 (1903).

Bowen, H. W., "Queer Diplomacy with Castro," *North American Review* 184 (March 30, 1907) 577–80.

———., "Roosevelt vs. Venezuela," *North American Review* 210 (September 1919) 414–17.

———., "Mr. Thayer and President Roosevelt," *North American Review* 210 (October 1919) 570.

Calvani, Arístides, "La Política Internacional de Venezuela en el Último Medio Siglo," in *Venezuela Moderna. Medio Siglo de Historia 1926–1976* (Caracas: Fundación Eugenio Mendoza, 1976) 389–488.

Carrera Damas, Germán, "Consideraciones sobre los Límites Históricos del Liberalismo en Venezuela," *Revista Paideia* 2:2 (January-March 1959), 107–8 (August 1975) 22–29.

"Castro Acclaimed on Arrival Here," *The Havana Post* (March 27, 1913).

"Castro Playing for Popularity," *Havana Telegraph* (February 28, 1913).

Clark, Floyd, "Castro the Ungrateful," *North American Review* 187 (April 1908) 569–77.

"Como Se Construía una Carretera (La Gran Carretera Transandina)," *BAHM*, 15: 77 (January-February 1974) 203–53.

Cooney, S., "Political Demand Channels in the Processes of American and British Imperial Expansion, 1870–1913," *World Politics* 27:2 (January 1975).

Dafert, F. W., "Observaciones sobre el Cultivo Racional del Cafeto," *Boletín del Ministerío de Fomento* 1:5 (November 1909) 349–54.

Davis, Norman H., "Wanted: A Consistent Latin American Policy," *Foreign Affairs* 9:4 (July 1931) 547–68.

de Armas Chitty, J. A., "La Economía Venezolana de Fines del Siglo XIX a traves del 'Boletín de la Riqueza Pública," *Anales de la Universidad Central de Venezuela* 41 (1956) 249–61.

De Booy, Theodor, "The People of the Mist. An Account of Explorations in Venezuela," *The Museum Journal* 9:3–4 (September–December 1918) 183–224.

———., "An Exploration of the Sierra de Perijá, Venezuela," *The Geographical Review* 6:5 (November 1918) 385–410.

———., “The Western Maracaibo Lowland, Venezuela,” *The Geographical Review* 6:6 (December 1918) 482–500.

Dennis, William Cullem, “The Orinoco Steamship Company Case before The Hague Tribunal,” *The American Journal of International Law* 5:1 (January 1911) 32–64.

Dozer, Donald Marquand, “Roots of Revolution in Latin America,” *Foreign Affairs* 27:2 (January 1949) 274–88.

“The Dutch and Venezuela,” *The Nation* 87:2268 (December 17, 1908) 595–96.

“El Ex-Presidente de Venezuela,” *Diario de Cádiz* (December 5, 1910).

“El Gobierno de Castro y la New York and Bermúdez Company,” *BAHM* 7: 41–42 (March-June 1966) 91–205.

España, Blas M., “Castro y Gómez,” *Venezuela. Ecos de una Tiranía* 21 (September 1906) 85–86.

“Executive Decree of Venezuela Concerning Foreign Claims, 13.11.12,” *Supplement to the American Journal of International Law. Official Documents* lx, 8:1 (January 1914) 174–75.

Fenton. P. F., “Diplomatic Relations of the United States and Venezuela, 1880–1915,” *Hispanic American Historical Review* 8:3 (August 1928) 330–57.

Giacopini Zárraga, J. A., “Revive con Su Ameno Verbo de la Batalla de La Victoria,” *Resumén* 7:81 (May 25, 1975) 56–62.

“H. W. Bowen Again,” *Washington Times* (March 30, 1904).

Harwich, Nikita, “Cipriano Castro: El Retorno,” *Resumén* 7:81 (May 25, 1975), 40–48.

———., “El Modelo Económico del Liberalismo Amarillo. Historia de un Fracaso, 1888–1908” in Boulton, Alfredo, ed., *Política y Economía en Venezuela 1810–1976* (Caracas: Fundación John Boulton, 1976) 203–46.

Henao Jaramillo, Jaime, “La Industria Cafetera de Venezuela,” *Revista del Instituto Nacional del Café* 3:10 (December 1941), 35–39.

Hendrickson, Embert J., “Root's Watchful Waiting and the Venezuelan Controversy,” *The Americas* 23:2 (October 1966) 115–29.

———., “Roosevelt's Second Venezuelan Controversy,” *Hispanic American Historical Review* 50:3 (August 1970) 482–99.

Henry, Philip Walter, “Has the United States Repudiated International Arbitration?” *North American Review* 185 (December 1907) 525–36.

Jahn, Alfredo, “Inmigraciones y Colonización en Venezuela,” *Boletín del Ministerio de Fomento* 4:8 (February 1913) 596–607.

Liscano, Juan, “Líneas de Desarrollo de la Cultura Venezolana en los Últimos Cincuenta años,” *Venezuela Moderna. Medio Siglo de Historia 1926–1976* (Caracas: Fundacíon Eugenio Mendoza, 1976), 588–681.

Livermore, Seaward W., “Theodore Roosevelt, the American Navy and the Venezuelan Crisis,” *American Historical Journal* 51:3 (April 1946) 452–71.

“Los Negocios de Castro, Gómez y Sus Ministros, 1905,” *BAHM* 17:89 (January-February 1976) 121–34.

Nava, Julian, “The Illustrious American: The Development of Nationalism in Venezuela under Antonio Guzmán Blanco,” *Hispanic American Historical Review* 45:4 (November 1965) 428, 527–43.

“A Nicely Timed Revolution,” *The Nation* 87: 2270 (December 31, 1908) 645.

Normano, J. F., "The British Offensive in South America," *Hispanic American Historical Review* 12:1 (February 1932) 93–100.

Osborne, John Ball, "Protection of American Commerce and Capital Abroad," *North American Review* 195 (May 1912) 687–700.

"Our Relations with South America," *The Nation* 88:2277 (February 18, 1909) 157.

Pierson, W., "Foreign Influences on Venezuelan Political Thought, 1830–1930," *Hispanic American Historical Review* 15:1 (February 1935) 3–43.

Platt, D. C. M., "The Allied Coercion of Venezuela 1902–03: A Reassessment," *Inter-American Economic Affairs* 15:4 (1962).

———., "British Diplomacy in Latin America since the Emancipation," *Journal of Inter-American Affairs* 21:3 (Winter 1967) 21–43.

"Promoters' Liability for Unrevealed Profits—The Asphalt Companies." From Transcript of Record, U.S. Circuit Court of Appeals for the Third Circuit, September Term, 1903. *The Land Title and Trust Company v. Henry Tatnall as Receiver of Asphalt Company of America etc.* in Ripley, William Z., ed., *Trusts, Pools and Corporations* (Boston: Ginn & Co., 1905) 370–80.

Rangel Lamus, Amenodoro, "Eustoquio Gómez" in Amado, Anselmo, ed. *Gente de Táchira (1900–1935)* vol. 2, (Caracas: BATT, 1974) 447–55.

Rios, Pompeyo, "Desarrollo Económico de Venezuela desde 1830 hasta 1920," *Revista de la Facultad de Agronomía* (Maracay) 3:3 (November 1964) 16–41.

Rippy, F., "C. Castro. A man without a Country," *American Historical Review* 55 (October 1949) 36–53.

———., "British Investments in Latin America at Their Peak," *Hispanic American Historical Review* 34:1 (February 1954) 94–103.

———., "The Venezuelan Claims of 1903–05: A Case Study in the Cost of Disorder, Despotism and Deficient Capital and Technology," *Inter-American Economic Affairs* 7:4 (1954) 65–77.

Salcedo Bastardo, J. L., "Las Autocracias Venezolanas, 1830–1935," *Boletín Histórico* 8:20 (January 1970) 73–89.

Silva, Carlos Rafael, "Bosquejo Histórico del Desenvolvimiento de la economía Venezolana en el siglo XX," *Venezuela Moderna. Medio Siglo de Historia 1926–1976*, (Caracas: Fundacíon Eugenio Mendoza, 1976), 491–587.

"Spanking Castro," *The Nation* 86:2235 (30 April 1908), 390–91.

Sullivan, William M., "La Élite Política del Castrismo: Ministros y Gobernadores (1899–1908)," *Boletín Histórico* 13:37 (January 1975) 92–110.

Thayer, W. Roscoe, "Bowen vs. Roosevelt," *North American Review* 210 (September 1919) 418–20.

"Una Interview con Matos," *Venezuela Conjuracíon Contra la Vida del General Juan Vicent Gómez Presidente de Venezuela y Sus Consecuencias* (Caracas: Imprenta Nacional, 1909) 417–420.

Vandenbosch, Amry, "Dutch Problems in the West Indies," *Foreign Affairs* 9:2 (January 1931) 350–52.

Velásquez, Ramón J., "Aspectos de la Evolucíon Política de Venezuela en su Utimo Medio Siglo" *Venezuela Moderna, Medio Siglo de Historia 1926–1976* (Caracas: Fundacíon Eugenio Mendoza, 1976), 3–385.

Veloz, Ramón, "Historia del Cambio en Venezuela desde 1830–1831 hasta 1942–1943," *Revista de Hacienda* 8:14 (September 1943).

ARCHIVES

United Kingdom, Public Records Office

Admiralty

ADM 128, Station Records, North America and West Indies.

Colonial Office

CO 295, Trinidad, Governor's Despatches, 1905–1909.

Foreign Office

FO 80, General Correspondence, 1900–1905.
FO 115, U.S. Embassy and Consular Archives.
FO 199, Venezuela, Embassy and Consular Archives, 1904–1909.
FO 368, General Correspondence, Commercial, 1906–1909.
FO 369, General Correspondence, Consular, 1906–1909.
FO 370, General Correspondence, Library, 1906–1909.
FO 371, General Correspondence, Political, 1906–1909.
FO 420, General Correspondence, Confidential Print, America, South and Central.

Venezuela

Academia de la Historia

Archivo del General José Manuel Hernández.
Archivo de Manuel Landaeta Rosales.

Palacio de Miraflores

Archivo Histórico de Miraflores.
Presidential Copybooks, 1906–1909.
Presidential and Secretary General's Correspondence, 1900–1909.

CONTEMPORARY OFFICIAL PUBLICATIONS

United States of America

Congressional Record, Proceedings and Debates, 1900–1909.
Department of Commerce and Labor, Bureau of Manufacture, "Monthly Consular & Trade Reports—Venezuela," 1900–1909.
State Department, "Papers Relating to the Foreign Relations of the United States of America—Venezuela," 1900–1909.

Venezuela

Ministerio de Hacienda, Dirección General de Estadística, Estadística Mercantil y Marítima, 1907–1909.
Ministerio de Hacienda, *Memoria*, 1908–1909.
Ministerio de Obras Públicas, *Memoria*, 1908–1909.
Ministerio de Relaciones Exteriores, *Libro Amarillo*, 1908–1909.
Ministerio de Relaciones Exteriores, *Cuenta*, 1908–1909.
Ministerio de Relaciones Interiores, *Memoria*, 1908–1909.
Recopilación de Leyes y Decretos de Venezuela, Vols. 1–60.

OTHER CONTEMPORARY SOURCES

Boletín del Archivo Histórico de Miraflores, Nos. 1–100.
Boletín del Archivo Nacional, 1924–1971.
Boletín del Ministerio de Fomento, 1909–1910.
Corporation of Foreign Bond-Holders (London), Newspaper Files, Vols. 7–11.
South American Journal (London), 1900–1909.

NEWSPAPERS

El Constitucional (Caracas), 1908–1909.
Gómez Unico, (San Juan) 1907.
The Times (London), 1908–1909.
Venezuela. Ecos de una Tiranía (Paris), February 1905 to December 1908.

UNPUBLISHED SOURCES

Burgraaff, John Winfield, "Civil Military Relations in Venezuela." (PhD. diss., University of New Mexico, 1967).
Carlisle, Douglas H., "The Organization for the Conduct of Foreign Relations in Venezuela, 1909–1953." (PhD. diss., University of North Carolina at Chapel Hill, 1951).
Carreras, Charles Edward, "U.S. Economic Penetration of Venezuela and Its Effects on Diplomacy, 1895–1906." (PhD. diss., University of North Carolina at Chapel Hill, 1971).
Demetriou, George J., "A Consideration of Some Aspects of the Problem of Legitimacy in Venezuela Politics, 1830–1953."(PhD. diss., University of Minnesota, 1954).
Duffy, Edward Gerald, "Politics of Expediency: Diplomatic Relations Between the U.S. and Venezuela During the Juan Vicente Gómez Era." (PhD. diss., The Pennsylvania State University, 1969).
Evans, K., "Anglo-American Relations: 1895–1908, with Special Reference to the Venezuelan Boundary Dispute." (MA. diss., University of London, 1955).
Harwich, Nikita Laureano, "Cipriano Castro and the 'Libertadora' Revolution. A Hypothesis in Historical Development" (Senior Honors History Seminar Paper, Duke University, 1971–2).

Hendrickson, Julius Embert, "The New Venezuelan Controversy: The Relations of the United States and Venezuela, 1904–1914." (PhD. diss., University of Minnesota, 1964).

Hood, Miriam, "A Phase in Anglo-Venezuelan Relations in the Latter Part of the Nineteenth Century and the Anglo-German Blockade, 1902–1903." (PhD. diss., The National University Cork, Ireland, 1971).

McBeth, B. S., "Juan Vicente Gómez and the Oil Companies." (PhD. diss., The University of Oxford, 1980).

Muñoz, Arturo, Guillermo, "The Táchira Frontier, 1881–1899: Regional Isolation and National Integration in the Venezuelan Andes." (PhD. diss., Stanford University, 1977).

Stann, E. Jeffrey, "Caracas, Venezuela 1891–1936: A Study of Urban Growth." (PhD. diss., Vanderbilt University, 1975).

Sullivan, William M., "The Rise of Despotism in Venezuela: Cipriano Castro, 1899–1908." (PhD. diss., The University of New Mexico, 1974).

INTERVIEWS

Ramón J. Velásquez, Caracas, 9 January 77, 5 February 77, 20 March 77, 9 July 77, and 21 August 77.

J. A. Giacopini Zárraga, Caracas, 1 April 77 and 25 July 77.

OFFICIAL PUBLICATIONS

United Kingdom

Diplomatic and Consular Reports

Consul de Lemos, "Venezuela—Report for the Year 1899 on the Trade and Commerce of the Consular District of Ciudad Bolívar," *PP*, vol. xcvii, 1900, pp. 529–35.

Acting Consul Andral, "Venezuela—Report for the Year 1899 on the Trade of the Consular District of Caracas," *PP*, vol. xcvii, 1900, pp. 535–57.

Consul de Lemos, "Venezuela—Report for the Year 1900 on the Trade and Commerce of the Consular District of Ciudad Bolívar," *PP*, vol. lxxvi, 1901, pp. 763–70.

Acting Consul Andral, "Venezuela—Report for the Year 1900 on the Trade of the Consular District of Caracas," *PP*, vol. lxxv, 1901, pp. 771–89.

Consul de Lemos, "Venezuela—Report for the Year 1901 on the Trade and Commerce of the Consular District of Ciudad Bolívar," *PP*, vol. cxi, 1902, pp. 553–59.

Acting Consul Andral, "Venezuela—Report for the Year 1901 on the Trade of the Consular District of Caracas," *PP*, vol. lxxxv, 1902, pp. 771–89.

Acting Consul Andral, "Venezuela—Report for the Year 1902 on the Trade of the Consular District of Caracas," *PP*, vol. lxxix, 1903, pp. 681–95.

Acting Consul Andral, "Venezuela—Report for the Year 1903 on the Trade of the Consular District of Caracas," *PP*, vol. ci, part II, 1903, pp. 451–65.

Acting Consul Andral, "Venezuela—Report for the Year 1904 on the Trade of the Consular District of Caracas," *PP*, vol. xciii, 1905, pp. 765–79.
Consul de Lemos, "Venezuela—Report for the Year 1905 on the Trade and Commerce of Ciudad Bolívar," *PP*, vol. cxxxix, 1906, pp. 903–11.
Acting Vice-Consul G. Haggard, "Venezuela—Report for the Year 1905 on the Trade and Commerce of the Consular District of Caracas," *PP*, vol. cxxxix, 1906, pp. 911–37.
Vice Consul F. F. Gray, "Venezuela—Report for the Year 1906 on the Trade and Commerce of the Consular District of Caracas," *PP*, vol. xciii, 1907, pp. 825–55.
Consul de Lemos, "Venezuela—Report for the Year 1906 on the Trade and Commerce of Ciudad Bolívar," *PP*, vol. xciii, 1907, pp. 855–61.
Consul C. H. de Lemos, "Venezuela—Report for the year 1907 on the Trade and Commerce of Ciudad Bolívar," *PP*, vol. cxvii, 1908, pp. 907–15.
Consul C. H. de Lemos, "Venezuela—Report for the Year 1908 on the Trade and Commerce of Ciudad Bolívar," *PP*, vol. xcix, 1909, pp. 643–53.
Vice Consul H. Tom, "Venezuela—Report for the Year 1906–1907 on the Trade of Venezuela and the Consular District of Caracas," *PP*, vol. xcix, 1909, pp. 653–85.
Vice Consul H. Tom, "Venezuela—Report for the Year 1908–1909 on the Trade of Venezuela and the Consular District of Caracas," *PP*, vol. ciii, 1910, pp. 2207–49.

United States of America

Senate

Calhoun, William J., "Wrongs to American Citizens in Venezuela," *Senate Document No. 413*, 60 Cong. sess. 1, 1907–1908.

Venezuela

Venezuela

Venezuela ante el Conflicto con las potencias Aliadas—Alemania, Inglaterra e Italia en 1902 y 1903 2 vols. (Caracas: Tip Universal, 1905).
Venezuela y la Compañía Francesa de Cables Telegráficos. Ruidoso Proceso. Documento Pubicados en El Constitucional (Caracas: Imprenta Nacional, 1906).
Documentos Importantes (Caracas: Imprenta Bolívar, 1906).
Conjuración contra la Vida del General Juan Vicente Gómez, Presidente de Venezuela y Sus Consecuencias (Caracas: Imprenta Nacional, 1909).

Congreso

Contestación al Mensaje Presidencial (Caracas: Empresa El Cojo, 1909).

Distrito Federal, Juzgado de Primera Instancia en loPenal

Alegatos ante la Corte Superior del Distrito Federal en la Causa Seguida contra el General Eustoquio Gómez por Homicidio (Caracas: Empresa El Cojo, 1909).

Presidencia

150 Años de Vida Republicana (1811–1961) (Caracas: Ediciones de la Presidencia de la República, 1966).

Alocuciones Presidenciales de Año Nuevo (1901–1971) (Caracas: Ediciones de la Presidencia de la República, 1971).

Index

About the Author

BRIAN S. McBETH trained as an economist and holds a doctorate in politics from the University of Oxford. He has been closely associated with the work of the Latin American Centre at St. Antony's College, Oxford. He has worked as a financial analyst in the city of London since 1979.